This is Philately

by

Kenneth A. Wood

Volume Three   Q-Z

Published by
Van Dahl Publications
Box 10
Albany, OR 97321

ISBN: 0-934466-04-1 (Volume 3)
ISBN: 0-934466-05-X (3 Volume Set)

Library of Congress Catalog Card Number: 82-70931

Printed in the United States of America.

QARKU POSTES I KORCES: This inscription identifies some early issues of Albania (q.v.).

Qatar: The State of Qatar comprises a peninsula jutting into the Persian (Arabian) Gulf from the Arabian shore.

It had been under the control of Bahrain (q.v.) until Turkey took over the area in 1872.

Following the defeat of Turkey by the British in World War I, Britain renewed an 1868 agreement with Qatar and undertook to assume responsibility for its defense and foreign affairs.

British forces were withdrawn in 1971, and Qatar became independent on Sept. 1 of that year.

The capital city is Doha (Ad Dawhah), and the peninsula has an estimated population of 220,000.

At the landward end of the peninsula there is a border with Saudi Arabia (q.v.) and the United Arab Emirates (q.v.).

The British established a postal service at Doha in 1950 and at Umm Said, a town south of Doha, in 1956.

At first, stamps of the British Postal Agencies in Eastern Arabia (q.v.) were used, and in 1957, British stamps overprinted "QATAR" and surcharged in naye paise (NP) and rupees were used. One hundred NP were equal to one rupee.

The Qatar Post Department took over on May 23, 1963, and since then has been responsible for stamp issues.

The unit of currency is the riyal (100 dirhams), which is currently 3.64 to the US dollar. The latest per capita income figure is $18,000.

The address of Qatar's philatelic bureau is Director, Philatelic Bureau, Dept. of Posts, Doha, Qatar, Arabian Gulf.

Qintar: A unit of currency used in Albania, 100 of which make up one lek.

It has also been spelled "qindar" and "qir.-darka."

Quadriglia: Italian word for "quadrille."

Quadrille: The term "quadrille" refers to the grid of small squares faintly printed on otherwise blank album pages.

In top-quality pages, the quadrille will be clear and distinct, but very faint, so as not to detract from the appearance when material is mounted on the page.

The purpose of the quadrille grid is to act as a mounting guide, and the center points at top, bottom, and sides, as well at the center of the page, are usually emphasized. (See Album.)

Quadrille: Foreign words for "quadrille" include gegittert (German), quadriglia (Italian), cuadriculado (Spanish).

Quadrille Paper: (See Paper, Quadrille.)

Qu'aiti State in Hadhramaut: (See Aden Protectorate.)

Qu'aiti State of Shihr and Mukalla: (See Aden Protectorate.)

Quality: A word referring to the state of a stamp or other philatelic item, as in "top quality." It is not a precise descriptive term. (See Condition.)

QUAN BUU: The inscription "QUAN BUU" is found on three military stamps issued by South Vietnam during the 1960s.

Quarter: Foreign words for quarter include un quart (French), viertel (German), quarto (Italian), and cuarta parte (Spanish).

Quarter Stamp: (See Stamp, Quarter.)

Quarto: Italian word for "one quarter."

Quartro: Numeral four (4) in Portuguese.

Quatre: Numeral four (4) in French.

Quattrino: A unit of currency used in the Italian state of Tuscany until 1860. There were 60 quattrino to the lira.

Quattro: Numeral four (4) in Italian.

Queensland: Queensland is a state in the Australian Commonwealth and occupies the northeast portion of the island continent.

It has a coastline of 3,236 miles, the longest of any Australian state except Western Australia. The capital of the state is the city of Brisbane.

Both the Spanish explorer Luis de Torres and the Dutch had discovered the Cape York Penin-sula, but it was not until 1770 that Captain James Cook discovered the east coast of what is now Queensland.

In 1823 John Oxley discovered the Brisbane River and established a penal settlement there. It was not until the mid-1800s that settlers sailed direct from Britain to Brisbane.

Political separation from New South Wales (q.v.) came in 1859, when Queensland's population numbered about 23,500.

A mining industry in Queensland was sparked by the discovery of gold in the 1850s.

By 1867, the colony's population stood at 100,000. Western migration had increased during that decade, and by 1870, the first railroad was operating.

During the 1950s, uranium was discovered at Mary Kathleen, and bauxite was found in quantity in the Cape York Peninsula, followed by the discovery of natural gas.

With an area of 666,700 square miles, Queensland had a population of 498,100 at the time of federation in 1901 and a 1979 population of 2,166,700.

The early stamps of the colony of Queensland featured the beautiful Chalon portrait of Queen Victoria (q.v.). Following federation, the stamps of the Australian Commonwealth replaced those of the colony.

Quelimane: Formerly known as Zambezia and administered by the Zambezia

QUEENSLAND

QUELIMANE

The administrative district of Quelimane had an area of 38,819 square miles.

Questa, House of: (See House of Questa.)

Quetzal (100 centavos): Unit of currency used in Guatemala (q.v.).

Quetzal Bird: The national emblem of the Central American country of Guatemala, the Quetzal bird *(Pharomachrus mocinna)* has been featured on many of that country's stamps.

It has been familiar to stamp collectors ever

Company, this administrative district of Portuguese East Africa is now a part of the People's Republic of Mozambique.

In 1544 a military post was established at the site of the present town of Quelimane to guard the delta of the Zambezi River.

Under the name of Zambezia, stamps were issued in 1894 comprising the numeral key type of the Portuguese Colonies inscribed "ZAMBEZIA." King Carlos key type stamps inscribed "ZAMBEZIA" came in 1898, a surcharged issue overprinted "PROVISORIO" in 1902, "REPUBLICA" overprints in 1911, with a final issue in 1914.

Meanwhile, in 1913, stamps of the Vasco da Gama issue for the Portuguese Colonies (q.v.), Macao, and Timor had been issued overprinted "QUELIMANE" and surcharged. In 1914 a set of the Ceres key type was issued inscribed "QUELIMANE."

since it first appeared as the main design element of a stamp in the 1870s.

As is common in the world of birds, it is the male that is the most beautiful with its spectacular long tail and specimens have been noted with a body length of 12 inches and a tail of up to 24 inches.

The Quetzal bird has also given its name to the currency unit of Guatemala which is currently at par with the US dollar.

q.v.: A Latin expression *(quod vide)* meaning "which see." It will be found used extensively in this work to direct the reader's attention to other references that will provide additional information.

Stamps from three of the few ''Q'' countries.

R

R: The letter "R" inscribed or overprinted on stamps of Colombia indicates use as registration stamps.

In 1916-17, Panama overprinted some stamps "R" and surcharged them to pay the registration fee. (See Stamps, Registration.)

R: The letter "R" is the only Roman alphabet inscription on the stamps of the Feudatory Indian state of Jind (Jhind).

The stamps are primitive in nature and were issued between 1874 and 1885.

Subsequent issues were released after the state became a Convention State, and these bear an English-language overprint or inscription. (See Jind.)

R: The letter "R" plus a surcharge on stamps of the French colonies general issue indicates that the stamps were for use on the island of Reunion (q.v.).

R: The letter "R," standing for "registered," is seen on labels or handstamped markings applied to registered mail.

Rab: (See Arbe.)

Rabaul: Rabaul was the capital of New Britain (q.v.), formerly part of German New Guinea, in the Bismarck Archipelago.

Following the ouster of the Germans by British forces in 1914, postage stamps were created by overprinting "G.R.I." (q.v.) on German New Guinea (q.v.) registration labels.

The labels bore the town names of Rabaul, Friedrich Wilhelmshaven, Herbertshohe, Kawieng, Kieta, and Manus.

Rag Paper: (See Paper, Rag Content.)

Rahmen: German word for "frame."

Rahmfarbe: German word for the color "cream."

Railway Air Mail Stamps: (See Stamps, Railway Air Mail.)

Railway Mail Service: As soon as railways grew beyond the novelty stage and began to spread throughout a country, it became obvious that they could be used to carry mail.

The first carriage of mail occurred as early as

A US railroad cancel after the 1949 change to Postal Transportation Service.

This is the British train that carried the first railway mail in 1830.

1830 on Britain's Manchester and Liverpool Railway.

Only a few years later, also in Britain, it was suggested that mail could be sorted en route, thus saving a great deal of time. So it was that in 1837, the first traveling post office began operating between Liverpool and Birmingham. Equipment to pick up and drop mail without stopping the train was also devised at about that time.

The French were also quick to utilize railways for carrying mail and by the early 1850s were attaching railway post offices to express trains.

In the US, it seems that mail was first sorted on a train in motion in July 1862, and Cabeen (*Standard Handbook of Stamp Collecting*) credits a postal clerk named W.A. Davis, of St. Joseph, Mo., with the suggestion. He is reported to have received $100 from the Post Office Department for his idea.

After this, the railway post office system spread and soon became the normal method of carrying mail over long distances.

As the US railroads declined after World War II, Highway Post Offices (q.v.) gradually replaced the RPOs, and by 1978 there was only one RPO route left. That was between New York and Washington, and soon it, too, was discontinued.

The HPOs did not last very long as they were replaced by jet aircraft as the prime mover of mail.

Duplex postal markings of the Railway Mail Service included "RPO" and the route designation in the circular date stamp with "RMS" in the killer portion.

In 1949 the Railway Mail Service became the Postal Transportation Service, and "PTS" replaced "RMS" in the postal markings.

During the period of use of RPO markings, they were also used by post offices aboard vessels on the run to Alaska and on ships on lakes and inland waterways, since these were under the administration of the Railway Mail Service. (See Ambulant.)

Railway Stamp: (See Stamps, Railway.)

Rainbow Proofs: (See Proofs, Rainbow.)

Rajasthan, Greater Union of: This was a 1947 union of 14 Indian states including the stamp-issuing Feudatory States of Bundi (q.v.), Jaipur (q.v.), and Kishangarh (q.v.).

Stamps of the three states were overprinted for use within the union, although each state reportedly continued to maintain its own postal facilities separately.

The Republic of India (q.v.) took over postal

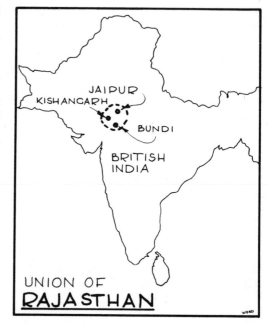

UNION OF RAJASTHAN

services in 1950, and the area now uses Indian stamps.

Rajpipla (Rajpeeple): For six years beginning in 1880, the Indian Feudatory State of Rajpipla issued its own stamps, which were valid only within its borders.

The state was located near Bombay and now uses the stamps of the Republic of India.

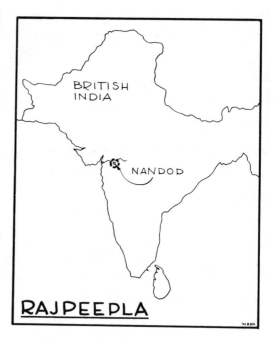

RAJPEEPLA

Rand: A unit of currency used in the Republic of South Africa since 1961 and also in South-West Africa (Namibia), Basutoland (Lesotho), Bechuanaland (Botswana), Swaziland, and until 1963 in Tristan da Cunha.

Rand: Dutch and German word for "margin."

Rappen: The rappen was a unit of currency used by Switzerland and the cantonal administrations in their stamp-issuing periods. It is still used by the Principality of Liechtenstein.

There are 100 rappen to the Swiss franc.

Rare: Foreign words for "rare" include zeldzaam (Dutch), rare (French), selten (German), and raro (Italian and Spanish).

Raro: Italian and Spanish word for "rare."

Rarotonga: When New Zealand assumed the administration of the Cook Islands (q.v.) in 1919, stamps of New Zealand overprinted "RAROTONGA" and surcharged in the native language in words were introduced.

In 1920 a set of stamps inscribed "RAROTONGA" was released. It continued in use until 1932, when stamps inscribed for the Cook Islands replaced them.

Ras al-Khaima: One of the sheikdoms forming the United Arab Emirates (q.v.), Ras al-Khaima is a fairly large and fertile area compris-

ing several small towns located on the Oman Peninsula between the Persian Gulf and the Gulf of Oman.

Until Feb. 10, 1972, when it joined the UAE, totals of 1,036 stamps and 70 souvenir sheets were released bearing the name of Ras al-Khaima. That figure does not include any imperforate varieties, according to R. Howard Courtney in *The Arab World Philatelist.*

The sheikdom had previously been a member of the Trucial States (q.v.).

Rasterdiepdruk: Dutch word for "photogravure."

Rastertiefdruck: German word for "photogravure."

Rate, Postal: A postal rate is a charge for transmitting an item of mail of a specific weight from one point to another using a particular classification of mail.

For instance, the current first-class letter rate within this country is 20c for the first ounce and 17c for each additional ounce.

A knowledge of postal rates effective in a given area at a particular time is of importance in most postal history studies.

Rauten: German word for "lozenges."

Rawdon, Wright, Hatch & Edson: The firm of Rawdon, Wright, Hatch & Edson

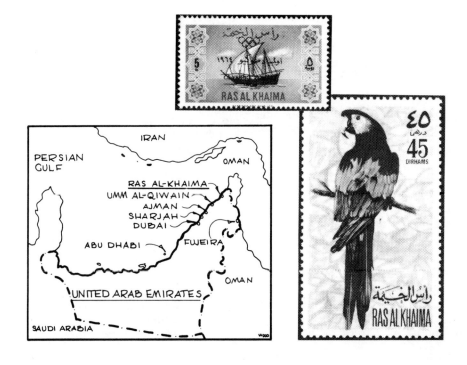

was a security printing company located in New York during the 19th century.

It printed the New York Postmasters' Provisionals, the US 1847 5c and 10c stamps, and the first stamps of the Colony of Canada, including the 3d Beaver and the famous 12d Black of 1851.

Rayons: The nickname "Rayons" is applied to the 1850-52 issues of the federal administration of Switzerland.

A "Rayon I" stamp.

The word "RAYON" followed by "I," "II," or "III" inscribed on the stamps designates a zone system for assessing postal charges.

R.B.: Prior to the introduction of stamps overprinted "O.S." in 1874 for general Official use, South Australia used a number of different overprints to indicate use by specific government departments.

"R.B." stood for Road Board.

Re: Italian word for "king."

Real: A unit of currency once widely used in Central and South America.

Reay, George H.: George H. Reay was a manufacturer of US stamped envelopes during the period from 1870 until the Plimpton issue of 1874.

Reay was noted for the fine engraving of the indicia on his envelopes.

RECAPITO AUTORIZZATO:

Inscription on Authorized Delivery stamps of Italy. This type of stamp permitted the delivery of a letter privately rather than via the normal postal system.

RECARGO: Inscription on Spanish War Tax stamp of 1898.

Receiving Mark: A receiving mark is a postmark applied to a piece of mail by the receiving post office. Usually found on the back of mail, these are commonly called "backstamps" by collectors.

At one time these marks were routinely applied, but today's volume of mail renders this impossible and they are now restricted primarily to registered mail.

One exception is mail carried on inaugural airmail flights, which requires backstamping in order to show that the mail was actually carried on the flight. (See Backstamp.)

Recess Printing: (See Printing, Intaglio.)

Rechts: Dutch and German word for "right."

Recomendada: Inscription on 1881 Colombian Registration stamp.

Recomendado: Inscription on 1925 Colombian Registration stamp.

Recorte: Spanish word for "cut square."

RECOUVREMENTS: An inscription on some postage due labels of Monaco.

Recutting: (See Retouching.)

Red: Foreign words for "red" include rod (Danish and Swedish), rood (Dutch), rouge (French), rot (German), rosso (Italian), vermelho (Portuguese), and rojo (Spanish).

Redonda: (See Antigua.)

Redrawn: The term "redrawn" refers to a stamp design that, while retaining its obvious similarity to the original printing, has been changed in some of its detail.

Sometimes a design will be redrawn to improve it or to correct some minor error of illustration or inscription.

There are cases in which a stamp design has been redrawn to overcome problems encountered in the production process.

Such an example is the US 15c air mail stamp of 1959, which was reissued in a redrawn form in 1961.

It had been found that during this stamp's printing on the Giori press, black ink tended to enter the area of the orange frame around the Statue of Liberty. This occured when the plate was wiped after being inked with the two colors and some black ink was wiped into the area supposed to be orange.

The redrawn design eliminated the orange

The original design is at the top, with the redrawn design featuring only a black frame around the Statue of Liberty below it.

frame and thus separated further the areas of black and orange.

George Brett *(The Giori Press,* Bureau Issues Association, 1961) notes that the direction of wipe was from right to left to minimize the staining of the orange areas by black ink, but since the frame completely surrounded the black vignette, staining on the left side was a more or less permanent condition.

As a point of interest, Brett also notes that the black aircraft area of the plate was not inked by the same roller that applied ink to the Statue of Liberty area because difficulty was experienced in properly inking both large and small areas with the one roller. When applying ink to a small area, the wear on the inking roller is greater than at another point where a larger area of color is involved, hence the use of two black inking rollers in that particular case.

The experience with this design well illustrates the necessity for the stamp designer to be aware of the production process and the potential problems that can be caused by not taking its limitations into consideration.

Reentry: The term "reentry" is used in recess/intaglio printing.

When, after some printing has been done, the subsequent application of the transfer roll (q.v.) does not exactly match the original plate impression, the result is termed a reentry.

Reapplication of the transfer role may be needed because of wear during printing, from damage to a subject on the printing plate, or because the original impression was not deep enough to print effectively.

The reentry can show as a partial doubling of the design where the transfer roller was not "entered" in the exact position as that of the original entry.

Deepening of an impression can sometimes be diagnosed from an examination of stamps printed before and after the reentry.

There are several types of work that are loosely termed "reentries":

Shifted Transfer: Where duplication at the edges of a stamp design occurs because of too much pressure being applied or too high a speed.

Fresh Entry: Where partial duplication occurs in an attempt to correct a misplacement. This is usually done before printing begins, and unlike other cases in which the doubling is purely accidental, here the intention is to shift the impression after erasing the original. The error here is that the original was not completely erased.

Reentry: This is basically a repair job as described above. (See Fresh Entry; Printing, Intaglio; Retouch; Recutting; Transfer Roller; Transfer, Short; and Transfer, Double.)

Reentry: Foreign terms for "reentry" include double frappe (French), nachgravierung (German), doppia incisione (Italian), and regrabado (Spanish).

REGATUL PTT ROMANIEI: This overprint on Hungarian stamps indicates use in occupied Romania following World War I.

REGIERUNGS DIENSTSACHE: Overprint and inscription on Official stamps of Liechtenstein.

Regional Issues, United Kingdom: (See Northern Ireland, Scotland, Wales, Isle of Man, Jersey, and Guernsey.)

Registered Mail: The system of registered mail that operates in and between most countries is a means of providing greater security for valuables in the mail system.

An item of registered mail should receive great care in handling and is recorded at each step in its journey.

A receipt is issued to the mailer showing the number assigned to the item, and the recipient must sign for it.

Many countries, including the US, have issued special stamps for registered mail. (See Stamp, Registration.)

Some postal administrations, especially in the British area, sell special postal stationery items in

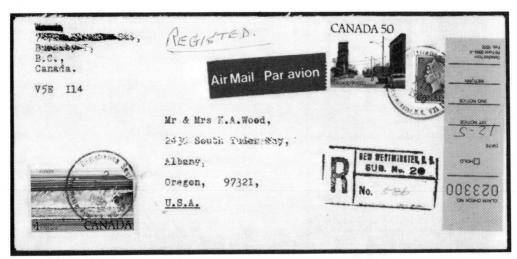

A typical registered cover with the stub of the receipt slip attached. It cost $1.67 Canadian including postage to send. Had it been going in the opposite direction the cost at that time would have been $3 plus postage.

the form of registration envelopes. These are strongly constructed and bear an imprinted indicium representing the registration cost and have blue lines printed through the center vertically and horizontally to identify them as registered mail. Many countries require such a marking, which is applied with a blue pencil when the special envelope is not used. (See Registration Label.)

Registration Label:
These labels are adhesive stickers applied to mail by a post office to show that the mail is registered and to provide a space to insert the registration number of that particular item of mail.

They usually include a large "R" on the left side and show the name of the originating post office plus a space for inserting the number. They may be printed in red or blue, with blue being the most commonly used.

Some countries, including the US, use a handstamp for this purpose.

The labels have no franking value and only indicate that the mail is registered and that the proper charges have been paid.

There is one interesting instance of a registration label acquiring franking power, and that was when stamp stocks ran low in New Guinea following its capture from the Germans in 1914.

The British occupation authorities overprinted German registration labels for use as postage stamps.

Colombia and Liberia have issued adhesive stamps specifically intended for use on registered mail. Each of these include, like the labels, space for the insertion of the number.

Registration Marks:
Registration marks are often found in the sheet margins of stamps printed in more than one pass through the

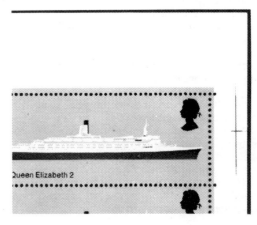

A stamp of Papua New Guinea reproducing the registration label that became a postage stamp.

An example of the use of a registered label by Great Britain and the handstamp registration marking utilized by the US Postal Service.

press. They usually take the form of two intersecting lines, sometimes contained within a circle.

They are intended to assist the printer in accurately registering, or positioning, multiple press passes.

Illustrated is a typical registration mark, found on the 5d denomination of the 1969 British ship set.

Registration Stamp: (See Stamp, Registration.)

Regno: Italian word for "kingdom."

REGNO D'ITALIA TRENTINO:
Overprint on Austrian stamps for Italian occupation of that province.

REGNO D'ITALIA VENEZIA GUILIA: Overprint on Austrian stamps for
Italian occupation of that province.

Regrabado: Spanish word for "reentry."

Regular Stamp: (See Stamp, Definitive.)

Regumming: Regumming is the act of applying new gum to a stamp in order to simulate its original condition, or to cover damage, such as a thin (q.v.), usually so that it may be sold on the philatelic market for a price higher than its actual condition warrants.

A regummed stamp is a faked stamp and should, when its true condition is known, command no more than the price of the same stamp without gum.

Unfortunately, regumming has reached a level of perfection that makes it virtually impossible for the average collector to distinguish genuine gum from the fake variety.

The high premium currently being paid for "original" gum without hinge mark has caused regumming to flourish. It is estimated, for example, by knowledgeable authorities that the majority of "mint, never-hinged" US 1893 Columbian high values bear fake gum. Thus it would seem sensible here to restrict the premium you will pay for the condition known as "mint, never-hinged" to the cost of regumming the stamp, usually stated to be about $5.

If you are in doubt, the services of an expertizing committee (q.v.) should be sought. (See also Mint and Unused.)

Reimpresion: Spanish word for "reprint."

Reimpression: French word for "reprint."

Reino: Spanish word for "kingdom."

Reis: The reis was a unit of currency once used in Portugal and the Portuguese colonies.

Reissue: A stamp is said to be reissued if it is again brought into use after being off sale for a period.

The use of this term does not appear to indicate whether the stamp is a new printing or simply stamps previously taken off sale.

The overprint "HABILITADO" on stamps of some Central or South American countries indicates that the stamps are reissues.

Relief Printing: (See Printing, Relief.)

Relief Roller: (See Transfer Roller.)

Relieve: Spanish word for "embossing."

Religion on Stamps, Collectors of:
The Collectors of Religion on Stamps (COROS) is an organization of collectors whose topical interest is all aspects of religious philately.

It publishes the *COROS Chronicle*, a bimonthly journal.

The organization was founded in 1943 and claims to be the oldest topical stamp society in the US.

The group has published a number of handbooks, including two currently available on Christmas stamps and one providing a checklist and biographies of protestant personalities on stamps.

However, the group is completely non-denominational and welcomes collectors interested in all faiths.

Further information is available from Viola Esau, Secretary, 600 West Orange Grove Rd., G-184, Tucson, AZ 85704.

Remainders: The name "remainder" is given to obsolete stamps of which quantities have been dumped on the philatelic market often at prices below their face value.

Sometimes the stamps are defaced by overprinting with a distinctive device, and when this is done, the objections to the practice cannot be strong, since the stamps can be recognized for what they are.

But when a country dumps stamps that can pass as genuine postally used stamps, then that country often forfeits its philatelic good reputation for an immediate profit.

The country of Ghana is an example. Initially, it enjoyed considerable popularity among collectors as one of the first African colonies to be granted independence. But when it began to dump remainders onto the philatelic market that had been canceled with a marking resembling a real postal cancel, it lost much of its popularity and, to this day, is widely ignored by the philatelic community. (See Cancelation, Bar; Seebeck.)

Rembrandt Press: The Rembrandt press is a type of press used in the photogravure production of postage stamps.

This press is used by the Note Issue Department of the Reserve of the Reserve Bank of Australia. It prints on paper pre-cut in sheet form and has five printing cylinders. Unlike the Chambon press, it does not have a built-in perforating capability.

The printing cylinders on the Rembrandt press are larger than the similar Chambon press (q.v.), and thus its output is greater. (See Printing, Photogravure.)

Renecke: (See Transvaal.)

Renverse: French word for "inverted."

Repaired: Foreign words for "repaired" include gerapeerd (Dutch), repare (French), repariert (German), riparato (Italian), and reparado (Spanish).

Repaired: The term "repaired" refers to a stamp that has been restored to simulate a condition better than it actually possesses. This can consist of adding a new margin or margins, mending a tear, filling a thin, applying new gum, etc.

This is usually done with the intent to defraud by selling the item at a higher price than its real state deserves and is fakery, impure and simple!

However, if a stamp has been enhanced in appearance, and such work is noted by marking the stamp permanently to that effect, and when the stamp is described as repaired when sold, there can be less objection to the practice.

The growing shortage of old stamps in the condition demanded by collectors is forcing more and more to accept lower condition standards. Unfortunately, it is also providing a beautiful opportunity for the faker to ply his nefarious trade, and all collectors should be very much on their guard when offered a bargain that looks too good to be true. It usually is.

Reparado: Spanish word for "repaired."

Repare: French word for "repaired."

Repariert: German word for "repaired."

Reply Coupon, International: International reply coupons are purchased from a post office and enclosed with a letter to prepay a response from the recipient in a foreign country.

The recipient can exchange it for postage on single-rate letter.

The required number of IRCs can be sent to prepay an air mail response.

The cost of an IRC is the return postage plus a premium.

Reply Portion: The term "reply portion" refers to the portion of a reply paid postal card that is used for the response. (See Postal Card.)

Reply Postal Card: (See Postal Card.)

Report: French and German word for "transfer."

Repoussage: "Repoussage" is the term given to the operation of knocking up a low point in a printing plate, either to bring it to the correct height for printing or to enable the plate to be retouched (q.v.).

This operation is performed from the back of the plate.

Reprint: Reprints are stamps produced from the original plates after the stamp has become obsolete.

Thus, reprints are not made for postal or revenue purposes, but for official records, as souvenirs, or for sale to collectors.

Such reprints should differ in some way from the original stamp by being in different colors, unperforated, etc.

Some collectors mistakenly use the term "reprint" to describe an additional or fresh printing of a definitive stamp.

Reprint: Foreign words for reprint include nadruk (Dutch), nachdruck (German), reimpression (French), ristampa (Italian), and reimpresion (Spanish).

REPUBLICA DE LA N. GRENADA: Inscription on first issue of Cauca, a state of Colombia (q.v.).

REPUBLICA ORIENTAL: Inscription on the 1864 issue of Uruguay (q.v.).

REPUBLICA PORTUGUESA: Identifies stamp of Portugal (q.v.).

REPUBLICA SOCIALE ITALIANA:
Identifies stamps of the Italian Socialist Republic (q.v.), the puppet state set up in Northern Italy in 1943 by the Germans.

Republik Malaku Selatan: (See South Moluccas Republic.)

REPUBLIQUE GEORGIENNE:
Identifies stamps of Georgia (q.v.), now part of the Soviet Union.

REPUBLIQUE LIBANAISE:
Identifies issues of Lebanon (q.v.).

REPUBLIQUE RWANDAISE:
Identifies stamps of Rwanda (q.v.).

REPUBLIQUE SYRIENNE: Identifies
stamps of the French Mandate over Syria.

REPUBLIQUE TUNISIENNE:
Identifies stamps of Tunisia (q.v.).

REPULO POSTA: Overprint on
Hungarian stamp indicates first air mail issue.

Research, Philatelic: Much of the
information recorded in philatelic literature is the result of painstaking research by individual collectors and groups working as teams, often over long periods.

What is research? For one thing, it represents more than the rediscovery of previously recorded information, although that is a necessary first step. It involves the discovery of new information and generally requires that some conclusions be drawn on the basis of that new information.

Many collectors are of the opinion that there is little new to be discovered, and judging from the enormus amount of information that has already been recorded in the vast quantity of philatelic literature, you can understand that opinion, even though it is incorrect.

By no means is everything known. Even a great deal of what has been discovered and recorded lies buried and unindexed in the literature and might as well never have been discovered in the first place. Philatelic libraries (q.v.) are doing some fine work in making recorded information more easily available to researchers, and the problem of locating that which is already known on a specific subject is being made easier.

There are several reasons for digging into the philatelic past, be it ancient or recent. One of these is to gratify the urge to be a detective that lurks in so many collectors, or simply to rise to the challenge of finding answers to questions. Another reason is a bit more commercial, but no less satisfying, and can be summed up by stating that the more you know about your subject, the greater will be your advantage in the marketplace. Many a scarce and significant item hides its true value from all except the knowledgeable.

To try to learn what is already known is the vital first step in research, but you need to determine exactly what it is you're seeking. So it is essential to establish a goal. Without one, how will you know when it is reached? Next, you must double-check the existing information as much as possible, to avoid starting off on the wrong foot. Membership in appropriate specialty groups is a good way to find out what is already available on a subject.

After double-checking all information and filling all possible gaps, a number of solutions may present themselves. Here is where logic, experience, and deductive abilities enter the picture as you verify and whittle down possibilities to the answer that best seems to fit the facts.

This will still be a hypothesis requiring confirmation, but it will be one based on logic and all available data.

The subjects of philatelic research are many. They can involve the technical production of a stamp in order to discover what caused a certain effect. To know how a particular printing defect came about, for example, is to be able to draw some conclusion as to its philatelic significance.

Or perhaps the object of your research may be the usage of an item, or some other aspect of postal history, such as the purpose of a puzzling postal marking.

Not the least important subjects concern recent, even current material and events. Much that is old has already been extensively researched and may well be too expensive to tackle, but recent material can be surprisingly little known and usually is more available for study.

In summary, determine what you want to know, establish what is already recorded, double-check it, and then pursue all possible avenues of inquiry. Be systematic and logical. Research requires logic as much as it does curiosity.

Finally, if you are fortunate enough to uncover new information, publish it, together with your conclusions. There is no shortage of opportunities, and publication will certainly be the easiest part of your task, but perhaps the most important.

Above all, do not wait until you think that you know all there is to know. If all researchers did that, there would be mighty little published!

Resellada: The word "resellada" means revalidted, or authorized for use after having been invalidated. Venezuela did this to stamps in 1900.

The catalogs reveal that it was done again in 1937, 1943, and 1951. (See Habilitado, Revalidado.)

RESELLO: Overprint applied to some issues of Nicaragua to revalidate them.

RESMI: Overprint, together with star and crescent, on stamps of Turkey to indicate Official status.

Rethymno: (See Crete, Austrian Post Offices in.)

Retouching: The name "retouch" is given to the result of manual alterations to the details

A poorly done retouch at the top of this early French stamp is clearly seen.

of a die or printing plate.

The term is also used to describe the "recutting" of a printing plate when it has become worn and a decision is made to strengthen the areas where the impression is beginning to show wear. But this is usually more extensive than simple retouching.

The later operation is also done manually and most often in the area of frame lines.

Return Letter Stamp: (See Stamp, Military Reply.)

Reunion: The Indian Ocean island of Reunion has been a French territory since 1638 and it is now an Overseas Department of France.

The island belongs to the Mascarene Island group, which also includes Mauritius, 130 miles to the northeast. Madagascar is some 400 miles to the west.

In 1649 the name Bourbon was given to the island, which had been settled in 1646 by mutineers deported from Madagascar.

During the Napoleonic Wars, the British occupied it for four years before returning it to France. Slaves were given their freedom in 1848 and granted the full rights of French citizenship in 1870.

The inhabitants raise sugar, perfume essences, vanilla, and spices. Rum is an important product.

The island has an area of 969 square miles, and its 1977 population was 490,000. The chief town is Saint Denis.

Reunion's first stamps were released in 1852 and comprised two primitive designs inscribed "Ile de la Reunion," which have been reprinted.

In 1885 stamps of the French Colonies

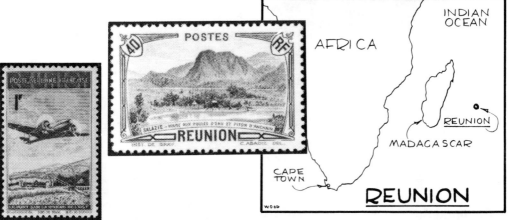

general issues were overprinted and surcharged for use on Reunion.

The Commerce and Navigation key type was released in 1892 inscribed "REUNION."

In 1907 a long pictorial set was issued, followed by another in 1933. Stamps of both sets were reissued overprinted "France Libre" in 1943. The final set came in 1947 and depicts some of the island's impressive scenery.

From 1949 until 1975, when the island became a French Department, stamps of France were released surcharged in CFA francs. Since then, the stamps of France have been used.

Revalidado: This word overprinted on stamps of Portugal indicates that they are revalidated after having been rendered invalid. (See Resellada.)

Revalidated: The term "revalidated" is applied to stamps that, having been invalidated or demonitized, are once again brought into use.

The stamps usually bear some overprint or surcharge to indicate their new status.

This term should not be confused with "reissue" (q.v.), which means the stamps are merely put into use once again after having been removed from sale for a period. (See Resellada, Revalidado.)

Revalued: An item of postal stationery is said to be "revalued" when it has an additional indicium imprinted beside the original one that alters the total denomination.

The illustrated item was originally a 6c stamped envelope, but the addition of the 1c

revaluation indicium converted it to a 7c item.

In recent years, as inflation has forged ahead, more and more revaluation of postal stationery has been done in order to avoid wasting large stocks held by the Postal Service.

Revenue Association, the American: (See American Revenue Association.)

Revenue Stamp: (See Stamp Revenue.)

Revenue Stamp: Foreign terms for revenue stamp include plakzegel (Dutch), timbre fiscal (French), stempelmarke (German), francobollo fiscale (Italian), and sello fiscal (Spanish).

Reverso: Spanish word for "back."

Rey: Spanish word for "king."

R.F.: Identifies stamps of France (q.v.). (See R.F. Overprint.)

RFD: (See Rural Free Delivery.)

R.F. Overprint: Many collectors are puzzled about the status of US stamps bearing the overprint "R.F."

Strictly speaking, these are not overprints but are more in the nature of control markings, similar in purpose to a perfin.

The "R.F." stands for "Republic Francaise" and was applied by French naval authorities during World War II to US stamps used on letters mailed by officers and men of the French naval forces stationed in North Africa.

They had been authorized by the US Navy to use US stamps on their mail to the US and Canada on the condition that the stamps be marked "R.F." by the French Naval postal authorities.

The letters also had to bear the return address of a member of the French Navy and had to be mailed and censored at a French Naval facility.

In addition to the 6c US air mail stamp in the 1941-44 series, the 6c US stamped air mail envelope was also used, and other US stamps are known to have been used.

The Aero Philatelist Annals issues of January-February, April-June, and July 1958 feature a three-part article on the "R.F." overprints by the late Henry M. Goodkind.

In part one, Goodkind reproduces a US Navy directive bearing the date of March 13, 1943 (although this is claimed by Goodkind to have been an error; the actual date, he says, should have been March 13, 1944), which sheds some light on the origin and purpose of the "R.F." overprints.

It is quoted as part of a May 11, 1948, letter from Joseph J. Lawler, third assistant US postmaster general, in response to a philatelic inquiry.

It reads: "Where no French postage is available and cancellation is made by a French post office, US Postage stamps may be used with the letters 'R.F.' over-printed thereon in accordance with the International Postal Convention Agreement.

"French postage affixed must be cancelled by a French postmark and US Postage by US or US Navy postmark, unless such US Postage has been over-printed as described above."

From this other material presented by Goodkind, it seems that the "R.F." was over-printed on stamps franking letters from French naval personnal addressed only to the US and Canada so that such mail could be identified. It was done at the request of US Naval authorities at Casablanca, North Africa.

In the case of the adhesive stamps, it seems certain that the "R.F." was mostly applied after the stamp had been affixed to the letter.

There are a number of variations in the markings, many being crude.

Manuscript markings are also reported by Goodkind.

As with most such primitive material, it is very likely indeed that forgeries were created, especially where the overprint is found on mint stamps or stamped envelopes.

R.G.: Prior to the introduction of stamps overprinted "O.S." in 1874 for general Official use, South Australia used a number of different overprints to indicate use by specific government departments.

"R.G." stood for Registrar General.

Rhineland Pfalz: The inscription "Rhineland Pfalz" means "Rhineland Palatinate."

Following World War II, France occupied this area of Germany, which comprised territory on both sides of the Rhine River, and issued stamps bearing this inscription. (See Germany, French Zone of.)

Rhine Palatinate: (See Germany, French Zone of.)

Rhodes: Ten postal administrations have operated on the island of Rhodes.

Now a part of Greece, Rhodes is set in the blue Aegean Sea a few miles off the Turkish coast. It is now considered one of the Dodecanese Islands (q.v.).

Despite its present minor status as one of the many Greek islands in a popular tourist area, Rhodes has an impressive history.

By 408 BC, the island was an independent state, and by 280 BC, one of the Seven Wonders of the World stood at the harbor entrance of the chief city of Rhodes.

This wonder was the bronze Colussus of Rhodes, said to have been 100 feet in height with a lighthouse in its head. It fell during an earthquake and lay in the harbor. The Saracens,

when they took the island, salvaged the bronze and are reported to have sold it to a scrap metal dealer.

Rhodes became part of the Byzantine Empire when the Saracens were evicted, and it remained so until 1309, when the Knights of St. John occupied the island and built the fortifications, parts of which can still be seen.

In 1522 the Turks took possession and for several hundred years ruled Rhodes while the island lay sleepily in the sun.

The Turkish postal service was not noted for its efficiency, and by the mid-19th century, other nations made arrangements to handle their own mail.

Between 1845 and 1948, postal administrations of Austria, Great Britain, Egypt, France, Germany, Greece, India, Italy, Russia, and Turkey had post offices on Rhodes.

This situation has resulted in a rich postal history and a large amount of varied stamps bearing cancelations of Rhodes.

The Austrians arrived in 1845; then came

RHODES

France and Russia, followed by the Egyptians, and finally, Turkey.

The Italians seized the island, together with the other Dodecanese islands, during the 1912 war with Turkey.

After World War I, Italian influence was strong, as Mussolini strove to impress the world with his Italian Empire.

When the Italians surrendered during WWII, their German partners took over the island.

At the end of the war, British and Indian forces occupied it and set up postal services using British stamps overprinted "M.E.F."

In 1947 Greece assumed responsibility for the island, and Rhodes is now part of that country.

Cancelations of Rhodes can be found on the stamps of Austrian Lombardy-Venetia, Austrian POs in Crete, and the stamps of Austria.

Italian handstamps were used for a period on the British "M.E.F." stamps.

During the period of its administration, Italy issued a number of stamps for Rhodes inscribed "RODI," including definitives, commemoratives, semi-postals, special deliveries, air mails, parcel post stamps, and postage due labels.

The island is 45 miles by 24 miles and has an area of 542 square miles and a population of about 100,000.

Rhodesia: (See Zimbabwe.)

Rhodesia and Nyasaland, Federation of: Existing from 1953 to 1963, the Federation of Rhodesia and Nyasaland included

Northern Rhodesia (q.v.), Southern Rhodesia (q.v.), and the Nyasaland Protectorate (q.v.).

Following the break-up of the federation in 1963, Northern Rhodesia became the Republic of Zambia (q.v.), Southern Rhodesia became Rhodesia (q.v.), and the Nyasaland Protectorate became the Republic of Malawi (q.v.).

Rhodesian Study Circle: The Rhodesian Study Circle is a group formed to further the collection and study of stamps and postal

history of the territories that formerly made up the Rhodesias and Nyasaland.

The North American chairman is John G. Joyce, 70 Glenvale Blvd., Toronto, ON, Canada, M4G 2V6.

R.H./OFFICIAL: British stamps of 1902 were overprinted "R.H./OFFICIAL" for use by heads of households at the royal residences around the country.

Only the ½d and 1d stamps of King Edward VII were overprinted.

Rial: Unit of currency used in Iran (q.v.). One rial comprises 100 dinars. Since 1970 the unit of currency in Oman has been the rial saidi.

RIALTAR SEALDAC NA HEIREANN: Overprint on stamps of Great Britain for use in the Irish Free State. (See Ireland.)

Riau (Riouw)-Lingga Archipelago:
The Riau-Lingga Archipelago comprises two groups of islands off the coast of Sumatra and south of Singapore off the tip of the Malay Peninsula, plus a considerable area on the island of Sumatra.

The Lingga Archipelago is the most southerly of the island groups, and the Riau group forms the southern shore of the Strait of Singapore.

The total area of the territory is 36,510 square miles, and the population was estimated in 1961 at 1,235,000. The capital city is Pakanbaru, located on Sumatra.

In 1954 stamps of Indonesia and the Netherlands Indies were overprinted "RIAU," vertically on some dominations and horizontally on others, in double-lined letters.

Horizontal overprints in solid letters on Indonesian stamps were issued in 1957, followed by similar overprints in double-lined letters in 1958 and 1960.

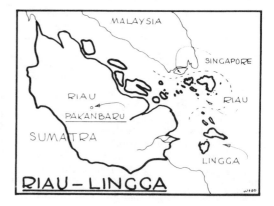

Ribbed: Foreign words for "ribbed" include geribbeld (Dutch), cannele (French), geriffelt (German), scanalatura (Italian), and acanalado (Spanish).

Riel: Unit of currency used in Cambodia beginning in 1955.

Right: Foreign terms for "right" include droite (French), rechts (Dutch and German), destro (Italian), and a la derecha (Spanish).

Rigsbank Daler: Unit of currency used by Denmark to 1875. It was made up of 96 skillings.

Rigsdaler: Unit of currency used in Iceland until 1876. It comprised 96 skillings.

Rijeka: (See Fiume.)

Riksdaler (Rixdaler): The unit of currency in Sweden from 1858 to 1874.

Riksdaler (Rixdaler) Banco: Unit of currency used by Sweden until 1858. It was made up of 48 skilling bancos.

Rilieve: Italian word for "embossing."

Rin: A unit of currency used by Japan. Ten rin made up one sen from 1876 to 1899.

Ringgit: The unit of currency used in Malaysia (q.v.).

Rio de Oro: Rio de Oro became part of Spanish Sahara in 1924. It consisted of territory

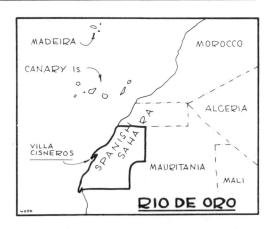

on the northwest coast of Africa and formed the southern part of the Spanish colony.

The capital city was Villa Cisneros, which had a population in 1960 of 1,900. It is located on the Rio de Oro peninsula about midway along the coast.

The peninsula is 23 miles long and has a maximum width of two miles. The coast of Rio de Oro extends from Cape Bojador in the north to Cape Blanco in the south.

Fishing and herding are the chief occupations of the population, which comprises mostly nomadic Arabs.

Rio de Oro had an area of 73,362 square miles.

Stamps were first issued in 1905 and continued until 1924, when stamps of Spanish Sahara (q.v.) were introduced.

The area was divided between Morocco and Mauritania but it is now Moroccan. The UN calls it Western Sahara.

Rio Muni: Rio Muni was a colony of Spain and part of Spanish Guinea until Oct. 12,

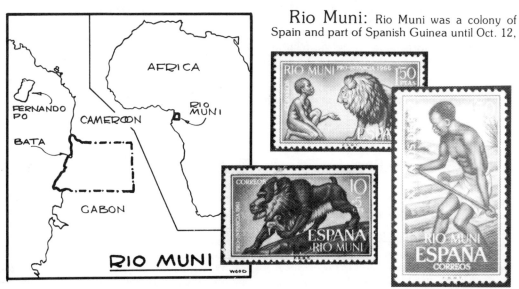

1968, when it merged with Fernando Po (q.v.) and the islands of Eloby, Annobon, and Corisco (q.v.) to become the independent nation of Equatorial Guinea (q.v.).

It is a large area of some 10,000 square miles located on the west coast of Africa between the countries of Gabon and Cameroon.

The population was estimated in 1960 at 183,400.

Its capital city is Bata, although the national capital of Equatorial Guinea is now Malaba (Santa Isobel) on the island of Fernando Po.

Cocoa, coffee, and timber are the mainstays of the economy. Spanish colonial stamps inscribed "Rio Muni" were used from 1960 to 1968, when Equatorial Guinea was formed.

Previously, stamps of Spanish Guinea were used.

Riparato: Italian word for "repaired."

Riporto: Italian word for "transfer."

RIS: Overprint of stamps of Dutch East Indies for the newly formed United States of Indonesia (q.v.).

Ristampa: Italian word for "reprint."

Ritaglio: Italian word for "cut square."

Riyal: A unit of currency used in Dubai (from 1966), Qatar (from 1967), Umm al Qiwain (from 1967), Hejaz (from 1928), and Saudi Arabia (from 1960).

Rizeh: Stamps issued by Russia in 1909 for use in the Turkish Empire were overprinted with the names of various Turkish cities in which there were Russian post offices.

These stamps overprinted "Rizeh" were issued in 1910 to commemorate the 50th anniversary of Russian post offices in the Turkish Empire.

R.O.: The letters "R.O." stand for "Rumelie Orientale." They were overprinted on stamps of Turkey for use in Eastern Rumelia (q.v.).

Robertsport: (See Harper.)

Rocket Mail: Although they were never a practical means of transporting mail, a number of experimental rockets have carried mail, these flights being mostly prompted by the desire to create philatelic covers.

Dr. Robert H. Goddard, the father of US rocketry, was working on a mail-carrying rocket as early as the World War I period, but mail was

not carried by rocket in the US until 1935. Even then, the flights were more in the nature of publicity stunts.

Mail-carrying rockets were first fired in 1931 in Austria, when Friedrich Schmiedl launched a rocket carrying 102 covers that bore Austrian postage stamps but were canceled privately. A number of similar flights took place in the following two years.

In the mid-1930s, Gehard Zucher (Zucker, according to some sources) fired rockets in England, Italy, Switzerland, and the Netherlands.

He even tried to fire a mail-carrying rocket from the European coast to England, according to Cabeen *(Standard Handbook of Stamp Collecting,* Crowell, New York, 1979), but it fell short.

What the British authorities' attitude was, or even whether they were aware of the attempt, is not recorded.

Certainly the flight, had it succeeded, would have posed a very considerable danger to any unfortunate Briton who may have been occupying the point of impact. Nevertheless, it was a remarkable example of events casting their shadows.

In India, Dr. Stephen Smith was very active in rocketry during the years between the two world wars. He made several mail-carrying firings and also used rockets to carry supplies to flood-isolated areas.

After a while, it became pretty obvious that rockets were not ideal as a means of transporting mail, since it was never certain exactly where the mail would be delivered!

And so the military took over and put the knowledge of rocketry to good (or bad) use during WWII. The most spectacular example was the German attempts to destroy London with their giant V2 rockets.

Since the war, rocket mail has been confined to the philatelically contrived stunt, and no serious rocket mail system has emerged.

You might want to label as "rocket mail" the Apollo 11 carriage of the die for the US 1969 Moon Landing stamp to the surface of the moon, and the canceling there of a souvenir cover, but even this was a stunt rather than a serious mail-carrying experiment.

A number of stamp-like labels have been issued to frank private rocket "mail," including two for a flight at Greenwood Lake, N.Y., in 1936.

In July 1936, mail-carrying rockets were fired between the US and Mexico, and two triangular labels were issued by the Loyal Service Post #37 of the American Legion, which conducted the flights.

Other similar labels have been issued for various rocket flights, according to Sanabria.

Attempts to send mail ashore by rocket from ships off Niuafo'ou Island (see Tin Can Mail Service) between 1902 and 1915 are reported by Clyde Carriker, but most was lost in the sea or fell in the dense jungle ashore.

Rocking In: When the transfer roll impresses its design into the plate that will form the printing surface, it is done with a rocking motion and is thus called "rocking in." (See Printing, Intaglio.)

Rod: Danish and Swedish word for the color "red."

RODI: Overprint and inscription indicates stamps issued for the Italian colony of Rhodes (q.v.).

Roessler, Albert C.: Albert C. Roessler (1883-1952) was a stamp dealer who was best known for his cacheted covers, and examples of his work are sought by collectors.

Roessler was born April 7, 1883, in Newark, N.J., and spent a portion of his early years in Colorado. He was a founding member of the Denver Stamp Club, established Dec. 13, 1905.

Within a few years he was established as a stamp dealer in East Orange, N.J., after a period of Nassau Street (New York) activity.

With the coming of air mail in the US in 1918, Roessler began the creation of cacheted covers.

His first cachet, according to Barry Newton (*A.C. Roessler: Photo Cachet Catalogue*, FDC Publishing Co., 1976), was for the first air mail flight between Washington, New York, and Philadelphia. He published *Air Mail Stamp News* from 1918 to 1938.

Something of a mystery man, Roessler would never permit his photograph to be published, and no confirmed pictures of him are known.

Dan Barber, in his "Via Air Mail" column in *Stamp Collector* (Sept. 13, 1980), reproduces two photographs which might be those of Roessler.

Roessler is reported to have gone out of the stamp business in 1940, and he died on Jan. 26, 1952.

Roi: French word for "king."

Rojo: Spanish word for the color "red."

Rojo Cobre: Spanish expression for the color "copper red."

Rojo Ladrillo: Spanish expression for the color "brick red."

Rojo Veneciano: Spanish expression for the color "Venetian red."

Rojo Vinoso: Spanish expression for the color "claret."

Rol: Dutch word for "coil (stamp)."

Roll of Distinguished Philatelists, The: The Roll of Distinguished Philatelists was established in the United Kingdom by the Philatelic Congress of Great Britain in 1921 to honor persons who have made significant contributions to philately.

The first to sign the roll was King George V, a knowledgeable collector who, while Prince of Wales, served as president of the Royal Philatelic Society, London.

Many of the US's leading philatelists have been honored by invitation to sign the roll. Each year a committee selects several names from among those nominated by any philatelic organization affiliated with the British Philatelic Federation, which was created in 1976 from the British Philatelic Association and the Philatelic Congress.

Roller Cancelation: (See Cancelation, Roller.)

Rollo de Sellos: Spanish expression for "coil (stamp)."

Rollo di Francobolli: Italian expression for "coil (stamp)."

Romagna: Once one of the Roman States (see Papal States), Romagna split from the group and became independent until 1860, when it became part of the Kingdom of Sardinia, later of the unified Kingdom of Italy.

Its capital was the city of Ravenna.

It issued its own stamps from 1859 until 1862, when Italian stamps replaced the local issues.

ROMAGNA

There are many reprints of the Romagna stamps, and forged cancelations on supposedly used copies are common.

ROMAGNE: Inscription on stamps of the Roman state of Romagna (q.v.).

ROMANA: The inscription "ROMANA" appears on the early issues of Romania (q.v.).

Romania: Located on the shore of the Black Sea, the Socialist Republic of Romania developed from the two principalities of Moldavia and Walachia.

Moldavia was formed in 1349, and Walachia had been created in 1330 by John Bassaraba as an escape from Hungarian domination.

Soon the two principalities increased in size and power, but they came under Turkish control, Walachia in 1411 and Moldavia in 1512. As Turkey tightened its hold, the two turned northward toward Russia for help.

In 1774 Russia defeated Turkey and obtained better treatment for Walachia and Moldavia.

The two states united in 1862 and were recognized by Turkey as the autonomous principality of Romania.

The Treaty of Berlin in 1878 recognized Romania's independence, and in 1881 it became a kingdom under Carol I.

Although trying to maintain good relations with the Austro-Hungarian Empire, the Russian Empire, and Balkan neighbors, Carol was partial to Austria.

On his death, however, his nephew Ferdinand came to the throne, and in 1916 he attacked Hungary. This was a disaster, and within six months his country was defeated and occupied.

When the Allies became victorious, Romania reentered the war on their side one day before it ended and, as a result of the territory acquired, doubled in size. Among the areas taken over was Russian Bessarabia, which was to cause problems later on.

When World War II loomed, Romania of-

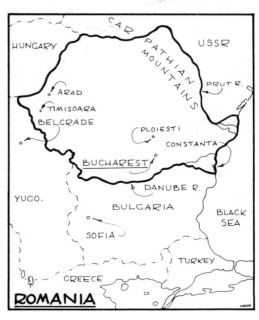

ROMANIA

ficially proclaimed neutrality but favored Germany. Soon it began losing territory it had previously gained, including Bessarabia, which was reoccupied by the Soviet Union.

Germany then occupied Romania on the pretext of protecting the oil fields from British attack.

Then allied, for better or for worse, with Germany, Romania took an active part in the invasion of the USSR, regaining Bessarabia and pushing far beyond.

But the good times did not last, as the Soviet Union came back in 1944 and drove into Romania, soon turning it into a Soviet satellite.

Since the early 1960s, Romania has been one of the more outspoken of the Eastern European countries under Soviet control, and it actually denounced the Soviet invasion of Czechoslovakia in 1968.

Relations with the West and with the People's Republic of China have been maintained, and Soviet troops have been prohibited from entering the country. Despite this, internal policies are said to be repressive.

The area of Romania is currently 91,699 square miles, and the population is estimated at 22,270,000. The latest per capita income figure is $3,100 and the literacy rate 98%.

Romania's unit of currency is the leu (100 bani). In 1981 it was 4.47 to the US dollar.

The first Romanian stamps were issued in 1865 and followed those of Moldavia and Moldavia-Walachia.

Over the years, the country's stamps have mirrored political events, and you can trace its modern history by leafing through the stamp catalog.

Since WWII, the stamp-issuing policies have closely followed the pattern of the other East European countries.

The address of the philatelic bureau is ILEX-IM, 3-13 Decembrie St., Box 136/137, Bucharest, Romania.

Romania, Austrian Occupation of:

When Romania attacked Hungarian Transylvania in June 1916, it was soundly defeated, and within six months the Austro-Hungarian Army was in control of the country.

During this occupation, Austro-Hungarian occupation stamps were issued.

They comprised two issues: the first in 1917 features Emperor Karl of Austria, and the second is similar except that the currency designation panel does not have a shaded background.

Romania, Bulgarian Occupation of:

Stamps were issued during the World War I oc-

cupation of Romania's Dobruja region by Bulgarian troops.

They consisted of Bulgarian stamps of the 1915 issue with an overprint including the date "1916-1917."

Romania, German Occupation of:

During World War I, Romania was defeated by the Central Powers and for a period was occupied by Germany, Austria-Hungary, and Bulgaria.

The German occupation authorities issued a number of occupation stamps, mostly German issues overprinted "M.V.i.R." (Militar Verwaltung in Rumanien — Military Administration of Romania) in various styles, including boxed and Roman, script, and German lettering.

In 1918 German stamps were issued overprinted "Gultig/ 9. Armee."

Romanian Occupation of Hungary:

(See Temesvar.)

Romanian Philatelic Club: The Romanian Philatelic Club caters to collectors of Romania and offers a quarterly bulletin, *Romanian Philatelic Studies.*

Information is available from Mark Fromer, 1519 East Eighth St., Brooklyn, NY 11230.

Roman Numerals: (See Numerals, Roman.)

Roman States: (See Papal States.)

Rombos: Spanish word for "lozenge."

ROMINA: The inscription "ROMINA" preceded by "R.P." was used on stamps of Romania during the period 1954-64.

'Roo: The name " 'Roo" is given to the first issue of the Commonwealth of Australia in 1913.

The design features a kangaroo, which in Australia is familarly known as a " 'roo," and a map of the country. The issue was designed by B. Young and remained in use for many years.

Rood: Dutch word for the color "red."

Rosa: German, Italian, and Spanish word for the color "pink." Also used for the color rose.

Rose: The German, Italian, and Spanish word for the color "rose" is rosa.

Rose: French word for the color "pink."

Rose Engine: Invented by Jacob Perkins of the famous security printing firm of Perkins, Bacon & Co., the Rose Engine was a device used to engrave complex geometric designs as seen on bank notes and many postage stamps. (See Engine Turning.)

Ross Dependency:

The Ross Dependency is an area of Antarctica under New Zealand administration.

The territory comprises a wedge of the Antarctic continent south of latitude 60 degrees south and between 160 degrees east and 150 degrees west.

It came under New Zealand control in 1923 and has an area of about 160,000 square miles. In common with other Antarctic claims, it is not recognized by the US.

The Ross Dependency was named for Sir James Clark Ross (1800-1862), a British rear admiral who commanded HMS *Erebus* and HMS *Terror* during an Antarctic expedition of 1839-43.

Stamps issues for the Ross Dependency are presumably intended mainly to support New Zealand's claim to the area rather than for actual postal purposes, and they feature ships (including HMS *Erebus)*, explorers Ernest Shackleton and Robert F. Scott, together with a map of the area, and various other asects of Antarctic exploration.

Rossica Society: The Rossica Society of Russian Philately was formed on April 14, 1929, in Yugoslavia by Eugene Arkhangelsky.

Its journal was first published in 1930 in Yugoslavia, then was moved to the Baltic states and later, just before World War II, to Shanghai. There was a gap of inactivity during the war, and the society was reestablished in 1952 in New York under A.A. Chebotievich.

Bilingual until the early 1960s, the journal has since been published only in English.

The society is currently based in Washington, D.C., and offers collectors interested in all aspects of Russian philately a number of benefits, including an expertizing service, as well as the journal.

Information is available from Dr. Kennedy L. Wilson, 7415 Venice St., Falls Church, VA 22043.

Rosso: Italian word for the color "red."

Rosso di Mattone: Italian expression for the color "brick red."

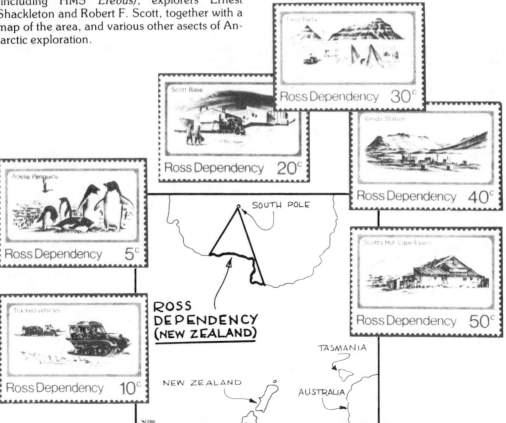

Rosso di Rame: Italian expression for the color "copper red."

Rosso Veneziano: Italian expression for the color "Venetian red."

Rostbraun: German word for the color "rust."

Rostov Issue: The name "Rostov Issue" is given to stamps issued in 1918-19 by the Don Government of South Russia that was set up by General Denikin during the fight against the Bolsheviks.

The first issue comprised surcharges on Russian stamps, and a single stamp issued in 1919 features a portrait of the Cossack leader, Ermak. (See Russia, South.)

Rot: German word for the color "red."

Rotary on Stamps Unit: (See American Topical Association Study Units.)

Rotary Printing: Foreign terms for "rotary printing" include rotatiedruk (Dutch), impression par cylindre (French), walzendruck (German), stampa rotativa (Italian), and impresion rotativa (Spanish).

Rotatiedruk: Dutch word for "rotary printing."

Roto: Spanish word for "broken."

Rotogravure Printing: (See Printing, Photogravure.)

Rouad (Ruad): Rouad Island, or Ile Rouad (Arwad), is located less than two miles

off the coast of Syria between Latakia (q.v.) and Tripoli.

A French post office operated on the island during 1916, and Blanc, Mouchon, and Merson key types inscribed "Levant" were overprinted "Ile Rouad." The first three stamps are relatively expensive, and good forgeries are reported.

A Phoenician city was located on the small, rocky island, which is about a mile in circumference.

Mentioned extensively in ancient times, the island was thought to have had a flourishing trade with Africa during the eighth century BC. It fell to Alexander the Great in 332 BC.

Rouble: The rouble is the unit of currency used in the USSR (q.v.). Chiefly British spelling.

Rouge: French word for the color "red."

Rouge Brique: French expression for the color "brick red."

Rouge Brun Terne: French expression for the color "Venetian red."

Rouge Cuivre: French for the color "copper red."

Rouleau de Timbres: French expression for "coil (stamp)."

Roulette: Foreign words for roulette include doorstik (Dutch), percage (French), durchstochen (German), foratura (Italian), and ruleta (Spanish).

Rouletting: Rouletting is a form of stamp separation that was once quite widely used, until it gave way to perforating (q.v.). It can still be found used in certain specialized applications.

In rouletting, unlike perforating, the paper is slit in various ways, leaving "bridges" of paper that can be easily torn apart, but no paper is removed.

In England about 1847, Henry Archer (See Archer, Henry) had experimented with a rouletting device before turning to the perforation equipment he devised as a means of separating

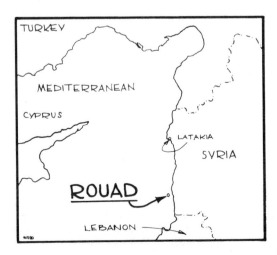

early British stamps that was more practical than merely hacking them apart with scissors. (See Perforation.)

He had found that the equipment he made to perform the rouletting operation tended to wear out quickly, and so he abandoned this method of separation.

Other countries, however, developed a great variety of rouletting methods. (The major types are illustrated, and their French names and English-language equivalents are noted.) Their names are derived from the shapes of the slits made in the paper.

The early issues of Finland are among the most outstanding examples of rouletting. The catalog notes that the form of rouletting is called "serpentine," in French, "Perce en Serpentin."

This is further subdivided into varying degrees, much as a perforation might come in a number of gauges. In this case, the depth of the large indentations is measured, and slight differences in the shape of the teeth are noted.

As can be the case with coarse perforations, here it is common to find damaged teeth, and stamps having this type of separation are seldom found in anything approaching perfect condition.

This is an excellent example of a case in which you must adjust your normal standards of condition so as to avoid a search for material in a condition that would be unreasonable to expect and very unlikely to be found.

Rouletting has been used in recent years to create unusual philatelic items. Where a large design is subdivided to form several stamps, the design may be perforated all around and then subdivided by rouletting. This is done so that the overall design is not marred by rows of perforations that would remove portions of the design.

A very good example of an item that could have benefited from this treatment is the US 2c Cape Hatteras se-tenant (q.v.) quartet of 1972.

Because they were small stamps, a large part of their design was lost to the perforating machine, and the attractive appearance was greatly marred.

An excellent example of how effective rouletting can be is the Chagall souvenir sheet issued by the United Nations Postal Adminsitration in 1967.

Two 1969 folklore designs released by Papua New Guinea illustrate a combination of perforating and rouletting. Here a larger perforated design is divided by rouletting into two separate stamps.

The small, so-called Bantam issues, which South Africa released during World War II as a paper conservation measure, are another exam-

ple of the effective combined use of perforation and rouletting.

A different method of rouletting that is almost a part of the printing operation is known as "rouletting in color" (in French, "Perce en lignes de couleur").

In this case, the stamps are printed from a number of separate cliches (q.v.), and between these cliches, which form the printing plate, are inserted notched rules.

The notches are raised so that when the paper is pressed against the inked plate, the notched rule slits the paper in the form of a series of straight cuts, or "Perce en Lignes."

The name "rouletted in color" comes from the fact that the projecting portion of the rule receives ink when the plate is inked prior to printing and thus transfers color to the area of the roulette, giving the impression that the paper has been rouletted along a dotted, colored line.

The 1865-73 issues of Luxembourg is an example of such rouletting, as is the Queensland 1d stamp of 1899.

Roumania: Spelling variation of Romania (q.v.).

ROUMELIE ORIENTALE: Overprint on stamps of Turkey for use in Eastern Rumelia (q.v.).

Routing Code Symbols: The name "routing code symbol" is given by the US Postal Service to those brightly colored round or rectangular (since about 1976) stickers often noted on a piece of mail when it is delivered.

These stickers bear either a black letter or numeral and are affixed to the top letter in a bundle intended for one destination.

The meanings of the various symbols are as follows:

"F" on blue: all items in bundle destined for the same address.

"D" on red: all items in bundle destined for the same five-digit ZIP code area.

"3" on green: all items in bundle destined for

the same area as determined by the first three ZIP code digits.

"C" on yellow: all items in bundle destined for the same city.

"S" on orange: all items in bundle destined for the same state.

Rowland Hill: (See Hill, Sir Rowland.)

Royal Blue:
Foreign terms for the color "royal blue" include bleu roi (French), konigsblau (German), assurro reale (Italian), and azul real (Spanish).

Royal Cypher:
A cypher (the mainly British variation of "cipher") comprises a set of initials, often ornate and usually in script lettering.

Britain's royal cypher combines the initials of the sovereign with the British crown.

It has been seen on various postage stamps, including the illustrated pair from Fiji, which features the royal cypher of Queen Victoria.

Royal cyphers also appear on British mailboxes, or piller boxes (q.v.) and they have also been used as overprints and watermarks.

Royal Philatelic Society, London:
The "Royal" was founded in April 1869 and is claimed to be the oldest existing philatelic society.

The society has had some illustrious presidents, including the Duke of York, later King George V, who continued as patron after he came to the throne.

In 1906 King Edward VII gave permission for the prefix "Royal" to be used.

The Earl of Crawford was another philatelic student who became president and whose name lives on in the society's highest honor, the Crawford Medal.

This medal is given to the person who contributes "the most valuable and original piece of philatelic work towards the study and knowledge of philately published within two years preceding the award."

The headquarters of the society is at 41 Devonshire Place, London.

Royal Philatelic Society of Canada:
Though there were several national philatelic organizations in Canada prior to World War I, the roots of the Royal Philatelic Society of Canada can be traced back to the founding of

the Winnipeg Stamp Society in 1919.

In 1920, according to Canadian philatelist Kenneth Rowe, who kindly supplied much of the information given here, membership was extended to collectors in all parts of Canada, and the name was later changed to the Canadian Philatelic Association.

The name was again changed, in 1923, to the Canadian Philatelic Society, and the headquarters was moved to Toronto. Incorporation came in 1926 — a move that was to be appreciated during subsequent depression-caused financial difficulties.

As with most philatelic societies, a journal is the cement that binds the organization together, and the Royal Philatelic Society of Canada has had a considerable number of official journals. However, in March 1950, the first issue of its own *Canadian Philatelist* appeared, and the society has published its own journal ever since. It appears bimonthly.

Following the end of WWII, a period of expansion accompanied postwar prosperity, and in 1959 the society received its greatest honor when it was granted permission to use the title "Royal," and the present name was born.

The society speaks for Canadian philately in the councils of the Federation International de Philatelie (FIP) and the Federacion Interamericana de Filatelia (FIAF), and a Canadian collector must be a member of the society or an affiliated chapter before being allowed to enter international competition.

The society played a major role in establishing the Philatelic Book Collection of the National

Library of Canada, and listings of new additions appear in the *Canadian Philatelist*.

The society introduced its own fellowship award in 1960, given for service to philately. So far, 39 such fellowships have been granted.

Membership information is available from The Royal Philatelic Society of Canada, Box 1054, Station A, Toronto, Ontario, Canada, M5W 1G5.

Royaume: French word for "kingdom."

ROYAUME DE CAMBODGE:
Identifies stamps of Cambodia (q.v.).

ROYAUME D'EGYPT: Identifies
some stamps of Egypt (q.v.)

ROYAUME DE L'ARABE
SOUDITE: Identifies some stamps of Saudi Arabia (q.v.).

ROYAUME DE MAROC: Identifies
stamps of the Kingdom of Morocco.

Rpf: This overprint, preceded by a numeral, found on stamps of Luxembourg, identifies stamps issued by the German forces that invaded and occupied the country during World War II.

The overprint represents an abbreviation of "reichpfennig."

RPO: The initials "RPO" in a postmark indicate that the item of mail was processed by a Railway Post Office. (See Railway Mail Service.)

RSA: The initials "RSA" stand for Republic of South Africa.

Ruanda-Urundi: Prior to World War I, Ruanda-Urundi was part of German East Africa. Following the expulsion of Germany, the occupied area was mandated to Belgium by the League of Nations in 1924.

It became independent after WWII. On July 1, 1962, Ruanda became the Republic of Rwanda (q.v.), and Urundi became the Republic of Burundi (q.v.).

The first stamps of Ruanda-Urundi came in 1924 and were Belgian stamps overprinted "RUANDA/URUNDI."

Stamps inscribed "RUANDA-URUNDI" were released in 1931 and feature various scenes in the mandated area.

In 1942 a handsome pictorial issue was released, followed by stamps reproducing various native carvings in 1948.

African animals are the subject of a 1959 set,

but with the coming of independence, stamps of Ruanda-Urundi were replaced by those of the two new republics.

Ruble: Unit of currency used in the USSR and associated areas, including the Russian Empire. Comprises 100 kopecks.

Rublis: Unit of currency used by Latvia until 1923. It comprised 100 kapeikas.

Ruckseite: German word for "back."

Ruhleben: Ruhleben was a World War I camp in Germany for British nationals. A variety of postal history material exists, and collections have been formed of it.

Ruleta: Spanish word for "roulette."

Rumania: "Rumania" is a spelling variation of Romania (q.v.).

RUMANIEN: This overprint accompanied by a surcharge was applied to German stamps by German forces occupying Romanian territory during World War I.

Running Chicken: (See Cancelation, Fancy.)

Running Turkey: (See Cancelation, Fancy.)

Rupee: A unit of currency used extensively for various periods in India and surrounding areas, including Aden (to 1951), Bahrain, British East Africa, Burma, German East Africa, Iraq (to 1908), Kuwait, Mesopotamia, Muscat, Pakistan, Somaliland Protectorate (to 1951), Tibet (to 1933), and Zanzibar (to 1908), plus several of the Indian native states.

It was also used at various periods in Afghanistan, British Indian Ocean Territory, Ceylon (Sri Lanka), Maldive Islands, Mauritius, Nepal, Seychelles, and Portuguese Timor.

Rupia: Unit of currency used in Portuguese India. It comprised 16 tangas.

Rupiah: Unit of currency used in Indonesia.

Rupie: Spelling variation of "rupee," used in German East Africa.

Rural Free Delivery: A giant step forward in US mail service was taken with the introduction of Rural Free Delivery on Oct. 1, 1896. The first routes were established in West

Virginia and based on the towns of Uvilla, Halltown, and Charlestown.

There were more than 80 routes in 29 states by 1896, each served by a horse-drawn RFD wagon.

By the 1960s, there were 32,000 routes, serving 34,000,000 patrons.

RFD postmarks were mostly of the straight-line type, which included a four-line inscription with the letters "R.F.D." on the top line and town, date, and state on the subsequent lines. The route number appeared in the killer portion.

"Mailed on Rural Route" is an endorsement marking, found in straight-line type and circular with a killer attached.

Russia:
The term "Russia" referred to an empire overthrown by the 1917 Russian Revolution.

It now refers only to the Russian Soviet Federated Socialist Republic (q.v.), one of the 16 "republics" that make up the USSR (q.v.).

The word "Russian" should only be used to denote the former Russian Empire, and it is so used in this work.

However, the error of referring to the USSR as "Russia" is common both within philatelic circles and without.

Russian stamp issues ceased following the revolution, and stamps of the new USSR were introduced.

Russian Offices in China:
(See China, Russian Offices in.)

Russian Offices in Turkey:
(See Levant, Russian.)

Russia, South:
Stamps of a number of anti-Bolshevist forces and governments in Southern Russia were issued during 1918-19 following the Russian revolution.

Included were the Don Territory Government, which used Russian stamps surcharged; the Kuban Territory Government, which issued Russian stamps and Russian Postal Savings Bank stamps surcharged; the Crimea Regional Government, which issued two Russian stamps surcharged, one of which was used as currency; the South Russian Government of General Denikin, which used specially designed stamps issued at Ekaterinodar inscribed "United Russia"; and General Wrangel's Government of South Russia, which issued surcharged Russian stamps.

Russian Soviet Federated Socialist Republic:
Prior to Aug. 19, 1923, when the first stamps of the Union of

Soviet Socialist Republic were issued, stamps were used under the title of Russian Soviet Federated Socialist Republic.

These began in 1918 with the well-known symbolic design of a sword severing the chains of the repressive Czarist regime, an example of which is illustrated.

RUSSUSCH POLEN:
Overprint on German stamps for occupation of Poland during World War I.

Rust:
Foreign words for the color rust include brun rouille (French), rostbraun (German), castagna (Italian), and castano oxidado (Spanish).

Rustenburg:
(See Transvaal.)

Rwanda:
The area of Ruanda (q.v.) was part of German East Africa prior to World War I and passed to Belgium, together with Urundi, now the Republic of Burundi (q.v.), as a League of Nations mandated territory in 1924.

Independence came on July 1, 1962, as the Republic of Rwanda. The latest per capita income figure is $178, making the country one of the less prosperous of the world's nations.

Virtually the entire work force is employed in agriculture, and the main crops are coffee, cotton, tea, and tobacco.

The area of the country is 10,169 square miles, and the population is estimated at 5,050,000. The capital city is Kigeli.

The unit of currency is the franc (100 centimes), which in 1981 was 92.84 to the US dollar.

Rwanda's stamp-issuing history began with independence, and it has been fairly prolific,

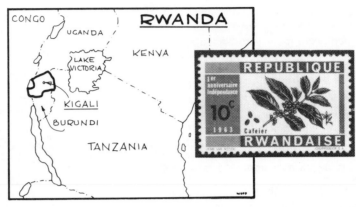

with a number of issues having themes unrelated to the country.

The address of the philatelic bureau is Direction Generale des PTT, Section Philatelique, Kigali, Republic of Rwanda.

Ryukyu Islands:
The Ryukyu Islands group is a chain of about 90 islands that extends south from Japan towards Taiwan. Prior to World War II, the islands made up the Okinawa prefecture of Japan.

After taking the islands, shortly before the end of the war, US forces occupied them, and a US military administration was set up.

In 1948 the islands became a stamp-issuing entity and continued to release stamps until May 15, 1972, when the islands were restored to Japan. They have now reverted to their status as part of Japan and use stamps of that country.

Coveted by both Japan and China, the history of the Ryukyus has, from the seventh century, been one of invasion, occupation, and the payment of tribute — sometimes to both Japan and China at the same time.

In 1879 the islands became part of Japan, which they remained until WWII.

The area of the islands is 921 square miles, and during the US administration period the population was about 943,000.

Prior to issuance of the first stamps, in 1948, a number of local issues had been created on the islands.

The stamps of the Ryukyu Islands soon became extremely popular with collectors both in Japan and the US. Despite this popularity, with the resulting temptation to issue more stamps, the Ryukyu postal authorities released fewer than 300 basic varieties during the 24-year stamp-issuing period.

Ryukyu Philatelic Specialist Society:
The Ryukyu Philatelic Specialist Society is a group dedicated to the collection and study of stamps and postal history of the Ryukyu Islands under United States administration. That period covers the years 1945 to 1972.

From the Dragon's Den is its quarterly journal, and the group offers members single-subject published studies.

The group also operates an expertizing service. Additional information is available from Lois M. Evans, Box 752, Quincy, MA 01269.

S: Prior to the introduction of stamps overprinted "O.S." in 1874 for general Official use, the British colony of South Australia created a number of different overprints to indicate use by a specific government.

"S" stood for Sheriff.

S: The letter "S," together with a crescent and star, overprinted on stamps of the Straits Settlements indicates stamps intended for use in Selangor, one of the states making up the Straits Settlements, during 1878-82.

S: The overprint "S" on air mail stamps of Columbia indicates that the stamp was sold in Switzerland to frank mail from that country to an interior point in Colombia and carried by the Colombian airline SCADTA (q.v.) during the early 1920s.

It was also necessary that such mail be franked with appropriate Swiss stamps.

The mail would be handed either to a Colombian consul or to an agent of the airline.

Saar, The:

The Saar, now the 10th state of the Federal Republic of Germany, is a hilly area of woodland and fields bisected by the valley of the Saar.

It is a coal-mining area, and there are blast furnaces and steelworks located in the valley between the capital city of Saarbrucken and the town of Volklingen.

The Saarland has an area of 991 square miles, and the population exceeds one million.

Although its inhabitants are German-speaking, the area had been ruled by the French for some 150 years up to the defeat of Napoleon, when it became part of the Prussian province on the Rhine, except for a small area ceded to Bavaria.

Following World War I, the Saar was placed under League of Nations control by the Treaty of Versailles. The coal mines were given to France in partial repayment for the suffering caused by the Germans.

Control by the League of Nations was to last for 15 years, with a plebiscite held at the end of that time.

When, in 1935, the vote was held, more than 90% of the population voted to rejoin Germany, and on March 1, 1935, the area became the Saarland Province of the Third Reich.

The territory issued its own stamps between 1920 and 1935 and again following WWII, during the period of French control, from 1947 to Jan. 3, 1948.

On that date, it obtained a semi-independent status and continued to issue stamps until two years after final reunion with the Federal Republic of Germany on Jan. 1, 1957. (See SAARLAND.)

France was allowed to continue working the Warndt coalfield on the French-Saar border and to make the River Moselle into a canal between Coblenz and Thionville.

The common language is German, but the

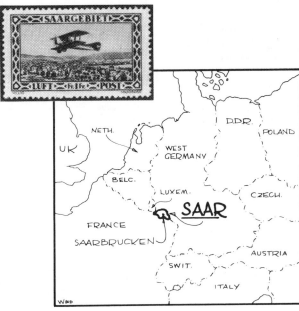

University of the Saarland at Saarbrucken is bilingual, with French and German used equally.

The industrialized belt along the Saar Valley contains most of the population. Chemical, glass, and ceramic industries are located there, in addition to iron and steel plants.

Despite its German status, the Saar maintains close links with French Lorraine, and the region is an important part of the European Coal and Iron Community.

The stamp-issuing period following WWII brought forth a number of attractive adhesives, among them the beautifully engraved Stamp Day issues.

During both stamp-issuing periods, many of the Saar's industrial and mining facilities were depicted on its stamps, together with examples of its architecture and culture.

After close to 40 years of turmoil and of being tossed back and forth as part of the spoils of war, the people of Saar are now enjoying a settled, secure life and using the stamps of the Federal Republic of Germany on their mail. (See SARRE, SAARGEBIET.)

SAARGEBIET: The overprint or inscription "SAARGEBIET" appears on some stamps of the Saar (q.v.).

The first use of "SAARGEBIET" was as an

overprint on stamps of Germany in 1920. The stamp issue of 1921 depicting various views within the territory was the first to use "SAARGEBIET" as an inscription. This continued until the area was incorporated into Hitler's Third Reich, and special stamps came to an end until after World War II.

When stamps were resumed in 1947 under the French administration, the inscription was changed to "SAAR."

SAARLAND: Although the Saar came under German control in 1957, stamps of the Saar continued from 1957 to 1959 but were inscribed "DEUTSCHE BUNDEPOST SAARLAND."

Sabah: Sabah was known as the British colony of North Borneo (q.v.) until 1963, when

it took the name of Sabah before joining the Federation of Malaysia (q.v.).

In 1964 Sabah used stamps of North Borneo overprinted "Sabah," and in 1965 and 1971, stamps bearing that name appeared as part of Malaysia's omnibus issues featuring orchids and butterflies.

Sachet, Stamp: Stamp sachets are containers of loose stamps sold in post offices vending machines. The container may take the form of a folder.

Great Britain has experimented with the use of a small card box in which to dispense stamps.

Since the stamps contained within these sachets are normal specimens, catalogs do not list such items. However, collectors specializing in countries which have produced sachets will usually include them, providing that the container is a product of a postal administration. (See Booklet, Stamp.)

Sachsen: The name "Sachsen" is German for Saxony. It is found inscribed on stamps of

the Kingdom of Saxony from the first issue, in 1850, to the final stamps, released in 1863.

Following World War II, the Soviet Union occupied the area of Saxony, and a large number of local stamps were issued from 1945 until regular issues were made available by the occupation authorities.

Within Saxony, a number of Oberpostdirektionen (Higher Postal Directorates, or OPDs) in various large centers issued their own stamps. These included Saxony (OPD Halle), West Saxony (OPD Leipzig), and East Saxony (OPD Dresden).

The stamp illustrated is one of several issued by OPD Dresden, although it bears no identifying inscription. (See Saxony, West and East.)

SAE: The letters "SAE" stands for "Stamped Addressed Envelope." If an SAE is requested, it means that an addressed envelope with postage affixed should be enclosed for use by the person responding.

In philately, it is considered polite to always include an SAE when making an inquiry. "SAE" is a variation of "SASE" (q.v.), which stands for "self-addressed, stamped envelope."

Sage Green: Foreign terms for "sage green" include vert sauge (French), salbeigrun (German), and verde salvia (Italian and Spanish).

Sage Type: (See Peace and Commerce Type.)

Saggio: Italian word for "essay."

Saguia al Hamra: (See Spanish Sahara.)

SAHARA ESPANOL: The overprint "SAHARA ESPANOL" appears on Spanish stamps issued for Spanish Sahara.

SAHARA OCCIDENTAL: A set of stamps inscribed "SAHARA OCCIDENTAL" was issued in 1924 for use in the Spanish colonies of La Aguera (q.v.) and Rio de Oro (q.v.).

St. Andrew's Cross: The name "St. Andrew's Cross" is given to the crosses printed on four blank spaces left in panes of some early stamps of Austria.

Such a marking is seen on the blank still attached to a stamp on the illustrated early Austrian air mail cover.

The same device has also been used on stamp-size blank "tabs" contained in some British stamp booklets.

The purpose of this is to prevent stamp forgers from having access to blank perforated and gummed stamp paper upon which to create forged stamps.

There is also a technical printing consideration that renders desirable the inclusion of a

This cover bears an Austrian stamp to which is attached a blank inscribed with a St. Andrew's Cross. A number of Austrian stamps were printed in sheets including blank stamp-sized perforated labels which it is said were inscribed with the St. Andrew's Cross to prevent blank paper becoming available to counterfeiters.

printing surface in such otherwise blank areas, and this is also the reason for the so-called "Jubilee Lines" (q.v.) on the sheet margins of many British stamps.

These additional printing surfaces help to reduce plate wear by balancing the inking roller. (See Pillar.)

St. Christopher: (See St. Kitts-Nevis-Anguilla.)

St. Helena: Once the tomb for an emperor, lonely St. Helena is a tiny, 47-square-mile speck in the South Atlantic Ocean.

When British government officials were pondering the problem of keeping the defeated Napoleon from making a comeback similar to that from Elba, they selected isolated St. Helena. And they chose well.

He lived there from 1815 until his death in 1821.

Of volcanic origin, the island is almost circled by high cliffs. Its only safe landing place is at James Bay, where the island capital of Jamestown is located.

Because of its warm but temperate climate, much exotic plant life thrives there along with that of less equatorial regions.

The island was discovered on May 21, 1502, by the Portuguese Joao da Nova Castella and named for the wife of the Emperor Constantine because it was sighted on her birthday.

The first known settlement was established in 1659 by the East India Company. In 1673 the Dutch captured the island but were soon expelled.

In December 1673, the East India Company in a new charter declared itself to be "the true

and absolute lords and proprietors of the island."

During Napoleon's exile, regular army troops garrisoned the island, which was ruled by a governor appointed by the British government.

After 1821, the East India Company resumed its control.

Two things led to St. Helena's decline: the coming of the steamship and the opening of the Suez Canal. Fewer ships passed that way and even fewer called.

During the South African War, the island was used as a place of detention for prisoners and at one time housed 6,000.

In 1922 the island of Ascension (q.v.) became a dependency of St. Helena, and in 1938 Tristan da Cunha was added.

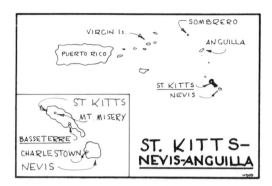

A small ship provides mail and passenger service between Cape Town, St. Helena, and London.

Despite its small size, the island has a rich postage stamp heritage. This began with the handsome first issue of 1856 and continued through the 1934 Centenary issue to the attractive definitive issue of 1976.

The island uses British currency, and stamps may be ordered from the Postmaster, Jamestown, St. Helena, South Atlantic.

St. Helena and Dependencies Philatelic Society:
The St. Helena and Dependencies Philatelic Society is an organization of collectors interested in the stamps and postal history of St. Helena, Ascension, and Tristan da Cunha.

A quarterly newsletter is published, a library is available to members, and auctions are held.

Information is available from Vivian W. Finne, Box 366, Calpella, CA 95418.

St. Kitts-Nevis-Anguilla:
The territory that made up St. Kitts-Nevis-Anguilla comprised the islands of St. Kitts (St. Christopher), Nevis (q.v.), and Anguilla (q.v.). The latter left the grouping in 1967.

The islands are located at the top of the chain of islands that swings east and south from Puerto Rico to South America. They are part of the Leeward Island group (q.v.).

St. Kitts is a long island with its maximum width at the northern end. It has an area of 68 square miles and an excellent climate, with less rainfall than other Caribbean islands.

The "backbone" of the island rises to 3,711-foot Mount Misery. The area of the island that is cultivated is mostly in sugar cane, the raising of which employs most of the island's workforce.

The islands were first sighted by Columbus in 1493 and colonized by the English under Sir Thomas Warner in 1623 to form the first English settlement in the Caribbean. For a time, the French had a toehold on St. Kitts but left in 1783.

The first stamps of the island were issued in 1870 under the name of St. Christopher. These were replaced in 1890 by the general issue for the Leeward Islands.

When stamps for St. Kitts were resumed in 1903, with the inscription reading "St. Kitts-Nevis," one of philately's more amusing bloopers occurred.

The stamp design purports to picture Columbus searching for new lands with a telescope. The only problem is that the telescope was not invented until about 100 years after Columbus died! But we should not blame the stamp designer — he merely reproduced the seal of the island.

Columbus is depicted using a telescope to search for new discoveries. The telescope, however, was not invented until many years after his death!

In 1952 stamps were changed to incorporate a new inscription reading "St. Kitts (or St. Christopher)-Nevis-Anguilla," and they continued to do so until 1980 even though Anguilla left the group to set up housekeeping on its own in 1967.

In common with the stamps of other islands that were once part of the British West Indies, St. Kitts-Nevis stamp issues have become more frequent in recent years, although St. Kitts-Nevis-Anguilla was by no means the worst offender in this respect.

The capital city of St. Kitts is Basseterre, and the population of St. Kitts-Nevis is about 50,000.

The unit of currency is the East Caribbean dollar (q.v.).

The address of the island's philatelic service is Postmaster, GPO, Basseterre, St. Kitts, West Indies.

On March 1, 1980, the postal administration of St. Kitts and Nevis were separated, and each island now issues its own postage stamps.

St. Louis Bears: The nickname "St. Louis Bears" is given to the Postmaster Provisional stamps (q.v.) issued in 1846 by the St. Louis postmaster.

The design reproduces the Missouri coat of arms, which includes two bears, hence the nickname.

The stamps have denominations of 5c, 10c, and 20c and are among the most famous rarities in US philately.

They were printed from copper plates of six subjects individually engraved by J.M. Kershaw.

The three stamps in the left column of the plate were of 5c denomination, and the right-hand column comprised 10c stamps.

Later, when 20c stamps were considered necessary to cover the double rate on a letter going more than 300 miles, the two upper 5c subjects were changed to 20c values. The plate was later restored to its original configuration, according to Scott's *Specialized Catalogue of United States Stamps.*

St. Lucia: The early settlers on the Caribbean island of St. Lucia did not fare very well. The first attempt to settle the island was by the British in 1605, but they were driven off by the stout-hearted Carib Indians, who also expelled the second wave in 1641 after that settlement had begun three years earlier.

Both Britain and France wanted the island, but they were forced to make a treaty with the Indians, promising to leave the island alone providing the Indians would not cause trouble elsewhere!

Any native inhabitants able to extract such respect from the powerful colonizing nations deserved better treatment than they received,

and the British and French continued to battle for possession of the island. After it changed hands 14 times during the next 100 years or so, it was occupied by Britain in 1803 and remained British until it achieved Associated Statehood status in 1967. It became independent on Feb. 22, 1979.

The 238-square-mile island is one of the Windward Islands and is located in the chain of the Lesser Antilles, to the south of Martinique and north of St. Vincent.

Of volcanic origin, the island has boiling sulphur springs, and its best-known landmarks are two tall rock formations known as the Pitons. Each rises higher than 2,000 feet from the sea off the southwest coast.

Bananas, coconuts, cocoa, and citrus are the main crops, and tourism is an important source of revenue. The population is estimated at 121,000, and the latest per capita income figure is $628. The currency is the East Caribbean dollar (q.v.).

The capital city of Castries has suffered several disastrous fires, most recently in 1948.

The island has been blessed with great natural beauty, and it has been similarly fortunate in its postage stamps. The first issue in 1860 is attractively different from the other early Victorian stamps of the British Empire.

But it was not until the 1936 King George V and the 1938 King George VI pictorial issues that the beauty of the island was really reflected on its stamps. These two sets are extremely attractive. The 2/- value of the latter set pictures the Pitons, and the 5/- stamp shows bananas begin loaded onto the Canadian National Railway's *Lady Nelson*, one of the passenger and cargo ships that used to ply the waters of

the eastern Caribbean between British Guiana and Halifax, Canada, on a regular schedule.

The 1948 Castries fire is recalled by a 1951 stamp appropriately reproducing a Phoenix rising from the ashes of the city.

With its recent issues, St. Lucia has lost much of the individuality its stamps once possessed, and there is little to distinguish many of them from the issues of neighboring islands.

Nonetheless, it has largely avoided the practice of issuing stamps primarily for sale to collectors, and its stamp-issuing policies have been reasonably restrained.

The address of the philatelic bureau is Postmaster General, GPO, Castries, St. Lucia, West Indies.

St. Pierre and Miquelon:

A small group of islands 10 miles south of Newfoundland's south coast, St. Pierre and Miquelon now make up a department of France. Their total land area is 93 square miles, and the population is reported at about 6,000.

Miquelon consists of Great Miquelon and Little Miquelon connected by the Isthmus of Langlade.

St. Pierre consists of an island of that name, the island of Ile-aux-Chiens, and other islets. St. Pierre is the capital and only town of significance.

The islands have little importance except as the center of the French cod-fishing industry.

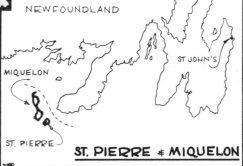

Britain obtained them in 1713 but returned them to France in 1816.

During World War II the islands supported General De Gaulle and his Free French forces.

The first stamps were those of the French colonial general issue handstamped with an overprint and surcharge, issued in 1885.

In 1892 stamps of the Commerce and Navigation key type were issued inscribed for the islands.

These were followed in 1909 by the first pictorial issue.

Collectors of Christmas issues may be interested in knowing that in 1941 a number of St. Pierre and Miquelon stamps were overprinted "NOEL 1941/ FRANCE LIBRE/ F.N.F.L." to mark the Christmas Day plebiscite in which the islanders opted for De Gaulle and freedom.

In 1942 a large number of various stamps of the islands were overprinted "FRANCE LIBRE/ F.N.F.L." These were largely bought up by speculators, and the remainders were sold at a premium by the Free French Agency in Ottawa, Canada. Most are expensive, and there are good forgeries around, so collectors should exercise caution when buying.

Since the war, a number of beautiful stamps have been issued by the islands. Even some postage due labels depict the cod-fishing industry, and others show a large Newfoundland dog.

Stamps of St. Pierre and Miquelon were discontinued on Sept. 15, 1979, when the islands became a department of France and French stamps went into use.

St. Thomas and Prince Island: (See Sao Tome and Principe.)

St. Vincent: An Associated State of Great Britain, St. Vincent is one of the Caribbean Windward Islands and is located south of St. Lucia and north of Grenada.

A number of the Grenadine Islands between St. Vincent and Grenada are attached to St. Vincent for administrative purposes.

The capital city is Kingstown and the island's populations is estimated at 120,000.

The island is volcanic, with its highest mountain being the active volcano of Soufriere, which erupted in 1821, 1902, and again in 1979, causing extensive damage.

Agriculture is the main occupation on the 133 square-mile island. Arrowroot is an important export, and the island is the world's main supplier. Bananas are now the most important single export. The unit of currency is the East Caribbean dollar (q.v.) and the per capita income is $250.

As with most of the Caribbean islands, St. Vincent changed hands between Britain and France a number of times, with a fair amount of resistance being distributed impartially by the native inhabitants. Like citizens in other areas, they eventually lost their home as a result of their audacity, and those few who survived were deported to an island off the Central American coast.

The first stamps of St. Vincent appeared in 1861 and, like those of St. Lucia (q.v.), did not conform to the usual pattern of Victorian postage stamps until the release in 1898 of stamps in the British Commonwealth key type.

The 5/- stamp of 1880, one of the British Commonwealth classics, is a handsome stamp

featuring the seal of the colony. For collectors unable to afford the stamp, St. Vincent used the same design on the high values of the 1955 series.

There has been something of a proliferation of stamps in recent years, including separate stamps for the Grenadines under St. Vincent's administration. Some catalogs do not recognize these latter stamps.

St. Vincent operates its own philatelic bureau, the address of which is Bureau Manager, St. Vincent Philatelic Service, GPO, Kingstown, St. Vincent, West Indies.

The unit of currency is the East Caribbean dollar (q.v.).

Salamanca: In 1868-69, provisional stamps were released for use in the Spanish province of Salamanca.

They consist of Spanish stamps handstamped with a double-line oval containing the words "HABILITADO NACION" between the two lines and "POR LA" in the center.

High quality counterfeits are known to exist of the three stamps so handstamped.

Salbeigrun: German word for the color "sage green."

S. Allan Taylor Society: The S. Allan Taylor Society is a group devoted to the collection and study of cinderella material (q.v.), including phantom and bogus material.

It is named for S. Allan Taylor, a famous creator of bogus stamps who also founded the first philatelic publication in the Western Hemisphere, the *Stamp Collectors' Record*.

The society publishes a journal and holds auctions of cinderella material.

Further information may be obtained from James C. Czyl, Box 69, Posen, IL 60469. (See Taylor, Samuel Allan.)

Salmon: Foreign words for the color "salmon" include saumon (French), lachs (German), and salmone (Italian).

Salmone: Italian word for the color "salmon."

Salonica: (See Levant, British: Levant, Italian Post Offices in.)

Salonicco (Salonica): (See Levant, Italian.)

Salonika: In 1911, Turkey issued a set of 18 stamps overprinted to mark the Sultan's visit to Macedonia.

Four different sets were issued, each bearing the name of a different city, one of which was "Salonika."

The others were Monastir, Pristina, and Uskub.

Salonique: Stamps issued by Russia in 1909 for use in the Turkish Empire were overprinted with the names of various Turkish cities in which there were Russian post offices.

These stamps overprinted "Salonique" were issued to commemorate the 50th anniversary of Russian post offices in the Turkish Empire. (See Trebizonde.)

Salung: A unit of currency used in Siam (Thailand). Four salungs made up one tical.

Salvador: (See El Salvador.)

Salvaged Mail: (See Crash Cover and Wreck Cover.)

Samenhangend: Dutch word for "se-tenant."

Samisch: German word for the color "buff."

Sammlung: German word for "collection."

Samoa: Jacob Roggeveen, a Dutch explorer, is credited with the discovery of the islands of Samoa in 1722.

Samoa was a native kingdom until competition between the US, Germany, and Great Britain concerning their "interests" in the islands during the late 19th century led to the islands' being divided between the US and Germany.

Britain had withdrawn from the argument.

American Samoa remains under US control and uses US stamps, but German Samoa was occupied by New Zealand shortly after the outbreak of World War I in 1914.

After the war, New Zealand obtained a mandate over the ex-German portion and on Jan. 1, 1962, it became the Independent State of Samoa. The official title was shortened to Samoa in 1977.

In addition to the two main islands of Savaii and Upolu, there are several smaller islands.

The total land area is 1,133 square miles, and the population is estimated at 160,000. The latest per capita income figure is $320. The unit of currency is the tala (100 sene), which in 1981 was .94 to the US dollar.

The capital city is Apia.

The islands are volcanic, with fertile valleys and rocky hillsides where the heavy rainfall has eroded the soil. The climate is tropical but equable.

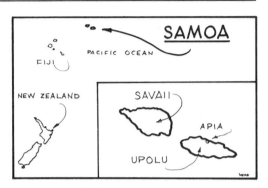

The chief crops are cocoa, coffee, coconuts, and bananas.

Stamps were first issued under the Kingdom of Samoa and are the well-known "Samoa Express" stamps.

During the German period, German stamps overprinted "Samoa" were used, followed by the German Kaiser's yacht colonial key type issues.

When New Zealand forces occupied the islands, the German stamps were overprinted "G.R.I." and surcharged in New Zealand currency. Stamps of New Zealand overprinted were later used.

Beginning in 1935, stamps were inscribed "Western Samoa" and continued thus until independence in 1962, when they were inscribed "SAMOA I SISIFO." The inscription "Western Samoa" was subsequently restored.

The address of the philatelic bureau is Supervisor, Philatelic Bureau, GPO, Apia, Samoa.

SAMOA I SISIFO: Identifies some stamps of Western Samoa (q.v.).

Samos: (See Aegean Islands.)

Sanabria: Nicholas Sanabria Co., Inc., of Ridgefield, Conn., published *The World Airmail Catalogue*. The last edition was published in 1966.

It lists much semi-official, proof, and essay air mail material not included in general catalogs.

Sanar: A unit of currency once used in Afghanistan. Twelve shahi made up one sanar.

Sand Dune States: The term "sand dune state" is a derogatory one applied to a country that issues an excessive number of gaudy stickers that serve little or no postal purpose in their own country and which are created solely for sale to the philatelic trade.

The term came about because of the policies of a number of desert sheikdoms along the shores of the Persian Gulf.

These states, which are now members of the United Arab Emirates, are pursuing a combined policy of a more conservative and responsible nature. This is in contrast to their former, agent-controlled policies of releasing floods of new stamps, few of which ever saw their supposed country of origin.

But the term "sand dune state" persists and proves that a rip-off reputation, once acquired, is very hard to lose.

Sandjak d'Alexandrette: The overprint "Sandjak d'Alexandrette" appeared on the 1938 stamps of Syria for use in the territory of Alexandretta (q.v.), later known as Hatay.

Sandwich Islands: When Captain Cook first discovered a group of islands in the central Pacific Ocean on Jan. 18, 1778, he named it the Sandwich Islands, in honor of the Earl of Sandwich.

The group later became better known as the Hawaiian Islands (q.v.), now a state of the US.

San Francisco Roulette: During 1907, the postmaster of San Francisco found a number of sheets of the 2c Shield type of 1903 with the horizontal perforations missing between the top two rows of stamps.

He had the missing perforation row rouletted and sold the stamps as normal. (See Kansas City Roulette.)

Sang: A unit of currency once used in Tibet. One sang was made up of 6-2/3 trangka.

Sanitary Fair Stamps: (See Stamp, Sanitary Fair.)

San Marino: The Most Serene Republic of San Marino claims to be the oldest state in Europe, and except for Monaco (q.v.) it appears to be the smallest.

It is thought to have been founded in the fourth century by a stonecutter from the island of Arbe, or Rab (q.v.), and is located in northern Italy about 14 miles south of Rimini.

With a few exceptions, such as a period under Cesare Borgia in 1503, it has maintained its independence, even to remaining neutral during World War II.

The three peaks of Mount Titano, each crowned by a castle, are the state's best-known landmarks and are featured on its coat of arms and many of its postage stamps.

It has an area of 24 square miles and a population estimated at 21,000. Government is by a Grand and General Council elected by the citizens.

San Marino is probably best known, both in the philatelic community and to the general public, for its numerous stamps and it is generally assumed that much of San Marino's revenue is derived from the creation of stamps.

In recent years, however, it has been a less prolific stamp issuer and other countries have expanded their production to the point at which San Marino is no longer exceptional in this regard.

The first stamps were issued in 1877 and a steady, if relatively modest, flow followed. It was during the 1960s that there were many issues featuring such non-San Marino-related subjects as birds, aircraft, ships (from this landlocked state!), automobiles, etc., but this has been reduced considerably, and the state is now quite popular with collectors.

The unit of currency is the Italian lira (100 centesimi).

Apart from stamps, sources of income are tourism, woolen goods, building stone, and the Italian government, which buys its monopoly on the sale of tobacco, playing cards, etc.

The philatelic bureau may be addressed at Philatelic Office, Republic of San Marino.

Sans: A French word meaning "without." For example, "sans gomme" means without gum.

San Sebastian: In 1937 a set of 12 stamps was issued for use in the Spanish province of Guipuzcoa, of which San Sebastian is the capital city.

The set consisted of stamps of the 1931-36 issue of Spain overprinted "ARRIBA/ ESPANA/ 1936."

Santa Cruz de Tenerife: A set of Spanish stamps overprinted "Viva Espana/ 18 Julio/ 1936" was issued in that year for use in the Department of Santa Cruz de Tenerife on Tenerife, the largest of the Canary Islands.

Santander: A department in the Republic of Colombia (q.v.), Santander is located north of the capital city of Bogota in mountainous country. Its capital is Bucaramanga.

There is an area of tropical lowlands to the western border, which is formed by the Magdalena River.

Santander is the principal oil-producing department of Colombia, and tobacco of high quality is grown there.

The first stamps of Santander were released in 1884, when the department was a state within the United States of Colombia.

Stamp issues continued until the early 1900s.

When the Republic of Colombia was formed in 1886, Santander, along with the other states, became a department in the new country. While many rights were given up, the departments retained the right to run their own financial affairs and to issue postage stamps.

Santim: A unit of currency used in Hatay. One hundred santims made up one Kurush.

The santim was also used from 1923, in Latvia, where 100 equaled one lat.

SAORSTAT EIREANN: This overprint was applied to British stamps in 1922 for use in the Irish Free State (Eire).

Sao Tome and Principe: The first settlers in what is now the Democratic Republic of Sao Tome and Principe (St. Thomas and Prince), which was discovered by the Portuguese in 1471, were convicts and exiled Jews who were put to work establishing sugar plantations. The slave trade, however, eventually became an important part of the islands' economy.

During the 1600s, the Dutch occupied the islands for a short time, and following their

SAO TOME + PRINCIPE

restoration to Portugal, the islands' importance declined.

Cocoa was introduced in the late 1800s and could have become a profitable crop, but European countries boycotted it because the labor used on the plantations bordered on slavery.

The islands remained a Portuguese colony until independence was achieved on July 12, 1975.

With a total area of 372 square miles, the country has a population estimated at 90,000. The islands are tips of extinct volcanos forming a submerged chain off the coast of Africa. The capital city is Sao Tome.

The latest per capita income figure is $270, and the unit of currency is the dobra, which in 1981 was 35.7 to the US dollar.

Stamps were first issued in 1869 and followed the usual Portuguese colonial pattern until independence.

Since then, stamp-issuing activity has been slight, and as far as can be ascertained, no philatelic services are offered.

Sarawak:
The romantic notion of settling in the East and becoming a white raja was one held by many European youngsters in the 19th century. For one man that dream came true.

He was James Brooke, who established a dynasty that lasted until 1946.

A wealthy, bored Englishman, Brooke was sailing in his armed yacht, **Royalist,** when he called at Singapore in 1838 and learned that a pro-British raja in Borneo was facing a rebellion in Sarawak. Brooke went to the capital city of Kuching and offered his services.

With Brooke's help, the rebellion was put down, and, as in the fairy tales, Brooke was rewarded by being made raja of Sarawak.

A good administrator, he established law and order and was knighted by Great Britain in 1848.

Returning to England, where he died in 1868, he appointed a nephew, Charles Johnson Brooke, as his successor.

Sir Charles was in turn succeeded by his son, Sir Charles Vyner Brooke. He proved to be the final member of the dynasty and ceded Sarawak to Great Britain in 1946.

Sarawak joined the Federation of Mayalsia (q.v.) in 1963.

Located on the northwest coast of Borneo, the region is about 450 miles in length, with a width ranging from 40 to 120 miles. It is about the same size as England, with an area of some 47,070 square miles.

Stamps were first issued on March 1, 1869, and they bear a portrait of Sir James Brooke.

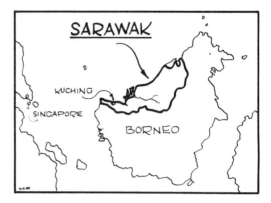

The three white rajas of Sarawak.

The two succeeding rajas continued to grace the country's stamps until 1946.

The final issue before the British took over is a fitting memorial to the dynasty. It commemorates the centenary of rule by the Brookes and very handsomely features their portraits.

During the Japanese occupation, which virtually ruined the country, stamps of Sarawak were handstamped with Japanese characters. When liberation came, stamps were overprinted "BMA" (British Military Administration).

With British aid, Sarawak moved rapidly towards independence, and in September 1963, the country merged with the independent nation of Malaysia, stamps of which it now uses.

Sardinia:
Sardinia is the second largest island in the Mediterranean and lies west of Italy and south of the island of Corsica.

It became part of Austria in 1708. Later, as an independent kingdom, it came to comprise not only the island but a large part of the Italian mainland and portions of what is now France, when Italian states became joined to the Kingdom of Sardinia prior to 1860.

On March 17, 1861, its name was changed to the Kingdom of Italy (q.v.).

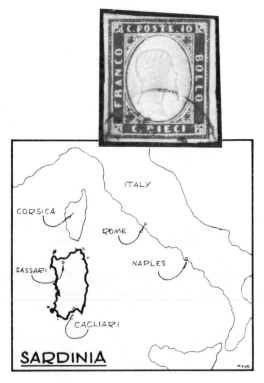

SARDINIA

In 1851 stamps had been issued by Sardinia featuring the profile of King Victor Emmanuel II, later to be the first king of a unified Italy.

The stamps have been reprinted, and forgeries and fake cancelations on used copies are plentiful.

The first stamps of the Kingdom of Italy were identical to those of Sardinia except that they were perforated.

Sark: One of the channel islands off the coast of France, Sark is part of the Bailiwick of Guernsey.

It has issued a number of local carriage labels valid only to frank mail from the island to the government post office.

These labels must be placed on the backs of letters, which must also bear the postage stamps of Guernsey applied in the usual way.

SARKARI: Overprint indicates Official stamp of the Indian state of Soruth.

SARRE: The overprint "SARRE" was applied to stamps of Germany and Bavaria in the post-World War I years for use in the Saar under League of Nations control.

This period lasted from Jan. 30, 1920, until the 1921 issue inscribed "SAARGEBIET" (q.v.) was released.

SASE: The abbreviation "SASE" means "self-addressed, stamped envelope." The "self" refers to the sender, who addresses the envelope and affixes the stamp for enclosure with a communication to which a response is desired. This allows a response at no cost and with minimum inconvenience to the other party.

In philatelic correspondence, it is considered good manners to enclose a SASE, and with the ever-increasing cost of postage, it is coming to be regarded as necessary if a response is expected. This is true whether the correspondence is personal or addressed to a commerical firm, especially if it does not pertain directly to a business transaction and is in the nature of a general inquiry. (See also SAE.)

Saseno: (See Italian Occupation of Saseno.)

SAS/Oceania: (See Society of Australasian Specialists/Oceania.)

Satang: Introduced in 1909, the satang was a unit of currency used in Siam (Thailand). One hundred satangs made up one tical and, later (in 1912), one baht.

Satz: German word for "set."

Saudi Arabia: Occupying most of the Arabian Peninsula, the Kingdom of Saudi Arabia was formed in 1932.

It comprises the dual monarchy of Hejaz-Nejd (q.v.) plus other areas of Arabia.

The formation of Saudi Arabia by King Ibn Sa'ud represented a change in policy from the traditional isolation of Arabia to one of contact and commerce with the West, and the king gradually guided his often puritanical people into the ways of the 20th century.

Saudi Arabia's boundary with its southern and eastern neighbors remains indefinite, although the area of the country is stated as 873,000 square miles. The population is estimated at 9,292,000.

The latest per capita income figure is $11,500, but the literacy rate is a low 15%.

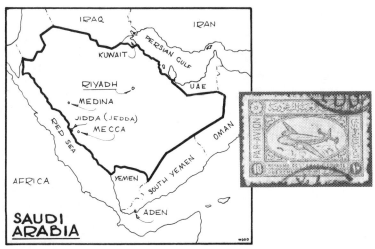

The unit of currency in Saudi Arabia is the riyal (100 halalas), which in 1981 was 3.36 to the US dollar.

Oil is the chief source of the country's wealth, although there is some agriculture with dates, wheat, barley, and fruit being grown.

The early stamps of the area were those of Hjaz, Nejd, and the dual monarchy of Hejaz-Nejd.

The first stamps of Saudi Arabia came in 1934 and feature the tughra, or cypher, of Abdul Aziz, as had some previous stamps of Hejaz-Nejd.

The address of the philatelic bureau is Division of Posts and Telegraphs, Philatelic Service, Riyadh, Saudi Arabia.

Saumon: French word for the color of "salmon."

Saurashtra, United States of: (See Soruth.)

Savings Stamp: (See Stamp, Savings.)

Saxony: The name "Saxony" dates back in recorded history to AD 200, when it was applied to an area including Holstein and the area around the lower reaches of the River Elbe.

In the course of time, the fortunes of the Kingdom of Saxony waxed and waned along with most of the other states that eventually came to form a united Germany.

Ownership, control, and borders all varied as alliances were formed, broken, and reformed; as marriages brought unions both romantic and political; and as the very whims of the nobility led to giving and receiving territory.

After the Seven Weeks War of 1866, during which Saxony sided with Austria, victorous Prussia forced Saxony to pay an indemnity and join the North German Confederation (q.v.).

As a result of the Franco-Prussian War, in which Saxony gave valuable help to Prussia, it was made a member state of the new German Empire.

Following World War I and the German revolution of 1918, Saxony became a free state under the Weimar regime. Its capital was Dresden.

When Germany was defeated in WWII, Saxony came within the Soviet zone of occupation and it eventually formed a "land" in the German Democratic Republic (q.v.). It has since been eliminated by division among neighboring administrative districts.

Saxony's first stamps were issued in 1850 and continued until they were replaced by the stamps of the North German Confederation, those of the German Empire, the Weimar government, the Third Reich, and then the German Democratic Republic.

In 1945, under the Soviet occupation, stamps were issued in the area of Saxony. These were inscribed "PROVINZ SACHSEN," and feature the arms of Saxony and various agricultural and industrial scenes. (See Saxony, West and East.)

Saxony, West and East: During the 1945-46 period of Soviet occupation of what is now the German Democratic Republic (East Germany), a number of local issues for the various provinces were released for use until the general issue for use throughout occupied Germany was issued.

The issues of West Saxony (Leipzig) compris-

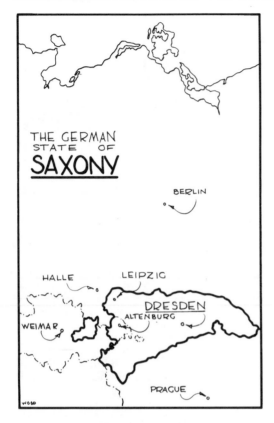

THE GERMAN
STATE OF
SAXONY

SCADTA: The letters "SCADTA" stand for Sociedad Colombo-Alemana de Transportes Aereos, an airline that operated in Colombia and that took over from the Compania Colombiana de Navegacion Aerea.

Both companies operated their own post offices and issued air mail stamps, which were required to be used to frank letters carried on the air mail service operated by the airlines in addition to government-issued stamps. SCADTA issues continued until 1932.

In addition, stamps of Colombia were sold in other countries for use on mail to Colombia. These were overprinted with various letters indicating the country in which they were sold, and applied to mail in addition to the required national stamps of the country. The overprinted Colombian stamps then paid for air mail service to interior points in Colombia.

Such mail would be handed to a Colombian consulate or an agent of the airline for transmission.

The letters applied to Colombian stamps as a control are: EU (United States), A-U Argentine and Uruguay), B (Belgium), Bo. (Bolivia), Br. (Brazil), Ca. (Canada), P plus a handstamped "C.Z." (Canal Zone), Ch. (Chile), CR (Costa Rica), C (Cuba), F. (France), A. (Germany), GB (Great Britain), I (Italy), H (Netherlands), P (Panama), Pe (Peru), E (Spain), Su (Sweden), S (Switzerland), and V (Venezuela).

Scanalatura: Italian word for "ribbed."

Scandinavian Collectors Club: The Scandinavian Collectors Club can trace its origins back to Nov. 25, 1935, when six collectors of Finland met in the Bronx to organize a Finnish-American Stamp Club.

In 1942 the group extended an invitation to collectors of all the Nordic countries, and at the suggestion of Harry L. Lindquist, the group was renamed the Scandinavian Collectors Club of New York. In 1959 the name was shortened to its present form.

Today, according to the club's publicity manager, Marvin D. Hunewell, the club has some 1,000 members and 15 active chapters in the US and Canada. Services to members include a quarterly club journal, the *Posthorn*, plus various specialized publications, handbooks, etc.; a sales circuit; library; and expertizing assistance.

The club also makes exhibition awards available for exhibits of Scandinavian material.

Further information is available from club secretary, Wayne P. Rindone, Box 276, Newtonville, MA 02160.

ed several designs, including the Leipzig coat of arms and the town hall. Some 36 items are listed by Stanley Gibbons.

East Saxony (Dresden) has 25 items listed, including stamps with a numeral design and a pair featuring Dresden buildings. (See Sachsen.)

S.C.: Prior to the introduction of stamps overprinted "O.S." in 1874 for general Official use, South Australia used a number of different overprints to indicate use by specific government departments.

"S.C." stood for Supreme Court.

Scarlet: Foreign words for the color scarlet include ecarlate (French), scharlach (German), scarlatto (Italian), and escarlata (Spanish).

Scarlatto: Italian word for the color "scarlet."

Scarpanto: An island in the Aegean Sea off the coast of Turkey. Once a part of the Italian

Dodecanese group (q.v.), it is now Greek and uses the stamps of that country.

From 1912 to 1932, stamps of Italy were overprinted "SCARPANTO."

Schagiw: (See Shagiv.)

Scharlach: German word for the color "scarlet."

Schermack Perforation: (See Perforation, Schermack.)

Schiefer: German word for the color "slate."

Schiff: German word for "ship."

Schiffspoststempel: German word for "ship cancelation."

Schilling: The schilling is a unit of currency used in Austria. It is composed of 100 groschen.

The schilling was also a currency unit used by the German states of Bergedorf, Hamburg, Mecklenburg-Schwerin, Mecklenburg-Strelitz, Schleswig-Holstein, as well as the island of Heligoland during its stamp-issuing period while a British colony.

Schleswig: Schleswig was the most northerly of the twin grand duchies of Schleswig-Holstein (q.v.) once located in northern Germany.

The Treaty of Versailles after World War I divided Schleswig into two parts.

In a 1920 plebiscite, North Schleswig voted for union with Denmark, and the south decided to remain with Germany.

A number of stamps were issued in 1920 for use in the area, inscribed "SLESVIG PLEBISCIT."

Later that same year the stamps were overprinted "1 ZONE."

Official stamps were also issued, and these were the regular stamps overprinted "C.I.S." (Commission Interalliee Slesvig.)

Schleswig-Holstein: The area of Schleswig-Holstein, once twin grand duchies, is located on the southern portion of the Jutland Peninsula, extending south to Hamburg.

Schleswig (q.v.) is to the north and Holstein to the south.

For years, Prussia, Denmark, and Austria argued and fought over them.

The Seven Weeks War of 1866, in which Prussia was victorious over Austria, resulted in Prussian control over the grand duchies, with only the northern border in dispute with Denmark.

After World War I, a plebiscite was held and North Schleswig became part of Denmark.

A motivating force behind Prussia's desire for domination over the area was the idea of a canal linking the Baltic with the North Sea.

Between 1887 and 1895, the Kiel Canal bacame a reality. It is more than 53 miles in length and runs from Kiel on the Baltic to the lower reaches of the River Elbe.

After WWII, Schleswig-Holstein became a "land" of the Republic of Germany (q.v.), with

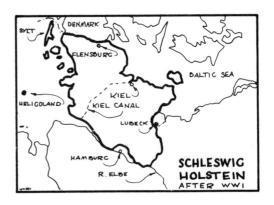

the administrative center being at Kiel.

Other towns in the present area are Lubeck, Flensburg, Rendsburg, plus the islands of Sylt and Heligoland (q.v.).

Stamps were issued for Schleswig-Holstein from 1850, with issues of 1864-65 for Schleswig and Holstein individually.

All stamps were superseded on Jan. 1, 1868, by those of the North German Confederation. Now, stamps of the Federal Republic are used.

Schokolade: German word for the color "chocolate."

Schwaren: A unit of currency used in the German state of Oldenburg. Twelve schwaren were equal to one silbergroschen.

Schwarz: German word for "black."

Schweizer: (See Transvaal.)

Scinde District Post: The inscription "SCINDE DISTRICT DAWK" appears on embossed stamps of the Scinde District of India that were issued on July 1, 1852.

There are three colors — white, blue, and red — and the design features the mark of the East India Company.

The stamps are listed as the first issue of India. They were released by authority of the British Commissioner in Scinde and became obsolete in October 1854. The Scinde District is in what is now Pakistan.

Scotland: After England, Scotland is the largest division of the United Kingdom of Great Britain and Northern Ireland.

In addition to its mainland portion, there are several hundred islands of various size off its coast, mostly comprising the Hebrides, Orkneys, and further north, the Shetlands.

Scotland has a total land area of 29,796 square miles and a population of about 5¼ million.

Edinburgh, near the Firth of Forth, is the capital, and across the country, Glasgow, on the Clyde is the industrial center.

Scotland is a mountainous country, and the Highlands occupy more than half of the area. The highest part of the UK is Ben Nevis, which rises to 4,405 feet.

Scotland was known in antiquity as Caledonia, and its inhabitants were a warlike race known as the Picts who offered stout resistance to the invading Romans. They caused them to retreat and build that massive 70-mile fortified wall known as Hadrian's Wall, remnants of which can still be seen.

Scotland's long history is marked by warfare, and when the tribes, and later the clans, were

not fighting each other, they were at war with England.

The Picts, Angles, Scots, and Britons all battled together and also had to contend with the invading Norsemen, who seized the various islands including the Orkneys, Shetlands, and Hebrides.

Scotland came together as one kingdom about AD 1018 under Malcom II, king of Alban, a state formed from two of the more important smaller kingdoms as he drove off the Norse invaders and the Northumbrians to the south.

His successor, Duncan I, also inherited the crown of Strathclyde, which gave Scotland all of the territory north of the Solway Firth and the River Tweed. It was Duncan who was assassinated by Macbeth, later made famous by Shakespeare.

Edward I of England brought Scotland under English suzerainty, and it was Scotland's resentment of this intrusion into its affairs that prompted an alliance with France in 1295. This French connection was to play a very significant part in the history of both England and Scotland.

Scottish friendship with France brought about the annexation by England. Although it was restored as an independent kingdom in 1328, that only resulted in a transfer of the strife to internal warfare, as the Scottish nobility bickered and fought among itself. Clan wars were common, and the war with England again flared and continued.

The friendship with France also continued and Mary, later Mary Queen of Scots, was born to James V and his French wife, Mary of Guise. Mary went to France in 1548 and married the heir to the French throne.

Protestant sentiment developed a wave of anti-French feeling in Scotland that was encouraged by Elizabeth of England.

Returning to Scotland following the death of her husband after only a year on the French throne, Mary became and remained a central figure in the struggle between Scotland and England until she was beheaded in 1587.

When Elizabeth died in 1603, James VI of Scotland inherited the crown of England and became the first sovereign to rule over a united England and Scotland.

The spirit of nationalism is still strong in Scotland, and in 1978 the UK government approved the creation of an elected Scottish Assembly.

Philately also reflects Scottish nationalism in the form of British regional issues. (See United Kingdom, Regional Issues.)

In 1958 regional stamps issues for sale at post offices in Scotland were initiated. Their design included the heraldic symbols of Scotland as well as the Wilding portrait of Queen Elizabeth II. Since 1971, the Machin Head portrait has been used with the symbols.

These stamps are also valid for postage throughout the UK.

In addition to the regional issues, there have been several aerogrammes with Scottish themes.

The regional issues for Scotland can be obtained from the British Post Office Philatelic Bureau, 20 Brandon St., Edinburgh, Scotland, EH3 5TT, United Kingdom.

Scott Catalog:
The most widely used stamp catalog in the US is that published by the Scott Publishing Co.

It is currently in four volumes plus a single-volume specialized catalog of the US. The latter volume features a large amount of detailed material on revenue stamps, postal stationery, etc.

The complete set is published annually. (See Catalog; Scott, John Walter.)

Scott, John Walter:
Called the "Father of American Philately," John Walter Scott (1845-1916) was an Englishman born in London. His interest in stamps was sparked while working for a London merchant, where the firm's foreign correspondence caused him to begin collecting.

In 1863 he moved to the US and settled in New York. He set himself up as an outdoor stamp dealer but soon sold his stock for $10 to William Brown (q.v.).

Now unemployed, he decided to join the army but was persuaded not to by Brown, who set him up with $100 worth of stamps, according to the *Museum Post*, bulletin of the Cardinal Spellman Philatelic Museum, Inc.

Business during the Civil War was not good, and Scott took Horace Greeley's advice and headed west on the trail of the gold rush. He ended up in Idaho, where in 1865 he lost everything in a fire in Idaho City, and he headed for California on foot.

After working for a while as a teamster in Sacramento, he returned to New York. His ship was wrecked near Panama, but he managed to reach New York and opened a stamp store at 34 Liberty St.

After putting out several price lists, he published his first catalog in 1868 and became editor of the *American Journal of Philately*. His first album was also published that year, and he married Minnie Peyton, by whom he had six children.

May 28, 1870, was a significant date, for it was on that day that Scott held the first stamp auction. (See Auctions.)

He returned to London in 1871 and while there was instrumental in arranging the first stamp auction in that city on March 18, 1872.

Back in New York, in 1886, he sold his title and interest to the Scott Stamp & Coin Co., but the necessity to earn a living made him reestablish a stamp store.

This involved him in legal action, as the Scott Stamp & Coin Co. objected. The case went to the Supreme Court, which ruled in Scott's favor, stating that no matter what the contract, no man can sign away his right to make a living by the only means available to him.

In a *Collectors Club Philatelist* article a few years after Scott's death, Dr. J. Brace Chittenden said of him:

"His knowledge of stamps, his intimate acquaintance with all the noted collectors of the last half century, his system of pricing stamps in his early catalogs solely from the evidence afforded by his stock, his service in establishing markets and establishing prices through auctions, his successful and often unique advertising, and more than this; his kindly sympathy and readiness to further the interest of every philatelic organization; these were the elements that afforded him the title, cheerfully credited by his contemporaries and even his enemies — The Father of American Philately."

Scudo:
The scudo was a unit of currency used by the Italian state of Romagna and other Roman States.

In both areas it was composed of 100 bajocchi.

Scutari di Albania:
(See Levant, Italian.)

A selection of Christmas seals.

S.d.N. BUREAU INTERNATIONALE DE TRAVAIL:

This overprint was applied to Swiss stamps for use from the International Labour Bureau.

Sea Green:

Foreign terms for the color "sea green" include vert de mer (French), seegrun (German), verde mare (Italian), and verde mar (Spanish).

Sea Horses:

This is the nickname given to the British King George V high-value stamps of 1913-34.

The design features Britannia, three horses and a profile of King George V.

The stamps were designed by Bertram Mackennal in denominations of 2/6, 5/-, 10/-, and £1 and are a popular, if increasingly expensive, subject for philatelic study.

J.A.C. Harrison, a free-lance engraver, engraved the die. The initial intaglio printing was by Waterlow and Sons, with De La Rue getting the contract in 1915 and relinquishing it to Bradbury Wilkinson in 1918.

It is possible to identify the various printings, and there are numerous varieties, including reentries, paper differences, shades, etc.

Seal, Christmas:

Christmas seals are sold at Christmas to raise money to fight tuber-

The magnificent "Sea Horse" design.

culosis and other lung ailments. They are placed on mail, officially on the back of envelopes, but often on the front, and they sometimes receive a postal marking.

They serve no postal purpose whatsoever, but they are collected. Thus they can confuse the newcomer to the hobby who may think that they have a postal function.

US Christmas seals are listed in the Scott *United States Specialized Catalogue.*

A Danish postal worker, Einar Holboell, is credited with the development of the seals, and by 1904 this method of raising funds was being used in the Scandinavian countries. The first US seal was issued in 1907, and they have appeared annually since then.

In contrast to the early seals, which came in sheets with a single design for each seal, modern designs can cover several seals or the entire sheet.

Seal, Post Office: (See Post Office Seal.)

Sea Post Office: Sea post offices
were full-service post offices established aboard ships.

The US Post Office Department operated sea post offices on many ships sailing on a schedule prior to World War II.

In most cases, they were operated jointly with the postal service of the destination country.

US-German Seapost markings: An item of mail handled on an eastbound voyage (top) and one addressed to the US. The first was mailed April 23, 1909; the second is dated July 23, 1897. (Illustrations courtesy of Everett Erle of Oakland, Calif.)

A selection of more recent sea post covers carried on the German liners *Bremen* and *Europa* shown courtesy of Everett Erle.

The service between the US and Germany is probably the best-known example, and postal markings identify such operations.

A ship bound for a German port would have a US post office staffed by USPOD personnel, and on the return voyage, the post office office would be German with a German staff.

Other countries using sea post offices were France, Italy, Belgium, Japan, the Netherlands, New Zealand, Spain, and Sweden, according to Cabeen *(Standard Handbook of Stamp Collecting,* Crowell, New York, 1979).

The onset of air travel and the decline of scheduled shipping service after WWII led to the elimination of the sea post office.

Seaway Invert: One of Canada's

more spectacular errors, the Seaway invert is a

variety of a 1959 stamp issued to mark the opening of the St. Lawrence Seaway.

A similar US commemorative was issued at the same time.

It is not known exactly how many of the Canadian stamps were fed into the press upside down to receive the second color impression, but one estimate from a Canadian source puts the figure at about 16 panes.

On Jan. 26, 1980, thieves made off with a block of 25 of the errors. This was the largest known block and belonged to Canada Post, which had loaned it for display in a Montreal shopping mall.

SECOURS GUERCHE: Inscription on
postal tax stamp of Saudi Arabia.

Sechs: Numeral six (6) in German.

Secret Marks: The term "secret
marks" refers to marks placed on US stamp dies handed over by the National Bank Note Company to the Continental Bank Note Company when the latter firm obtained the contract for

producing US postage stamps on May 1, 1873.

The marks were applied so that the subsequent printings could be identified.

Konwiser *(American Stamp Colelctor's Dictionary,* Minkus, 1949) quotes Stephen Rich, writing in the *Stamp Specialist,* 1949, as stating that the markings were applied by the National Bank Note Company before surrendering the dies to Continental.

Brookman *(The 19th Century Postage Stamps of the United States,* Lindquist, 1947) seems to imply that the marks were applied by Continental when he states: "In 1873, the Continental Bank Note Company obtained the printing contract and in order that its work could be distinguished from that of its predecessor, secret marks were added to the dies...."

John N. Luff in *Postage Stamps of the United States,* 1902, states that it was Continental that placed the marks on the dies turned over to them by the National Bank Note Co.

The weight of evidence seems to indicate that Continental placed the secret marks on the dies to indicate that such stamps were printed by that firm, not that National added them to indicate that such stamps were not printed by that firm.

These secret marks are illustrated and described in the US stamp catalogs. (See Bank Note Issues.)

On the 7c denomination featuring Edwin M. Stanton, the secret marks consist of two small semi-circles on the ends of the lines that almost encircle the lower right-hand ball at the bottom right of the stamp design as shown on the stamp at the left.

Secures aux Refugies: Inscription on semi-postal stamps of Syria.

Seebeck, Nicholas F.: Though Nicholas Frederick Seebeck the man seems to be something of a mystery — being variously described in philatelic literature as "a New York stationer associated with the Hamilton Bank Note Engraving and Printing Company of New York," its "general manager," an "agent" of the company, its "president," and a "stamp dealer" — there is a lesser degree of mystery about what he did.

His actions during the last decade of the 19th century live on, and even today the label "Seebeck" is still applied to something undesirable in terms of stamp issuing, especially in Latin America.

Even countries in that area that had nothing to do with Seebeck have suffered by mere proximity to the four countries that were for a short time associated with him.

Despite the lack of agreement as to his relationship with the Hamilton Bank Note Co., it seems certain that he acted on its behalf when, in early 1889, he offered to supply El Salvador, Honduras, and Nicaragua with stamps and postal stationery at no cost to them, in return for certain privileges.

To the far-from-prosperous governments, it seemed like a very good deal indeed.

On May 4, 1889, in Managua, Nicaragua, a contract was signed between the Director General of Posts and Telegraphs of Nicaragua and the Hamilton Bank Note Engraving and Printing Co. of New York as represented by its general manager, N.F. Seebeck, according to Clyde Gentle, writing in the May 6, 1977, issue of *Stamp Collector*.

Gentle went on to reproduce the terms of the contract as it appeared in the June 22, 1889, *Official Gazette* as follows:

"(1) Mr. Seebeck assumes responsibility for the Hamilton Bank Note Company to furnish the Government of Nicaragua, without any cost to the latter, all stamps needed for franking postal and telegraph correspondence up to a total of two million stamps, also postal cards, stamped envelopes with imprinted postage, up to a total of 225,000 pieces, for a period of one to two years.

"(2) The Government shall, at its discretion, change the stamps each year or each second year on January 1st and at the same time shall demonetize those of the preceding period. The design shall be the same for all denominations of each issue; they shall only differ in color. With each new issue the design shall be substantially different from the previous ones.

"(3) Simultaneously, with the signing of the contract, the Government orders from Mr. Seebeck all stamps needed for the year 1890, submitting design, size of issue, color, and quantity of each individual denomination. The Hamilton Bank Note Company has to deliver the complete order not later than November 15, 1889, to a Government representative in New York.

"In the future, the Government will, every year or every second year, order from the Hamilton Bank Note Company in a similar manner a new issue to be delivered not later than November 15 of the respective year.

"(4) The stamps shall be steel engraved of artistic workmanship and best quality.

"(5) As compensation for the free delivery of the first issue for 1890, the Government shall surrender to the Hamilton Bank Note Company all stamps, covers, and postal cards of the current 1882 issue and any older issues still in supply on December 31, 1889.

"In the same manner the Government shall deliver to the Hamilton Bank Note Company, each succeeding year or biannually, all remaining supplies of the preceding period that have been demonetized according to paragraph 2 of the contract, delivery to be at Managua in each instance not later than during February of the following year.

"(6) The Government permits the Hamilton Bank Note Company to sell to stamp collectors the supplies so obtained from the Government and authorizes the Hamilton Bank Note Company to re-issue any denomination when the supply is exhausted in order to be able to satisfy collectors' demand.

"(7) The Government can under no condition sell current stamps at more than a 10% discount of face value. Stamps used to frank telegrams shall be destroyed together with the originals (presumably, telegram forms are meant — Author).

"(8) In case the Hamilton Bank Note Company fails to deliver on time, it loses its rights to the latest remaining supplies and the Government has the right to cancel the contract.

"(9) Should the quantities ordered by the Government and supplied by the Hamilton Bank Note Company not cover the demand, the company is obligated upon request by the Government to supply up to one million additional pieces over and above the quantities stipulated in paragraph 1.

"(10) This contract is for the period of ten years."

A few weeks prior to the signing of the above contract with Nicaragua, the Hamilton Bank Note Co. entered into similar contracts with El Salvador and Honduras.

Two years later, Ecuador signed a similar contract with Henry N. Etheridge of the Hamilton Bank Note Co.

The issue of these countries under the Seebeck agreement are reported to be Nicagagua and El Salvador 1890-99, Honduras 1890-95, and Ecuador 1892-96.

These arrangements soon brought the countries into disrepute among collectors, and in North America the Seebeck issues, as they came to be called, were pretty much ignored.

Gentle notes, however, that they have been extensively studied by European philatelists who offer the following reasons for their philatelic unpopularity:

"In the more conservative era of philately in the early 1890s, the annual issuance of long, new stamp sets with high face value was considered almost a crime by collectors.

"The issuance of stamps with face values up to 10 pesos ($5 US) by Nicaragua and, to some extent, by El Salvador and Ecuador was validly criticized. This represents a face value far exceeding that required for postal needs in those countries.

"Objections were raised because the stamps could be sold by Seebeck at a substantial discount from face value after demonetization.

"European collectors objected to Seebeck's right to reprint the issues.

"Eventually there existed a widespread uncertainty as to which stamps were originals and which were reprints. Even when the differences became known, the difficulties of identifying the reprints increased the unpopularity of genuine and reprint alike.

"When it was discovered that many stamps had been canceled to order or bore fraudulent cancelations, the measure of philatelic dislike greatly increased to the point where there was almost a complete boycott against collecting them."

Gentle reports the suggestion that the boycott of the "Seebecks" arose because the collectors of that time were reluctant to purchase long sets.

"However," continues Gentle, "when the contracts with the Hamilton Bank Note Co. were in force, the governments of the 'Seebeck countries' were solely interested in obtaining stamps needed for their postal and telegraph services at no cost.

"There was no intention of picking philatelists' pockets, because collectors knew that after a year had passed they could obtain stamps of the previous year below face value, thus over-the-counter sales to collectors could hardly be expected."

Gentle also notes the possibility that the high denominations may have been used in settling interdepartmental accounts and subsequently destroyed.

The greatest objection to the Seebeck arrangements is claimed by Gentle to be the permission to reprint the stamps, plus the fact that many exist in canceled-to-order (q.v.) condition and with counterfeit cancelations.

It has been claimed that reprints were not produced until 1899, shortly after Seebeck's death, but this is by no means certain.

Seebeck himself, being a stamp collector, is said to have understood why his actions were something less than popular in the philatelic community. Gentle reports that he offered to cancel the contracts he had negotiated on behalf of the Hamilton Bank Note Co. if the respective governments would agree and give guarantees that they would not negotiate similar agreements with any of the printing firm's competitors.

Gentle credits Joseph B. Leavy, writing in the journal of Stanley Gibbons of London, for the initial news of reprints.

Leavy's definition of reprints were only those stamps that were printed on thick, porous paper that the Hamilton Bank Note Co. first used for the 1899 postage dues of El Salvador. The reprints exist on this paper with and without watermarks.

For years it was not known that the Phrygian Cap watermark is horizontal on this thick, coarse paper; the original paper used for the 1895-98 issues has the Phrygian Cap always vertical.

Leavy's revelations caused great confusion among collectors and catalog editors, but gradually the catalogs began to recognize these differences.

German philatelists have done considerable research on the Seebeck issues, and information was published in that country as early as 1910.

It is accepted, according to Gentle, that there are no known reprints of the Nicaraguan Seebeck issues of 1890, 1891, 1892, and 1895. There were several printings of the 1894 issue, but the status of these is not clear.

It has been stated that Seebeck, instead of reprinting after the stamps were demonitized, had had excess quantities printed before the stamps were delivered. Because these stamps were printed during the time they were valid for postage, it would be difficult to consider these anything but originals, whether they were ever delivered to the respective countries' postal authorities or not.

But since neither official documents of the governments involved nor any records that may have been kept by Seebeck are known, printing quantities of original deliveries or of reprints must remain a matter of speculation.

Nonetheless, there is evidence of a growing philatelic interest in the Seebeck issues, and fresh information may yet be uncovered.

One thing is certain: the name "Seebeck" is firmly enshrined in philatelic terminology.

Cabeen *(Standard Handbook of Stamp Collecting,* Crowell, 1957) reports, as a sidelight, that Seebeck made an unsuccessful attempt to sell advertising space on the back of stamps printed for Ecuador by the Hamilton Bank Note Co.

Cabeen notes the possibility that Seebeck might have originated the idea that New Zealand used in 1893 when it issued stamps bearing commercial messages on their backs.

Seegrun: German word for the color "sea green."

SEGNATASSE: Inscription on postage due labels of Italy, Italian Colonies, San Marino, and Vatican City.

SEGURO POSTAL: Inscription on Insured Letter Stamps of Mexico. (See Stamp, Insured Letter.)

SEGURO SOCIAL DEL CAMPESINO: Overprint on Postal Tax stamps of Ecuador.

Sei: Numeral six (6) in Italian.

Seidenfaden: German word for "silk thread."

Seis: Numeral six (6) in Portuguese and Spanish.

Seite: German word for "side."

Seiyun, Kathiri State of: (See Aden Protectorate.)

Selangor: Selangor is a part of Malaysia (q.v.) located on the west side of the Malayan Peninsula.

It has a population of well over one million and a land area of 3,167 square miles.

Unrest among the Chinese tin-mine workers in the late 19th century led the British to proclaim a protectorate over the area in 1874 to restore order.

In 1895 Selangor joined the original Federated Malay States (q.v.).

Its chief city of Kuala Lumpur is also the present capital of Malaysia.

Tin, rice, and rubber constitute the main economic base, but pineapples are also grown and exported.

Selangor's first stamps were released in 1878 and consisted of stamps of the Straits Settlements (q.v.) handstamped with a circle containing a crescent, star, and the letter "S."

A number of "SELANGOR" overprints followed until 1891, when the Tiger key type inscribed "SELANGOR" was issued.

From the inception of the Federated Malay States in the late 1890s until 1935, the Leaping Tiger design was used for the low values, with the Elephant design being used for the high-value stamps.

After 1935, stamps picturing the sultan were released. Some bear only the word "MALAYA" in the English language.

The Japanese produced overprints on Selangor's stamps during their World War II occupation.

Post-WWII issues continued the prewar style, except that a pictorial issue featuring various scenes and a portrait of the sultan was released in 1957.

This continued until the advent of the Malaysian Federation. In 1965 and 1971, stamps inscribed "SELANGOR" again appeared as part of two Malaysian omnibus issues.

Sello: Spanish word for "postage stamp."

Sello da Tasa: Spanish word for "postage due."

Sello de Correos: Spanish expression for "postage stamp."

Sello Fiscal: Spanish word for "revenue stamp."

Selten: German word for "rare."

Selvage (Selvedge): The border of paper around a sheet or pane of stamps is called the selvage (selvedge).

Though it is often mostly blank, it has at times been imprinted with various production markings such as plate or cylinder numbers, jubilee lines (q.v.), registration marks, electric eye perforation marks, printers' imprints, public service messages, including "Mail Early" and "Use ZIP Code," and even advertisments. There is a growing trend toward the use of commemorative inscriptions.

The use of marginal inscriptions is nothing new. Indeed, the very first stamp, the Penny Black (q.v.), included the following messages on each side: "Price 1d. Per Label. 1/- Per Row of 12. £1 Per Sheet. Place the Labels ABOVE the address and towards the RIGHT HAND SIDE of the Letter. In Wetting the Back be careful not to remove the Cement." Also, the plate number was located in each corner of the sheet.

When stamps are produced in sheets containing a number of panes, into which the sheet is cut after printing, the gutters separating the panes become the pane selvage after they are cut apart.

Selvedge: (See Selvage.)

Semi-Official Air Mail Stamp: (See Stamp, Semi-Official Air Mail.)

Semi-Postal Stamp: (See Stamp, Semi-Postal.)

Sen: A Japanese unit of currency. The sen was also used in a number of Asian areas, including the Ryukyu Islands (to 1958), Indonesia, Malaya, and West Irian.

Sene: A unit of currency used in Western Samoa since 1967. One hundred sene equal one tala.

Senegal: The French became established on the coast of West Africa after the area had been first settled by the Portuguese in the 1400s.

The colony France established was based on the capital city of Dakar, and French influence gradually spread into the interior.

During World War II, Senegal stayed with the defeated French and its puppet Vichy regime. But after the Allied liberation of North Africa, Senegal decided that it had better change sides

and pledged itself to General De Gaulle and his Free French administration.

In 1924 Dakar and surrounding territory had been made a special territory, but in 1946 it was reunited with Senegal, which was made semi-autonomous in 1958.

From April 4, 1959, to Aug. 20, 1960, it united with the Sudanese Republic to form the Mali Federation (q.v.). When Senegal withdrew, the Sudanese Republic became the Mali Republic, and Senegal became the Republic of Senegal.

In December 1981, Senegal merged with the Gambia to form a country known as Senegambia (q.v.).

The country's agricultural economy has been hard hit by recent long droughts, which have brought famine.

The latest per capita income figure is $342, and the literacy rate is 10%.

Senegal has an estimated population of 5,660,000. The unit of currency is the CFA franc (q.v.).

Senegal's stamp-issuing history began in 1887 when stamps for the French colonial general issue were surcharged. In 1892 stamps of the Commerce and Navigation key type were released inscribed "SENEGAL & DEPENDANCES."

The first pictorial issue came in 1906 and was inscribed "AFRIQUE OCCIDENTALE FRANCAISE SENEGAL."

Stamps bearing just the word "SENEGAL" were issued beginning in 1935 and continued until 1944, when it became part of French West Africa.

When independence came in 1960, stamps inscribed "REPUBLIQUE du SENEGAL" made their appearance, and these continue.

Senegal has followed the usual pattern of stamp issues for African countries, and a fairly large number of stamps have been produced since the early 1970s.

Senegambia: In December 1981, The Gambia (q.v.) and the Republic of Senegal (q.v.) agreed to a merger under the name of Senegambia, which became effective Feb. 1, 1982.

Under the treaty signed by the two countries, they will retain their separate identities and governments, but merge their economic and monetary systems and armed forces. They will coordinate their foreign policies.

Last July, the leader of The Gambia, Sir Dawda Jawara, invoked a 1965 mutual defense treaty and called on Senegal to help put down a coup that was attempted while he was in London attending the wedding of Prince Charles and Lady Diana Spencer. This pointed up the advantages of a merger of the two countries.

Senegambia and Niger: What is now the Republic of Mali (q.v.) began as the French colony of Senegambia and Niger.

The colony issued a set of stamps in 1903. They were the Commerce and Navigation key type inscribed "SENEGAMBIE ET NIGER."

The name was changed to Upper Senegal and Niger, and stamps inscribed "HT.SENEGAL-NIGER" were issued from 1906 until 1920, when the colony became French Sudan, which later would become the Republic of Mali.

Sengi: A unit of currency once used in Zaire. It was 1/100th of a li-kuta.

Senit: A unit of currency used in Tonga. The senit has been 1/100th of a pa'anga since 1967.

Sent: A unit of currency used in Estonia. One hundred sents were equal to one kroon.

Sentimo: A unit of currency used in the Philippines since 1946. One hundred sentimos make up one peso.

Sepia: Foreign words for sepia include sepia (French, German, and Spanish) and seppia (Italian).

Seppia: Italian word for "sepia."

Sept: Numeral seven (7) in French.

Serbia: Once an independent kingdom, Serbia is now one of the six constituent republics forming the People's Republic of Yugoslavia (q.v.).

Beginning in 1866 and continuing to 1920, it issued its own stamps as the Kingdom of Serbia.

It had one more period of philatelic identity while under German occupation during World War II, when the Germans attacked and occupied the Balkans.

This second stamp-issuing period lasted from 1941 until the country's liberation at the end of the war. Since then it has used the stamps of Yugoslavia.

Originally from Galacia, the Serbs emigrated to what became Serbia about the year AD 637. During the 1100s, Serbia was an important power in the Balkans and by the 14th century included Bosnia, Albania, Macedonia, Thessaly, part of Bulgaria, and portions of Greece.

In 1389 the Serbs were routed by the Turks,

treaties with Russia; and Germany had an arrangement with the Austro-Hungarian Empire.

And so the invasion of Serbia lit the fuse of the bomb the explosion of which was to extinguish the lights of Europe and sacrifice an entire generation.

The first attack was repulsed by Serbia, and this inflicted some 50,000 casualties. By early September, all the Austro-Hungarian armies had been able to do was establish two small bridgeheads across the rivers Sava and Drina.

After this period of humiliation, another effort was made, and the Serbian capital of Belgrade was taken. But the Serbs counter-attacked and sent the Austro-Hungarian forces in headlong retreat.

At this point, the invaders came to the reasonable conclusion that they needed some help in subduing the tiny country, and Bulgaria was persuaded to knife Serbia in the back, or, to be more accurate, in the east.

Forced to retreat, Serbia was now in deep trouble, and the government was compelled to leave the mainland and establish itself on the island of Corfu (q.v.).

At the end of the war, Serbia joined with neighboring areas to form the Kingdom of the Serbs, Croats, and Slovenes, which became Yugoslavia.

During WWII, the Germans invaded the area, and once again Serbs saw their country occupied. However, with liberation, Yugoslavia arose again, but with a Communist-oriented government.

The country then entered a period of peace and relative prosperity under its leader, the late President Tito.

and for the next 350 years, the country was a Turkish province.

In 1718 a large part of Serbia became Austrian, but it reverted to Turkey in 1739.

Despite being shuttled between other warring nations, the Serbs managed to retain their national identity, and in 1829 the country achieved a semi-independent status.

Complete independence came in 1878, and in 1882 Serbia became a kingdom.

The Balkans fermented and bubbled until 1914, when the Austro-Hungarian Empire invaded Serbia in retaliation for the killing by Serbian student Gavrilo Princip of the Archduke Ferdinand of Austria and his wife on June 28, 1914, during a visit to Sarajevo.

Following the assassination, Austria-Hungary delivered a harsh ultimatum. Serbia accepted it in part and, after continued pressure, offered to submit the case to the International Tribunal at The Hague, but Austria-Hungary was bent on war and invaded Serbia on July 28.

It was the coming into effect of the various treaties between the major powers that drew all of Europe into WWI. Russia was pledged to help Serbia; France and Britain were linked by

Serbian Occupation of Hungary:
(See Baranya.)

SERBIEN: Overprint on stamps of Bosnia and Herzegovina for use during Austrian occupation of Serbia during World War I.

Serge Beaune: The Serge Beaune principle of multicolor printing was patented in the 1920s and is the principle on which the Giori and similar presses is based.

Briefly, it involves the inking of recess printing plates with up to three colors at one time.

This involved the application of ink from various inking rollers that have been cut away so as to apply ink only to the portion of the plate desired.

Modern presses using this principle can apply up to nine colors. (See Printing, Intaglio.)

Serie: Dutch, French, Italian, and Spanish word for "set."

Series: This term is usually applied to a set (q.v.) of definitive stamps that may be released and added to over a period of years.

These additions usually comprise new denominations, color changes, etc., made necessary by postal rate changes, stamp booklet make-up, coil stamps, and so on.

SERVICE: Overprint on many stamps of India, Burma, Indian states, Ceylon, Pakistan, etc. Indicates conversion to Official use status.

SERVICE DE LA SOCIETE DES NATIONS: Overprint on stamps of Switzerland for Official use by the Geneva-based League of Nations.

SERVICIO ORDINARIO: Overprint on air mail stamps of Nicaragua to validate them for ordinary use.

Sesquicentennial: A sesquicentennial is the 150th anniversary of an event. It is an anniversary for which a set of commemorative stamps or a single stamp is often issued.

An example is a US stamp issued on Aug. 3, 1927, to mark the sesquicentennial of the Battle of Bennington and the independence of the state of Vermont.

Set: A printing term used in stamp production to describe the act of composing type or the arrangement of cliches (q.v.) from which a sheet of stamps is to be printed.

The term "set" is also used to describe the arrangement of a stamp printing plate, as in "100-set."

Set: This term is used to describe a group of two or more stamps with a single commemorative theme or a definitive series (q.v.) such as the US Americana or the British Machin Head sets.

Sets are usually, but not always, issued at one time, though definitives are commonly released over a period of years as new denominations are required, colors changed, etc.

The 1977 British set marking Queen Elizabeth II's Silver Jubilee had an additional denomination added because of a postal rate change after the set appeared, but all are considered one set.

Nowadays, many commemorative sets consist of four to six stamps, although there is no fixed quantity. Some sets are extremely long. One of the longest must surely be the 1958-60 issue from Turkey consisting of more than 130 stamps. And there are only two denominations in the whole lot!

Set: Foreign words for set include serie (Dutch, French, Italian, and Spanish) and satz (German).

Sete: Numeral seven (7) in Portuguese.

Se-tenant: Foreign terms for se-tenant include samenhangend (Dutch), se-tenant (French), zusammendruck (German), combinazione (Italian), and combinacion (Spanish).

Se-tenant: A term that, in philately, refers to any two or more different, unseparated stamps.

A stamp from a stamp booklet with an adjacent stamp-sized tab bearing an advertisement, a postal service message, or some printed design is said to be "se-tenant with" the tab.

In describing such a variety, the expression "se-tenant" is usually qualified as "pair se-tenant" or "se-tenant block of four," etc.

At one time, printing plates were made up of small units called cliches (q.v.) that printed a single stamp. It sometimes happened that one cliche wore or became damaged and required replacing. This has caused errors when a cliche of another but similar stamp has been accidently substituted, thus creating a se-tenant variety.

There is a well-known US se-tenant variety that new collectors might assume came about in just such a way.

It is the 5c denomination in a sheet of 2c stamps of the Washington type.

However, when you find out that this stamp was printed from a plate consisting of a single piece of metal into which the stamp impressions were rolled under pressure, the mystery deepens.

How is it that there are three 5c stamps in a sheet of 400 2c stamps (two in one pane of 100 and one in another)?

Cabeen, in his *Standard Handbook of Stamp Collecting,* explains that when the plate had all the various stamp impressions rolled in, three were found to be unsatisfactory and were marked to be redone. This involved erasing the defective impressions and replacing them with new ones.

Unfortunately, through an error, the impression of the 5c denomination was substituted for the defective 2c impressions.

This was not noticed at the time, according to Cabeen, and the stamps were printed and distributed. When the mistake was discovered, post offices made a check of all stocks, but some had already been sold and got into philatelic circulation.

Occasionally you hear of blocks of twelve 2c stamps containing a vertical pair of 5c stamps in

A US se-tenant block of four commemorative stamps.

A British booklet pane of se-tenant stamps.

A British vending machine strip that sold for 1/-.

the center, or blocks of nine stamps with a single 5c stamp in the middle. (See Five-cent Error.)

In recent years, the use of se-tenant sheet arrangements for commemorative stamps has become so prevalent that it sometimes seems to be the rule rather than the exception it once was, and the novelty such arrangements once had is completely gone.

At one time, most se-tenant arrangements were the result of stamp booklet make-up requirements, where it is convenient to have stamps of different denominations and also desirable that the total cost should be an even amount.

The 1977 US $1 vending machine booklet, with its seven 13c stamps and one 9c denomination, is a good example. The 9c stamp can be found se-tenant with a 13c stamp either vertically or horizontally. It can also be the upper left stamp in either a block of four or in the complete pane.

Another se-tenant variety takes the form of a vending machine strip.

An example from Great Britain is a strip comprising two 2d stamps and one each of 1d, 3d, and 4d, totaling 1/-, which was a convenient coin widely used prior to decimalization.

Following the switch to decimal currency, a similar strip was issued containing two 1/2p, two 1p, and one 2p stamps.

These are only a few of the many se-tenant varieties available, but they will suffice to indicate the wide range of such material.

Set-off: This term refers to the accidental transfer of an image or partial image from the face of a sheet of stamps to the back of the following sheet before the ink has completely dried during the printing process.

This reversed impression occurs when the following sheet is deposited on top of the still-wet ink of the previous sheet.

It can also occur in offset printing after the press has been run without paper. When this happens, a sheet of paper may pick up an impression that had been previously deposited on the impression cylinder because there was no paper to receive it. This is more correctly known as a blanket print.

Set Solid: The term "set solid" refers to sheets of stamps that are printed in such a format that they are not separated into panes by gutters.

Sette: Numeral seven (7) in Italian.

Seville: In 1936 a set of 12 Spanish stamps overprinted "Sevilla/ "VIVA/ ESPANA"/ Julio-1936" was issued for use in that Spanish province.

This was followed by a similar issue, using a different typeface for the overprint, and a single Special delivery stamp.

The date "Julio-1936" marks the beginning of the Franco regime.

Sex: Numeral six (6) in Swedish.

Seychelles: Located in the Indian Ocean to the northeast of Madagascar, the Republic of Seychelles is now independent.

It began in 1768 as a French settlement until it was taken over by the British in 1794 and governed from Mauritius until 1903.

The main island in the 85-island group is Mahe. The entire group has an area of about 150 square miles, with the capital city of Victoria being located on Mahe. The population is about 70,000.

Copra, cinnamon, and vanilla are the economic mainstays, with fishing also being important.

The latest per capita income figure is $1,030, and the unit of currency is the rupee, which in 1981 was 6.65 to the US dollar.

The Seychelles' first stamps came in 1890 and were in the unattractive British Colonial key type design. Unfortunately, this key type design persisted through the reigns of King Edward VII and King George V.

It was not until the 1938 King George VI pictorial issue that collectors had any real cause to look twice at the islands' stamps. This latter issue was unusual in that during an age of intaglio-printed Commonwealth stamps, it was printed by photogravure.

Since then, a number of attractive issues have helped to make up for the dreariness of those early stamps, and much of the flora, fauna, and scenery of the islands have been depicted.

Following independence in 1976, the new country apparently has experienced a distinct drift to the left in its politics, judging from a 1977 issue marking the 60th anniversary of the Russian revolution!

The address of the Seychelles philatelic office is Seychelles Philatelic Bureau, General Post Office, Mahe, Seychelles, Indian Ocean. (See also Zil Eloigne Sesel.)

SF: Stands for Soldater Frimaerke. Overprinted for military stamps of Denmark on two values of the 1913-28 definitive issue.

S.G.: Stamps of Sudan perforated "S.G." are official stamps issued beginning in 1913, according to Gibbons.

The major English-language catalogs do not list these issues.

The "S.G." stands for Sudan Government.

Stamps of Sudan overprinted "S.G." were first issued in 1936. From 1902 to 1912, Official stamps were overprinted "O.S.G.S." (See "AS.")

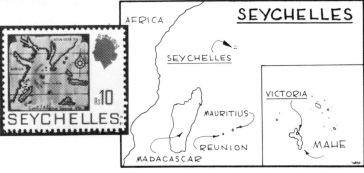

S.G.: Prior to the introduction of stamps overprinted "O.S." in 1874 for general Official use, South Australia used a number of different overprints to indicate use by specific government departments.

"S.G." stood for Surveyor General.

SH: The first issue of Schleswig-Holstein (q.v.) features the letters "SH" in the upper corners of the design. This is the only clue to their identification.

The stamps were issued in 1850 and bear the coat of arms of the former duchies.

The stamps are in denominations of one and two schillings. They are imperforate and are printed on paper containing silk threads.

Shade: (See Color, Shade.)

Shagiv: A unit of currency used in the Ukraine and Western Ukraine.

Shahi: A unit of currency used in Persia (Iran) prior to 1881. It was also used in Afghanistan.

Shanghai: An important city in China, Shanghai is located on the Hwang Pu River, a tidal inlet of the Yangtze River.

The famous International Settlement was formed there in the mid-1800s.

A postal system that was independent of the Chinese postal system was set up, and stamps were issued from 1865 to 1898.

Inscriptions on these many and varied issues include "SHANGHAI LPO," "SHANGHAI LOCAL POST," "SHANGHAI MUNICIPALI-

TY," plus a number of various surcharges and overprints.

An issue was released in 1893 overprinted "1843/ JUBILEE/ 1893" to mark the 50th anniversary of the first foreign settlement.

Shanghai, US Postal Agency: (See China, US Postal Agency in.)

Sharjah: A sheikdom on the Persian Gulf, Sharjah is now a member of the United Arab Emirates.

Together with its Gulf of Oman dependencies of Dhiba, Khor Fakkan, and Kalba, Sharjah joined the UAE on Dec. 2, 1971.

Including the chief town of the same name, it has a population of about 5,000.

During the period that followed the break-up of the Trucial States (q.v.), and before the formation of the UAE, Sharjah released 1,247 stamps plus 14 souvenir sheets, not counting imperforate issues, according to R. Howard Courtney writing in *The Arab World Philatelist*.

SHCO: The letters "SHCO" appear in the corners of a shield on postal tax stamps of Mozambique.

Sheet: An arrangement of stamps as they come from the printing press. Sheets are often subdivided into smaller units called panes (q.v.) before distribution to post offices.

Many US commemorative stamps are printed in sheets of 200 that are cut into four panes of 50 stamps each; the smaller definitives come in four-pane sheets of 400.

Special sheet arrangements are used to produce stamps intended for stamp booklets (q.v.) so that these can be guillotined into booklet panes.

Souvenir sheets (q.v.) are usually printed in

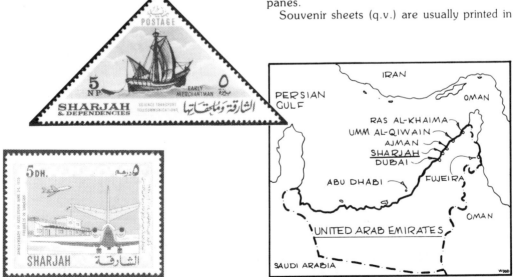

multiples and then separated. The US CAPEX souvenir sheet of 1978 was produced in sheets of six. This souvenir sheet is unusual in that it is separated from the others in the entire sheet by perforations instead of being guillotined apart.

Many British Commonwealth areas have stamps that are produced in twin-pane sheets that are not separated by the printer. This is the source of the popular gutter pairs (q.v.), which occur when stamps from both sides of the gutter are left attached.

The world's first government adhesive postage stamps, the Penny Black and the Twopenny Blue of 1840, were produced in sheets of 240, which rounded out to a price of £1 (or 240 pence) for the Penny Black and £2 (or 480 pence) for the Twopenny Blue. Thus, the composition of a sheet was originally determined by a convenient price unit.

Sheet: Foreign words for sheet include vel (Dutch), feuille (French), bogen (German), foglio (Italian), and hoja (Spanish).

Sheet Numbers: Numbers are often printed on the selvage of sheets of stamps as a check on quantities printed.

They should not be confused with plate or cylinder numbers, which are printed in the color or colors of the stamp.

The consecutive numbers can also be found on the backs of some stamps, for example, some issues of Spain and Andorra.

Shekel (1,000 agorot): Unit of currency used in Israel (q.v.).

Shensi-Kansu-Nighsia: Regions of the Communist administration in Northwest China for which stamps were issued from 1946 to 1949, prior to the formation of the People's Republic of China. (See Northwest China under China, Regional Issues of.)

Shift, Coil: When coil stamps are produced from printing cylinders comprising two (usually) plates curved and fitted around the cylinder, there may be a slight misalignment of the plates in relation to each other.

Thus, when the stamps are printed, a periodic variation in the position of the stamp design may be noticed. This occurs between the last stamp of one plate and the first of another. Pairs or strips showing this condition are known as coil shift pairs or strips.

Quite often, this shift is accompanied by a line in the color of the stamp that is printed between two stamps showing the shift. Such pairs are known as "line pairs" (q.v.) and result when two plates do not meet perfectly. The gap between plates will pick up ink and print, much as an engraved line on an intaglio printing plate picks up ink and transfers it to the paper.

Regardless of whether a line appears between the two stamps, a coil shift indicates a joint between two plates.

Coil shifts are sometimes called "jumps" because the design "jumps" up or down from one stamp to another. This term is mostly found in connection with misalignments on Canadian coil stamps.

Shifted Transfer: (See Reentry.)

Shilling: A unit of currency used in the United Kingdom prior to decimalization and widely used within the British Commonwealth until most Commonwealth members also converted to decimal currency. Twenty shillings made up one pound sterling. (For the correct expression of the shilling, see "Shilling Mark." See also British Currency.)

Shilling Mark: The shilling mark is used in the correct designation of British shillings and fractions thereof.

It is a virgule (or slash) between the whole shilling figure and the fraction and is used thus: "2/6" is two shillings and sixpence; "2/-" represents two shillings.

Ship Cancellation Society, the Universal: (See Universal Ship Cancellation Society.)

Note the shift in position of the impression between the second and third stamps in this strip of four coils.

Ship Letter: A ship letter is one carried by a ship not normally engaged in the carriage of mail.

Henry Bishop (q.v.) is credited with beginning the system whereby ship letters were brought into port by captains and placed in the mail service.

Bishop paid the captains one penny for each letter they brought to him for delivery by his postal service. This system was later made official, and special markings were applied to such mail.

These markings would read "Ship Letter," "Loose Ship Letter," or "Posted at Sea," with the name of the port of entry.

As mail carriage by contract grew and private vessels carried less mail, the practice declined. By the beginning of the 20th century, only a few markings saw occasional use.

The earliest British ship-letter markings date from the early 1700s and were straight-line markings. Later, curved types went into use, followed by oval markings.

The East India Company had a special arrangement by which mail was carried, and some ports had special India letter markings. This practise ceased in the 1840s.

Ships on Stamps Study Unit: (See American Topical Association Study Units.)

Short Paid: The marking "short paid" on a cover indicates that insufficient postage was applied and that there is postage due.

Short Set: The term "short set" refers to the lower denominations of a series of stamps. In particular it was once used to describe sets of British Commonwealth stamps to the 1/- denomination.

Collectors with modest budgets could buy short sets without having to take the high values.

Collectors who buy short sets when they can obtain the complete series often have cause for regret, since it is usually the higher values that become the most desirable. Thus, when they do try to fill the gaps, it is often those very stamps that they neglected that have most risen in cost.

It is a relatively accurate generalization to say that higher-value stamps tend to rise in price the most and the less-expensive lower denominations usually remain low priced.

Short Transfer: (See Transfer, Short.)

S.H.S.: The letters "S.H.S." were overprinted on stamps of Bosnia and Herzgovina and Hungary for use in Croatia-Slavonia during 1916. These are considered early issues of Yugoslavia.

Siam: (See Thailand.)

Siberia: Following World War I and the Russian Revolution, a number of Anti-Bolshevist governments sprang up in Siberia.

The following areas and regimes issued stamps: Admiral Kolchak government; the Ataman Semyonov regime in Transbaikal Province; Amur Province; Far Eastern Republic (q.v.); Priamur and Maritime Provinces; and, finally, Soviet Union issues for the Far East.

SICILIA: The Word "SICILIA" is a partial inscription found on stamps of the Kingdom of the Two Sicilies. (See Sicily, Two Kingdoms of.)

Sicily, Two Kingdoms of: In the 12th century, Roger II, Count of Sicily and Duke of Apulia and Calabria, assumed the title of King of Sicily. His domain was sometimes called the Kingdom of the Two Sicilies, because the southern part of the Italian Mainland over which he ruled was known as "Sicily on this Side of Cape Faro."

In 1282, however, the kingdom was split up, but in 1816 King Ferdinand of Naples united the kingdoms and declared himself King Ferdinand I of the Kingdom of the Two Sicilies.

The capital city was Naples.

Ferdinand died in 1825 and was succeeded by

THE **KINGDOM** OF THE **TWO SICILIES**

his son, Francis I, who was followed by his son, Ferdinand II, in 1830.

After unrest developed in Sicilian portion of his kingdom, Ferdinand wreaked such barbarous vengeance on his subjects that, in 1859, Britain intervened to curb his cruelty.

It was during this period that he gained the nickname of "King Bomba" for his habit of shelling villages that he believed deserved punishment. (See "Bomba Heads.")

It must have been with considerable relief that his subjects found their land merged with that of Sardinia, prior to the formation of a unified Italy (q.v.).

In 1858 a set of nine stamps was issued for the mainland portion of the kingdom under the name of Naples. The stamps feature the coat of arms of the Bourbon dynasty and the Cross of Savoy.

A year later, in 1859, a set of stamps was released under the name of Sicily. These stamps feature the portrait of the infamous "King Bomba."

Side: Foreign words for "side" include zijkant (Dutch), cote (French), seite (German), lato (Italian), and lado (Spanish).

Siderography: Siderography, the art of creating a printing plate from a design engraved in steel, is part of the process known as intaglio printing (see Printing, Intaglio). The craftsmen who engaged in this skilled task are siderographists.

Sieben: The numeral seven (7) in German.

Sienna: Foreign words for "sienna" include terre de Sienne (French) and sienna (German, Italian, and Spanish).

Sierra Leone: A republic within the British Commonwealth, Sierra Leone was founded in 1787 and was used as a settlement for freed slaves and those liberated from apprehended slave ships.

There are estimated to be some 60,000 of their descendents living in the country.

The capital city of Freetown is located on a hilly part of the coast and has the finest harbor in West Africa.

The Republic of Sierra Leone is on the bulge of West Africa, between Liberia and Guinea. It has an area of 27,925 square miles and a population estimated at 3,470,000.

The economy is based on cocoa and coffee, with minerals including diamonds, iron, and bauxite. The latest per capita income figure is $199, and the literacy rate is a low 15%. The unit of currency is the leone (100 cents), which in 1981 was 1.14 to the US dollar.

The colony was granted independence in 1961 and became a republic in 1971.

The first stamps were issued in 1859 and feature the profile of Queen Victoria.

In 1896 the British colonial key type was introduced and remained in use through the reign of King Edward VII and well into that of King George V, until the pictorial issue of 1932.

The Wilberforce issue of 1933 is one of the modern classic issues of the British Commonwealth. It marked the centenary of the death of William Wilberforce, the Englishman who fought for the abolition of slavery.

Soon after independence in 1961, there came the modern period of the free-form, self-stick gimmick issues, and there have been a large number of long, expensive sets of these stickers interspersed with a few normal postage stamp issues.

Though Sierra Leone was once popular with the world's collectors, interest has greatly diminished as a result of this collector-aimed material.

A philatelic bureau is located at GPO, Gloucester St., Freetown, Sierra Leone.

Silbergroschen: A unit of currency used in the German states of Brunswick, Hanover, Mecklen-Strelitz, Oldenburg, and Schleswig-Holstein.

It was also used in the North German Confederation, the northern district of the German Empire, and the northern parts of the Thurn and Taxis postal system.

In general, the silbergroschen was 30 to the thaler.

Silesia, Eastern: Eastern Silesia was located on the border of the newly formed states of Czechoslovakia and Poland following World War I. It had previously been part of the Austro-Hungarian Empire.

Since neither of the two new countries could agree, a plebiscite was planned for 1920, and stamps of both Poland and Czechoslovakia were released overprinted "SO/ 1920." the "SO" stood for "Silesie Orientale" (Eastern Silesia).

Because of Czech opposition, however, the plebiscite was never held, and the Allied powers divided the area between the two countries.

The Paris Conference of Ambassadors awarded 491 square miles of the area to Czechoslovakia, with the remainder of the 1,987 square-mile total going to Poland.

The final boundary divided the town of Teschen (in Polish, "Cieszyn," and in Czech, "Tesin").

Silesia, Upper: Prior to World War I, Silesia was part of Germany, but, at the end of the war, because of its mixed German and Polish population, a boundary dispute arose and a plebiscite was planned. On Feb. 20, 1920, stamps were issued for use in an area called Upper Silesia until its future could be decided.

The plebiscite failed to decide the matter, and the Polish population, under Polish Plebiscite Commissioner Wojciech Korfanty, rebelled.

Stamps were issued by Korfanty, and these are noted but not listed by the Scott catalog, which states that these were a private issue and not recognized by the Inter-Allied Commission of Government.

Nonetheless, Jozef L. Brodowski, writing in the Jan. 18, 1982, issue of *Stamp Collector*, contends that the stamps were legally issued by the Polish Military Organization under Korfanty.

The fighting ended in 1921, when the League of Nations awarded much of the disputed area to Poland, with the rest going to Germany.

Stamps issued by the plebiscite authorities were of several designs and included a number of surcharges. Stamps for Official use were also released, consisting of a handstamped overprint "C 1. H.S." in a circle and a straightline "C.G.H.S.," both on German stamps.

Scott lists a total of 51 Official stamps.

Meanwhile, Lower Silesia had been retained by Germany, since its population was German. An area known as Eastern Silesia (q.v.) was divided between Poland and Czechoslovakia.

This is the design used for the Korfanty issue.

An Upper Silesian plebiscite issue.

Silk Thread: Foreign terms for "silk thread" include fil de soie (French), seidenfaden (German), filo di seta (Italian), and filamento de seda (Spanish).

Silver Tax Stamp: (See Stamp, Silver Tax.)

Sily: Unit of currency used in the Republic of Guinea (q.v.).

Simi: An island in the Aegean Sea off the coast of Turkey. Once part of the Italian Dodecanese group (q.v.), it is now Greek and uses Greek stamps.

Sinaloa: A provisional revolutionary government in the Mexican state of Sinaloa issued two stamps in 1929.

Federal forces, however, put down the revolution before the stamps could be used. Copies canceled by favor are known. (See Mexico.)

Sin Dentar: Spanish word for "imperforate."

Singapore: At the crossroads of Southeast Asia, Singapore has long been an important seaport and trading center.

It is now the fourth largest port in the world, and the estimated 2,390,000 citizens of the 226-square-mile country enjoy a per capita income of $2,279, second in Asia only to that of Japan.

The Republic of Singapore, on an island at the very tip of the Malay Peninsula, began life as an East India Company trading post established in 1819 by Sir Thomas Stamford Raffles.

Its name reportedly comes from the combination of the Sanskrit words "singa" and "pura," meaning "lion city."

Its strategic position soon made it a colonial seaport and naval base of great importance.

In 1942 it fell to the invading Japanese, while Britain was otherwise engaged with the Germans, and remained under Japanese occupation until its liberation at the end of the war. It was then made a crown colony, and it became self-governing in 1959.

In 1963 it merged with Malaysia (q.v.), but the union was not a success because the large Chinese population in Singapore was overwhelmed by the Malay population in the rest of Malaysia.

It was agreed in 1965 that the marriage should be terminated, and Singapore became an independent nation outside the Malaysian Federation.

Prior to World War II, the colony had been one of the Straits Settlements (q.v.) and used the stamps of that unit. Beginning in 1946, as a Crown Colony, it had its own stamps. At first they were inscribed "SINGAPORE," but in 1949 this was changed to include the word "MALAYA."

Since independence, Singapore has issued a moderate number of stamps featuring various aspects of Singapore's life and culture, including issues designed to encourage tourism.

The unit of currency is the dollar, which in 1981 was 2.12 to the US dollar.

The address of the philatelic office is Philatelic Bureau, Philatelic Services Dept., Eighth Floor, World Trade Center, Maritime Square, Singapore 0409.

Sinistro: Italian word for "left."

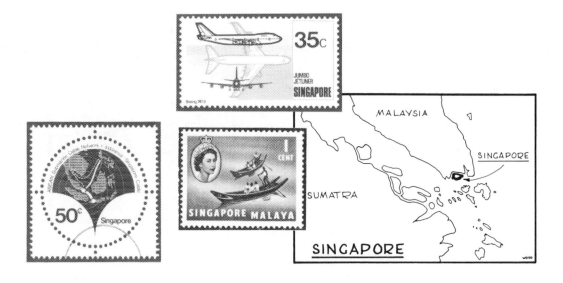

Sinkiang: An outer province of China, Sinkiang issued stamps from 1915 to 1945. These issues consisted of overprints on Chinese stamps.

In 1949, Sinkiang was served by stamps of the Northwest China Liberation Area.

Sinking Fund: (See Caisse d'Amortissement.)

Sir Codrington Error: (See Error, Design.)

Sirmoor: Sirmoor was an Indian Feudatory State located in the Punjab. Its capital city was Nahan.

It issued its first stamps in 1879 and continued until March 31, 1901. They were valid for use only within the state.

Official stamps were also issued, and these can be distinguished by the overprint "On/ S. S./ S." in the form of a diamond.

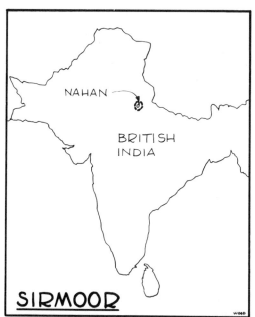

Six: Numeral six (6) in French.

Size: Foreign words for "size" include format (French and German), formato (Italian), and tamano (Spanish).

Sju: Numeral seven (7) in Swedish.

Skatikas (Skatiku): A unit of currency used in Lithuania prior to 1922. One hundred skatikas made up one auksinas.

Skilling: A unit of currency used in Denmark (96 to the rigsbank daler), Iceland (96 to the rigsdaler), and Norway (120 to the specie daler).

Skilling Banco: A unit of currency used in Sweden prior to 1858. There were 48 skilling banco to the riksdaler (rixdaler) banco.

Sky Blue: Foreign terms for the color "sky blue" include bleu ciel (French), himmelblau (German), azzurro cielo (Italian), and azul celeste (Spanish).

Sky Train: (See Glider Mail.)

Slate: Foreign words for the color "slate" include ardoise (French), schiefer (German), ardesia (Italian), and pizarra (Spanish).

Slav Alphabet: (See Alphabet, Cyrillic.)

Sleeper: The term "sleeper" refers to a stamp or other philatelic item that is considerably scarcer than its price would indicate.

It may well be from a currently unpopular area of the hobby with low demand that will not have made its scarcity obvious.

The knowledgeable collector is often able to pick up a bargain by buying such an item when he comes across it in the course of his collecting activities.

In a related field, when a collector is seeking a new area of interest, he can often build up an interesting collection at low cost relative to the scarcity of the material by selecting a currently unpopular area, merely because he is not competing with other collectors for the available supply.

It should be emphasized, however, that this is best done on the basis of philatelic knowledge and purely for philatelic enjoyment.

Its advantage is not that the collector will

make money, but that he will get more philately for the amount of money spent, since he will be outside the field of operations of the investors and speculators and thus be unaffected by the artifically high prices that investment activity will create.

As always, philatelic knowledge is the key to wise and rewarding collecting.

SLESVIG: The inscription "SLESVIG" identified plebiscite issues of Schleswig (q.v.).

Slovakia: The central province of Czechoslovakia, Slovakia was established as a pseudo-independent state by the Germans following their 1939 "carve-up" of the country.

With its capital at Bratislava, the new "country" had an area of 14,850 square miles and a population of 2,50,000, which had a surprising amount of initial of freedom.

Despite early good conditions, the people

gradually became less and less enthusiastic about their German "partners," and in August 1944, as Soviet troops began a westward drive, they revolted.

Unfortunately, the Soviety army did not arrive until early 1945 and were thus of little use in helping the partisans in their fight.

Bratislava was liberated on April 4, 1945, and Slovakia was restored to Czechoslovakia.

Beginning on Jan. 18, 1939, Slovakia issued its own stamps. The first issues were overprints on the stamps of Czechoslovakia.

Strangely, in the midst of the war, Slovakia was at first something of an oasis. Allowed an unusual amount of freedom, the inhabitants even found time to stage a national stamp show in May 1942 and to issue a set of four stamps to mark the event! (See also Czechoslovakia; Bohemia and Moravia; and Carpatho-Ukraine.)

Slovenia: (See Ljubljana, Italian Occupation of; and Ljubljana, German Occupation of.)

SLOVENSKY STAT: Overprinted on stamps of Czechoslovakia for use in Slovakia.

S.M.: Prior to the introduction of stamps overprinted "O.S." in 1874 for general Official use, South Australia used a number of different overprints to indicate use by specific government departments.

"S.M." stood for Stipendiary Magistrate.

Small: Foreign words for "small" include klein (Dutch, German), petit (French), piccolo (Italian), and pequeno (Spanish).

Smallest Stamp: See Odd-shaped Stamps.

Smaragdgrun: German word for the color "emerald."

Smeraldo: Italian word for the color "emerald."

SMIRNE: Overprint on stamps of Italy for use in the Turkish city of Smyrna.

S.M.O.M.: The letters S.M.O.M. stand for "Sovereign Military Order of the Knights of Malta."

Headquartered in Rome, the organization has issued "stamps" that it claims are valid for postage.

Though some countries, including Italy, have recognized these stamps, they are not generally accepted in the international mail, and the Universal Postal Union (q.v.) does not recognize them.

Smorto: Italian word for "dull," as in dull color.

Smyrna: (See Levant, Italian.)

Smyrne: Stamps issued by Russia in 1909 for use in the Turkish Empire were overprinted with the names of various Turkish cities in which there were Russian post offices. Smyrne was one of the cities.

These overprinted issues commemorated the 50th anniversary of Russian post offices in the Turkish Empire. (See Trebizonde.)

Snowshoe Thompson: A giant among mail carriers, "Snowshoe Thompson" operated in the High Sierras between California and Nevada, and his exploits are the stuff of which legend is made.

Like all legendary figures, accounts of his adventures vary in detail, but it seems certain that he was born in Norway as John Tostensen and came to this country as a child. He changed his name to John Thompson when he went West in 1851 to seek gold in the California Gold Country.

The monument to Snowshoe Thompson that stands at the summit of Interstate 80, north of Lake Tahoe. It is the work of American sculptor Angus Kent Lamar of Chickasha, Okla., and was made possible by the Snowshoe Thompson Lodge of the Sons of Norway and a number of skiing organizations. (Photo courtesy of Pacific Gas and Electric Co. *Progress* and Ted W. Fuller, Editor.)

Konwiser *(American Stamp Collectors Dictionary,* Minkus, New York, 1949) reports that in 1855 Thompson contracted with T.J. Matheson of Murphy's Camp in Calaveras County, Calif., to carry mail in the winter between Placerville, Calif., and the Carson Valley, Nevada.

For $200 a month, he agreed to carry mail without regard for the depth of snow in a mountain range famous for its massive snow falls.

Although he came to be called "Snowshoe," he is said to have used oak skis weighing 25 pounds that he made himself.

A monument to "Snowshoe," located at New Summit, north of Lake Tahoe on Interstate Highway 80, features a large figure of him on his skis, holding a balance pole, and wearing the backpack in which he is reputed to have carried up to 60 pounds of mail.

For several winters, he made up to four round trips per month over the mountains.

Ernest A. Wiltsee *(The Pioneer Miner and Pack Mule Express,* Quarterman Publications, Lawrence, Mass., 1976) notes that Thompson began his mail service in 1853 carrying mail both winter and summer, continuing it until the pass was open to stage coaches in the late 1850s.

It was Thompson who brought out for assay the first ore from the Comstock Lode, which sparked the rush to Nevada.

S.O.: Overprint on stamps of Czechoslovakia for Eastern Silesia. "S.O." stood for Silesia Orientale.

Soaking: Soaking is the operation of removing a stamp from the paper to which it has been affixed.

Before beginning this operation, you should take some precautions.

Isolate all doubtful cases, including stamps stuck on colored or manila paper, stamps with colored cancels, precancels, pieces of colored air mail envelopes, etc. These are best soaked separately, since the colors can run and stain the rest of the material. Some may require a treatment such as floating (q.v.) or the use of a sweatbox (q.v.).

The material to be soaked should be fed into tepid water and stirred around so that all pieces are exposed to the water. If you dump a wad into the water, it may not get soaked clear through.

After stamps begin to float free, remove and give them a bath in clean water; otherwise, dissolved gum in the first water may remain on the stamps.

Wet paper is extremely delicate, and stamps can easily be damaged, so handle with care. This is a time when the advice to use tongs should be ignored. Fingers are apt to do less damage than are tong tips!

After rinsing, the stamps may be placed face down on white paper towels so that excess moisture can evaporate.

When almost dry, but while the paper is slightly damp, the stamps can be placed between layers of white paper towels and pressed. After a few hours they will be ready for mounting.

Despite a very tenacious gum being used on some current US definitives, I have not had any become stuck to the drying paper during pressing, but the possibility should be guarded against by making sure that the stamp is only barely damp before pressing.

In addition to colored envelope paper, cancels, etc., there are some stamps that will run, especially if the soaking water is too warm.

The 1980 US Edith Wharton stamp is an example, as are many other stamps printed in purple. Treat these separately and with care. Beware also of early red US stamps, especially the early postage dues, stamps printed on chalky paper, and some early photogravure-printed stamps.

Then there are those early stamps that were deliberately printed with fugitive ink. They will require sweatbox (q.v.) treatment, and even then you must be careful.

A modern problem is the horrible coated paper used for many recent US commemoratives. The canceling ink does not penetrate the paper, and if you are not careful, one careless swipe with a thumb can wipe off that beautiful socked-on-the-nose circular date stamp.

With the extra-sticky gum used on Austrian stamps, for example, several changes of water may be necessary, since I have found that even the gum suspended in the soaking water will redeposit itself. You may have to actually rub the back of the stamp to get it all off, but be very careful.

Finally, if there is doubt about the results, there is no reason why a nicely canceled stamp should not be left on paper. Just trim it neatly, being sure not to cut off any of the cancelation, and place it in your collection.

Sobre: Spanish word for "envelope" or "cover."

Sobrecarga: Spanish word for "overprint."

SOBRE CLOTA PARA MULTOS POSTALES: This inscription identifies a Mexican parcel post stamp.

SOBREPORTO: Colombian stamps inscribed "SOBREPORTO" were used to pay an additional fee for mail to countries with which Colombia had no postal agreement. A set of three such stamps was issued in 1866.

Sobretasa: Spanish word for "surcharge."

SOCIEDADE DE GEOGRAPHIA DE LISBOA PORTE FRANCO: This inscription identified Portuguese franchise stamps to benefit the Geographic Society of Portugal

SOCIEDADE HUMANITARUA CRUZ DA ORIENTE: This inscription is found on postal tax stamps of Mozambique.

SOCIEDADE PORTUGUEZA DA CRUZ VERMELHA PORTE FRANCO: This inscription identifies Portuguese franchise stamps issued for the benefit of the Red Cross.

SOCIETE/ des/ NATIONS: Overprint on regular stamps of Switzerland in 1922-23 for Official use by the League of Nations.

Societies, Philatelic: Few hobbies are blessed with so many general and specialty organizations as philately.

Virtually every town has its local stamp club, and there are national organizations devoted to just about every aspect of philately imaginable. Many of the larger, national societies also have chapters located in large cities around the country.

Lying between major national groups — like the American Philatelic Society (q.v.), the Society of Philatelic Americans (q.v.), and the American Topical Association (q.v.) — and local stamp clubs is a mass of specialty groups and study units, many of which are as national and international in their membership as are the larger organizations.

This is as true of other countries as of the US, and many collectors of a specific country or topical interest are members of foreign organizations devoted to their interest. Indeed, it is common for many national organizations to have a membership list that is international.

There are organizations devoted to the collection and study of such material as revenues, postal stationery, US philately, ship and maritime postal markings, essays and proofs, postal history, first-day covers, air mail material, plate numbers, space philately, errors-freaks-oddities, meter stamps, perfins, permits, precancels, plus major and minor political entities, and just about every topical subject you could imagine.

These organizations can be contacted through the addresses contained in this work or through local stamp clubs, dealers, or the philatelic press.

Many of the smaller groups are chapters of one of the major national societies, and inquiries can also be directed to the APS, SPA, or ATA.

Most commercial philatelic publications also maintain files of societies, addresses, and an inquiry accompanied by an SASE will usually get you the information desired.

Society for Czechoslovak Philately:
(See Czechoslovak Philately, Society for.)

Society for Hungarian Philately:
(See Hungarian Philately, Society for.)

Society for Thai Philately: (See Thai Philately, Society for.)

Society for the Suppression of Speculative Stamps: Founded in Great Britain in 1895, the Society for the Suppression of Speculative Stamps (SSSS) attempted to persuade stamp-issuing authorities to refrain from issuing stamps the chief purpose of which was to raise money from their sale to collectors.

A measure of the organization's failure is the fact that most of today's stamps are produced with philatelic sales very much in mind.

Postal administrations are openly courting collectors and make no secret that their stamps are aimed directly at collectors.

The Black Blot Program of the American Philatelic Society (q.v.) is a current attempt to achieve results sought by the SSSS, and it appears to be achieving a similar degree of success.

Society of Australasian Specialists/ Oceania: The Society of Australasian Specialists/ Oceania is a group of collectors interested in the South Pacific islands, Australia, New Zealand, and their associated territories.

The society publishes a journal, *The Informer*, which features material relating to the area. It also publishes handbooks and makes them available to members at reasonable prices, holds periodic auctions, and operates a sales circuit.

Information is available from the society at Box 82643, San Diego, CA 92138.

Society of Costa Rica Collectors:
(See Costa Rica Collectors, Society of.)

Society of Indo-China Philatelists:
(See Indo-China Philatelists, Society of.)

Society of Israel Philatelists: (See Israel Philatelists, Society of.)

Society of Philatelic Americans:
Soon after the founding of the American Philatelic Association in 1886, young collectors in the South began to complain that it was dominated by "old fogies" and "Yankee old fogies" at that!

So it was that in February 1894, the Southern Philatelic Association was formed with 19-year-old J.M. Chappell Jr. as president and 15-year-

old J. Hugh Conley as treasurer.

Membership was then limited to residents of the former Confederate states, but this requirement was soon eased.

By 1914, many members favored a change to a name more in keeping with a national membership, and in 1918 the SPA became the Society of Philatelic Americans.

Now, the SPA boasts an international membership and offers a sales service, an exchange department, and special rates on insurance.

An expertization service, slide programs, and the monthly *SPA Journal* are additional membership benefits.

Membership information is available from the executive secretary, Robert B. Brandeberry, Box 9041, Wilmington, DE 19809.

Socked-on-the-Nose Cancel: (See Cancelation, Socked on the Nose.)

Sol: A unit of currency used in Peru. It comprises 100 centavos.

SOLDI: The inscription "SOLDI" is found on stamps of Lombardy-Venetia from 1858. It represents a unit of currency used in the area.

Solidus: The solidus was a gold coin of Rome from which the names shilling (British),

schilling (Austrian), skilling (Scandinavian), etc., are said to be derived.

It was equal to 12 denarii (see Denarius), according to the *Random House Unabridged Dictionary, 1966 edition.*

Solomon Islands: Formerly known
as the British Solomon Islands, this South Pacific island group became the Solomon Islands in 1975. It achieved self-government status on Jan. 2, 1976, and independence on July 7, 1978.

The group comprises a chain of islands with an area of 11,500 square miles, spread over 375,000 square miles of ocean, and has an estimated population of 222,000.

The Solomons generally are a continuation of the sweep of islands spreading to the southeast from New Ireland that, together with Bougainville, is part of Papua New Guinea (q.v.).

The islands were discovered by the Spanish explorer Alvaro de Medana in 1568. De Medana made an unsuccessful attempt at colonization, but it was not until the 18th century that any detailed exploration by Europeans was done.

Great Britain declared a protectorate over most of the islands in 1893, with Germany taking similar action to the north. The islands of Bougainville and Buka came within the German Protectorate.

The Solomons were the scene of bitter fighting during World War II, and names such as Guadalcanal, Savo Island, and The Slot have been immortalized in that war's history.

The 1977 population of the island group was estimated at 200,000, with Malaita being the most thickly populated. The chief crop and main export is copra, the dried meat of the coconut.

The first stamps were issued in 1907 and bear the inscription "British Solomon Islands Protectorate." This was changed to "British Solomon Islands" with the 1913 issue.

The definitive series of 1939 offers an attractive glimpse of an apparent island paradise, and you can understand the desire of the Englishman who during the 1930s is reported to have wanted to get as far away from the threat of a European war as he could.

It was hardly his fault that he made the monumental error of judgment of choosing Guadalcanal!

Since WWII, stamps of the Solomon Islands have continued to feature the country's scenic beauty and its primitive culture.

A 1974 set marking the 100th anniversary of the Universal Postal Union is unusual in that it depicts examples of the ancient Oriental art of origami, or paper folding.

The unit of currency in the Solomons is the Australian dollar, and the latest per capita income figure is $300.

The address of the philatelic bureau is Controller of Posts and Telecommunications, Philatelic Section, GPO, Honiara, Solomon Islands, South Pacific.

Solot: A unit of currency once used by
Siam (Thailand). The solot was 32 to the salung.

Somala (Somalo): A unit of currency
used in Somalia after 1950. It comprised 100 centesimi. Authorities differ as to the correct spelling.

Somalia, Italian Administration: In
1950 the British handed the administration of the ex-Italian colony of Italian Somaliland back to Italy as the Trust Territory of Somalia.

This administration lasted until 1960 when the country became the independent Republic of Somalia which later would become the Somali Democratic Republic (q.v.).

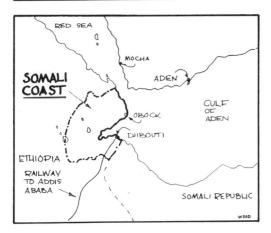

Somali Coast: Located in a strategic position at the southern end of the Red Sea, the French Somali Coast was established in 1888.

The town of Djibouti became the territory's capital in 1892, and work was begun on a rail link with Addis Ababa, the capital of Ethiopia.

The first stamps of the Somali Coast were issued in 1894 and consist of overprints on the Commerce and Navigation key type stamps of Obock.

From then on, the colony issued a stream of attractive stamps that reflect the country and its people and add color to a collection of French colonial stamps.

The country consists mostly of arid desert, with temperatures averaging a high of 104 degrees F. and a low of 73 degrees F. Annual rainfall is less than five inches.

The population is largely nomadic and moves over wide areas with flocks of sheep, goats, and herds of camels.

Mountains rise from a coastal plain to a height of 6,600 feet, and the coastline is deeply indented by the Gulf of Tadjoura.

The free port and capital city of Djibouti is the country's major economic asset. It serves the interior and Ethiopia via the Djibouti-to-Addis Ababa railway.

The main export of the country is marine salt, and some 6,500 metric tons are exported annually.

After the Italian conquest of Ethiopia in 1936, the French fortified the Somali Coast, but a Vichy regime controlled the colony from 1940 to 1942, when the area declared for General De Gaulle and the Free French.

In 1967 the area became the French Territory of Afars and Issas, following a referendum on independence.

Critics claimed that the French interfered in the voting to ensure a continuation of French control. They were accused of a massive expul-sion of Somali residents that made the resulting 60% vote in favor of France a foregone conclusion.

Finally, on June 26, 1977, the territory became Africa's 49th independent country, and it is now known as the Republic of Djibouti (q.v.). The future of the new country is not bright, as both the adjoining countries of Ethiopia and Somalia have long had claims on the area.

The stamps of the Republic of Djibouti are now used.

Somali Democratic Republic:

The Somali Democratic Republic obtained its independence on July 1, 1960, as the Republic of Somalia.

It was formed from the ex-Italian colony of Italian Somaliland and the British-administered Somaliland Protectorate (q.v.).

As early as the seventh century, Arabs and Persians had developed trading posts around what is known as the Horn of Africa.

Despite these early contacts, exploration of the interior only began after the British established a base at Aden in 1839.

Soon, there was intense competition among colonial powers for control of the area. This resulted in the creation of French Somaliland (q.v.), Italian Somaliland, and the British Somaliland Protectorate (q.v.).

During World War II, Italian forces, which had already conquered Ethiopia, occupied the British Protectorate in 1940, but they were defeated and driven out of the entire area, in-

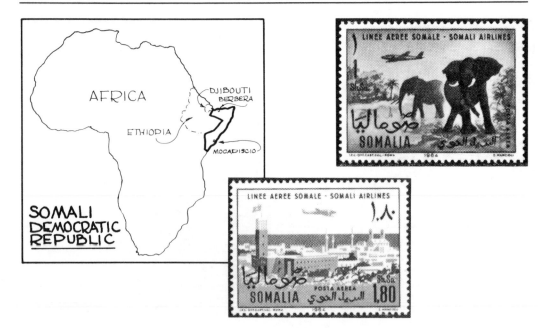

cluding Ethiopia, in 1941. From 1943, stamps of Great Britain overprinted "E.A.F." (East Africa Forces) were used.

Italian Somaliland was under British military administration until 1950, when the Italians were allowed to establish a government under United Nations supervision with the objective of preparing it for independence within 10 years. Stamps inscribed "Somalia" were used.

Since independence, the Somali Democratic Republic has clashed with Ethiopia over the long-standing border dispute concerning ownership of the Ogaden region of Ethiopia.

In 1969, in a bloodless coup, a revolutionary council seized power, abolished the assembly, and changed the country's name to the Somali Democratic Republic.

The poor nation's economy is mainly agricultural, with a current per capita income of about $105.

The capital city and chief port is Mogadiscio, with the second city and port being the old British Protectorate capital of Berbera.

The currency unit is the shilling (100 centesimi). It is about 6.30 to the US dollar.

The address of the philatelic bureau is Philatelic Section, Ministry of Posts and Telecommunications, Mogadiscio, Somali Democratic Republic.

Somaliland Protectorate: In

1882, in order to protect the trade route to India via the Suez Canal and the Red Sea, Great Britain occupied territory along the African shore of the Gulf of Aden.

In 1887 a British protectorate was proclaimed over the area. At first administered as a dependency of Aden, located across the gulf on the Arabian shore, the area came under the British Foreign Office in 1898 and was handed over to the Colonial Office in 1905.

The protectorate was occupied by Italy in 1940 but was recaptured by British forces in 1941.

By pre-arrangement, the protectorate was

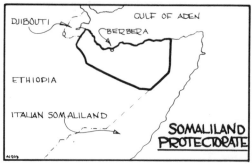

given its independence a few days before the ex-Italian colony of Italian Somaliland became independent, in order that the two might merge and form the Republic of Somalia, which is now the Somali Democratic Republic.

Stamps were first issued for the protectorate in 1903 and comprised Indian stamps overprinted "British Somaliland."

In 1938 a series of King George VI definitive stamps inscribed "Somaliland Protectorate" was issued. Designs feature a Berbera Blackhead sheep on the low denominations and a map of the protectorate on the high denominations.

Somerset House: Somerset House in London is the headquarters of Britain's Board of Inland Revenue.

A number of stamps have been produced in its printing facilities. These include the 1847-54 embossed issues of Great Britain and some early King George V stamps, in particular the 6d denomination, which was produced at Somerset House until well into the 1930s.

Sonora: During the 1913-16 civil war in Mexico, the Mexican state of Sonora issued a number of stamps for use in the state.

SOOMAALIYA: Partial inscription on stamps of the Somali Democratic Republic (q.v.).

Soort: Dutch word for "variety."

Soprastampa: Italian word for "overprint."

Sort: Danish word for "black."

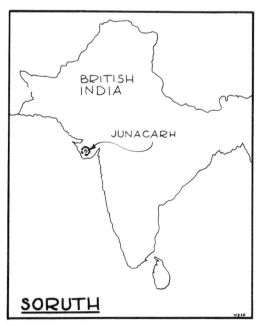

SORUTH

Soruth: An Indian Feudatory State, Soruth issued its first stamps in 1864. These

were handstamped individually in watercolor.

In 1923 the name was changed to Sourashtra and in 1929, to Saurashtra.

A group of 217 of the area's states was formed in 1948, known as the United States of Saurashtra.

This included the stamp-issuing feudatory states of Jasdan, Morvi, Nowanuggur, and Wadhwan.

The issues of the union were replaced by the stamps of the Republic of India in 1950.

Earlier, Official stamps were overprinted "SARKARI."

Sottile: Italian word for "thin."

Soudan: The overprint "Soudan" together with an Arabic inscription is found on the stamps of Egypt for use in the Sudan in 1897.

SOUDAN Fais: Overprint on stamps of French colonies for use in French Sudan.

SOUDAN FRANCAIS: Inscription on stamps of French Sudan.

Soumi: Identifies stamps of Finland (q.v.).

Sourashtra: (See Soruth.)

South Africa: In 1909 the British Parliament created the Union of South Africa, which combined the four former colonies of the Cape of Good Hope, Natal, Transvaal, and the Orange Free State. (See under the individual colony names.)

The union came into being on May 31, 1910. On May 31, 1961, the union became a republic and the country withdrew from the British Commonwealth, other members of which had opposed South Africa's policy of racial discrimination.

Under the South African government's policies of apartheid, blacks are paid lower wages than whites, are only permitted to engage

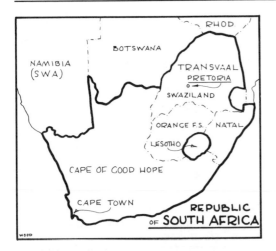

in certain types of work, and cannot vote or run for public office. Thus, the white minority is able to keep control of the country.

Upon the outbreak of World War I, there was considerable pro-German sentiment on the part of the Boers, but this was overcome. South African forces moved into German South West Africa, expelling the Germans, and afterwards obtaining a League of Nations mandate over what became known as South-West Africa (Namibia).

In recent years, the Republic of South Africa refused to give up the territory, and the United Nations does not recognize South African authority over what is now known to the rest of the world as Namibia. The UN has issued several stamps calling attention to the illegal occupation of Namibia, still called "South West Africa" by the government of the Republic of South Africa.

The republic supported the Allies during WWII, but because of continuing pro-German feeling among the Boers, it did not institute conscription into the military services, which remained on a volunteer basis.

The republic has an area of 471,819 square miles (excluding Namibia) and a population estimated in 1976 at 29,290,000.

South Africa is the world's largest producer of gold, diamonds, and other minerals, including copper, platinum, uranium, and vanadium.

The latest per capita income figure is $1,296 and the literacy rate 35%.

The rand (100 cents) is the unit of currency and in 1981 was .82 to the US dollar.

The first stamp of the Union of South Africa was issued in 1910 and commemorated the opening of the Union Parliament on Nov. 4, 1910.

Beginning in 1926, stamps were issued in both English and Afrikaans versions. The stamp versions alternated in sheets, thus providing se-tenant (q.v.) pairs.

After 1952, stamps were inscribed in both languages, thus eliminating the se-tenant pairs. Two exceptions are the 1955 Voortrekker Covenant issue and the 1966 Fifth Anniversary of the Republic issue.

During WWII, the unusual "bantam" stamps were produced. These were perforated in units of either two or three with the individual small stamps being rouletted between.

Since 1967, the stamps of the republic have been inscribed "RSA."

The address of the Republic of South Africa's philatelic bureau is Philatelic Services, GPO, Pretoria 0001, Republic of South Africa.

The service also sells stamps of South-West Africa (Namibia), plus the "homelands" of Transkei, Bophuthatswana, Venda, and Ciskei. (See South Africa, Homelands of.)

South Africa, Homelands of:

Following World War II, the policy of separation of the races in what was the Union of South Africa became official, and in 1959 the South African government passed legislation for the establishment of what it calls "Bantustans," or "homelands."

The first such homeland to obtain its own

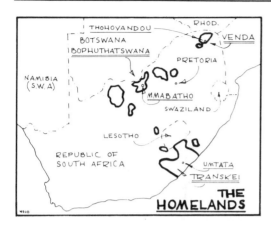

THE HOMELANDS

postage stamps was Transkei, which began issuing stamps in 1977. The second stamp-issuing homeland was Bophuthatswana, formed in 1977, followed by Venda, created in 1979, and Ciskei, in 1981.

None of these areas have received any political recognition outside the Republic of South Africa, and their stamps have no validity in the international mail, although the English Stanley Gibbons catalog notes that the issues of Transkei appear to be tolerated and lists them.

The US Scott catalog includes these issues in its "For the Record" section but does not accord them catalog status.

South Arabian Federation: (See Federation of South Arabia.)

South Australia: Occupying about one eighth of the land area of Australia, the

SOUTH AUSTRALIA

state of South Australia contains 380,000 square miles and is located in the south-central part of the country.

Settlement dates from December 1836, but Matthew Flinders had explored the area in 1802.

At first dependent on the British Colonial Office in London, the settlement grew, and following the discovery of large copper deposits together with expanding wool and wheat production, the settlers became largely independent of support from Britain.

In 1851 South Australia became the first portion of the British Empire to effect a complete separation of church and state.

The capital city of Adelaide — a handsome city with broad, tree-lined streets — is named for the consort of King William IV.

In 1979 South Australia had a population of 1,287,600.

The state has two climatic regions: a warm, dry area with very little rain in the north, and a Mediterranean-type region with moist winters and hot, dry summers in the south.

South Australia's stamp-issuing period began in 1855 and continued until issues of the Commonwealth began following federation.

As a change of pace from the procession of stamps bearing the royal profile, a stamp was issued in 1899 featuring the Adelaide Post Office.

Another unusual item is a tiny ½d stamp of 1883. An 1894 stamp, although giving half its area to Queen Victoria, managed to include a palm tree and a kangaroo.

South Bulgaria: (See Eastern Rumelia.)

South China: (See China, Regional Issues.)

Southern Cameroons: (See Cameroons, U.K.T.T.)

Southern Nigeria: The British Protectorate of Southern Nigeria, which had been formed in 1900 absorbed the Niger Coast Protectorate in the same year, and united with Lagos in 1906 to form the colony of Southern Nigeria.

It merged with Northern Nigeria (q.v.) to form the colony of Nigeria, which later became the Republic of Nigeria (q.v.).

Southern Rhodesia: (See Zimbabwe.)

South Georgia: (See Falkland Islands Dependencies.)

South Kasai: South Kasai was an area

around the town of Bakwanga in the Republic of Zaire (q.v.).

During the unsettled period following the independence of the Belgian Congo — which had become the Congo Democratic Republic (later the Republic of Zaire) — South Kasai in 1960 declared its own independence and did not rejoin the CDR until October 1962.

Two stamp issues were released in 1961, and it is reported that stamps were prepared and placed on sale in Belgium but not sent to South Kasai.

South Lithuania: (See Lithuania, South.)

South Moluccas: The South Moluccas Republic was a short-lived entity in the Moluccas, or Spice Islands. These islands lie between the Celebes (Sulawesi) and New Guinea.

The South Moluccas group comprised the islands of Buru, Ceram (Seram), and Ambon, according to Dr. Robert E. Florida writing in *Stamp Collector* (Jan. 1, 1977).

Some of the inhabitants of these islands wanted to be independent of Indonesia when that country was formed after World War II from what had been the Dutch East Indies.

For a short time during 1951, a provisional government existed, but Indonesia's military forces brought the islands under its control, and the provisional government went into exile in the Netherlands.

It is this government-in-exile that is presumed to have issued a number of stamp-like labels inscribed "REPUBLIK MALAKU SELATAN" that has come onto the philatelic market in large quantities since 1951. These labels are still encountered, and since none are listed in the ma-

jor catalogs, they tend to confuse collectors.

Florida lists nine issues released from 1951 to 1974, a selection of which is illustrated. He states that it is doubtful that any of these items ever did postal duty in the islands.

Another label inscribed "REPOEBLIK MALOEKOE SELATAN" is known, and stamps of the Dutch East Indies overprinted "RMS" are rumored to exist.

South Orkneys: (See Falkland Islands Dependencies.)

South Russia: (See Russia, South.)

South Shetlands: (See Falkland Islands Dependencies.)

South Vietnam: (See Vietnam, Socialist Republic of.)

South Vietnam, National Front for the Liberation of: Also known as the Viet Cong, this was a Communist guerrilla organization that operated in South Vietnam from December 1960 until it gained control of the entire country in May 1975. At that time, South Vietnam surrendered and US troops were withdrawn.

During its fight for control of South Vietnam, the Viet Cong issued stamps for use in the areas it controlled.

The first issue appeared in 1963 and comprised three stamps showing the Viet Cong flag and two in other designs. Various issues continued until the unification of Vietnam under the Communists on July 2, 1976.

Currency used was the dong (100 xu), which fluctuated and was not tied to the North Vietnamese dong, according to Gibbons.

South-West Africa: The area now known either as South-West Africa or Namibia was made a German protectorate in 1884. It is twice the size of California with a present population of about 994,000.

The German colony was surrendered to the Union of South Africa in 1915 and was mandated to that country by the League of Nations.

Since the formation of the United Nations, however, South Africa has refused to recognise any UN authority over the area. Many other nations, plus the UN Security Council, have condemned South Africa for its illegal hold over the mandated territory.

The fact that SWA/ Namibia has the world's largest uranium mine, and untapped riches in diamonds, copper, and other minerals, might have some bearing on the dispute.

The UN made the area's official name

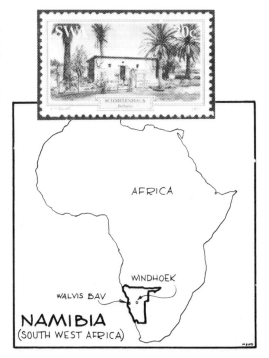

"Namibia" in 1970, and the International Court of Justice has declared that South Africa is exercising illegal control.

The first stamps for South West Africa were stamps of Germany overprinted "DEUTSCH-SUDWESTAFRIKA," issued in 1897. These were followed in 1900 by the Kaiser's Yacht key type.

The first stamps under South African occupation came in 1923. these were South African stamps overprinted "SOUTH WEST/ AFRICA" on every other stamp and "ZUID-WEST/ AFRIKA" on the remainder. There are a number of variations of these overprints.

In 1931 the first specially designed stamps were released. They take the same bilingual format as did those of South Africa.

Since 1968, stamps have been inscribed "SWA."

The capital of the area is Windhoek, and the only deep-water port is Walvis Bay. South African currency is used.

The address of the philatelic bureau is the same as for South Africa: Philatelic Service, GPO, Pretoria 001, Republic of South Africa.

Southwest China: (See China, Regional Issues.)

Souvenir Card:

Souvenir cards have been issued for a number of years by the US Post Office Department (and later the US Postal Service), the Bureau of Engraving and Printing, and since 1972, by the United Nations Postal Administration.

They are commonly known as USPS cards, BEP cards, and UNPA cards.

Souvenir cards have no franking value and are in no way postal items. They are issued to commemorate a stamp exhibition or convention, or, in the case of the UNPA cards, are issued in conjunction with a UN stamp issue.

The BEP cards are mostly issued for domestic philatelic exhibitions or numismatic events. They feature altered reproductions of US stamps or currency items.

The first BEP card was issued on March 13, 1954, in honor of the Postage Stamp Design Exhibition in Philadelphia.

Sizes of the cards has varied from 6 x 9 inches up to 8½ x 10½ inches.

The forerunner of the USPS cards is considered to be the Philatelic Truck sheet (q.v.), issued during the 1938-41 national tour of the Philatelic Truck, from which it was given free.

The 1960 souvenir card for the First International Philatelic Congress in Barcelona, Spain, is the first in the current series.

These USPOD and USPS cards are generally issued in conjunction with a foreign international philatelic event, although there have been several exceptions.

They usually feature amended versions of US postage stamps and sometimes also a stamp of the country in which the event is being held.

The most usual size for these cards is 6 x 8 inches.

Souvenir Card Collectors Society:

The Souvenir Card Collectors Society is an organization for collectors of souvenir cards issued by the US Postal Service, Bureau of Engraving and Printing, United Nations Postal Administration, American Bank Note Co., and foreign postal administrations.

It publishes a quarterly journal, the *Souvenir Card Journal*, which provides in-depth articles

This BEP souvenir card was released during the US Bicentennial celebrations.

The US Postal Service issued this souvenir card in honor of ROCPEC '78, a stamp exhibition held in the Republic of China (Taiwan).

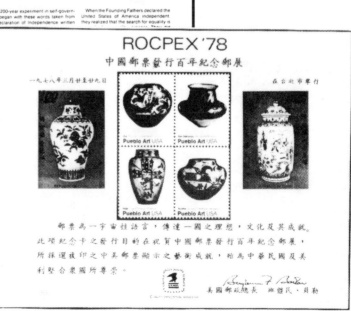

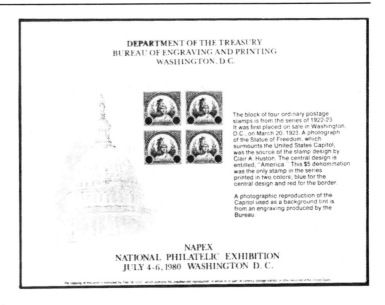

A BEP souvenir card issued for NAPEX, a national stamp show held in Washington, D.C. in 1980.

and a forum for the exchange and sale of souvenir cards.

Information concerning the organization and its activities may be obtained from the group at Box 7116, Rochester, MN 55903.

Souvenir Sheet: A souvenir sheet is a small sheet of stamps issued for a specific commemorative purpose and having a commemorative inscription or artwork in its border.

It may contain from one to as many as 25 stamps.

Some confusion results from the British use of the term "miniature sheet" (q.v.) to describe what is called in the US a "souvenir sheet." US terminology reserves the use of "miniature sheet" to describe a small sheet of stamps that is not commemorative in nature.

The first souvenir sheet is claimed to be a sheet of 10 stamps issued by Luxembourg in

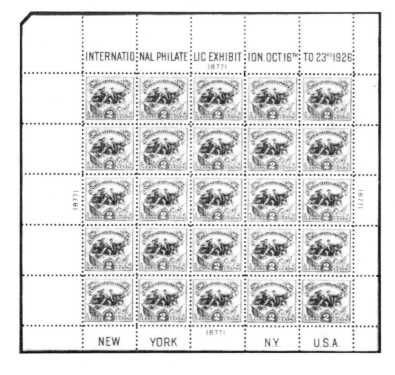

This is the famous "White Plains" souvenir sheet, the first such item to be released by US postal authorities. It was issued Oct. 18, 1926 to mark a stamp exhibition held in New York Oct. 16-20 of that year.

Canada's first souvenir sheet, issued to honor CAPEX in 1978.

1906 to commemorate the accession of Grand Duke William IV to the throne.

Up to the 1970s, souvenir sheets were pretty much reserved for special occasions, and the major countries continued to observe restraint, issuing them primarily to mark major philatelic events.

Indeed, it was not until 1978 that both Canada and Great Britain released their first souvenir sheets.

The first US souvenir sheet was the so called "White Plains" sheet, issued Oct. 18, 1926, to honor the international philatelic exhibition held in New York Oct. 16-20.

The sheet contains 25 of the 2c stamps issued for the 150th anniversary of the Battle of White Plains and bears a commemorative inscription in the sheet margin.

In recent years, many of the world's smaller countries have begun to tack souvenir sheets onto virtually all of their commemorative stamp issues. These sheets sometimes duplicate the stamps in the set, sometimes add a high face-value stamp to the set, and sometimes reproduce the stamps in imperforate condition. There are cases in which souvenir sheets have even been released in both perforated and imperforate versions.

Therefore, any special significance that a souvenir sheet may once have possessed has pretty much disappeared, and such items have become routine.

Though some of the older souvenir sheets, especially from some European countries, have achieved considerable value, the majority of modern sheets are not highly regarded by collectors, who look upon them merely as attempts by postal administrations to increase the revenue from philatelic sales.

Certainly little other justification can be seen for most modern souvenir sheets.

Souvenir Sheet: Foreign terms for "souvenir sheet" include velletje (Dutch), bloc-feuillet (French), gedenkbogen (German), foglietto (Italian), and hoja bloque (Spanish).

Sovraprezzo: Italian word for "surcharge."

Sower, The: The Sower is one of the best-known French stamp designs.

Entitled *La Semeuse* (The Sower), the design is by Oscar Roty and in various versions was current from 1903 until World War II, and it was even reintroduced in 1961.

Its first format included a sun and horizon and was intaglio printed from a die engraved by Eugene Mouchon.

In 1906 a single, solid-background 10c denomination appeared with ground under the feet of the sower, but in the same year the series continued with the solid background but without the ground.

The 10c and 35c values exist with both thick and thin numerals and lettering.

The design was used in the 1927 Strasbourg Exhibition souvenir sheet and was also surcharged 1/2c on 1c to convert it to a newspaper stamp. The 10c value of the first issue was also overprinted "F.M." in 1906 for use as a military stamp.

The reintroduced Sower design of 1961 came

shortly after France revalued its currency on the basis of 100 old francs to one new franc.

Little is known of the model who posed for Roty and whose form was to become so well known.

The October 1980 issue of Britain's *Philatelic Magazine* quotes a Dutch correspondent who reports that the model was Charlotte Ragot, 30 years old when she posed for *La Semeuse* in 1887.

The design was first used for an agricultural medal, then on coins, before its use in the long line of "Sower" stamps.

SOWJETISCHE BESATZUNGS ZONE: Overprint on German stamps for use in the Soviet Zone of occupation following World War II.

SP: On stamps of Luxembourg, the overprint "SP" indicates that they are Official stamps. The letters stand for "Service Publique."

SPA: The initials "SPA" are those of the Society of Philatelic Americans (q.v.).

Space Filler: A space filler is generally defined as a stamp that, though not of high quality, is good enough to fill a space in a collection until a better copy can be found.

There are several schools of though concerning space fillers. There are collectors whose standards would not permit them to fill a space with a less-than-perfect stamp; others would be quite happy with a stamp that did not look too bad but that could not expect to find a permanent home there.

If a collector's condition standards, especially for older material, are so high that additions are few and far between, the result could well be a loss of interest because of the few acquisitions being made.

Another consideration is that much of the older material in top condition is already beyond the means of all but the affluent.

A further point to consider is that much of the original-gummed, never-hinged material has been faked, and unless you are very careful, you risk paying a very high premium for what is nothing more than faked material.

Thus, the acquisition by collectors of stamps in a lightly hinged state, but with original gum, would not only make dandy space fillers, but might turn out to be very wise purchases.

But this is not what the average collector considers to be space fillers. Space fillers are the presentable-appearing stamps that have some slight defect, perhaps a small thin, a nibbed perforation, or centering that is just a bit off.

Heavily canceled stamps are not considered good space fillers, because their poor appearance tends to lower the apparent standard of the whole collection.

Just as a collector of socked-on-the-nose (q.v.) stamps will start out with a stamp showing a segment of the CDS and try to upgrade the specimen until that perfect copy turns up, many collectors get as great a thrill from upgrading a space filler as the perfectionist will receive from filling the space to his satisfaction.

Space Topics Study Group: The Space Topics Study Group is an organization devoted to serving the collector of space material. Its bimonthly journal, *The Astrophile*, features a great deal of information including checklists, NASA data, and other information related to space philately.

Among the group's benefits are four auctions each year and a service whereby a committee will dispose of a deceased member's collection on behalf of the estate.

Details are available from Les Winick, 2121 Maple Rd., Homewood, IL 60430.

Spain: Although but a shadow of its once-glorious self, Spain has made amazing economic progress in the past 20 years and now ranks as one of the world's major industrialized nations.

The Phoenicians established colonies along Spain's Mediterranean coast beginning in about the 11th century BC and were followed by The Carthaginians, who founded Barcelona in 228 BC.

Next came the Romans, who occupied and organized the Iberian Peninsula on which Spain is located, making it one of the most properous parts of their large empire.

But dark days were to follow as Teutonic invaders from Eastern Europe laid waste to the entire peninsula. A weakening Rome appealed to the Visigoths, or Western Teutonic people, and their armies became the dominant power in the area.

To continue this outline of Spain's many-faceted history, the Moorish invasion and occupation came in AD 711, and by 719 they were in control of the Iberian Peninsula and had even penetrated the Pyrenees into France.

But a small area in the north of Spain retained its Christian rule in the form of the Kingdom of Asturias. From this small seed sprouted the resistance that was to regain the peninsula for Christianity.

In the meantime, the Moors had made the area one of the most advanced in Europe. It became a center of learning, with universities teaching medicine, mathematics, philosophy, and literature. The work of Aristotle was revered there long before he was known in Christian Europe.

But by the beginning of the 13th century, Moorish power was declining, although it hung on in small pockets until well into the 1400s.

The year 1469 was a landmark one in Spanish history, for in that year Isabella, Queen of Castile, married Ferdinand, King of Aragon. The union of their two kingdoms set the stage for future Spanish greatness.

Although it must be noted that Isabella was responsible for the introduction of the Inquisition and Ferdinand stole property from the Jews of Spain to further his ambitions, the single most important act of the royal couple was to finance a man with a dream. This man was not only to discover vast hitherto unknown lands but was responsible for the foundation of an empire the wealth and territory of which was to stretch around the world.

His name was Christopher Columbus, and his voyages of discovery led directly to Spain's richest and most powerful period. Much of the Americas came under rule of the Spanish, who literally bled it, exterminating whole populations in the process of extracting all the gold and other treasure they could cart home to Spain.

In addition, much of Italy, the Netherlands, and Burgundy came under Spain's control.

The heady wine of power led another Spanish king, Philip II, to vent his wrath against England, which was suspected, rightly, of aiding the Dutch in their struggle to escape from his rule.

Confident of Spain's superiority at sea, Philip

constructed a great armada in 1588 and sailed off to teach the English a lesson. Unfortunately, a combination of bad weather and the refusal of the English to be terrified led him to disaster, and the armada was destroyed.

From this point, Spain's power began to wane. During the brief lightning flash of Napoleon's power, the Spanish crown went to him, and he gave it to his brother Joseph.

The Peninsula War of 1808-14 was the first setback for the French, and Spain regained its royal family with the help of Britain; such are the strange international bedfellows made of necessity, a situation not unknown even today.

Following the restoration of the Spanish crown to Spain, its inhabitants found that much of the oppression eliminated by Napoleon was being reinstituted. In 1820 a revolt was successful in bringing about eventual reform.

Meanwhile, Spain's empire in the Americas was dissolving as country after country threw off its harsh control.

The Spanish-American war of 1898 showed how weak Spain had become, and it was easily defeated by the United States, losing what few areas of the Americas it had managed to retain.

Things muddled along under various governments until the king was ousted in 1931, and the scene was set for the 1936 revolt of the army under General Franco that inaugurated the bitter and bloody Spanish Civil War and led to a long-lived dictatorship.

The war became a testing ground for World War II as Germany and Italy aided Franco, and the Soviet Union helped the government.

Spain was neutral in WWII and refused German overtures to join the Axis against the Allies.

Franco died in 1975, but he had previously designated Prince Juan Carlos as king. Juan Carlos has done much to liberate Spain and has reinstituted free elections. The remnants of the empire have been given their freedom, and there are only a few tiny areas left to testify to Spain's powerful past. These include the Balearic Islands, the Canary Islands, and the enclaves of Ceuta and Melilla in Morocco.

Spain has an area of 194,883 square miles and a population estimated at 37,430,000. Its latest per capita income figure is $5,500, and the unit of currency is the pesata (100 centimos), which in 1981 was 89.26 to the US dollar.

The first Spanish stamps were issued in 1850 and continued in a normal fashion until 1930, when an outstanding period of stamp design and production began.

The opening issue in this period was a spectacular set honoring the painter Goya and reproducing some of his paintings, including the famous *La Maja Desnuda,* which triggered international horror in conservative circles but delighted young collectors! In the context of the times, it must be admitted that it was startling and brought Spain into the forefront of the philatelic community.

That issue and the Columbus issue that followed remain a highlight in Spanish postage stamp production.

Modern photogravure stamps of Spain suffer from the handicap of a coated paper that neither stands up to handling nor does justice to the designs printed thereon.

When the occasional intaglio-printed stamps come along, the contrast is startling. The series of Spanish castles and the more recent Kings and Queens of Spain series are outstanding examples of excellent stamp production, as is the beautiful 1964 set of ships on stamps.

The address of the philatelic bureau is Direccion General de Correos, Servicio Filatelico Internacional, Madrid 14, Spain. S. Nathan of Barcelona reports, however, that the bureau will not handle individual orders and does not respond to inquiries.

Spain, Carlist Stamps: Stamps were issued in certain Spanish provinces by the self-proclaimed King Carlos VII beginning in 1873 and continuing until 1876, when they were banned.

The provinces were Alava, Biscay, Guipuzcoa, Navarre, Catalonia, and Valencia.

The stamps all bear a portrait of King Carlos. Some have been reprinted, and fake cancelations are known on all issues.

Spandrel: The word "spandrel" describes the triangular space between the curve of an

arch and the rectangular frame enclosing it.

In philately, the term is used to describe the triangular areas in the corners of a stamp having a round or oval central frame surrounded by a square or rectangular one.

For instance, the two Canadian stamps illustrated feature maple leaves in the spandrels of one and crowns in those of the other.

Spanish Guinea: (See Equatorial Guinea, Republic of.)

Spanish Morocco: (See Morocco, Spanish.)

Spanish Numerals: (See Numerals, Spanish.)

Spanish Sahara: An overseas province of Spain, Spanish Sahara was located in northwest Africa. Its coastline ran from just south of Cape Juby (q.v.) to Cape Blanco.

Its southern portion was Rio de Oro (q.v.), and the northern part was known as Saguia al Hamra. The total land area was 102,703 square miles.

The climate along the coast is relatively temperate, but in the interior the daily temperature range can be from 52 degrees F. to 112 degrees F.

Because the population is largely nomadic and ignores unimportant things like national boundaries, the figure is hard to pin down and, it is estimated, can range from 25,000 to 60,000.

The only towns of significance are the capital of Aaiun (al-Aiun), with a 1960 population of 5,251; Villa Cisneros (1,961); and La Guera (363). Villa Cisneros must import its drinking water.

Camel, sheep, and goat raising are the main occupations, and there is some commercial fishing.

Stamps for Spanish Sahara were first issued

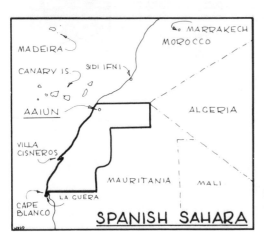

SPANISH SAHARA

in 1924 in the form of a set depicting a Tuareg and camel that was released for use at La Guera (q.v.) and in Rio de Oro (q.v.). They are inscribed "POSESIONES ESPANOLAS DEL SAHARA OCCIDENTAL."

Later stamps were inscribed "SAHARA ESPANOL."

In 1976 Morocco annexed two-thirds of Spanish Sahara. Mauritania took the rest but later handed it over to Morocco.

The United Nations does not recognize the annexation and refers to the area of Spanish Sahara as Western Sahara.

Spanish West Africa: Beginning in 1949, Spanish postal authorities released stamps inscribed "AFRICA OCCIDENTAL ESPANOLA" for use in Rio de Oro and Saguiet el Hamra — both of which made up Spanish Sahara — and Ifni (see under individual names).

A set of 16 stamps appeared in 1950 depicting various scenes in the territory.

Spanish Western Sahara: (See Spanish Sahara.)

Special Delivery Stamp: (See Stamp, Special Delivery.)

Special Handling Stamp: (See Stamp, Special Handling.)

Specialization: The term "specialization" in philately has come to have a meaning that is not what it originally conveyed.

Nowadays, it is not uncommon to hear a new collector claim to be specializing, when what he really means is that he is concentrating on a limited area of collecting as opposed to collecting the entire world.

He does not necessarily mean, as the term "specialization" once implied, that he is collecting in greater depth, but just on a more limited basis.

To collect the stamps of Canada, as opposed to general collecting, is not to be a specialist.

If a collector were to concentrate, however, on a narrow field in greater depth than if he were collecting more widely, then he could be said to be a specialist.

One who collects and studies the Machin Heads of Great Britain in all their infinite variety, giving attention to production details of the plate layout of the booklet panes, would be a specialist, not because the Machin Heads represent a more narrow field than would the entire British area, but because the individual is collecting in much greater detail and is studying the material collected.

You must study in addition to collecting, if you are to merit the title of "specialist."

There are many aspects of study in all areas of the hobby. In direct relation to stamps or postal stationery, you may study production (art, printing, paper, gum, color, etc.), the design of a stamp (topic), or its usage (postal history).

And each one of these categories can be subdivided into many smaller and even more deeply specialized areas.

You may become so deeply immersed in postal history that you will relegate the stamp to a comparatively minor role in the overall specialty. Indeed, you may not even be concerned about stamps, adhesive or otherwise, at all!

Your interest may focus on some aspect of stampless covers, ship letters, disinfected mail, air mail, etc., or you might concentrate on the stamp in its original form — as a handstamped marking of some kind.

So, if you collect the stamps of France instead of a larger area, for reason of cost, preference, or whatever, you are more correctly a limited collector rather than a specialist.

No particular status or lack of it should be applied to any of the titles that are used. What is important is using a title or label in a precise and accurate manner.

Special Printings:
The name "Special Printings" was given to U.S. stamps reprinted in 1935 and made available to the public imperforate and ungummed, because of Postmaster General Farley's actions in giving such favor items to his friends. (See Farley's Follies.)

Specie Daler:
A unit of currency used in Norway prior to 1877.

Specimen:
An individual philatelic item, as in "a beautiful specimen."

Specimen:
Foreign words for specimen include specimen (Dutch and French), muster (German), mostra (Italian), and muestra (Spanish).

Specimen:
So-called "specimen" stamps are those that are either overprinted or perforated with the word "specimen" or a foreign-language equivalent.

Some authorities include in the definition stamps produced by security printers and submitted to postal administrations, but these would appear to be more accurately termed essays (q.v.) or samples.

Specimen stamps are actual stamps so mark-

This official stamp is one of the 1875 special printings, and thus the overprint is a form of cancelation rather than to indicate a true specimen stamp.

Although distributed to the philatelic press for publicity purposes, that purpose is effectively frustrated by the heavy "SPECIMEN" overprint on this Kiribati stamp.

ed to prevent their use for their intended purpose.

At the Universal Postal Union (q.v.) meeting in Paris, in 1878, it was ruled that each country should send three copies of each new stamp to every member country for reference purposes. Though there was no stipulation that the stamps be marked "specimen," some countries especially those of the British Commonwealth, did mark them. Most US stamps issued from 1851 to 1904 can be found with a specimen overprint.

The USPOD overprinted special printings of obsolete US stamps for sale at the 1876 Philadelphia Centennial Exposition.

Some foreign countries overprint their own language equivalents of the word "specimen." Spain uses "MUESTRA," and Germany uses "MUSTER."

Speculation:
Speculation is the buying of philatelic material, usually contemporary and often commemorative issues, in quantity in the hope that immediate demand will render it more valuable and thus provide a quick profit when sold.

Speculation is almost always short-term, as opposed to investment (q.v.), which is usually long term.

Speculation in modern issues can sometimes be linked to attempts to "corner" a specific item with the idea of creating an artificially high price before quickly unloading. High-pressure advertising combined with attractive "buy" ads can tip-off such attempts to rig a market.

Such activities require a relatively large supply of inexpensive material, since the aim is to generate mass hysteria among a large number of inexperienced collectors, each of whom is made to believe that he is onto a good thing.

Speculative Issues: A speculative issue is generally considered to be one for which no obvious postal purpose exists and that is primarily intended for sale to collectors.

Nowadays, with even major and once extremely conservative stamp-issuing entities shamelessly courting philatelic sales, the term has lost much of its meaning and has become fuzzy indeed.

You can say with a considerable amount of justification that most of today's commemorative issues are speculative in nature.

Even such a former stronghold of conservatism as Great Britain caters to what it believes to be the wishes of collectors.

Former whipping-boys like Monaco, San Marino, Liechtenstein, etc., are now models of philatelic rectitude when compared with states such as Equatorial Guinea, Liberia, and a number of former British West Indian islands.

Today, the term "speculative" would be better applied to these and to the privately hyped issues of uninhabited islets, printed-to-private-order postal stationery oddities, etc.

Sperati, Jean de: The famous French stamp forger Jean De Sperati of Aix-les-Bains began his work soon after World War I and over the next several decades is believed to have forged about 550 different stamps, some more than once.

His downfall came during WWII when he was accused of smuggling unused stamps out of France and thus violating currency restrictions.

Since the stamps he was accused of smuggling appeared to be genuine and of great value, he was placed in the position of having to prove them to be forgeries! This he did, despite the testimony of experts who claimed them to be the real thing.

He was cleared of the smuggling charge but was then charged with forgery, despite his claim that he always sold the items as facsimilies and marked them on the back. Since this latter operation was done in pencil, his motives might well be questioned!

In the early 1950s he lost on appeal and went out of the forged stamp business. With failing eyesight, he sold all his equipment, duplicates, plates, etc., to the British Philatelic Association.

De Sperati was a perfectionist who was proud of his work and was said to become enraged if one of his productions should be expertized as genuine!

Cabeen (*Standard Handbook of Stamp Collecting*, Crowell, New York, 1965) reports that De Sperati was not only an expert forger but was extremely clever. For instance, he would forge a valuable inverted center variety by removing the frame from a normal genuine stamp and replacing it with an inverted one, knowing that the genuine center would receive the most scrutiny!

De Sperati died, very much unmourned by the philatelic world, in 1957 at the age of 73.

Spesso: Italian word for "thick."

Spif: "Spif" is a British term for a stamp with perforated letters or a device made up of a series of small holes and intended as a control over the unauthorized use of stamps belonging to business firms.

Departments of various governments have also used this means of identifying stamps used by those departments.

L.N. and M. Williams in *Fundamentals of Philately* (American Philatelic Society, State College, Pa., 1971) attribute the following meaning to the term "SPIF": "Stamp Perforated with the Initials of Firms or Societies," and "Stamps Perforated for Insurance against Fraud." These stamps are generally termed "perfins" (q.v.) in North America.

Spitsbergen: (See Svalbard).

Split: A stamp divided into two or more parts and used at a corresponding fraction of its normal face value was once called a "split." It is a term seldom heard today. (See Bisect.)

SPM: Overprint found on general issue stamps of the French Colonies for use on the French islands of St. Pierre and Miquelon (q.v.), twin islands off the south coast of Newfoundland.

Spoon Cancelation: (See Cancelation, Spoon.)

Sports Philatelists International: Sports Philatelists International is a group for collectors of philatelic material dealing with sports.

There are a number of study groups within the organization. The group's services offered include checklists, handbooks, a bimonthly

Journal of Sports Philately, a sales department, auctions, and a translation department.

Information is available from C.A. Reiss, 1410 Illuminating Bldg., Cleveland, OH 44113.

Squared Circle Cancelation: (See Cancelation, Squared Circle.)

Square Pair: The term "square pair" refers to two triangular stamps that are joined on the hypotenuse, or long side, of the triangle thus forming a square.

Sri Lanka: The Portuguese were the first Europeans to occupy the island of Sri Lanka, located off the southern tip of India, when they established settlements in the early 1500s.

The Dutch arrived in 1658, and the British came into possession of the island in 1796.

Under the name of Ceylon, the one-time colony became an independent member of the British Commonwealth in 1948. It changed its name to the republic of Sri Lanka on May 22, 1972.

Unemployment, economic problems, terrorist activities, and food shortages plagued the nation under the government of Mrs. Bandaranaike, who had succeeded her husband, the prime minister who was assassinated in 1959.

Her government was ousted in the election of 1977, and the more conservative United National party worked to restore stability.

The island covers an area of 25,330 square miles. It is 270 miles long, with a width at its widest point of 140 miles. It is separated from the tip of India by the 33-mile-wide Palk Strait.

The population is estimated at 14,740,000.

Sri Lanka's history can be divided into two parts. The first saw outside influence from Asia; the second comprised the coming of the Europeans.

The early settlers came from India about 500 BC and the Buddhist religion was also imported from India in about 300 BC.

Following the Portuguese and Dutch attempts to dominate the island, the British established a system of government, and the island became a Crown Colony in 1802.

Coffee and tea were the two chief crops, but the coffee was wiped out by disease in the 1880s. Rubber was also an important early crop, as was copra (coconuts).

With the opening of the Suez Canal, Ceylon's capital, Colombo, became a port of worldwide importance.

As the British prepared the island for self-government, many government posts came to

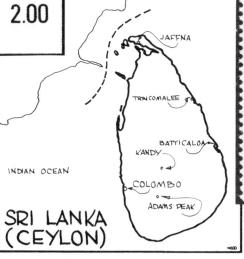

be occupied by Ceylonese, and although World War II delayed the process, self-government was granted in 1948.

The island's stamp-issuing history began in 1857 with the release of the Pence issue, now regarded as one of the world's classic issues. Decimal currency, based on the rupee, came in 1872.

The various British colonial key types were used, and it was not until the 1935 King George V pictorial definitive issue that the stamps of Ceylon once more became attractive.

Recent issues have seldom come even close to that 1935 issue in terms of beauty or quality.

Since Ceylon became Sri Lanka, stamp issues have become very similar to those of neighboring India.

The unit of currency remains the rupee (100 cents), which in 1981 was 18.35 to the US dollar.

The latest per capita income figure is $168.

Sri Lanka's philatelic office is located at Philatelic Bureau, Ceylonco House, Colombo 1, Sri Lanka.

SS: The letters "SS" are a common abbreviation of souvenir sheet.

SSSS: (See Society for the Suppression of Speculative Stamps.)

S.T.: Prior to the introduction of stamps overprinted "O.S." in 1874 for general Official use, South Australia used a number of different overprints to indicate use by specific government departments.

"S.T." stood for Superintendent of Telegraph.

STAATSMARKE: Inscription on some Official stamps of Wurttemberg.

STADT BERLIN: Inscription on stamps used in the Soviet Zone of Berlin following World War II.

Stahlblau: German word for the color "steel blue."

Stain: Foreign words for stain include tache (French), fleck (German), macchia (Italian), and mancha (Spanish).

Stamp: Nowadays, the word "stamp" carries with it a degree of ambiguity. Not only is it used when referring to an adhesive postage or revenue stamp, but it also describes the act of impressing something on an object, as in the case of applying a postal marking to an item of mail.

The object to which the inscription is applied is said to be "stamped."

Prior to the introduction of what we now refer to as a "stamp" (an adhesive stamp), the meaning of the word was clear.

Now, confusion often results from attempts by purists to retain the term for such impressions, while in common usage, the word is generally understood to refer to an adhesive "stamp."

In his proposal for the adhesive postage stamp, Sir Rowland Hill (q.v.) used the term in its original sense when he described it as "...a bit of paper just large enough to bear the stamp and covered at the back with a glutinous wash...."

In other words, Hill envisioned an adhesive "stamp" as a piece of gummed paper *bearing* a stamp.

The original sense of the word "stamp" is retained in the expression "the letter is stamped" to describe a letter with an adhesive postage stamp affixed.

It would seem, in view of the widespread use of "stamp" to describe an adhesive stamp, that use of the term to refer to a marking applied to mail or a document would better be avoided; else we could reach the ultimate confusion of saying that "the stamp is stamped" when we really mean that the adhesive postage stamp has been canceled by some form of postal marking!

Webster's Third New International Dictionary states, in part, the following under the word "stamp":

"3a: to impress or mark (something) with a symbol or design in intaglio or relief with ink or coloring."

Also, "4b: to impress (something) with an official mark, stamp, or adhesive label to certify that a government or state tax or duty has been paid."

Also, "7a: a stamped or printed device or slip of paper issued by a government or state at a fixed price and required by law to be affixed to, or stamped on, various papers or matter as evidence that the government charge or tax is paid."

Webster defines a postage stamp as "an adhesive stamp or an imprinted stamp on a piece of postal stationery issued by a postal service for use on mail matter as evidence of prepayment of postage." (I am grateful for permission to reprint the above from Webster's *Third New International Dictionary*, copyright 1976 by G. C. Merriam Co., publishers of the Merriam-Webster Dictionaries.)

Stamp, Acknowledgment of Receipt: Several countries have issued stamps to pay for an acknowledgment of receipt service.

The stamps usually include the letters "AR" either in the design or as an overprint, and they mean "Aviso de Recepcion." The inscription in full is found on a pair of stamps issued by El Salvador in 1897.

Other countries that have used such stamps include Chile, Colombia, and Montenegro.

This was an international Universal Postal Union-recognized service.

Stampa in Offset: Italian expression for "offset printing."

Stamp, Air Mail: An air mail postage stamp is one issued to prepay air mail postal rates.

Some catalogs segregate these stamps, while others include them in a single chronological listing with other issues.

The Scott catalog in the US gives the prefix "C" to air mail stamps.

The first government-issued air mail stamps were released by Italy in May and June 1917. (See Air Mail.)

The US Post Office Department issued its first such stamps on May 13, 1918, to frank mail car-

These two stamps are generally considered to be the world's first official, government-issued air mail stamps. They were issued in May and June 1917 respectively.

ried on a service between Washington, Philadelphia, and New York.

Soon after that, the air mail craze grew and grew, and it continued to be a very popular collecting area for many years.

There were special air mail albums, and for a number of years the Sanabria catalog listed all

A selection of the world's air mail stamps.

air mail stamps in some detail. The last edition of the catalog was published in 1966.

The carriage of mail by air eventually became so routine that the romance associated with the devil-may-care, white-scarf-'aflutter aviator has quite disappeared. Today's image is of a graying airline pilot carrying a briefcase containing a flight plan instead of a parachute and a thermos bottle.

Thus the collection of air mail stamps has tended to merge into the area of postal history, and in that sense, the enthusiasm for air mail material is still riding high, as witness the prices of earlier covers.

Even before World War II, the British Empire "All Up" scheme was carrying mail by air to the farthest points of the empire at regular postal rates. In the years since the war, although the rates are somewhat higher now, the mail has routinely flown.

Because air mail stamps are intended for the specialized purpose of franking mail to be carried by air, they usually bear a special inscription.

Depending on the language of the country, it is likely to be one of the following:

For English-speaking countries, the inscription will be "Air Mail." Other commonly seen air mail inscriptions are "Poste Aerienne" (French-speaking areas), "Legiposta" (Hungary), "Correo Aero" (Spain and Spanish-speaking areas), "Luftpost" (Sweden, Norway, and Denmark), "Posta Aerea" (Italy), "Flugpost" or "Deutsche Luftpost" (Germany), "Flugfrimerki" (Iceland), "Poczta Lotnicza" (Poland), "Luchtpost" (Netherlands), and "Correio Aereo" (Portugal). (See Air Mail; Zeppelin Mail; Balloon Mail; Stamp, Semi-official Air Mail.)

Stampalia: An island in the Aegean Sea off the coast of Turkey. Once part of the Italian Dodecanese group (q.v.), Stampalia is now Greek and uses Greek stamps.

Stamp, American Foreign Service: Stamps bearing this inscription are actually Consular Service Fee stamps and were used to indicate payment of fee for services.

They were affixed to documents or receipts. (See Stamp, Consular Service Fee; Stamp, Revenue.)

Stampa Rotativa: Spanish expression for "rotary printing."

Stamp Bisect: (See Bisect.)

Stamp, Boating: The Federal Boating Stamp was a US revenue stamp indicating payment of a certificate fee for boats of more than ten horsepower.

The tax went into effect April 1, 1960, when two stamps were issued, in denominations of $1 and $3.

The $3 stamp was to pay for the Coast Guard certificate; the $1 value covered a charge to replace lost or destroyed certificates.

The US Post Office accepted applications for certificates and passed them to the Coast Guard. (See Stamp, Revenue.)

Stamp, By Post: A By Post stamp is one issued for a local post and restricted in its validity to a specific route or region.

Though not listed in the general catalogs, By Post stamps were used to frank mail carried within their area and with the consent of the national postal authority.

They are considered to have served a need that the national postal service did not.

A number of these services operated in Scandinavian countries.

Stamp, Carrier: Carrier stamps in the US are those that were issued to pay postage for the delivery of letters to or from a post office in the area in which they were issued.

In the US from 1851 to 1863, such carrier stamps were issued by both the federal government (Franklin and Eagle types) and locally by private carriers.

The March 3, 1851, Act of Congress declared streets and highways in many cities to be post roads, and letter carriers were appointed in accordance with an Act of July 2, 1836, according to Konwiser (*American Stamp Collectors Dictionary*, Minkus, New York, 1949).

Stamp, Cigarette Tube: Cigarette Tube Stamps are US revenue stamps indicating the payment of the tax on cigarette tubes, which a smoker would use to make his own cigarettes.

The first stamp was a 1c value released in 1919. Together with another 1c stamp issued in 1929, it was an overprint reading "CIGTTE./TUBES" on the documentary issue of 1917.

In 1933 specially designed 1c and 2c stamps were issued. (See Stamp, Revenue.)

Stamp, Cinderella: A definition of Cinderella stamps is probably one best handled by exclusion rather than by inclusion.

If you exclude government-issued postage stamps and stationery, then what is left usually qualifies as Cinderella material.

The Cinderella Stamp Club, based in Great Britain, defines Cinderella material as "...local stamps, telegraph stamps, fiscals (revenues),

1

2

3

4

5

A selection of Cinderella labels; in this case patriotic and propaganda labels from France (1 and 3), Great Britain (2 and 5) and the US (4).

A local post Cinderella stamp issued by Western Airlines to frank its airletter service. The label must be used in conjunction with regular US postage.

Event publicity labels are Cinderella items, too. Above are five philatelic labels from the US, Czechoslovakia, Colombia, Australia, and Norway. Below are a trio of aviation event labels from Switzerland and France.

A selection of Cinderella local post labels. When items such as these are used on mail, they must be accompanied by regular government postage stamps of the area. Some are well known, such as the Hutt River Province label from Australia,   the Lundy Island label of Great Britain, or Herman Herst's Shrub Oak Local Post carried by his dog "Alfie." Little is known about the item at the top center, presumably from Aden.

A typical Christmas Seal, also a Cinderella item. This is a 1930 one from the US.

bogus and phantom issues, Christmas seals, registration labels, and advertising and exhibition labels."

It could also include such items as Britain's railway stamps, the university stamps of Oxford and Cambridge, air mail etiquettes, propaganda labels, Easter seals, etc.

The newcomer to philately would probably do best to regard as Cinderella material that which is not listed in the general catalogs, although it should be noted that some of the more specialized catalogs do include such Cinderella material as revenues, post office seals, etc.

This is not to imply that material not included in general catalogs is not collectible — far from it. But it is something that should be collected on the basis of knowledge.

The fields of Cinderella philately are broad indeed, and although there are many sunlit uplands, there are also some dark, dank corners that can trap the unwary into obtaining material that is not what it is represented to be.

As in all areas of philately, knowledge is the key. When collected with knowledge, Cinderella material can offer a great deal of pleasure.

Stamp Clubs: (See Society, Philatelic.)

Stamp, Coil: Coil stamps are printed in rolls for use in vending machines. Stamp rolls may be produced with the design either horizontal or vertical, and such stamps will be imperforate at top and bottom or at the sides.

Examples are illustrated from the US, Canada, and Sweden.

Coil stamps used in vending machines in Great Britain are perforated all around, although in the course of making up rolls, perforations on two opposite sides may be partially trimmed. Some British coils can be distinguished by having the watermark sideways. (See Orangeburg Coil.)

Coil stamps from the US, Canada, and Sweden.

Stamp, Commemorative: This

classification of postage stamp accounts for the vast majority of stamps issued in recent years.

The commemorative stamp is a special stamp issued either as a single value or in the form of a set, sometimes of various denominations. It is issued to honor a person, an event, or an anniversary, in limited, although often very large, quantities.

Additional printings are sometimes made, although this is the exception.

Commemorative stamps are on sale for a specified period, usually a few weeks, and unsold remainders are usually destroyed. Most responsible postal administrations then announce the quantity sold.

Some countries may keep them for sale to collectors through their philatelic sales bureaus until stocks are sold out, but in many cases the stamps are sold out before the normal selling time has expired.

I recall visiting the philatelic branch of the Mexican Post Office in Mexico City in the late 1960s and finding stamps on sale at face value dating back to the 1930s!

The commemorative stamp has become the "glamor star" of the stamp world largely because of the amount of publicity it receives, and there are collectors who appear to believe that it is the only type of stamp to collect!

A style of releasing commemorative stamps that has become common in recent years is that phenomenon known as the omnibus issue (q.v.). This occurs when a number of different countries all release stamps commemorating a common event.

The first extensive example was the 1935 King George V Silver Jubilee issue of the British Commonwealth. Since then there have been very many, some of considerable interest, others of horrendous monotony. Then there is even the recurring omnibus, such as the annual Europa stamps.

Such "combined philatelic operations" are heavily publicized, and indeed, "hyped" might not be too strong a term, so that they often appear to the collector to have an importance far beyond reality.

Though most stamps currently being issued are commemorative, there are many that can hardly be thought of as commemorative in nature. Stamps showing a country's fish, insects, flora, landscapes, etc., are not true commemoratives because they merely picture a subject, usually but not always relevant to the issuing country.

These could more properly be called "special" stamps, to distinguish them from true commemoratives or definitives. Presently, Australia

categorizes its stamps in such a fashion; rather strangely, the US commemorates Christmas each year with what it terms "special" issues!

Nevertheless, commemorative stamps are issued in profusion, with large printings being common. This is because postal administrations have found that they are very appealing to collectors, and since no postal service has to be rendered on stamps sold to collectors, such sales represent large profits.

A factor additional to the raising of revenue from philatelic sales is that of propaganda, and there are few countries that do not use commemorative stamps as a propaganda medium to some degree.

Stamps of the Communist nations are very heavily oriented in that direction, and even those of the US often mark this country's achievements, quality of life, battle victories, etc., and might be classed as national propaganda stamps.

An important reason for the popularity of commemorative stamps is that they are usually large and colorful. And, of course, a significant degree of popularity must be attributed to their strong advertisement by dealers and postal administrations.

A few commemorative stamps are well designed and represent the best in high-quality production, but sadly, many modern issues are tasteless in conception and garish in execution.

Topical collecting (q.v.) was largely made possible by the fantastic variety of subjects found on commemorative stamps.

Now, we have a situation in which stamps are being deliberately created for the maximum degree of attraction they will have for collectors by featuring as many different topics as possible.

Commemorative stamps are not a recent development, although their history does not go back quite as far as the beginnings of the adhesive postage stamp.

What was the first commemorative is still a subject for debate. It is generally accepted that a set whose first denominations of which were issued in 1888 by the then-British colony of New South Wales is the first adhesive issue to actually mark an anniversary with a specific inscription. It commemorates the centenary of the first British settlement in Australia, and the lower values can still be obtained for a modest price.

It has been claimed that an 1871 stamp from Peru, said to note the 20th anniversary of South America's first railroad, is actually the first commemorative, but the stamp, unlike the NSW issue, does not bear a commemorative inscription.

L.N. and M. Williams in their book *The Postage Stamp* mention that several local posts

These stamps are part of what is thought to be the world's first official, government-issued commemorative set. They were released in 1888–89 by New South Wales to mark the 100th anniversary of the British colony in Australia.

A selection of the many thousands of commemorative stamps from around the world.

in Germany released commemorative stamps in 1887. One, issued by the Privat-Brief-Verkehr, marks a sharpshooting contest held at Frankfurt-on-Main. It bears a commemorative inscription and, in the opinion of the Williams brothers, constitutes the first commemorative adhesive postage stamp.

However, it was not a government postal service issue, and thus we come back to the 1888 New South Wales issue.

The first US commemorative adhesive postage stamps are those of the 1893 Columbian issue, although items of postal stationery had appeared in 1876 in the form of stamped envelopes to honor the centenary of the US.

This latter issue is considered by many to be the first postal commemorative issue of any type.

Most collectors seek commemorative issues in mint condition, but it can be a stimulating challenge to collect them postally used. Even those from major countries can be difficult to find, and those of the smaller nations are extremely scarce.

There are two main reasons for this scarcity. One is that in many cases the major portion of the printing will be distributed to the philatelic trade without even being sent to the country's post offices. The second is that the stamps placed on sale at local post offices are only available for a limited time.

Stamp, Consular Service Fee: US
consular service fee stamps went into use on June 1, 1906, and were affixed to documents or receipts to show that the consular service fee had been paid.

The stamps ranged in denomination from 25c to $20.

The first issue was inscribed "American Consular Service Fee Stamp," and subsequent issues bear the inscription "American Foreign Service Fee Stamp."

Use of these stamps ceased on Sept. 30, 1955. (See Stamp, Revenue.)

Stamp, Cordials, Wines: Stamps bearing the words "CORDIALS" or "WINES" or both are US revenue stamps indicating the collection of a tax on such products.

There are almost 200 such stamps, in denominations ranging from 1/5 of a cent to $4,000. The designs vary, but all feature the denomination and inscription of an engine-turned background. (See Engine Turning.)

First issued in 1914, they were discontinued Dec. 31, 1954, according to Scott. (See Stamp, Revenue.)

Stamp, Customs Fee: Customs fee stamps were US revenue stamps intended to indicate payment of various customs fees, excluding customs duties.

A set of eight stamps was issued in 1887 in denominations ranging from 20c to 90c and varying in the detail of the design background.

Use of the stamps was discontinued on Feb. 28, 1918, according to Scott. (See Stamp, Revenue.)

Stamp Dealer: A stamp dealer is one who buys and sells stamps and related philatelic material as a business for profit.

It need not be a full-time occupation, and many dealers are involved on a part-time basis to augment their income or as a retirement occupation.

Comparatively few maintain retail shops, although those that do are often among the biggest and best known firms.

In days gone by, Nassau Street in New York was known for its many retail stamp businesses. Now, rising costs have driven most into other areas.

One of philately's most famous philatelic addresses is 391 Strand in London, England. Most of the world's collectors would recognize that as the address of Stanley Gibbons, although the firm has long since outgrown it.

The majority of the more modest stamp dealers operate on a mail-order basis from their homes and contact their customers by means of advertisements in the philatelic press.

In recent years, a new kind of dealer has appeared. This is the "bourse" dealer, who travels to the many stamp shows and commercial bourses held in all parts of the country. Although many will also operate a mail-order business, some do no other form of stamp dealing.

Another type of stamp dealer is the philatelic auction firm. These operations will hold periodic auctions (q.v.), and their profit comes from the commission on sales paid by the seller or the buyer and seller. (See Auction; Approval; Bourse.)

Stamp, Definitive: The definitive, or regular, stamp is the workhorse of the stamp world. Usually issued in an extended range of denominations and used over a fairly long period, sometimes many years, it performs the basic job of franking everyday mail.

Though they are often small in size and can be drab in appearance, definitive stamps often embody much philatelic interest. This is because their extended use requires periodic reprinting, which may be reflected in shade varieties, per-

Just a few of the definitive stamps that offer so much philatelic interest.

foration differences, variations of watermark and gum, plus differences in design caused by the use of several printing plates or by the touching up of worn plates.

The same definitive may even be produced by more than one printing method.

Not only can different printings often be distinguished and accompanying variations discovered, but definitive stamps can also be produced on a number of different papers during their lifetime.

As postal rates change, new denominations are added and denominations no longer needed become obsolete — sometimes after a short life and without warning.

Definitive stamps may be found in booklet form with all kinds of attractive combinations joined together (see Se-tenant) in booklet panes.

Definitive stamps are those usually found in vending machines. These are often produced in coil format (q.v.) and sometimes have two opposite edges imperforate.

The smart collector is one who keeps his definitive collection up to date, and "getting them when they are first issued" is always good policy.

There are a number of beautiful definitive issues, and among the best is Great Britain's Machin Head series. The Canadian 1967 Centennial definitives are full of interest and present a challenging and tangled mixture of paper, perforations, and plates — all of which adds enormously to their interest.

The US Americana series soon became philatelically interesting, with a number of booklet variations.

Some of the world's most fascinating philatelic problems have been posed by definitive issues, and Canada's Admirals of 1912, the French Sowers, and the Greek Hermes Heads, are just a few that come to mind.

No consideration of definitive stamps would be complete without a mention of Austria's magnificent Landscapes series. This issue will surely counter the argument that definitives are visually unappealing. Indeed, they are far more attractive than many commemorative issues.

They have that combined beauty that only a set in a consistant format can offer, and their engraving is superb and colors vivid and pure.

A word should be said about another interesting and fairly recent aspect of definitive collecting (and also of some commemoratives), and that is the chemical tagging (q.v.) applied to stamps to enable letters to be processed by automated equipment.

Interesting experimental work has been done, and this is pretty much confined to definitive stamps. There are some early experiments by the US Post Office Dept., and Great Britain's graphite lines experiment is another example.

The term "definitive" has also been used as an antonym to a "provisional" (q.v.) stamp, but this is not generally used.

Stamp, Department:

Department stamps are those issued for use by a specific government department.

A number of countries have issued such stamps, including the US, Great Britain, and some of the British Commonwealth nations.

Department stamps are correctly classified as Official stamps. (See Stamps, Official.)

Stamp, Documentary:

A documentary stamp is a revenue stamp (q.v.) intended to be affixed to an official or business document to indicate that a tax or fee has been paid.

Adhesive documentary revenue stamps were used in the United States from 1862 until Dec. 31, 1967.

The illustrated documentary stamp was issued July 1, 1962, and is a commemorative revenue stamp, marking the centenary of the Internal Revenue Service. It depicts the IRS building in Washington, D.C.

Stamp, Duck:

(See Migratory Bird Hunting Stamps.)

Examples of British stamped paper dating from the 1880s.

Stamp Duty:

Stamps of the Australian colony of Victoria (q.v.) bearing the inscription "Stamp Duty" are valid postage stamps.

From Jan. 1, 1884, revenue and postage stamps became acceptable for either use.

Gibbons states that all stamps inscribed "Stamp Duty" printed after that date are true "Postage and Revenue" stamps, whereas those produced prior to Jan. 1, 1884, are really "Postal Fiscals," since they had been created solely for revenue purposes and were only later valid as postage.

Stamped Envelope:

A stamped envelope is an envelope bearing a printed impression often simulating an adhesive postage stamp, called an indicium.

Despite the unsuccessful Mulready envelopes (q.v.), Great Britain issued a stamped envelope in conventional form on Jan. 29, 1841. (See Postal Stationery.)

Stamped Paper:

The term "stamped paper" is used to describe paper bearing an impressed revenue indicium. Such paper is used for documents on which a revenue tax is imposed, and the indicium indicates that the tax was paid when the paper was purchased.

Stamped to Order:

(See Printed to Private Order.)

Stamp, Embargoed:

(See Prohibited Stamps.)

Stamp, Europa:

Sept. 15, 1956, was the issue date of the first of the annual Europa stamps.

The six countries joining in this first cooperative issue were Belgium, France, Germany, Italy, Luxembourg, and the Netherlands. The issue had been agreed upon at a meeting in Paris on Jan. 20, 1956.

A number of artists had submitted designs,

**The first Europa
stamp design.**

and that of the French artist Daniel Gonzague
was selected the winner.

His design featured the word "Europa" in a
vertical format.

Europa stamps have been issued each year
since then. Originally they were in a common
design, but now they conform to a common
theme.

The last year of the common-design theme
was 1973, when the following countries participated:

Andorra (French and Spanish), Belgium,
Cyprus, Finland, France, Germany, Greece,
Iceland, Ireland, Italy, Liechtenstein, Luxem-
bourg, Malta, Monaco, Netherlands, Norway,
Portugal, San Marino, Spain, Switzerland,
Turkey, and Yugoslavia.

The 10th anniversary year of 1969 saw a
record number of countries taking part including
these not listed above: Austria, Denmark, Great
Britain, and the Vatican.

Since 1973, the Europa omnibus issues have
been much more interesting and attractive,
because, while the common theme has been used, each country has designed its own stamps
within that theme. (See CEPT.)

Stamp, Express: The term "express"
is used to describe a class of stamp that pays the

fee for special handling of an item of mail. (See
Stamp, Special Delivery.)

Stamp, Fiscal: (See Stamp, Revenue.)

Stamp, Franchise: A franchise stamp is
one that is supplied by a postal administration

free of charge to an individual or organization
for the purpose of franking mail from that individual or organization.

A number of countries have issued franchise
stamps, including France, Germany, Portugal,
Spain, and Switzerland.

Organizations so favored have included the
Red Cross, a TB organization, rifle clubs, etc.

Spain has granted franchise stamps to two individuals, Diego Castel and Antonio Fernandez.
The stamps were used to mail copies of books
they had written.

The German franchise stamps of 1938 and
1942 were for use by the Nazi Party.

The sole French franchise stamp is a 90c
denomination overprinted "F" in 1939 for use by
refugee Spanish soldiers.

Stamp, Insured Letter: Mexico is one
country that has issued a number of stamps to
prepay insurance on mail. The first issue appeared in 1935.

The designs have always had some form of

"security" motif. Illustrated is the design currently in use. It bears the inscription "SEGURO
POSTAL" used on all those stamps.

Stamp, Late Fee: "Too late" or "late
fee" stamps were applied to mail to indicate
payment of a special fee that would ensure ac-

ceptance of the item after the normal closing of a mail.

The colony of Victoria, in Australia, issued a "Too Late" stamp on Jan. 1, 1855.

In 1923 Denmark issued a late fee stamp bearing the overprint "GEBYR," followed in 1926 by a stamp inscribed "GEBYRMAERKE." The stamps were used until 1934.

Colombia issued late fee stamps beginning in 1886 inscribed "RETARDO," and Ecuador overprinted and surcharged a postal tax stamp in 1945, to indicate payment of a late fee.

Stampless Cover:

A stampless cover is a piece of mail that passed through a mail service without being franked by an adhesive postage stamp or postal indicium.

An example would be a soldier's letter during wartime that was passed free, sometimes with an inscription "O A S " (On Active Service). Stampless covers have also come about during times of disaster when adhesive postage stamps were not available.

Thus, it is not necessary that a stampless cover be one that dates from a time before adhesive stamps were used. Though pre-stamp covers are always dated prior to the use of adhesive stamps, a stampless cover is not necessarily a pre-stamp cover.

A cover that has lost its adhesive stamp for some reason, as when mail becomes damaged by water and the stamp become separated from the envelope, is not properly regarded as a stampless cover. (See Pre-Stamp Cover.)

Stamp, Life Insurance:

Life insurance stamps are issued by New Zealand and are Official stamps for use by the Life Insurance Department of the New Zealand government.

The first such stamps were issued in 1891, and since then more than 60 of these attractive stamps have been issued.

All designs feature lighthouses, one recent issue featuring beautiful seascapes portraying the various lighthouses around the coast of New Zealand.

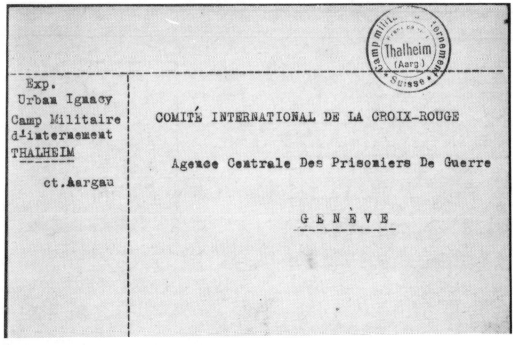

A stampless cover from a Swiss World War II internment camp.

Stamp, Local:

Local stamps, unlike local postage stamps (q.v.), are privately produced to frank mail carried by the individual or organization issuing the stamps to the nearest government post office.

They are not valid for any other purpose, and when the mail so franked is deposited at a government post office, official postage stamps must be applied. Nowadays, the local stamps are supposed to be affixed to the backs of envelopes in order for them to be accepted into the government postal system.

There are some very famous local stamps, and one of the best known is the 1847 *Lady McLeod* local issue of Trinidad.

The *Lady McLeod* was a ship plying the waters of the Gulf of Paria between Port of Spain and San Fernando, and its owner, David Bryce, created the 5c stamps to frank the mail he carried.

Unlike most local stamps, this issue is included in the Stanley Gibbons catalog, which lists it as Trinidad #1. The issue date is given as April 24, 1847.

In more recent years, there has been something of a flood of private local stamps that serve no real postal purpose and are created more to gain publicity and for sale to collectors than for any postal use.

Some of the most notorious of these have originated from tiny islets around the coast of the British Isles. In some cases, these islands have no permanent population, and the owner often lives miles away on the mainland.

There is an amusing story concerning the owner of one minute rock off the Scottish coast who waxed very indignant when he found out that someone was issuing "stamps" for his rock, and he demanded a piece of the action!

Another type of local stamp has appeared in recent years, sparked by postal strikes. This is the "strike local," which comes about when a government waives its postal monopoly during strikes by government postal workers.

When this happened in Great Britain a few years ago, many services sprang up, complete with stamps ranging from crude quickie jobs to elaborately produced multicolored productions.

Though many services did actually carry mail, it seems very likely that others were more of an excuse to create and sell stamps to collectors.

Strike locals have also been produced in Canada in similar situations. (See British Private Local Issues; Stamps, Local United States.)

The famous "Lady McLeod" local stamp of Trinidad shown on a stamp of that country on its 125th birthday.

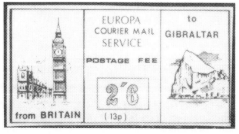

A selection of British local stamps issued during a postal strike in that country and supplied by John G. Carberry, a collector specializing in the postal history of British postal strikes.

Stamp, Local Postage: Local postage stamps are defined as official government issues that have a restricted validity.

They are not valid outside the area or service for which they were issued, nor can they be used in the international mails. They should not be confused with local stamps (q.v.), which are privately produced.

Zemstvos, or stamps of the Russian rural posts, are an example of local postage stamps, since they were authorized by the Russian government to fill a postal need that could not be met by the Imperial Postal Service. (See British Private Local Issues.)

Stamp, Local United States: Prior to the mid-1840s, the United States Post Office did not deliver mail to homes or businesses.

This caused a large number of private companies or carriers to come into existence to fill this gap in mail service. Until 1861, most cities had some form of private mail service between post offices and private and commercial addresses, and between addresses within a city.

As the US Post Office began to institute home delivery, the private local posts were gradually eliminated.

Many of these local posts issued their own stamps, some of which were quite elaborate, others primitive in the extreme.

Stamp, Marine Insurance: (See Floating Safe Stamp.)

Stamp, Military: Military stamps have been issued by a number of countries either to frank mail of men serving in their military forces or to indicate that no charges are to be levied on such mail.

The first military stamps appear to be a set issued in 1898 by Turkey. They are unusual, octagonal-shaped stamps and were intended for use by Turkish forces occupying Thessaly.

The military government in Austrian-occupied ex-Turkish territory in the Balkans issued military stamps inscribed "MILITAR K.u.K. POST." to indicate a state of military government.

Denmark issued military stamps during World War I overprinted "S.F." (Soldater Frimaerk).

WWII Belgian military parcel post stamps can be identified by the overprint "M."

Italian military post stamps bear the overprint "P.M." (Posta Militare). France has issued regular stamps overprinted "F.M." (Franchise Militaire) and also utilized specially designed stamps, including an attractive one depicting the French flag.

Finland is another country that has issued military stamps, and these comprise specially designed items usually inscribed "KENT-TAPOSTIA" or similar.

After the defeat of Japan in World War II,

A cover franked with a US Blood's Penny Post local tied with a chemical cancel that discolored both local stamp and cover.

Australian occupation forces in that country were provided with Australian stamps overprinted "B.C.O.F. - JAPAN - 1946."

Military stamps were issued for Syria beginning in 1942, when the Vichy regime was eliminated and Syria was liberated by British and Free French forces. These were followed in 1943 by semi-postals and air mail stamps including a souvenir sheet.

These issues, however, like the British stamps overprinted "B.M.A." and similar issues, are more occupation stamps than items intended for use by military forces.

Military stamps — qualifying as such — without question come in profusion from, of all places, peaceful Switzerland.

These are really labels issued to Swiss servicemen to indicate that their mail is not to be assessed postage charges.

Other military stamps include several items issued by Germany during WWII, of which the famous Afrika Corps label is a well-known ex-

ample. (See Afrika Corps Label; B.C.O.F. - JAPAN - 1946; British Forces in Egypt; C.E.F.; Feldpost; Finland; F.M.; I.E.F.; M; M.E.F.; P.M.; and Swiss Soldier Stamps.)

Stamp, Military Reply: A military reply stamp is one sent by a member of armed forces to a correspondent to be used to frank, completely or partially, a reply.

Sweden used such stamps from 1929, with the last being issued in 1951.

The gummed stamps were affixed below the flap of the free military envelope used by the soldier, sailor, or airman for his letter.

The recipient removed and used the stamp to frank a reply. It was valid for the domestic postal rate.

The *Facit Catalog* lists 11 main types with a number of varieties.

Stamp, Motor Vehicle Use: Motor vehicle use stamps were US revenue stamps indicating payment of a fee for the use of a vehicle. The stamp was to be displayed on the vehicle.

The stamps were issued from 1942 until 1945. (See Stamp, Revenue.)

Stamp, Mourning: A number of stamps have been issued to mourn the passing of a head of state or similar prominent figure, but few have been as attractive or as sincere as the beautiful stamp illustrated.

This is part of a set of eight semi-postal stamps issued in 1935 by Belgium to mourn the death in

an automobile accident of Queen Astrid of Belgium.

Other mourning stamps have paid tribute to Chancellor Engelbert Dolfuss of Austria, King Albert of Belgium, and President Hindenburg of Germany, all in 1934.

Greece's King Constantine (in 1936) and King George (in 1947) rated mourning stamps, and a number of other countries have so honored their dead leaders.

More recently, a new phenomenon has come upon the scene. This is the so-called omnibus tribute, when almost before an internationally known figure has been decently buried, a veritable mass of philatelic material of every shape, size, and denomination is foisted upon the philatelic world by countries with at least a tenuous relationship with the deceased figure.

The mass of gimmick material for Sir Winston Churchill and President John F. Kennedy made it obvious that money rather than mourning was the real motive.

Stamp, Narcotic Tax: Narcotic tax stamps are US revenue stamps that came into use after the Revenue Act of 1918 imposed a tax on narcotics such as opium.

The stamps were placed on the drug containers to indicate payment of the 1c per ounce tax.

The tax was repealed in 1971, and the use of revenue stamps was discontinued on April 30 of that year.

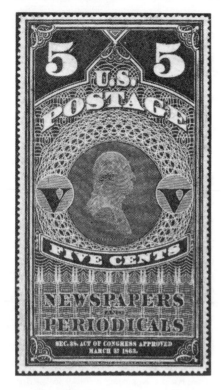

The first US newspaper stamps were 51x95mm monsters.

A newspaper stamp from Austria. Note the lack of any inscription.

Stamp, Newspaper:

Newspaper stamps were issued by a number of countries to show prepayment of postal charges on newspapers, journals, and periodicals.

They were first issued by Austria in January 1851, and since then they have been issued by countries around the world, including Belgium (inscribed "Journaux Dagbladen"), Brazil (inscribed "Jornaes"), Czechoslovakia, Bohemia and Moravia, France, (inscribed "Journaux"), Denmark, Fiume, Germany (inscribed "Zeitungs Marke"), Hungary, New Zealand, Portugal and colonies (inscribed "Jornaes"), Philippines (inscribed "Impresos"), Poland (overprinted on Austrian stamps), Turkey, Uruguay (inscribed "Prensa"), and the US.

Stamps issued jointly by the British, French, and US forces occupying Austria at the end of World War II. The stamps were for the use of the civilian population in the three zones of occupation.

The first US issue appeared in 1865 and comprised 51 x 95mm monsters. In 1875 a handsome set depicting various female figures was placed in use, and the same or similar designs were in use until newspaper stamps were discontinued on July 1, 1898.

The US newspaper stamps were used to reflect postage paid on bulk shipments of newspapers. From 1875, the stamps were not placed on the newspapers but on the memorandum of mailing and were retained by the Post Office.

Stamp, Occupation:
Occupation stamps are those issued by an invading or occupying power. Many such stamps have been

This stamp celebrated the US defeat in the Philippines at the beginning of the war in the Pacific during 1942.

issued in the years since adhesive postage stamps have been in use.

Many were created as a result of both World Wars I and II.

Some of the more attractive are those issued by the French for their zone of occupation in Germany following WWII.

The stamp illustrated was an overprint on a Philippine stamp issued by the invading Japanese to "commemorate" the fall of the Bataan Peninsula and Corregidor Island at the start of WWII in the Pacific.

Stamp, Official:
The term "Official" refers to a postage stamp issued for use by a department of government.

As with the adhesive postage stamp itself, the idea of Official stamps originated in Great Britain with the famous "VR" Penny Black of 1840.

This stamp had the letter "V" in the upper left corner and "R" in the upper right. Since it was never officially released, it properly belongs in the "prepared for use but never released" category. A few seem to have "escaped," since used copies are known to exist.

A great many countries have issued Official stamps, including the US. In 1873 the US Post Office Department issued stamps for use by various branches of the government.

Their designs feature inscriptions for the

Two Canadian Official stamps.

Dept. of Agriculture, the Executive Branch, Dept. of the Interior, the Justice Dept., the Navy Dept., the Post Office Dept., the Dept. of the Treasury, and the War Dept.

The stamps were in use for some seven years.

The USPOD also released imprinted Official envelopes between 1873 and 1884, and an Official postal card appeared in 1913.

New Zealand is a country that has had a number of interesting Official stamps, including the attractive Life Insurance Dept. issues featuring lighthouses. (See Stamp, Life Insurance.)

Switzerland has also been a prolific producer of official stamps, a number of which have been used by the various agencies of the League of Nations and the United Nations.

Official stamps of Indian and the Indian native states can be recognized by the overprint or inscription "Service" on many stamps.

Great Britain's Official stamps have included "department" issues for the Office of Works, the Army, the Board of Education, the Royal Household, and the Admiralty. All are overprints on the stamps of Queen Victoria and King Edward VII.

Canada's official stamps were first perforated with the letters "OHMS," then overprinted with "O.H.M.S." Later this was changed to "G." (See Flying "G".)

The world's first Official stamps are claimed to be an 1854 issue of Spain.

Overprints and inscriptions designating Official usage have included the word "official" in various spellings according to the language of the country, plus "B" (Belgium), "OS" (Australia and states), "E" (Bavaria), "Dienstmarke" (Germany), "Hivatalos" (Hungary), "Pjonustu" (Iceland), "Servizio di Stato" (Italy), "Regierungs Dienstsache" (Liechtenstein), "Armenwet" (Netherlands), "Offentlig Sak" (Norway), "OB" (Philippines), "Tjanste" (Sweden), and "Resmi" (Turkey).

There are others in various languages and alphabets.

Stamp, Parcel Post:

A number of interesting stamps have been issued to frank parcels, including those of the US and the small "twin stamps" of Italy.

Stamps issued specifically to frank parcels have been used by the postal administrations of a number of countries.

The US issue came in 1912 and comprised 12 stamps in similar format and, strangely, all in the same color. It was this latter factor that contributed to the many headaches they caused postal workers and made it only too easy to confuse the 1c and $1 denominations.

The 20c stamp in the series was the very first stamp to depict an aircraft carrying mail, although by 1912, mail had been carried through the air on many occasions.

The stamps had been authorized to frank fourth-class mail (parcel post), under an Act of Congress of Aug. 24, 1912.

A series of five parcel postage due labels was issued at the same time, and a parcel post special handling stamp was released in 1925. These latter stamps were to ensure that fourth-class franked with the stamps received first-class handling.

From July 1, 1913, the US parcel post stamps became valid to prepay postage on all classes of mail.

Italy seems to have been the first country to use parcel post stamps. In 1884 it issued a set of stamps inscribed "PACCHI POSTALI" and depicting the profile of King Humbert I.

Later Italian parcel post stamps took the form of stamps perforated vertically down the center. One half was placed on the waybill, the other affixed to the mailer's receipt. Similar stamps were used by the Italian colonies and also by San Marino.

The Belgian National Railways have used parcel post labels since 1879, although these were not official government postage stamps, and Cabeen (*Standard Handbook of Stamp Collecting,* Crowell, New York, 1965) suggests that they be termed "express labels."

Later, Belgium did issue actual parcel post stamps inscribed "Colis Postal-Post Collo' or "Colis Postaux-Post Colli."

These items are affixed to the waybill and eventually find their way onto the philatelic market.

The inscription "ENCOMIENDAS" identifies the parcel post stamps of Uruguay, and more than 100 of the stamps have been issued.

Other countries that have issued parcel post stamps include Afghanistan, Austria, Belgian Congo, Bulgaria, Denmark (inscribed "POSTFAERGE"), Greenland (inscribed "PAKKE PORTO"), Haiti, Hungary (inscribed "Csomag" or "Cs"), Iran (inscribed Colis Postaux), Mexico, Peru (inscribed "Porte de Conduccion"), Portugal (inscribed "ENCOMENDAS POSTAIS"), Romania (inscribed "TAXA DE FACTAGIU"), St. Pierre and Miquelon (inscribed "Colis Postaux"), and Tunisia.

Stamp, Personal Delivery:

Only Czechoslovakia and Bohemia and Moravia are known to have issued personal delivery stamps. These stamps ensured delivery only to the person to whom the letter was addressed.

The Czech stamps were first issued in 1937 and were triangular in format. One denomination was issued in both blue and carmine.

In 1946 a further similar stamp was issued.

During the Germans' occupation of Czechoslovakia, they established a puppet state called Bohemia and Moravia (q.v.), and it was under this regime that another pair of personal delivery stamps was issued. The stamps took the same format as the Czech issues.

Stamp, Playing Card:

Playing card stamps are US revenue stamps that were placed on packs of playing cards to indicate payment of a tax.

Such stamps were included in the first general issue of US revenue stamps, but in 1894 a separate category of such stamps was created and the stamps were used until the tax was eliminated in 1965. (See Stamp, Revenue; Stamp, Private Die Proprietary.)

One of the shortlived US parcel post stamps.

An Italian parcel post stamp comprising two parts.

After World War I, if you did not know what country you lived in, you might have used a plebiscite issue such as this on your mail, until you voted for the country of your choice from the alternatives offered.

Stamp, Plebiscite:

At the end of World War I, as the political map of Europe underwent drastic changes, populations at times found themselves suddenly living in another country.

In order to eliminate as much unsettlement and unrest as possible, where populations of one ethnic group might not wish to become part of a country dominated by another, a number of plebiscites were held, in which the populations voted on whether they favored integration into one country over another.

Such plebiscites took time to organize and hold, and the stamps that were required and issued during the period of doubt are known as plebiscite issues.

Areas in which plebiscites were held and that were provided with temporary postage stamps include Schleswig, Carinthia, Allenstein, and Silesia.

The stamp illustrated was issued for use in Upper Silesia, which until WWI was part of Eastern Germany. Because the plebiscite result was a virtual draw and the German and Polish populations were evenly split, the League of Nations divided the area between Germany and Poland.

Stamps for Upper Silesia were in use from 1920 until the final disposition of the territory.

Stamp Position:

In order to make it simple to indicate a specific stamp in a sheet, a system is used whereby every stamp has a number. This is determined by numbering stamps starting at the upper left stamp in a sheet and continuing along the top row, then returning to the left stamp in the second row, etc.

Thus, the first stamp of the first row would be #1, and assuming a sheet of 10 x 10, containing 100 stamps, the last stamp in the top row would be #10. The second row would begin with stamp #11, and so on.

This means that if you wanted to pinpoint stamp #43, it can easily be found as the third stamp in the fifth row.

Stamp, Postage and Revenue:

Postage and revenue stamps are valid for both postal and revenue use.

Many examples may be found in British and British Commonwealth issues.

They can be easily identified by the inscription "Postage/ Revenue" in various formats, and there is certainly no excuse for not recognizing the illustrated stamp's dual purpose!

When buying used copies of high-denomination stamps with such dual validity, you must beware of fake postal cancelations applied to stamps that have had a revenue marking removed, since the revenue use is much

more common and does not command the price of a genuine, postally used stamp (See Stamp, Revenue.)

Stamp, Postage Due: (See Postage Due Label.)

Stamp, Postal Fiscal:

A postal fiscal stamp is a revenue stamp that has been properly authorized for postal purposes and has been so used.

Stamp, Postal Note:

On Feb. 1, 1945, the US issued a set of 18 postal note stamps.

These were intended to supplement regular money order service and were affixed to money orders to make up odd amounts. They came in denominations of 1c to 10c, 20c, 30c, 40c, 50c, 60c, 70c, 80c, and 90c and were discontinued on March 31, 1951.

Jon Rose (*Stamp Collector*, Jan. 27, 1979) states that although used copies of all values are common, mint examples of the higher denominations are harder to find. Rose also notes that these items exist on cards with first-day cancelations.

Stamp, Postal Scrip:

Stamps of Canada inscribed "Postal Scrip" are intended for use in remitting small amounts.

When first issued in 1932, they were inscribed "Postal Note" and were used for making up odd

amounts on postal money orders. When inscribed "Postal Scrip," they could be redeemed at any Canadian post office and were thus ideal for small remittances.

They are now redeemed only when attached to money orders, according to Dr. Holmes (*Specialized Philatelic Catalogue of Canada and British North America*, Ryerson, 1959). (See Stamp, Postal Note, for similar US issues.)

Stamp, Postal Tax: (See Tax Label, Compulsory.)

Stamp, Postmasters' Provisionals:
On July 1, 1845, an Act of Congress became effective in the US establishing uniform postal rates at 5c for a single-rate (one half ounce) letter up to 300 miles and 10c for a single-rate letter traveling more than 300 miles. The rates doubled, tripled, etc., at every additional half ounce.

Drop letters (q.v.) were set at 2c.

Congress, however did not authorize the postmaster general to issue postage stamps until the Act of March 3, 1847.

There was, therefore, a period of uniform rates but with no stamps available, and individual postmasters created what are now known collectively as postmasters' provisionals.

The first one to appear was during July 1845 in New York City. Several followed in other parts of the country until the 1847 5c and 10c stamps became available July 1, 1847.

The postmasters' provisionals are now among the major rarities of the world. They were issued by postmasters at Alexandria, Va.; Annapolis, Md.; Baltimore, Md.; Boscawen, N.H.; Brattleboro, Vt.; Lockport, N.Y.; Millbury, Mass.; New Haven, Conn.; New York City; Providence, R.I.; St. Louis, Mo. (the famous St. Louis Bears); and Tuscumbia, Ala.

In some cases, these provisionals took the form of imprinted stamps on envelopes, and others were adhesive stamps.

During a period at the beginning of the Civil War in the Confederacy (q.v.), between the withdrawal of US stamps and the introduction of Confederate stamps, postmasters created their own provisionals.

Such action continued on a sporadic basis during the war.

In many cases, these issues comprised envelopes with post office handstamps applied along with the word "paid."

Postmasters' provisionals were not confined to the US and the Confederacy, and a number of other countries have used them.

Among these issues are the famous Perot and Thies stamps of Bermuda (q.v.), plus some of Colombia, Peru, and Mexico.

Stamp, Potato Tax:
US potato tax stamps came into use under the Agricultural Adjustment Act of 1935.

They were in use for a little more than one month before the act was declared unconstitutional.

It was intended that potato growers should be given a crop allotment and pay a tax of ¾c per pound on any excess grown.

The stamps range in denomination from ¾c to $1.50. (See Stamp, Revenue.)

Stamp, Precancel:
A precancel in its most simple form is a postage stamp canceled before it is sold in order to streamline the subsequent mail-handling procedure.

The Precancel Stamp Society provides the following definition:

"A precancel stamp, or precancel, is an adhesive postage stamp (or revenue stamp) that has been canceled, under proper authority, with a device designed solely for this purpose before being affixed to mail (or taxable) matter."

From the US *Postal Manual* comes another definition: "Precanceling means the cancelation of postage stamps, stamped envelopes, or postal cards in advance of mailing."

This enlarges the field to include postal stationery.

The first precancel is claimed to date from the very first US government-issued postage stamps. It is reported that on Sept. 1, 1847, the postmaster at Wheeling, Va., began using what some consider a precancelation device. This took the form of a large, seven-line grid in red that was carefully placed over a block of four stamps so that each stamp received a quarter of the impression.

The next reported attempt at precancelation comes from Fort Bridger, Utah Territory, on March 1, 1858, when the postmaster used his printing press to impress "Fort Bridger U.T. March 1, 1858" in two lines on his stock of 3c stamped envelopes.

Another early town named imprinted on a

stamp as a precancel came on Oct. 22, 1857, when Cumberland, Me., put its name on the 1c and 3c stamps of 1857.

The first foreign precancel is claimed to have been issued by France in 1868.

US precancels, with the exception of the earlier issues (See Lansing Spider) consist of a combination of lines and the town or city name.

Some are produced at the Bureau of Engraving and Printing, as part of the stamp's production, for those cities using precancels in enormous quantities. These are called "bureau precancels," or "bureaus." Other precancels are applied locally and are known as "local precancels," or "locals."

Some US precancels also bear dates, and these are known as "dateds." The large mail order companies used this form of precancelation to a considerable extent.

Dated precancels before 1918 are considered classics, and the mail order houses used dateds from 1938.

On May 23, 1903, the US Post Office Dept. specified that precancels were to include city and state names within two lines. Revenue stamps have also been widely precanceled in the US.

In September 1978, the US Postal Service decided that the city and state designation was not necessary, and since then only two parallel lines have appeared on bureau precancels.

Precancel collecting is a popular branch of philately, and there are active collector organizations and a large amount of precancel literature.

Because of the vast quantity of different varieties, most collectors specialize in some aspect of precancel collecting.

Typical examples of US "dated" precancels used in enormous quantities, especially by the large mail order houses, which began to use them from 1938 on.

You may collect a city or state, specific stamp of different towns, either bureaus or locals, dateds, etc.

It is one of the few areas of our hobby where the emphasis is still on trading, and there are few expensive varieties.

A word of warning: If you have handstamped "local" precancels, do not try to soak them off paper. There is a danger that the water soluble ink used will dissolve, and you will be left with a beautiful unused stamp! So, if in doubt, trim neatly and leave it in paper.

A number of foreign countries have used precanceled stamps, with various methods of designating them.

Canada has used a series of code numbers and also a number of lines across stamps. Austria, Belgium, France, Hungary, and the Netherlands are also among precancel-using nations.

The first foreign equivalent of bureau prints were the Belgian precancels of 1906. According to Konwiser (American Stamp Collector's Dictionary, Minkus, New York, 1949), all Belgian precancels are bureau prints. French precancels from 1920 to 1934 are also considered to be the same as bureau prints.

I am grateful to Stamp Collector's precancel columnist, James Kingman, for much of the information presented here.

A Dutch precancel from the town of Hertogenbosch, one of the more than 100 towns that used this form of roller precancel. They are usually hard to read and closely resemble postal cancelations.

A selection of US precancels.

Some foreign precancels.

The US 1970 experimental Christmas precancels, which
were supplied to post offices in 68 cities in an attempt to
ease the task of handling Christmas mail.

Stamp, Private Die Proprietary:

Private Die Proprietary stamps are commonly called "Match and Medicine" stamps or "M & Ms."

These stamps were used to seal the container of an item and indicated that the tax had been paid. They were usually torn when the container was opened.

Items requiring them included matches, proprietary medicines, perfume, playing cards, etc.

The issues were prompted by the Revenue Act of 1862, which sought to raise money required by the great drain on the economy caused by the American Civil War.

Manufacturers were allowed to have stamps produced for their own particular product, bearing their name and trademark. Though they paid for the die and printing, they received a discount ranging up to 10%.

There is a large variety of these private die proprietary stamps.

The law requiring the taxes was repealed effective July 1, 1883, according to Scott.

Cabeen (Standard Handbook of Stamp Collecting, Crowell, New York, 1979) states that a few such stamps were used during the Spanish-American War. (See Stamp, Revenue.)

Stamp, Prohibited: (See Prohibited Stamps.)

Stamp, Quarter: At least three stamp-issuing entities have released stamps made up of four quarters that could be used intact or divided into four parts, each worth one quarter of the total face value.

Spain issued such stamps in 1872 and 1873; the German state of Brunswick issued a similar stamp in 1857; and in 1856 and 1864 Mecklenburg-Schwerin released stamps that could be divided into four parts.

Stamp, Railway: In Belgium, the railroad system operates a parcel post service and since 1879 has issued special stamps. These stamps are popular with railroad collectors, and the catalogs list more than 400 varieties.

Designs range from symbolic winged railroad wheels to beautifully engraved representations of various locomotive types. Many of the stamps include the French/ Flemish bilingual inscription "Chemins de fer/ Spoorwegen," and some feature "Postcollo/ Colis Postal" or "Postcolli/ Colis Postaux."

Since the World War II years, the stamps have also included the letter "B" enclosed in an oval in their design.

In Great Britain, special stamps have been used to frank letters carried on the trains of various railway companies.

This is more in the nature of an express service and the stamps are used in addition to normal postage stamps.

Since 1957, the Talyllyn Railway in Wales has issued a number of attractive local stamps (q.v.) picturing various aspects of the popular tourist attraction.

As recently as 1971, British Railways issued a 15p railway stamp for use by its London Midland Region.

Stamp, Railway Air Mail: In Great Britain during the 1930s, most domestic air services were operated by the railway companies.

On April 12, 1933, the Great Western Railway began an air service carrying mail and passengers between Cardiff and Plymouth, with a stop at Haldon Aerodrome to serve Torquay and Teignmouth.

At first, a railway newspaper parcel stamp was used to indicate payment of the 3d air mail fee in addition to the normal British postage. But on May 15, 1933, a handsome adhesive picturing a Westland Wessex aircraft used on the route was released.

For a few months this service staggered along but lost money, and it was abandoned on Sept. 9, 1933.

A number of other adhesives were issued for use by several non-railway air services in Great Britain during the 1930s. As late as the 1960s, British European Airways was using such stamps to denote payment of the air mail fee.

In March 1934, the four large railway companies in Great Britain — the London, Midland, and Scottish (LMS), the London, North Eastern Railway (LNER), the Great Western Railway (GWR), and the Southern Railway (SR) — joined forces to form the Railway Air Service. Payment of the 3d air mail fee was indicated by a handstamped impression, and no further stamps were issued until the 1950s when British European Airways reintroduced items similar to those previously noted.

Back in the 1930s, the railway companies quite rightly saw that air travel was going to give them some heavy competition, but the time was not ripe, and before air travel in Britain had really developed, World War II intervened.

The relatively short distances and the enormous rail network, with its excellent service of fast and comfortable trains, postponed the development of an economic passenger and air mail service in Great Britain. This is in contrast to countries like the US, where distances were enormous and surface transportation less fully developed.

A cover bearing a Great Western Railways air mail local stamp, which paid the air mail fee. The regular British stamps paid the normal mail cost. (Cover from the collection of Dr. Perham Nahl, reproduced courtesy of the owner.)

Stamp, Registration: A number of countries have issued stamps specifically for use in paying the special fee on registered mail.

The US issued a single stamp inscribed "REGISTRY" on Dec. 1, 1911. It had a denomination of 10c, which in those days paid the registration fee — a far cry from today's inflated cost.

The use of this registration stamp was discontinued on May 28, 1913, but later usage is possi-

ble as post offices were permitted to use up stocks on hand.

The South American country of Colombia has issued registration stamps, many of which feature a space for inserting the registration number of the item of mail, similar to the labels commonly seen on registered mail.

The letter "R" overprinted on early Colombian air mail stamps represents payment of the registration fee on mail carried by the airline Sociedad Colombo-Alemana de Transportes Aeroes, or SCADTA (q.v.). The "R" stands for "Registro."

Some stamps of Panama are overprinted "R" and surcharged for use as registration stamps.

Stamp, Regular: (See Stamp, Definitive.)

Stamp, Restricted: (See Prohibited Stamps.)

Stamp, Revenue: Revenue, or fiscal, stamps are intended to indicate the collection of a tax or payment of a fee. In a broad sense, you might say that postage stamps are a category of revenue stamps — which would surely delight the heart of any avid revenuer.

At one time, revenue stamps were as widely collected as postage stamps. As the number of postage stamps proliferated, however, collectors found it necessary to limit their area of collecting, and catalog editors had to limit the size of the general catalogs, so revenue stamps were largely eliminated.

The lack of a single, up-to-date worldwide catalog of revenue stamps has had an inhibiting effect on revenue collecting, although the active American Revenue Association (q.v.) in the US has done a great deal to stimulate a renewed interest in this branch of philately, and its members have been responsible for a considerable body of literature on the subject.

There is an enormous number of revenue stamps from almost every country, and some have literally issued thousands if you include national, regional, and local revenue stamps.

Although the first adhesive revenue stamps

One of the best-known designs in the field of US revenue stamps, this proprietary stamp is commonly called the "Battleship Stamp."

are said to be the Austrian issues of Lombardy-Venice in 1854, the imprinting or embossing of revenue "stamps" on documents pre-dates adhesive postage stamps by at least 200 years.

One early form was the attachment to a document of a strip of thin metal that was then embossed with something resembling a notary's seal, which "tied" the metal to the document.

The design and format of revenue stamps are as varied as are those of their contemporary postal issues. Indeed, some would claim that they offer even a greater variety of subject, size, and design.

Topical collectors should not ignore the possibilities offered by revenue stamps, which could well be included in topical collections when appropriate.

Among US collectors, the most popular revenues would have to be the extremely beautiful migratory bird hunting stamps (q.v.), or duck stamps as they are popularly known.

These are large, beautifully designed and engraved reproductions of various types of waterfowl. They are issued annually, and the designs are selected from competition among wildlife artists.

One of the major attractions of revenue collecting is that, unlike postage stamps, the great majority of revenues are not issued with a view to their purchase by collectors.

The US has had a large amount of varied revenue stamps, including the stamps of 1765 that were intended for almanacs, newspapers, and general use, but not for tea, the tax on which, according to Cabeen, (Standard Handbook of Stamp Collecting, Crowell, New York, 1979), was not paid with stamps!

An interesting branch of US revenue stamp collecting includes the stamps used by the many firms making perfumes, playing cards, matches, and proprietary medicines, and on which the firms were permitted to have their names and trademarks.

These are full of the atmosphere of a bygone age and provide an intriguing glimpse of the merchandising methods used so long ago.

Tax paid stamps are another form of revenue.

Their application to an article or container indicates that the applicable tax has been paid although the stamps bear no denomination.

Telegraph stamps are another form of revenue stamp and have been issued by many countries. (See Stamp, Postal Fiscal; Stamp, Documentary; and Stamp, Private Die Proprietary.)

Stamp, Sanitary Fair: Sanitary Fair stamps were local stamps issued for bazaars and fairs held in various northern cities by the US Sanitary Commission during the Civil War.

The stamps paid for the carriage of mail from the fair to the nearest US post office.

The US Sanitary Commission was established in 1861 to use public contributions to provide medical attention and nursing to wounded Northern troops and to supervise sanitary conditions at camps and hospitals.

The fairs were held to raise funds, and the local stamps were issued for eight of the events.

Though not officially recognized, the stamps were permitted in this worthy cause and are listed by Scott in its US Specialized Stamp Catalogue.

Stamps were issued at fairs held at Albany, N.Y.; Boston, Mass.; Brooklyn, N.Y. (two fairs — one in December 1863 and another in February-March 1864); New York, N.Y.; Philadelphia, Pa.; Springfield, Mass.; and Stamford, Conn.

Another function adopted by the Sanitary Commission was to forward soldiers' unpaid and postage-due letters.

Most of the designs of the local stamps were primitive. Several feature eagles, one design depicts a bird carrying a letter, and another pictures a soldier greeting two women.

Scott notes that in several cases imitations exist.

Stamp, Savings: Beginning in 1911, the US Post Office Department issued savings stamps, which were redeemable as a credit to postal savings accounts.

During World War II, these stamps featured a design showing a Minute Man and were inscribed "U.S. Postal Savings."

The Post Office Savings account system ended March 28, 1966.

From 1954 until June 30, 1970, similar stamps were issued inscribed "United States Savings Stamp" and were redeemable for US Savings Bonds. From 1958, these Minute Man designs feature the US flag in the background.

Stamps for a similar purpose were issued by the Treasury Department from 1917 to 1943 inscribed "United States War Savings," and these were redeemable for US Treasury War Certificates, or Defense or War Bonds.

There was also a Treasury Savings stamp issued in 1921.

Stamp, Semi-Official Air Mail: In the early days of air mail, private companies operating air services carried mail and often issued their own private labels to indicate pay-

A Canadian semi-official air mail stamp.

ment of the fee for carriage by air, over and above the normal postage as indicated by government postage stamps.

Though the air mail stamps were not official, their use was tolerated.

Some of the best-known of these semi-official lables are those issued by Canadian airlines. Many of the small airlines operating in the vast expanses of Canada issued semi-official stamps, which were supposed to be affixed to the back of mail.

The Colombian airline SCADTA (q.v.) was also a user of such stamps, as were the railway air services in Great Britain prior to World War II.

Other countries in which airlines used semi-official air mail stamps include Australia, Belgium, Chile, Costa Rica, Denmark, Ecuador, France, Germany, Greece, Honduras, Hungary, Italy, Monaco, Newfoundland, New Guinea, New Zealand, Poland, Portugal, Sweden, Switzerland, and the United States.

Stamp, Semi-Postal: A semi-postal stamp is a means of raising funds for some purpose in addition to paying the postal charges on an item of mail to which it is affixed.

A British term for such a stamp is "charity stamp."

A semi-postal usually bears two figures, the normal figure of denomination and one representing the amount of the surtax, for example, "15c + 5c." The cost of such a stamp is the sum of these two figures.

In the Scott catalog, semi-postal stamps are listed separately with the prefix letter "B." In most cases, the stamps are commemorative in nature.

Strangely, it was the then ultra-conservative British Post Office that is claimed to have introduced this means of raising money. In 1890 it released a 1d postal card to mark the anniversary of penny postage. The card was sold at 6d, with the additional 5d going to a fund for postal workers.

It was not long before the idea of adapting this fund-raising device to adhesive postage stamps began to spread, and in June 1897 the British colony of New South Wales jumped into the fund-raising race with both feet. Two stamps were released for Queen Victoria's Diamond Jubilee in 1897, with denominations of 1d and 2½d and surtaxes of 1/- and 2/6 respectively — 12 times face value!

The stamps were printed in several colors and must have been considered quite spectacular at the time of their release. The designs feature

Semi-postal stamps from New Zealand, Spanish Sahara, and France.

symbolic renditions of charity, and the surtax was for the support of a home for consumptives.

Three years later, the neighboring colony of Queensland adopted the idea to raise money for a patriotic fund in connection with the Boer War, then raging in South Africa.

Thus was born the idea of using the postage stamp as a fund-raising object.

Since the use of semi-postal stamps to frank mail is optional, it has been stamp collectors striving for completion who have likely been the greatest contributors to the charities.

In most cases, the surtax (q.v.) is a fraction of the face value, but some countries, following the rather extreme example of New South Wales, have tacked unreasonably high amounts to the normal face value of the stamp. Belgium has been an outstanding offender in this respect.

Right from the beginning, stamp collectors have disliked semi-postal stamps. When the 1897 New South Wales pair was announced, the *London Philatelist* expressed itself as being "...confident that this issue will meet with profound dissatisfaction and contempt."

Other publications were equally opposed to the new gimmick, and the London firm of Stanley Gibbons not only avoided listing them in its catalog but warned collectors not to waste money on them, according to L.N. and M. Williams *(The Postage Stamp,* Penguin Books, London, 1956). So much for public condemnation!

But perhaps the actions of British collectors spoke loudest if belatedly, because, when Britain issued its first semi-postal stamp on Jan. 22, 1975, the 4½p + 1½p stamp proved to be a financial flop.

A number of countries released annual semi-postal sets, and where a policy of restraint is observed and a worthy cause benefits, the issues have been popular with collectors.

Examples are the annual New Zealand Health stamps, the French Red Cross issues, and the Netherlands' Child Welfare sets.

Some of the most popular of all the annual semi-postal issues, however, are the Swiss Pro Juventute and Pro Patria sets, and these have become the highlights of the Swiss stamp-issuing year.

The Federation Internationale de Philatelie (FIP) has a policy of boycotting semi-postal issues for which the surtax exceeds 50% of the postal face value of the issue.

Stamp Shows: (See Philatelic Exhibitions.)

Stamp, Silver Tax: Silver tax stamps were US revenue stamps intended to indicate

the payment of tax on profits realized from the sale of silver.

The stamps comprise the 1917 documentary issue overprinted "SILVER/ TAX." They were in use from Feb. 20, 1934, to June 4, 1963. (See Stamp, Revenue.)

Stamps on Stamps Centenary Study Unit: (See American Topical Association Study Units.)

Stamp, Special Delivery: A special delivery stamp is one used to indicate the payment of a special delivery, or express, fee on an item of mail.

In the US, special delivery stamps were first issued Oct. 1, 1885, when special delivery service was inaugurated at free-delivery post offices

and at post offices in communities having a population of 4,000 or more.

The following year, the service was extended to all US post offices.

Special delivery services in a number of countries are called "express services," and their stamps are inscribed "Express," "Expre," "Express Delivery," "Expresso," etc., depending on the language of the country.

Some of the foreign-language inscriptions for special delivery stamps include "Surgos" (Hungary), "Urgente" (Spain and Colonies), "Poskilat" (Indonesia), "Entrege Immediata" (Cuba), and "Entrega Especial" (Dominican Republic).

Stamp, Special Handling: The US Postal Act of February 1925 provided for a 25c special handling stamp, which, when added to the normal postage on fourth-class matter, would entitle it to special handling. It was then handled as first-class.

The 25c stamps was issued April 11, 1925. This was followed by 10c, 15c, and 20c stamps, released on June 25, 1928, which covered revised rates effective July 1928.

Other countries have used special handling stamps. Austria issued its first such stamps in 1916. They were triangular in format with the long side at the top instead of the more usual ar-

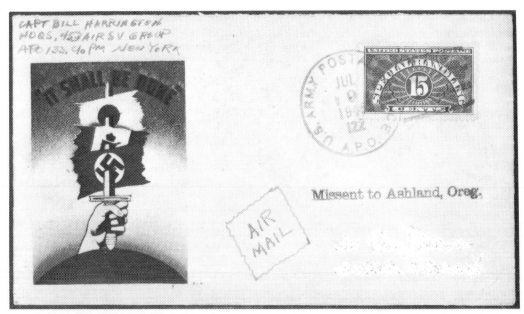

A fourth-class special handling stamp used on a letter from a serviceman at the end of World War II.

rangement. These issues continued until 1922, but in a less unusual format.

Bosnia used special handling stamps, which bear the inscription "Militarpost Eilmarke."

Stamps, Prohibited: (See Prohibited Stamps.)

Stamp, Stereoscopic: On Dec. 29, 1956, Italy marked the first anniversary of its admission to the United Nations with a pair of stereoscopic stamps.

The design consisted of globes in red and green that when viewed through special glasses, take on a three-dimensional effect.

The special glasses were supplied with an Italian ministerial bulletin that described the printing process.

Stamp, Swiss Soldier: (See Swiss Soldier Stamp.)

Stamp, Tax Paid: A tax paid stamp is a revenue stamp that is affixed to a container to indicate that a particular tax has been paid.

It bears no monetary denomination but has a quantity denomination and thus is usable regardless of variations in the actual amount of tax paid.

Italy's stereoscopic stamps. When viewed through a special viewer they appear to become three dimensional.

Stamp, Telegraph: Telegraph
stamps are special stamps — either adhesive, for affixing to telegraph forms, or imprinted thereon — that reflect payment of the cost of a telegram.

Generally, they are considered revenue stamps.

In Great Britain, postage and revenue stamps, good for either purpose, served to prepay the cost, and the Stock Exchange Forgery (q.v.) involved a British 1/- postage and revenue stamp.

There have been official British telegraph stamps, as well as a number issued by various

A Dutch telegraph stamp.

private telegraph companies.

In Spanish-speaking countries, telegraph stamps are inscribed "TELEGRAFO."

The first telegraph stamp is reported by Otto Hornung *(Illustrated Encyclopedia of Stamp Collecting,* Hamlyn, London, 1970) to have been issued by Prussia in 1864.

Postage stamps have been overprinted to convert them to telegraph stamps.

The 5c and 1.75fr denominations of Algeria's 1936-41 issue were overprinted "E.F.M." and surcharged with a new denomination to prepay the cost of telegrams sent by Allied servicemen in 1943. The letters "E.F.M." stand for "Emergency Field Message."

In the US, a large variety of telegraph stamps was issued by the various private telegraph companies in the late 1800s and early years of the 20th century.

The Scott *United States Specialized Stamp Catalogue* devotes some 10 pages to a listing of these stamps.

Stamp, Tobacco Sale Tax: Tobacco
sale tax stamps were US revenue stamps created to indicate payment of a tax on the sale of tobacco above quotas established by the Secretary of Agriculture under the Agriculture Adjustment Act of 1935.

Like the potato tax stamps, they were discontinued when the act was declared unconstitutional.

The stamps range in denomination from 1c to $20 and comprise overprints reading "TOBACCO/ SALE TAX." on values of the 1917 Documentary Issue. (See Stamp, Revenue.)

Stamp, University Colleges: (See
College Stamps, Universities.)

Stamp, War Tax: During World War I,
many of the British colonies issued stamps overprinted "WAR TAX" and sometimes surcharged with an additional denomination.

These stamps were intended to raise funds, over and above the cost of postage, for wartime use.

Some of the stamps so overprinted were really revenue stamps that were required on mail and represented a tax.

Canadian stamps inscribed "War Tax" were revenue stamps, and those inscribed "1Tc" were good for 2c postage, with the additional 1c going to the war effort.

War tax stamps from Fiji and the Gold Coast.

The first war tax stamps had been issued by Spain in 1874 and bore the inscription "Impuesta de Guerra," or "Impto de Guerra."

Similar overprints were produced on the stamps of Puerto Rico during the Spanish-American War of 1898.

Standing Helvetia: This name refers to
the 1882-1907 issue of Switzerland, which shows the standing figure of Helvetia instead of the seated figures as on previous issues.

In 1907 Switzerland reverted to the use of a seated figure.

Stanislav: The name "Stanislav Issue" is
given to the 1919 stamps of the Western Ukraine issued during its brief independence following World War I.

The issues comprised Austrian stamps overprinted and surcharged. (See Ukrainian Soviet Socialist Republic.)

Star Plates: On certain US stamps issued during 1908, and again in 1925, the Bureau of Engraving and Printing experimented with the spacing between stamp subjects on the printing plate.

In 1908 a spacing of 3mm was provided between one column and the next for the six outer columns of stamps in an attempt to compensate for unequal paper shrinkage and thus improve the centering of the perforations between stamp impressions.

Plates so spaced were identified with an open star located between the printer's imprint and the plate number.

On one plate of each of the 1c and 2c stamps, a smaller solid star was used, and these stamps command a much higher price.

The 1925 experiments were another attempt to improve the location of perforations between stamps and involved the vertical spacing of stamp columns over the entire plate. Spacing on these star plates was increased from 2-3/4mm to 3mm.

Both five-pointed and six-pointed stars were used on these plates.

Star Route: The term "Star Route" refers to a postal route on which US mail is carried by a contractor who must guarantee speed and security.

States Admitted to the United States of America: States in order of admission to the Union are:
1. Delaware (Dec. 7, 1787).
2. Pennsylvania (Dec. 12, 1787).
3. New Jersey (Dec. 18, 1787).
4. Georgia (Jan. 2, 1788).
5. Connecticut (Jan. 9, 1788).
6. Massachusetts (Feb. 6, 1788).
7. Maryland (April 28, 1788).
8. South Carolina (May 23, 1788).
9. New Hampshire (June 21, 1788).
10. Virginia (June 25, 1788).
11. New York (July 26, 1788).
12. North Carolina (Nov. 21, 1789).
13. Rhode Island (May 29, 1790).
14. Vermont (March 4, 1791).
15. Kentucky (June 1, 1792).
16. Tennessee (June 1, 1796).
17. Ohio (March 1, 1803).
18. Louisiana (April 30, 1812).
19. Indiana (Dec. 11, 1816).
20. Mississippi (Dec. 10, 1817).
21. Illinois (Dec. 3, 1818).
22. Alabama (Dec. 14, 1819).
23. Maine (March 15, 1820).
24. Missouri (Aug. 10, 1821).
25. Arkansas (June 15, 1836).
26. Michigan (Jan. 26, 1837).
27. Florida (March 3, 1845).
28. Texas (Dec. 29, 1845).
29. Iowa (Dec. 28, 1846).
30. Wisconsin (May 29, 1848).
31. California (Sept. 9, 1850).
32. Minnesota (May 11, 1858).
33. Oregon (Feb. 14, 1859).
34. Kansas (Jan. 29, 1861).
35. West Virginia (June 20, 1863).
36. Nevada (Oct. 31, 1864).
37. Nebraska (March 1, 1867).
38. Colorado (Aug. 1, 1876).
39. North Dakota (Nov. 2, 1889).
40. South Dakota (Nov. 2, 1889).
41. Montana (Nov. 8, 1889).
42. Washington (Nov. 11, 1889).
43. Idaho (July 3, 1890).
44. Wyoming (July 10, 1890).
45. Utah (Jan. 4, 1896).
46. Oklahoma (Nov. 16, 1907).
47. New Mexico (Jan. 6, 1912).
48. Arizona (Feb. 14, 1912).
49. Alaska (Jan. 3, 1959).
50. Hawaii (Aug. 21, 1959).

Stationery: (See Postal Stationery.)

STATI PARM: The inscription "STATI PARM" is found on the first issue of the Italian state of Parma (q.v.). It is an abbreviation for "Stati Parmensi."

Stato di Conservazione: Italian expression for "condition."

Steel Blue: Foreign words for "steel blue" include bleu acier (French), stahlblau (German), azzurro acciaio (Italian), and azul acero (Spanish).

Steel Engraving: The art of engraving stamp designs on steel dies that are then hardened and used to produce printing plates. (See Printing, Intaglio.)

Steendruk: Dutch word for "lithography."

Steindruck: German word for "lithography."

Stellaland: Stellaland was a Boer republic set up in what is now part of the Republic of South Africa. It was previously known as British Bechuanaland. Its headquarters was at Vryburg.

The republic lasted only a short while during 1884-85 before being taken over by British forces. Great Britain refused to recognize the "country" and sent an expeditionary force to eliminate it.

A set of five stamps was issued inscribed "REPUBLIEK STELLALAND" in 1884, and a single 4p stamp was issued in 1885 surcharged "TWEE."

Ste. Marie de Madagascar: An island off the east coast of Madagascar, Ste. Marie de Madagascar became a French colony in 1750. It

lies to the north of the Madagascan town of Tamatave, and its chief town is Ambodifototra.

With an area of 64 square miles, the island has a population estimated at about 8,000. It became a part of Madagascar in 1896.

A set of stamps in the French Colonial Commerce and Navigation key type inscribed "Ste. Marie de Madagascar" was issued in 1894.

The area is now included in the Democratic Republic of Madagascar (q.v.).

Stempel: Dutch word for "postmark."

Stempelmarke: "Stempelmarke" is a German word for a revenue or tax stamp.

The illustrated example is from Austria and is dated 1916. Both front and back are illustrated in order to show the security underprinting on the back.

Stephan, Dr. Heinrich von: Dr. Heinrich von Stephan (1831-1897) has been called the father of the Universal Postal Union (q.v.).

He was director of posts for the North German Confederation and dreamed of an international agreement for postal communications, which were still in a terrible state of confusion, despite efforts of Montgomery Blair (q.v.) and the Paris conference of 1863.

The lack of uniform postal rates, nonrecognition of one country's stamps by another, and the complicated accounting necessary to

reimburse countries through which mail traveled all combined to create a degree of confusion difficult to comprehend.

Von Stephan wanted to do something to sort this all out and establish international standards.

In 1868 he proposed a plan calling for a postal congress of nations to draft an agreement for international postal affairs.

He was, in effect, proposing on an international scale what Sir Rowland Hill (q.v.) had done for the British Post Office.

An international postal congress was arranged for 1869, but the Franco-Prussian War intervened, and the meeting was not held until 1874, in Switzerland.

At this postal congress, the General Postal Union (later the Universal Postal Union) was born, and Von Stephan's dream was realized.

Stereoscopic Stamp: (See Stamp, Stereoscopic.)

Stereotype: A stereotype is a duplicate of an engraving made by means of a plaster-of-Paris or papier-mache mold, the latter usually called a mat.

The operation of making such duplicates is known as stereotyping.

S. THOME E PRINCIPE: This inscription identifies stamps of St. Thomas and Prince Islands.

Stich: German word for "engraving."

Stickney, Benjamin R.: Benjamin Stickney (1871-1946) was the inventor of the web-fed rotary press that bears his name.

The press was used by the Bureau of Engraving and Printing to print many US stamps. It used two curved plates to make up a printing cylinder.

Stiffener: In order to protect a philatelic cover on its journey through the mails, something should be placed inside it to prevent it from being creased and damaged by mail-handling equipment.

It is usual to place what is called a stiffener in the envelope. This is usually a piece of card about the weight of a postal card.

A stiffener also helps to ensure that a cover will receive a good impression, or strike, of whatever cancel or postal marking the cover receives.

In the case of cacheted covers, it is not unusual for the stiffener to have information printed on it that tells about the event or person noted by the cachet.

Stockbook: A stockbook is a book containing pages having a number of strips forming pockets into which stamps may be inserted for storage.

The strips may be of manila, glassine, or acetate. The transparant acetate strips are generally preferred, since the stamps are visible without having to be removed from the pocket.

Glassine strips are fragile and easily torn, and the manila strips tend to stretch and then do not hold their contents securely.

The better stockbooks also have some form of interleaving to protect material on facing pages from rubbing together.

Most collectors use some form of stockbook, and there is no question that such storage is the best method of protecting material pending its mounting in a collection.

Many modern stamp albums with some form of built-in mounts are really a form of stockbook.

Stock Exchange Forgery: One of the most famous examples of the use of forged stamps to defraud a postal administration was the so-called Stock Exchange Forgery.

It was also one of the most successful, since the individuals involved were never caught. Indeed, the caper was not even discovered until 25 years later in 1898, when London stamp dealer Charles Nissen came upon some copies of the British 1/- stamp of the 1867 issue used on telegram forms.

The British Post Office also ran the telegraph service, and thus regular postage stamps were used in payment.

Nissen felt that there was something wrong with the stamps. They were blurry in appearance, and some of the corner letters were in combinations that should not exist on genuine stamps.

He reported the matter to the Post Office, and an investigation was begun, but after so many years it was impossible to find the culprit or culprits.

Since all of the forged stamps were canceled at the Stock Exchange Post Office in London, they became known as the Stock Exchange Forgeries.

Apparently, a post office clerk would take the forged stamps to work and during the day would either sell them over the counter or affix them to telegram forms and pocket the money.

S. TOME: The Portuguese spelling of St. Thomas.

Stotinki: A unit of currency used in Bulgaria. One hundred stotinki equal one lev.

Straight Edge: The term "straight edge" refers to stamps that are usually perforated normally but that have one or two adjacent sides imperforate.

This comes about when stamps are printed in sheets having no margins on one or more sides, or containing gutters along which the sheets are

Two US straight-edged stamps.

One of Canada's unpopular straight-edged stamps.

divided into panes. Thus, the outside stamps will have one or more sides left imperforate.

Both the US and Canada have issued stamps in this format.

Such stamps, despite their relative scarcity compared with the normally perforated stamps from the rest of the pane, have never been popular with collectors.

This unpopualrity explains why many of the scarcer stamps in straight edge condition have had their imperforate sides faked to simulate perforations, in order that they may be sold at much higher prices.

Stamp booklets from a number of countries contain small panes of stamps that are imperforate around the edges, thus creating stamps with one or two adjacent sides imperforate.

Straight-edge stamps should not be confused with coil stamps (q.v.), which will have two opposite edges imperforate.

Small Canadian stamp booklets exist containing panes of three stamps in a horizontal strip have the outer stamp imperforate on top, bottom, and right hand side, with the other two stamps imperforate at top and bottom. However, these can be distinguished from coil stamps by their perforation, which measures 12 on the booklet stamps and 9½ on the coils.

During the 1960s, Canada issued several commemorative stamps from sheets laid out to produce straight-edged stamps.

I am indebted to Canada Post for supplying the following information concerning this interesting, if unpopular, episode in Canadian stamp manufacture:

The British American Bank Note Company was awarded a contract to produce certain stamp values beginning in 1968. The suggestion to issue straight-edged stock distributed to post offices (with normally produced stamps bearing marginal inscriptions being specially produced for the philatelic branch) had been considered for several years. Because the firm's new web-fed presses had this capability, the decision was made to use it to produce first-class domestic rate stamps and certain commemorative issues.

The advantages were lower paper cost and better post office housekeeping, according to the CPO.

An 8mm selvage (q.v.) was required on one edge of the sheet at the "bottom" to serve as a gripper in the press operation. This selvage was also used to staple 50 sheets of stamps to a cardboard cover, which was part of the security packaging at that time.

It was necessary for the printing firm to arrange the size of the printing cylinder to provide for the straight-edge condition, and individual stamp size was set at 24 x 20mm.

Each sheet of 100 stamps (10 x 10) required 240mm plus 8mm of selvage for a total of 248mm. The cylinder circumference was set at 744mm to accomodate three sheets around.

Slitting devices were used to cut off any side trim where the outside perforations would normally be located. The marginal imprints were located outside the slitter positions, so that the production of stamps for post office distribution would have the inscription cut away.

A cross-cutting device cut the web into individual sheets at the position where the top row of perforations would normally be located.

For the production of stamps to be sold to collectors from the Philatelic Service at Ottawa, two changes were made on the press. First, the slitter wheels were moved to a position outside the area of the marginal inscriptions, and perforating pins were added at the point where the slitter wheels were located for the straight-edge production.

This produced panes that were imperforate at the top only and contained selvage bearing marginal inscriptions separated from the adjacent stamps by perforations.

Because the circumference of the printing cylinder had been fixed at 744mm, it was not possible to eliminate the straight edge across the web.

After about three years, a decision was made to return to the normal method of stamp production by increasing the cylinder circumference to 768mm.

This resulted in a standard production format for the three firms printing Canada's postage stamps.

By 1971, Canadian stamps were being produced as before, and the straight-edge experiment was over.

Straits Settlements: The Straits Settlements was an administrative grouping of Malacca (q.v.), Penang (q.v.), and Singapore (q.v.). Stamps of India, some overprinted with a crown and surcharged, were used until 1867, when issues of the Straits Settlements went into use.

In 1906 the island of Labuan (q.v.), located off the coast of Borneo, was included in the Straits Settlements and used the group's stamps until its administration was transferred to North Borneo.

The colony group was broken up when Singapore was made a separate colony. Malacca and Penang became part of the Malayan Union (q.v.), later the Federation of Malaya (q.v.).

Straw: Foreign words for "straw" include juane paille (French), strohgelb (German), giallo pallido (Italian), and amarillo pajizo (Spanish).

Street Car Mail Service: Between
1893 and the 1920s, street car mail systems were operated in Baltimore, Boston, Brooklyn, Chicago, Cincinnati, Cleveland, New York, Pittsburg, Rochester, St. Louis, San Francisco, Seattle, and Washington.

Beginning in 1903, letter boxes were installed on street cars in a number of US cities. The boxes were attached to the front or rear of the car, according to Konwiser (The American Stamp Collector's Dictionary, Minkus, 1949).

Cabeen (Standard Handbook of Stamp Collecting, Crowell, New York, 1957) reports that by Dec. 5, 1892, a service that included sorting, canceling, and distribution was in operation in St. Louis. A special cancel went into use on Feb. 3, 1893, reading "Street R.P.O. No. 1."

Then came similar services in Brooklyn in 1894; Boston, Philadelphia, New York, Chicago, and Cincinnati in 1895; and Washington, Baltimore, San Francisco, and Rochester in 1896. These were followed by Pittsburgh in 1898, Seattle in 1905, Cleveland in 1908, and Omaha in 1910.

In 1899, states Cabeen, the street car mail services were transferred from the Railway Mail Service to the postmasters of the cities concerned.

The development of the mail truck, with its greater flexibility and mobility, soon caused the decline of the street car services, although Baltimore's existed until 1929.

Streifen: German word for "strip."

Stretta: Italian word for "cut close."

Stretto: Italian word for "narrow."

Strike: The impression of a postal marking. The term is usually used in conjunction with a condition description, such as "excellent strike," "poor strike," etc.

Though its use implies the description of a handstamped marking, the term is also used to describe machine cancels, roller cancels, etc., but this use is imprecise.

The extremely high quality of a philatelic

Strikes: A good one from Alaska, a bad one from Algeria, and an awful one from Mexico.

A strike of philatelic quality.

strike should not be used to judge the quality of a strike on run-of-the-mill items of mail.

Philatelic strikes are applied under ideal conditions with special care. This treatment cannot be expected on regular mail.

Strip: Foreign words for "strip" include strook (Dutch), bande (French), streifen (German), striscia (Italian), and tira (Spanish).

Strip: A strip of stamps comprises three or more stamps joined either vertically or horizontally. More precise usage requires that a vertical strip be called a column and a horizontal strip be termed a row.

Striscia: Italian word for "strip."

Strohgelb: German word for the color "straw."

Strook: Dutch word for "strip."

STTVUJA or VUJNA: These overprints are found on stamps of Yugoslavia and were created for use in Zone B, Trieste.

Su: The overprint "Su" on an air mail stamp of Colombia indicates that the stamp was sold in Sweden to frank mail from that country to an interior point in Colombia and carried by the Colombian airline SCADTA (q.v.).

It was also necessary that such mail be franked with appropriate Swedish stamps.

The mail would be handed either to a Colombian consulate or to an agent of the airline.

SU: Overprint on stamps of the Straits Settlements identifies stamps for Sungei Ujong.

Subject: The term "subject" is used to refer to the individual stamp printing units that make up a printing plate.

The number of subjects will vary, with a quantity of 200 in four panes of 50 being very common for US commemorative stamps.

At one time, these units were made up individually and were then locked together to form a printing plate.

These individual units were known as cliches (q.v.).

Submarine Mail: Mail has been carried in many different and unusual ways.

During times of war, the unusual often becomes the most practical, and it is difficult to apply normal standards of judging philatelic respectability. Thus it is with the best-known instance of submarine mail — one that used special postage stamps.

It came about in 1938, during Spain's civil war, when the Spanish Republican government was desperately short of foreign currency.

In his "Spotlight on Spain" column in *Stamp Collector* (Oct. 7, 1978), S. Nathan tells how the idea was born to raise foreign currency by philatelic means.

The Agencia Filatelica Oficial in Barcelona is credited with the idea of instituting a submarine mail service using special stamps to frank covers that would be carried on an underwater journey.

A set of six stamps, plus a souvenir sheet including three stamps, was produced, which the British Gibbons catalog lists in denominations of 1p, 2p, 4p, 6p, 10p, and 15p. Nathan notes that the souvenir sheet contained the 4p, 6p, and 15p denominations.

Only the lower values are reported to have been placed on sale when the stamps were released at Barcelona on Aug. 11, 1938. They were sold out in a few days.

The fund-raising idea was given a practical twist by using the submarine C4 to carry mail from Barcelona to Menorca, the only island in

A Spanish submarine mail stamp.

the Balearic group left in Republican hands. It was dangerous for surface vessels to attempt the voyage to the island city of Mahon, but a submarine could do it with much less risk.

The first and only voyage began on Aug. 12, 1938, when *C4* carried more than 300 registered covers and 100 ordinary covers bearing full sets of the stamps, plus 100 maximum cards with 1p stamps, and 200 smaller Agencia Filatelica Oficial covers, some of which were franked with the souvenir sheet and some with only the 1p stamp.

A large quantity of ordinary mail for the islanders was also taken along.

C4 arrived at Mahon on Aug. 13, 1938, and mail was unloaded while mail for the return journey was received. Nathan states that only 25 special submarine mail covers were carried back to the mainland.

The return voyage began on Aug. 14 and ended at Barcelona on the evening of Aug. 18.

American newspaper reporter Werner Kell traveled on *C4* and described the trip in a March 11, 1939, article in the *Saturday Evening Post*, titled "Stamp War."

Though the "mail service" was primarily intended as a justification for the existence of the special stamps, both stamps and covers are becoming increasingly sought after and fetch high prices when offered.

The years have given a patina of respectability to the submarine stamps, and they are an interesting example of one of philately's more unusual aspects.

The Scott catalog does not list these stamps but notes their existence in the appropriate place in its listing for Spain. It is stated that the stamps were sold at twice face value.

Another example of submarine mail concerns the two epic voyages of the German submarine *Deutschland* to the US and back to Germany during World War I.

Both voyages took place in 1916, before the US entered the war. Mail was carried and bore a special "Deutsche Tauchboot-Seepost" marking, according to Prince Dimitry Kandaouroff *(Collecting Postal History*, Larousse and Co., New York, 1974).

The Canal Zone was the location of yet another instance of submarine mail, when the US submarine *C3* carried souvenir mail through the canal between Cristobal and Balboa on May 7, 1919.

The mail was carried as souvenirs for those who subscribed to a Victory Loan drive.

Official envelopes without adhesive stamps were postmarked at Cristobal, and a receiving mark was applied at Balboa.

The mail was billed as "The First Ocean to Ocean Submarine Mail."

At a recent auction, one of these covers realized a price of $42.50.

Sucre: A unit of currency used in Ecuador. It comprises 100 centavos.

Sudan: The Democratic Republic of the Sudan has a permanent place in philately for its familiar Camel Postman (q.v.) stamp design. This is one of philately's classic designs and is said to be the work of Colonel Stanton of the British Royal Engineers stationed in the Sudan during the 1890s. The design remained in use for some 50 years.

The area that is now the Sudan was a Coptic country until the Arabs introduced Islam in the 1400s. The northern part of the land was known as Nubia.

Egypt took over the area in the early 1800s, and it eventually became the Anglo-Egyptian Sudan.

Toward the end of the 19th century, Mohammed Ahmed, the self-styled "Mahdi," led his dervishes in a rebellion that took the life of the British administrator, General Gordon, at Khartoum.

In 1898 an Anglo-Egyptian force under

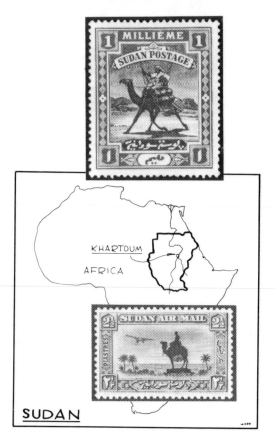

SUDAN

General Kitchener defeated the Mahdi at the Battle of Omdurman and avenged Gordon's murder. Britain and Egypt continued to operate the condominium government.

After World War II, Egypt began to demand that the agreement with Britain be terminated and in 1951 proclaimed Farouk king of Egypt and the Sudan. Britain, however, ignored the move.

In 1953, after Farouk was ousted, Britain and Egypt agreed to a three-year transition period for Sudanese independence, and the country achieved that state on Jan. 1, 1956.

Since then there has been considerable instability, and the country has vacillated between East and West.

When the US ambassador and a Belgian diplomat were murdered, the govenment freed the murderers and allowed them to leave the country.

With an area of 967,491 square miles, the Sudan is the largest country in Africa. It has a population estimated at 18,690,000. The Sudan is poor, with the latest per capita figure reported at $320 and a literacy rate of 20%.

The unit of currency is the Egyptian pound (100 piastres), which is about .50 to the US dollar.

The first stamps, issued in 1897, were overprints on Egyptian stamps, but the Camel Postman design soon followed. It continued in use for more than 50 years, the last example being released in 1954, when a trio of stamps marking self-government appeared.

Since then, stamps have been mostly political in nature and symbolic in design.

A 1931 air mail design depicting the statue of General Gordon and a 1901 postage due label showing a River Nile gunboat are outstanding and well known.

The address of the philatelic bureau is Director General, Posts and Telegraphs Department, Philatelic Section, Khartoum, Sudan.

Suez Canal Company: Shortly after the Suez Canal was opened in the late 1860s, the Suez Canal Company issued a set of four stamps to frank letters carried through the canal in its ships.

The stamps appeared in July 1868 but were withdrawn on Aug. 16, 1868, and demonetized on Aug. 31 of the same year, according to Gibbons.

The stamps had a common design featuring a steamship of the period. The inscription reads "CANAL MARITIME DE SUEZ," and the denominations are 1c, 5c, 20c, and 40c.

The Gibbons catalog notes that many forgeries exist both mint and used.

SUID AFRIKA: Inscription on some stamps of South Africa. Usually found on stamps se-tenant with English-language inscription or as part of a bilingual inscription on one stamp.

S. UJONG: Inscription on some stamps of Sungei Ujong.

Sulphuretted: Stamps originally printed in certain colors, notably shades of orange and orange-browns, will often become blackened over the years because of the action of gases in the atmosphere on constituents in the ink. These stamps are said to be sulphuretted.

It is possible to restore the original color by the use of hydrogen peroxide. (See Color Changeling.)

SULTANAT D'ANJOUAN: Stamps of the Commerce and Navigation key type of the French colonies inscribed "Sultanat d'Anjouan" were for use on the Comoro island of Anjouan (q.v.).

Sunday Delivery Labels: "Never on a Sunday" might be an appropriate title for the labels attached to Belgian stamps used between 1893 and 1914.

Also known as "Dominical Labels," they bear

A Belgian stamp with Sunday delivery tab attached.

the inscription "Ne pas livrer le Dimanche" (French) and "Niet Bestellen op Zontag" (Flemish), both translating as "Do not deliver on Sunday."

Because of religious objections to the Sunday delivery of mail, the Belgian Post Office decided to give mailers a choice as to whether their mail was to be delivered on Sunday or not.

If there was no objection, the mailer simply removed the perforated label, or tab, from the stamp before applying it; if Sunday delivery was not desired, the tab was left attached to the stamp.

Nowadays this problem no longer exists, since Sunday delivery of mail is a thing of the past in most countries, and Saturday deliveries also in many places!

The terms "Bandalette" and "Banderole" are sometimes used to describe these labels, which should only be collected attached to the stamps.

The Scott catalog notes that its prices are for the stamp with label attached; prices for stamp without label are about 50% of that figure.

There are several variations of the inscription. Some are in the form of a single line across the label for each inscription; another has an inscription on each side divided by a vertical line.

The Netherlands is reported to have had a separate label that mailers could apply to their letters to control Sunday delivery, according to Cabeen (*Standard Handbook of Stamp Collecting*, Crowell, New York, 1979).

Bulgaria has used stamps that were compulsory if mail was to be delivered on Sundays and holidays.

There was a charge for these stamps, and the money thus raised went to support medical and rest facilities for postal workers. Issued between 1925 and 1941, the stamps picture examples of these facilities.

Sungei Ujong: Sungei Ujong was a small state on the Malay Peninsula that was merged into the state of Negri Sembilan in 1895.

Beginning in 1878, Sungei Ujong had used the stamps of the Straits Settlements (q.v.) with various overprints either spelling out the name or using the letters "SU" and in a number of cases also bearing a surcharge.

In 1891 special stamps in the Leaping Tiger and Tiger Head key types were issued inscribed "S. UJONG."

After 1895, the area used the stamps of Negri Sembilan.

Suomi: Inscription found on the stamps of Finland.

Superb: A grade above very fine (q.v.), "Superb" is a term used for its impressive effect.

Since it represents a standard of condition that must be virtual perfection, its use is not often justified. (See condition.)

Supplementary Mail: Supplementary mail was that taken into a mail system after the normal closing time.

At New York, it represented mail taken to a ship after the mail pouch had gone on board. A fee was charged for this service, and items were marked "Supplementary Mail."

The service was also provided in the case of train departures. (See Late Fee.)

Surcharge: French word for "overprint."

Surcharge: Foreign words for "surcharge" include toeslag (Dutch), surtax (French), zuschlag (German), sovraprezzo (Italian), and sobretasa (Spanish).

Surcharge: A surcharge is an impression applied to an existing stamp in order to change its denomination or face value (q.v.).

It is often incorrectly called an overprint (q.v.), which is the term used to describe an inscription that changes the purpose of a stamp or that has a commemorative message.

An exception would be the case of a stamp surcharged with an additional amount that thus converts a stamp to a semi-postal (q.v.). An example from the Belgian Congo is illustrated. In this case, it would be accurate to refer to the surcharge as a surtax, but in other instances such a reference would not be correct.

Stamps can be surcharged to convert them to another denomination to fill a need caused by a temporary shortage or because of a currency change.

In recent years, the trend to decimal currency in various British areas has caused a number of sets to be surcharged pending preparation of stamps in the new currency.

Some of the most dramatic surcharges occur on the stamps of Germany during the inflation period in the 1920s (q.v.) and on Chinese stamps immediately following the end of World War II.

In 1923 surcharges of up to ten thousand million marks on 100-million-mark German stamps represented uncontrolled inflation at its most horrifying and were a contributing factor in the rise to power of Hitler and, thus, the onset of World War II.

Chinese inflation surcharges are equally as frightening as those of the earlier period in Germany. Surcharges of $5,000,000 on a $20 stamp do indicate something terribly wrong with a country's economy.

Wartime conditions and inflation are probably the most important factor in causing surcharges,

A selection of surcharged stamps. The two bilingual stamps from the Belgian Congo (1) bear a "+25c" surcharge, thus converting them to semipostal, or charity, stamps (q.v.). This surtax (q.v.) was intended to finance a monument to the dead of World War II. The Bahamas stamp (2) illustrates a surcharge made necessary by the country's conversion to decimal currency. The German stamp (3) is an example of an inflation surcharge of one thousand million marks (1,000,000,000) on a 100-mark stamp. The Tristan da Cunha (4) and Canadian stamps (5 and 6) bear normal surcharges to change their denominations.

with philatelic sales also rating pretty high as a probable cause, at least in the early days of our hobby.

Philatelic publications in the 19th century tended to get very uptight and editorialized strongly against a stream of apparently unnecessary surcharges emanating mainly from French and British colonial areas.

Though some undoubtedly resulted from poor communications, it seems clear that even in those days philatelic considerations played a big part in the creation of surcharged stamps.

A glance at the catalog listings of such places as French Guiana, Benin, British Honduras, Ceylon, North Borneo, Seychelles, etc., will indicate what appears to be either shockingly bad postal administration or a surprisingly well developed idea of what collectors of stamps could contribute to postal revenues.

Editorializing about the French colonial surcharges in the December 1893 issue of the Stanley Gibbons *Monthly Journal*, the editor wrote: "It is more than 12 months since about 320 varieties of the absolutely unnecessary articles (surcharges) were let loose upon the philatelic market, and it seems doubtful whether any of these have yet reached the places for which they were supposed to be intended."

In the same publication, in April 1894, the editor commented as follows on a report that a surcharged issue of Ceylon was to be officially destroyed!

"We trust that this will be the last issue of surcharged stamps from this country and that this will be a warning to many other places, especially in Asia, where the same thing has been going on so largely of late years." So much for the philatelic popularity of surcharged stamps!

A less-common form of surcharge occurs when a stamp is authorized to be bisected and the two halves are surcharged with a denomination, as when in 1882 Dominica created a bisected stamp by surcharging each half of a 1d stamp with a "½" denomination in three different varieties.

SURCHARGE POSTAGE:
Inscription found on postage due labels of Trinidad and Trinidad and Tobago.

Surface Printing: (See Printing, Relief.)

Surinam: Who can say which country got the best of the deal when Britain gained New Amsterdam in exchange for Surinam?

The swap occurred in 1667 under the Treaty of Breda, when Britain added the city of New Amsterdam, now better known as New York to its American colonies while the Netherlands received the South American colony of Dutch Guiana, now the Republic of Surinam.

The British had colonized the coast of South America in the area of Surinam beginning in the early 1600s.

During the Napoleonic Wars from 1799 to 1802 and again from 1804 to 1816, the British reoccupied the colony, but at the end of the period they recognized Dutch rights and restored the area to the Netherlands.

In 1922 it became a part of the Kingdom of the Netherlands and became independent as the Republic of Surinam on Nov. 25, 1975. The capital city is Paramaribo.

The country has an area of 63,250 square miles and a population estimated at 404,000. The per capita income figure is relatively high at $1,240, compared with $437 for neighboring Guyana. The unit of currency is the guilder, which in 1981 was 1.79 to the US dollar.

Surinam's first stamps were issued in 1873, and they subsequently followed a pattern similar to those of the Netherlands.

A 1967 issue commemorates the 300th anniversary of the Treaty of Breda and reproduces contemporary views of New Amsterdam, Paramaribo, and the Netherlands.

Over the years, the country has released a number of attractive issues picturing its people, culture, and scenery, and there has been a fair quantity of semi-postal issues.

The address of the philatelic bureau is Postal Administration, Philatelic Department, Paramaribo, Surinam.

Surtax: French word for "surcharge."

Surtax: A surtax is the non-postage amount in the total cost of some postage stamps. It appears on semi-postal stamps (see Stamp, Semi-Postal) as a separate figure, usually in the form of "10c + 2c" or similarly.

The additional amount, or surtax, is generally devoted to some charitable purpose and is a method long used to raise funds.

Svalbard: Formerly known as Spitsbergen, Svalbard comprises a group of islands about 400 miles north of Norway.

The group has a land area of about 25,000 square miles and was incorporated as Norwegian territory in 1925, although a Norwegian post office is reported to have been established years earlier.

Although Svalbard has never had its own official postage stamps, there have been local issues, including the item illustrated.

This is one of two denominations (10-ore brown and 20-ore red) reportedly issued in 1896 by a steamship company.

Sutton (*Stamp Collector's Encyclopedia,* Bonanza, 1966) reports that labels inscribed "Arctische Post" and "Polar Post" were created by a Captain W. Bade in 1897-98. Bade was master of a ship on the run from Norway to Svalbard. Sutton, however, states that these were souvenir labels for tourists and served no postal function. There have been other similar labels.

The main resource of the islands is coal. The

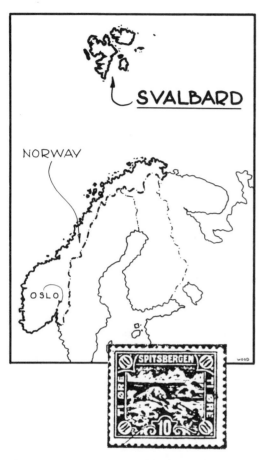

islands have rich deposits, and one mine at Barentsburg is operated by the Soviet Union.

A number of local stamps (or labels) are illustrated and noted in the *Handbook of Local Posts* by Hurt and Williams and published as volume six of *Billig's Specialized Catalogues.*

Inscriptions on the items, several of which feature a hunter and polar bear motif, vary between "Spitsbergen" and "Spidsbergen."

Svart: Swedish for "black."

SVERIGE: Inscription identifies stamps of Sweden (q.v.).

SWA: The inscription "SWA" identifies stamps of South-West Africa (q.v.). The letters are also found as an overprint on stamps of South Africa (q.v.).

Swan River Settlement: "Swan River Settlement" is an old name for the Australian colony of Western Australia, now a state of the Australian Commonwealth.

The name is sometimes found used in old stamp albums and in the philatelic literature of the period.

It does not appear to ever have been used in any official sense, and the colony's stamps were all inscribed "Western Australia" and sometimes "West Australia."

Swan's Inverted Frame: One of the world's rarities is a stamp from Western Australia (q.v.) that has been incorrectly named for many years.

It is the 4d stamp in the 1854 issue from the Australian colony and it appears to have its center inverted in relation to the frame. Nonetheless, it is not the center that is inverted, but the frame!

In philately's early days, collectors were not very familiar with stamp production methods, and it was a great puzzlement to determine how the variety could have come about at all. So it should not surprise us that they assumed that it was the center that was at fault, and since it sounds so much more impressive to speak of the "inverted swan" than a mere upside-down frame, the name stuck.

The fact that the stamp is printed in only one color contributed to the confusion, since "invert" errors usually occur in stamps printed in more than one color where separate passes through the press are required for each color.

In such a case, it is easy to see how a sheet could be sent through the press the wrong way for a subsequent color application.

But a stamp printed in one color offered no such obvious solution.

What did happen is that in the course of making up the design to be transferred to a lithographic printing stone, one frame was applied upside down. So all the centers and all but one frame were correct.

In making up the design sheet for the 4d denomination, the printers had laid out, correctly spaced, the centers of the stamps in a 60-stamp, twin-pane arrangement.

Then, according to L.N. and M. Williams (*Stamps of Fame,* Blandford Press, London, 1949), frames bearing the new 4d denomination were applied to complete the layout of the 120 designs.

It was one of these individual frames that was applied incorrectly. The completed sheet was transferred to the stone from which printing took place. The Williams tell us that it was during printing that the mistake was noted and corrected.

No one knows how many of the error were produced before it was discovered and corrected, and the few copies in existence command high prices.

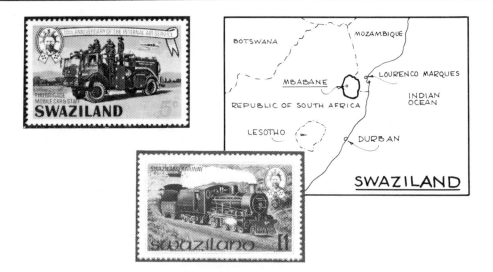

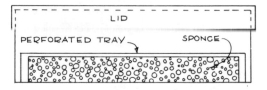

Swaziland: Swaziland is a kingdom located near where the southern border of Mozambique meets that of the Republic of South Africa.

After first being under Boer administration and then that of the governor of the Transvaal, Swaziland came under British protection in 1907.

The Swaziland royal house can be traced back for some 400 years and is one of the few remaining African dynasties

Independence was granted in 1968 and the country became a constitutional monarchy, but in 1973 the king repealed the constitution and took absolute power.

There is a customs union with the Republic of South Africa, and many citizens of Swaziland hold jobs in the republic, thus providing a significant source of income for their country.

Swaziland's area is 6,705 square miles, and the population is estimated at 550,000. The per capita income is $530 and the literacy rate is 36%.

Timber is important to the country's economy, as is the growing of corn, cotton, rice, pineapples, sugar, and citrus.

The unit of currency is the lijangeni (100 cents), which in 1981 was .82 to the US dollar.

The first stamps of Swaziland were those of the South African Republic issued in 1889 overprinted "SWAZIELAND."

From 1895, stamps of the Transvaal and its successor, the Union of South Africa, were used until 1933, when stamps of Swaziland were resumed.

The address of the philatelic bureau is Swaziland Stamp Bureau, Dept. of Posts and Telecommunications, Box 555, Mbabane, Swaziland.

Sweatbox: A sweatbox is a container with a lid. At the bottom is a damp pad or piece of sponge on top of which is a perforated tray, mesh, or similar material.

A stamp to be "unstuck" is placed on the tray and the container closed.

Some experimentation is necessary to

establish the length of time required to cause the stamp to separate from whatever it is stuck to.

This method of removal of stamps from paper or other stamps will allow a certain amount of gum to remain, but there is no way of unsticking stamps that will not cause some permanent damage to the gum.

Sweden: Sweden is a constitutional monarchy sharing the Scandinavian peninsula with Norway and fronting on the Baltic Sea.

It also includes the Baltic islands of Oland and Gotland.

By the first part of the ninth century, Christianity was being taught in Sweden by Frankish missionaries.

Before the 12th century had ended, King Eric IX had conquered Finland but was killed when Denmark attacked Sweden and began a long series of wars between the two countries.

In 1397 the Union of Kalmar united Sweden, Denmark, and Norway. But even during the

SWEDEN

100 years that the union endured, Danes were fighting the Swedes.

In the 16th century, Sweden entered a period of expansion, even to the point of occupying parts of Estonia and Poland.

Under Gustavus II, Sweden obtained Karelia and Ingermanland and became the greatest power in the Baltic area. But in 1709, Sweden was defeated by Russia and lost much of its territory across the Baltic.

During the Napoleonic Wars, Denmark was made to give up Norway to Sweden, but after Napoleon's defeat Sweden owned no territory in Europe.

The Congress of Vienna recognized Norway as part of Sweden. In 1905, however, Norway obtained its independence.

Sweden maintained its neutrality in both World Wars I and II.

The country's latest per capita income figure is $9,274, and the literacy rate is 99%. Recently, high wages have inhibited exports, and the economy has cooled.

The country's area is 173,665 square miles, and the population is estimated at 8,312,00. Industry provides the country's mainstay, but Sweden is virtually independent in food production.

The unit of currency is the krona (100 ore), which in 1981 was 4.76 to the US dollar.

Sweden's first stamps were issued in 1855 and feature the country's coat of arms. They were inscribed "SVERIGE," and the inscription continues in use.

Swedish stamps are known for the high quality of their design and production. Most issues are engraved and intaglio printed. Booklet and coil formats are mostly used.

The address of the philatelic bureau is PFA, Postens Frimarksavelining, S-105 02 Stockholm, Sweden.

Swedish Numerals: (See Numerals, Swedish.)

Swiss 'Rayed Star' 5c: As if to prove that major discoveries can still be made, even in the area of 19th-century material, a previously unknown variety of an 1878-80 Swiss postage due label was found in 1980.

H.L. Katcher of the Swiss specialist stamp firm The Amateur Collector Ltd., of London, England, was sorting a quantity of Swiss 1878-

80 postage dues when he noticed a rayed 1c that looked "different." Soon he saw why: the 1c label had a "5" as the numeral of denomination.

Since, up to then, the 1c was the only denomination with a rayed star in the background, this was indeed a "find." It currently is the only known copy, thus placing it in the company of such exotic items as the British Guiana 1c magenta of 1856 and the Swedish three-skilling banco color error, both of which are the only known representatives of their kind.

This Swiss postage due is canceled "Bissegg," according to Katcher, and is said to be a sound copy, although somewhat off center.

How did the variety come about? It was originally intended, says Katcher, that all values of that issue should have the rayed star background, but during the printing of the 1c it was found that the lines forming the rays were too fine and quickly clogged with ink.

Permission was granted by the postal authorities to remove the star and rays from the other denominations in the series.

The frames were all printed from a printing base made up of 200 cliches (250 cliches were made). Figures of denomination were added in

a separate press run. Thus no printing plates were duplicated from the cliches.

When the rays and star were removed, it should have been impossible to produce any further postage dues with a rayed star background.

Katcher offers the possible explanation that during later printing, one cliche became damaged and was replaced with one of the extra 50, which may not have had the rayed star removed.

Another possibility, according to Katcher, is that during the application of the 1c numeral, one may have become defective and could have been accidently replaced with a numeral "5."

Yet a third answer might be that since the printer was not happy with the results of the 1c value using the rayed star, he might have made up a small "plate" using some numeral "5s" to show postal authorities how poor the results would be, and it might be that this single copy "escaped" from a sheet the printer kept for his records.

Regardless of how it may have come about, it is interesting that such an item should have remained undiscovered for more than 100 years. Swiss experts are reported to have authenticated the item as being genuine.

Swiss Soldier Stamps: Swiss soldier stamps are issued to those serving in Swiss military units and are placed on their mail to indicate it is not to be assessed postal charges.

The first such stamps is reported to have been issued in 1915, and over the years a very large number of different designs have appeared. It is estimated that there are now more than 3,000 different soldier stamps.

Their collection is a popular sideline in Swiss philately. Amateur Collector Ltd., in its *Switzerland Catalogue*, though it does not list them individually, stating that there are too many, does offer them in packets of all different examples up to a quantity of 1,000. The publisher notes that Swiss soldier stamps are listed in the Sulser catalogue/ handbook. (See Stamp, Military.)

Switzerland: Known to the Romans as Helvetia, Switzerland is a federal republic comprising 23 cantons, or districts.

The Swiss Confederation gained independence from the Holy Roman Empire in 1648.

It has not been involved in a foreign war since 1515, and its policy of armed neutrality has kept it out of NATO and the United Nations,

although it is the headquarters of a number of UN agencies.

In the period between the two world wars, it was the headquarters of the League of Nations.

Switzerland is located in central Europe adjoining Italy, Austria, Liechtenstein, West Germany, and France. The capital city is Bern, and the largest city is Zurich.

The area of the country is 15,941 square miles, and the population is estimated at 6,343,000.

It is a mountainous country, with most of its area located between the Alps and the Jura Mountains. The principal river system is the Rhine and its tributaries.

The economy is based on industry, including machinery and watches. Cheese and chocolate, banking, and tourism are also important.

The per capita income figure is $15,455, and the literacy rate is 99%. The unit of currency is the Swiss franc (100 centimes), which in 1981 was 2.02 to the US dollar.

The first stamps were the cantonal issues for Zurich (1843), Geneva (1843), and Basel (1845).

The first federal issue came in 1850, and since then Switzerland's stamps have continued to reflect its history, culture, and scenic beauty. The country's semi-postal issues include the annual and popular Pro Juventute and Pro Patria issues.

There have also been a number of Officials and issues for the international organizations located in the country.

The address of the philatelic bureau is Philatelic Service PTT, Parkterrasse 10, CH-3030 Bern, Switzerland.

Switzerland, International Bureaus:

When the League of Nations was formed following World War I, it established its headquarters in Geneva, Switzerland.

The Swiss Post Office provided special stamps for use from the league offices from 1922.

These were Swiss stamps overprinted "SOCIETE DES NATIONS," "SERVICE DE LA SOCIETE DES NATIONS," and "COURRIER DE LA SOCIETE DES NATIONS."

The International Labor Office used Swiss stamps beginning in 1923. They were overprinted "S.d.N. Bureau International du Travail," "SERVICE DU BUREAU INTERNATIONAL DU TRAVAIL," and "COURRIER DU BUREAU INTERNATIONAL DU TRAVAIL."

Issues for the International Labor Office continued after WWII under the United Nations (q.v.), and from 1952 specially designed stamps were used.

The International Bureau of Education used Swiss stamps from 1944 overprinted "COURRIER DU BUREAU INTERNATIONAL D'EDUCATION," "BIE" (vertically), and "BUREAU INTERNATIONAL D'EDUCATION."

Specially designed stamps were issued beginning in 1958.

The World Health Organization used Swiss

stamps from 1948 overprinted "ORGANIZA-TION MONDIALE DE LA SANTE" until 1957, when specially designed stamps were released.

The International Organization for Refugees used Swiss stamps from 1950 overprinted "ORGANIZATION INTERNATIONALE POUR LES REFUGIES."

The United Nations European Office used Swiss stamps from 1950 overprinted "NATIONS UNIES/ Office Europeen," and specially designed stamps inscribed "NATIONS UNIES/ HELVETIA" until Oct. 4, 1969, when United Nations stamps in Swiss currency denominations were put into use. These have continued.

The World Meteorological Organization has used specially designed stamps since 1956. They are inscribed "ORGANISATION METEOROLOGIQUE MONDIALE/ HELVETIA."

The International Bureau of the Universal Postal Union has used specially designed stamps since 1957. They are inscribed "UNION POSTALE UNIVERSELLE."

The International Telecommunication Union has used specially designed stamps since 1958. They are inscribed "UNION INTERNA-TIONALE DES TELECOMMUNICATIONS."

Sydney Views: The 1850-51 issues of the Australian colony of New South Wales feature the seal of the colony, which incorporates what

is said to be a view of the capital city of Sydney.

The issues have thus come to be known as the "Sydney Views." (See New South Wales.)

These stamps have been extensively studied for their numerous variations of paper, color, and engraving. Nowadays their high price places them out of reach of any but wealthy collectors.

Syli (100 caury): Unit of currency used in the Republic of Guinea (q.v.)

Syllabic Characters: Syllabic characters are small characters believed to denote plate numbers on stamps and postal stationery of Japan in 1874-75.

Syncopated Perforations: (See Perforations, Syncopated.)

Syria: The area that is now the Arab Republic of Syria possessed an advanced culture as early as the 16th century BC.

Syria has known many masters in the years since then, including the Egyptians, Hittites, Chaldeans, Persians, and Romans.

Alexander the Great conquered it, and since Jerusalem was then within its borders, it was a target of the Crusades.

The widespread fighting to which the country was subjected made it poor, and the Mongol invasion of 1260 completed the ruin.

Syria was included in the Turkish Ottoman Empire, where it remained for 400 years, until the end of World War I.

The opening of the Suez Canal in 1869 removed much of Syria's importance as an overland route to the East.

World War I had a great impact on Syria, as General Allenby's forces liberated it from Turkish rule, promising independence in return for Arab help against the Turks.

At the war's end, the area came under French occupation, as the British retained Palestine and Trans-Jordan, giving control of the Lebanon-Syria area to the French.

France obtained a mandate from the League of Nations and divided the area into Lebanon and Syria, with several areas receiving short-lived autonomy.

French rule generated great anti-French sentiment, especially when France refused to ratify a treaty it had worked out with Syria to grant its freedom. The best Syria got was the status of an autonomous republic under French control in 1934.

After the fall of France during WWII, the Vichy government gained control of Syria, and a joint British-Free French force liberated the country in 1941.

The Free French promised independence, and Syrian elections were held in 1943. Full independence came on Jan. 1, 1944. But still the French persisted in trying to hang on to direction of Syrian afairs, and fighting broke out in 1945. The British army intervened and extracted the French, and Syria became a member of the United Nations shortly thereafter.

Political instability has marked the postwar years, and there have been many changes of government.

In 1958 Syria and Egypt merged to form the

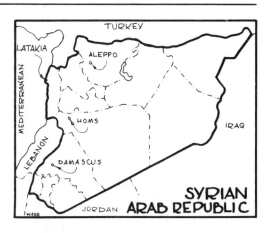

United Arab Republic, but the marriage was weak, and in 1961 the divorce became final.

Syria has remained a firm foe of Israel. The disputed Golan Heights, from which Syria had long shelled settlements in Israel, were taken in 1967 and are still occupied by Israeli forces.

In 1976 Syrian troops entered Lebanon to control the civil war raging in that country.

Syria covers some 71,498 square miles and has a population estimated in 1978 at 8,980,000. Most of the inhabitants live in the western part of the country, especially along the 100-mile coastal strip. The latest per capita income is $702.

The first Syrian stamps were those of France in 1919 overprinted "T.E.O." (Territoires Ennemis Occupes) and surcharged in Egyptian currency.

The overprint was later changed to "O.M.F."

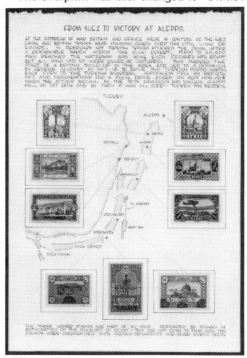

A page from a topical collection about World War I which illustrates the British campaign against Turkey that resulted in the creation of Syria.

(Occupation Militaire Francaise). From 1920, stamps were in Syrian currency.

During the 1930s, stamps were released showing many of Syria's scenic and historical attractions.

The brief marriage with Egypt sparked identical stamp designs, but in different currencies, making it simple to distinguish the Syrian and Egyptian issues.

For a brief period in 1919, the British "E.A.F." stamps of Palestine were handstamped "The Arab Government" in Arabic and used in parts of Syria.

The unit of currency is the Syrian pound, which in 1981 was 3.93 to the US dollar.

The address of the philatelic bureau is Receveur Principal des Postes, Service Philatelique, Damascus, Syrian Arab Republic. (See Alaouites; Kilis; Latakia; Lebanon; and Levant, French.)

Szechwan: (See China, Regional Issues of.)

Szeged Issues: Szeged is a town in Hungary just across the border from Yugoslavia, to the north of Belgrade.

In 1919 a Hungarian National Government was set up there by Admiral Horthy, while the town was occupied by French forces as a result of the World War I defeat of the Austro-Hungarian Empire.

Hungarian stamps were released overprinted "MAGYAR NEMZET KORMANY" (Hungarian National Government) around the sides and top, with "Szeged, 1919" at the bottom.

Some stamps were also surcharged, and numerous counterfeits exist.

Admiral Horthy was educated at the Austro-Hungarian Naval Academy at Fiume. At the end of WWI, he organized the National Government, which was successful in opposing a Communist government under Bela Kun.

Some ''S'' country stamps.

T: Prior to the introduction of stamps overprinted "O.S." in 1874 for general Official use, South Australia used a number of different overprints to indicate use by specific government departments.

The overprint "T" stood for Treasurer.

T: The letter "T" represents the internationally recognized symbol for "postage due." When it is either stamped or written on an item of mail, it indicates that the item is insufficiently

prepaid and that there is additional postage to be collected.

The letter "T" is often incorporated in a circular or rectangular box together with the amount due.

It stands for the French word "taxe."

In recent years, the use of special postage due labels (q.v.) has declined, and it is common to see the "T" marking on short-paid international mail.

T, TAX, or TAXE: These markings applied by handstamp indicate postage due. Usually accompanied by manuscript amount due (See T, above.)

T: The letter "T" in a circle overprinted on stamps of Peru indicates stamps for the province of Huacho (q.v.).

T (in four corners): A stamp with a numeral in the center and the letter "T" in the four corners is a 1901-22 postage due label of the Dominican Republic.

T: The letter "T" perforated in stamps of Tasmania indicates an Official stamp.

Tab: When a portion of the selvage of a stamp sheet is left attached to a stamp, it is described as a tab.

Sometimes, these margin portions bear an in-

scription, and such stamp issues are often collected with the inscribed tab still attached. The stamps of Israel are a good example of the popularity of collecting stamps with tabs. Israel's stamps are normally printed in sheets in which the bottom row of stamps only can exist with attached tabs.

The term "tab" can also be used to describe that portion of a booklet pane that is used to fasten it into a stamp booklet. The method of binding the panes can be either by stapling, stitching, or gluing.

Booklet panes are considered more desirable when collected with the narrow binding tab still attached.

Tablet: The term "tablet" is used to describe an area in a stamp design that is set off to contain the denomination by framing or boxing an area within which the denomination is located.

This tablet or panel is most commonly seen on key type issues such as those used by various British colonies for so many years. The French Peace and Commerce key type is another good example.

Tache: French word for "stain."

Tael: A unit of currency used in China until 1897. It was composed of 10 mace.

Tagging: (See Phosphorescent.)

Tahiti: Tahiti is one of the Society Islands located in the South Pacific. Its capital city is Papeete, which is now the capital of French Polynesia (q.v.).

From 1882, it had its own stamps. At first, these were overprints on stamps of the French Colonies, but later, the issues of the French Oceanic Settlements were overprinted.

The last issue was a pair of Red Cross stamps released in 1915.

Tai Han (Tae Han): This is the name sometimes used for the country of Korea within that country.

According to the *Encyclopedia Britannica*, it was used generally from 1897 to 1910. (See Korea.)

Taille-douce: French term referring to intaglio printing. (See Printing, Intaglio.)

Taiwan: The island of Taiwan (Formosa) contains the Republic of China. (See China.)

Taka (100 paisa): Unit of currency used in Bangladesh (q.v.).

TAKCA: Inscription on early postage due labels of Bulgaria.

TAKSE PULU: Inscription on postage due labels of Turkey.

Tala: A unit of currency used in Western Samoa. It is made up of 100 sene.

Talari: An alternative spelling of the Ethiopian "thaler."

Tamano: Spanish word for "size."

Tambala: A unit of currency used by Malawi since 1970. One hundred tambala equal one kwacha.

Tanga: A unit of currency used in Portuguese India. There were 16 tangas to the rupia.

Tanganyika: (See Tanzania.)

TANGER: The inscription "TANGER" identifies Spanish stamps for use in Tangier, North Africa, and was also used on French stamps for use in Tangier's International Zone from 1918 to 1924.

Tangier: Beginning in 1927, British stamps were overprinted "TANGIER" for use at British post offices in the Tangier International Zone. They were discontinued on April 30, 1957.

Stanley Gibbons notes that such stamps were

also valid for use in Great Britain from 1950 and warns collectors that stamps postmarked in Great Britain are worth considerably less than those used in the Tangier International Zone. (See Morocco.)

Tangier, French Post Offices in: (See Morocco.)

Tangier, Spanish Post Offices in: In 1929 Spain issued stamps for use at its post offices in the International Zone of Tangier, an enclave around the city of Tangier located on the Atlantic coast of Morocco, just to the west of the Strait of Gibraltar.

A total of 46 stamps was issued, according to Scott, and they included regular issues, semi-postals, air mails, a special delivery stamp, and a semi-postal special deliver.

The stamps are inscribed "TANGER." (See Morocco, Spanish; and Morocco.)

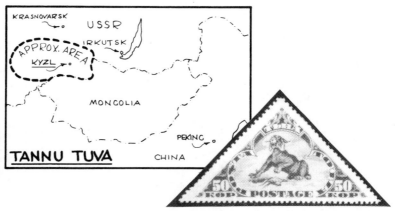

Tannu Tuva:
Now incorporated into the USSR, Tannu Tuva is known as the Tuva Autonomous Soviet Socialist Republic. The capital and chief city is Kyzl.

Russia began to eye the area in 1870 and by World War I had made it a protectorate. For all practical purposes, the area then was already part of Siberia.

Its inhabitants, however, took advantage of the confusion caused by the 1917 revolution in Russia to proclaim independence under the name of Tannu Tuva.

China and Mongolia protested its separation from Mongolia, and a commission was appointed to determine its status. The result was that Mongolia recognized the independence of Tannu Tuva in 1926. But the Russian bear had not changed, despite its revolution, and in 1944 the area was taken over by the USSR and continues as a part of that country.

Its area is about 64,000 square miles, and the population is believed to be about 65,000.

With independence came the first stamps. Issued in 1926, the first set depicts a symbol described as a "wheel of eternity."

This was followed in 1927 by a set of stamps in various shapes featuring scenes of the country.

Controversy has surrounded the issues of 1934-36. These are large, in assorted sizes and shapes, and picture the landscape of Tannu Tuva, its wildlife, and its people. Young collectors of the 1930s loved them, even though catalogs did not recognize them and they were generally regarded as bogus.

Nonetheless, the Gibbons catalog now includes them with a statement that the editors are satisfied that the stamps were in fact available for use in the country and were so used. Other catalog editors continue to have their doubts.

With the Soviet takeover, stamps of Tannu Tuva ceased.

Tanzania:
The United Republic of Tanzania began its philatelic life as the colony of German East Africa, but its history goes back a great deal further.

From the first century AD, there was trading between Arabia and the coastal area of what is now Tanzania.

The Portuguese and French were active in the area, and the slave and ivory trades prospered, causing penetration by Arab traders as far as Lake Nyasa (Lake Malawi).

Sir Richard Burton and John Hanning Speke explored East Africa, and David Livingston traveled through the area trying to halt the trade in slaves.

Missionary interest began to develop by the 1860s, but it was Germany that introduced European influence in what was to become Tanzania.

Dr. Karl Peters and Gustav Nachtigal were the founders of the German Colonial Society in 1884. The unification of Germany in 1870-71 led to the development of an intensely nationalistic state with the ambition of catching up with other European nations in the acquisition of a colonial empire.

An Anglo-German agreement in 1886 divided East Africa, with Germany taking the southern portion. In 1891 the German government declared a protectorate over what then became German East Africa.

The Germans' administrative methods did not endear them to the natives, and there was considerable unrest, which was not effectively put down until 1907.

World War I cost Germany its colonial empire, including German East Africa, which, even though cut off from the sea when the British occupied Mafia Island (q.v.) at the mouth of the Rufiji River, was successfully defended until the end of the war.

The Treaty of Versailles gave Britain a man-

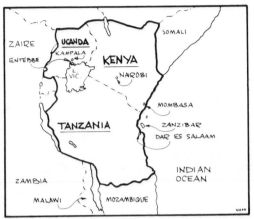

date over the area except for Ruanda-Urundi, which was transferred to Belgian administration in 1918 and is now the republics of Burundi (q.v.) and Rwanda (q.v.).

The Kionga area became a Portuguese mandate in September 1919 and is administered by the Republic of Mozambique to this day.

Renamed Tanganyika Territory, the country made considerable progress until the depression and WWII caused setbacks in economic growth.

In December 1961, Tanganyika became independent under Prime Minister Julius Nyerere.

On Dec. 9, 1962, it became a republic within the British Commonwealth. The new republic and the People's Republic of Zanzibar (q.v.) merged in 1964 to become the United Republic of Tanzania.

The first stamps of the area came in 1893 under the German administration and were stamps of Germany surcharged for use in the colony. These were followed in 1900 by the Kaiser's Yacht key type inscribed "Deutsch Ostafrika."

In 1916 stamps of Nyasaland were issued overprinted "N.F." (Nyasa-Rhodesia Force), and in 1917 stamps of Kenya were overprinted "G.E.A." German East Africa stamps were overprinted "Mafia Island" (q.v.), and Indian Expeditionary Force stamps overprinted "I.E.F." were used.

Belgian Congo stamps were also overprinted and used in the area of Belgian occupation.

Stamps under the British mandate were released in 1922 inscribed "Tanganyika," and in 1927 this was changed to "Mandated Territory of Tanganyika."

From 1935, Tanganyika was part of a postal union and used stamps inscribed "Kenya, Uganda, Tanganyika." These continued until 1963, although issues of the independent state of Tanganyika began in 1961.

Following a 1967 issue inscribed "Tanganyika and Zanzibar," stamps with the inscription "Tanzania" have been used. Zanzibar joined to form that country on July 1, 1968.

Tanganyika, later Tanzania, shared the issues of the East Africa Postal and Telecommunications Administration from 1964 to 1977. (See East Africa.)

One issue in 1966 bearing the name of Tanzania was valid only in Zanzibar.

The population of Tanzania is estimated at 17,400,000, and the latest per capita income figure is $253.

The unit of currency is the shilling, which in 1981 was 8.23 to the US dollar.

The address of the philatelic bureau is East Africa Posts and Telecommunications, Dept. of Posts, Box 9070, Dar-es-Salaam, Tanzania.

Tapling, Thomas Keay:

Thomas Keay Tapling (1855-1891) was a collector by 1865 and continued his interest in philately through his years at Harrow and at Cambridge University.

After completing his education, he joined the London Philatelic Society, later the Royal Philatelic Society, London, and became one of the early philatelic students.

He worked in a day when there was little literature to aid the philatelist, and collectors had to learn by gaining knowledge from the study of the actual material.

His will specified that after his death the enormous collection he had accumulated was to go to the British Museum and that it was not to be dispersed or sold by the museum.

The collection was mounted and placed on public display.

In addition to his comprehensive collection,

the name of Tapling lives on in the form of the Tapling Medal, which is awarded by the Royal Philatelic Society, London, for the best paper read to the society during the two years prior to the award.

Tartu: (See German Occupation of Estonia.)

TASA: Inscription on postage due labels of Uruguay.

TASA POR COBRAR: Inscription on postage due labels of Cuba.

Tasmania: Although its discoverer, the Dutch navigator Abel Tasman, named it Van Diemen's Land for the then-governor general of the East Indies, the shield-shaped island to the south of Australian mainland now bears his own name.

Tasman had come across the island in 1642, during a voyage to discover a route from the Indian Ocean to the Pacific.

Later it was visited by both British and French explorers, including Cook, Bass, Flinders, Furneaux, and Bligh.

The British were the first to establish a settlement. In 1804 they landed at the site of what is now the capital city of Hobart. A second settlement followed in 1806 at Launceston, and the island became a British colony in 1825.

The first stamps came on Nov. 1, 1853, in the form of very primitive profiles of Queen Victoria. These were followed by the extremely beautiful stamps featuring the Chalon Portrait (q.v.) of the Queen.

The earliest settlers, both free and convict, had come from Norfolk Island. By 1828 the total population had reached 17,000; by 1848 it was 70,000.

A period of economic depression ensued between 1857 and 1880 as a result of the discovery of gold in Victoria and the protectionist policies of that colony on the mainland.

The economy, however, improved after 1880 as local industries and agriculture developed.

In 1901 Tasmania became a member of the Australian Federation and is now its smallest state.

Even today, the absence of a large local market is a handicap, but the island is fortunate in possessing two-thirds of Australia's hydroelectric capacity.

In 1961 the total population of Tasmania was some 115,900.

The island is separated from the mainland of Australia by the 150-mile-wide Bass Strait and has a length of 180 miles with a width of 190 miles.

The total area, including King Island, the Furneax group, and Macquarie Island, is 26,215 square miles.

With federation and the arrival of Australian stamps, the issues of Tasmania ceased.

Reportedly, Tasmania has the dubious honor

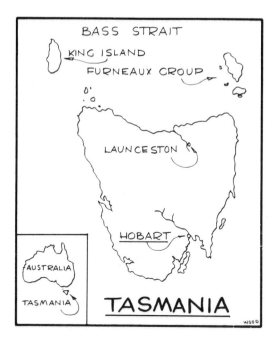

TASMANIA

of being the only country to possess a postmaster who suggested that philately be outlawed!

In 1864, following a number of requests for a stamp that proved bogus, the harrassed postmaster expressed regret that the hobby had come to Tasmania and suggested that it be banned by law, according to Robson Lowe's *Encyclopedia*.

TASSA GAZZETTE: Inscription identifies a newspaper tax stamp of the Italian state of Modena. It was issued in 1859 and represented a tax collected on newspapers mailed from foreign countries.

Tavola: Italian word for "plate."

TAXA DE FACTAGIU: Inscription found on some Parcel Post stamps of Romania.

TAXA DE GUERRA: War tax overprint found on stamps for Portuguese Africa, Portuguese Guinea, Portuguese India, and Macao. It translates as "war tax."

TAXA DE PLATA: Inscription on postage due labels of Romania.

TAXA DEVIDA: Inscription on postage due labels of Brazil.

Tax Label, Compulsory: Compulsory tax labels are adhesives that must be applied to mail at specific times in addition to normal postage.

Many countries have used this method of tax-

Compulsory tax labels of Berlin and Colombia.

ation to raise money for specific purposes.

The illustrated label from Berlin was used to help pay the cost of mail-handling during the blockade of Berlin by the Soviet Union in 1948.

The label from Colombia was to raise money for a new communications building.

Such labels pay no part of the postal charges and thus can be considered Cinderella items.

Tax Paid Stamp: (See Stamp, Tax Paid.)

TAX RECEBIDA: Inscription found on 1946 air mail issue of Mozambique.

Taylor, Samuel Allan: A man who would become infamous in the world of philately, S. Allan Taylor (1838-1913) was born in the small fishing village of Irvine, Ayrshire, a few miles south of Glasgow, Scotland.

In 1850 he went to the US, later moving to Montreal, where in 1864 he began publishing

The rogue himself.

The Stamp Collector's Record, the first philatelic publication in North America.

A few years later, after moving to Boston, he became leader of the Boston Gang, a group of philatelic forgers. One of his most audacious exploits was the creation of a bogus stamps for "Kers City Post" on which he reproduced his own likeness! He also is said to have added a phony 10c value in the 1872 issue of Prince Edward Island.

He was three times charged with counterfeiting, in 1887, 1890, and 1891, but according to Dr. Varro E. Tyler *(Philatelic Forgers: Their Lives and Works,* Robson Lowe, London, 1976), the charges were either dropped or sentence was deferred. It seems, however, that he was sufficiently alarmed to give up his life of philatelic crime.

Taylor is buried at Everett, Mass.

In his book, Tyler quotes the following from Taylor's last price list: "These cancelled facsimile stamps have been provided for the purpose of meeting the wants of that class of collector whose object is knowledge of the stamp issues of the world, and not aimless acquisition. They are cancelled and have holes around the edges and serve every purpose of originals." A fitting memorial to a rogue with a highly developed, if somewhat warped sense of humor. (See S. Allan Taylor Society.)

TC: The overprint "TC" on stamps of Cochin were for use in Travancore-Cochin, a state in India.

TCHAD: Inscription identifies stamps of Chad, in Central Africa.

Tchad, Republique du: (See Chad.)

Tchongking (Chungking): In 1902 an Indo-Chinese post office was opened in Chungking.

From 1903, stamps of Indo-China were overprinted "TCHONGKING," or "Tch'ong K'ing," and surcharged with the denomination in Chinese characters.

T.C.Postalari: This inscription is found on a 1931 set of Turkey issued to mark the Second Balkan Conference.

TE BETAAL: Inscription on postage due labels of South Africa and South West Africa.

TE BETALEN PORT: Inscription found on postage due labels of the Dutch East Indies, the Netherlands, Surinam, and the Netherlands Antilles.

Teeth: The projecting portion or tips of a stamp's perforations. Prior to separation, they make up the bridge between the perforation holes.

The term "teeth" can also be applied to similar projections left by some rouletting patterns.

TEHERAN: In 1902 stamps of Persia were overprinted "P.L. Teheran," with the letters "P.L." standing for "Poste Locale."

Telecommunications Study Unit: (See American Topical Association Study Units.)

Telegraph Stamp: (See Stamp, Telegraph.)

Temesvar Issues: Temesvar was a town in the Hungarian portion of the Austro-Hungarian Empire prior to the end of World War I.

Hungarian stamps were overprinted during the 1919 Serbian occupation.

The overprints read "Banat, Bacska 1919" in various forms, together with surcharges and "Koztarsasag" (republic) overprints.

The area was later divided between Yugoslavia and Romania, with the town of Temesvar going to Romania. It is now named Timisoara and is located south of Arad (q.v.).

Hungarian stamps were also surcharged for use in the Temesvar area by Romanian occupation authorities, which took over when the Serbian army evacuated.

Tempo: A unit of currency once used in Korea. It was composed of 100 moons.

T.E.O.: Stands for "Territories Ennemis Occupes" and is found overprinted on French stamps for use in occupied Syria during World War II.

T.E.O. CILICIE: Overprinted on stamps of Turkey for use in occupied Cilicia during World War I.

Terne: French word for "dull," as in dull color.

Terre de Sienne: French expression for the color "sienna."

TERRES AUSTRALES ET ANTARCTIQUES FRANCAISE: Inscription on stamps of the French Southern Antarctic Territories.

TERRITOIRE DE FEZZAN: Inscribed on stamps for use during the French occupation of Southern Libya.

TERRITOIRE DE L'ININI: Overprinted on stamps of French Guiana for use in the interior province of Inini.

Territorial Cover: A territorial cover in US philatelic terminology is one bearing postal markings indicating that it originated in a territory of the United States.

Such covers are widely sought by students of US postal history.

TERRITORIOS DEL AFRICA OCCIDENTAL ESPONOLA: Identifies stamps of Spanish West Africa.

TERRITORIOS ESPANOLES DEL GOLFO DE GUINEA: Inscription on some early stamps of Spanish Guinea.

Teruel: In 1868-69, provisional stamps were issued for use in the Spanish province of Teruel.

They comprise seven values of Spain's regular issue handstamped "HPN" in an oval.

Good forgeries of these are known, according to Scott.

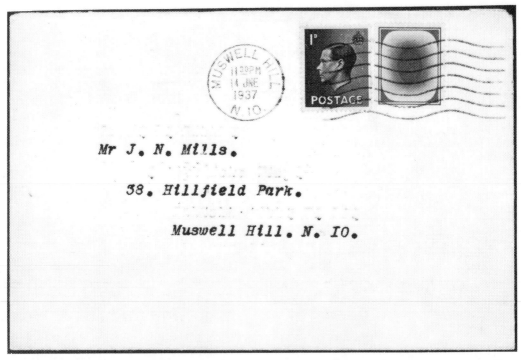

A British testing label that passed through the post in 1937 as a ½d stamp to make up the then letter rate of 1½d. This is the so-called "Poached Egg Stamp."

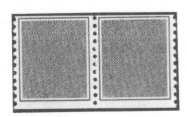

Two types of US testing labels.

Testing labels: These are labels simulating postage stamps and are used to test postage stamp vending machines.

In Great Britain during the 1930s, a type of label used for this purpose became known as a "Poached Egg Stamp" because of its supposed resemblance to that dish.

About 1936-37, a quantity of these labels "escaped" into philatelic hands. Some of these labels were used on cover and passed through the British postal system without being assessed postage due.

The cover illustrated bears a King Edward VIII 1d stamp and a green "Poached Egg Stamp," which passed as a ½d stamp to make up the then-current 1½d letter rate.

A later British testing label is inscribed "For Testing Purposes Only."

The United States Post Office has also used similar testing labels, and two types are illustrated.

These gummed, stamp-size labels are produced in coil format in order to exactly duplicate the action of a stamp in a vending machine.

Tete: A district of Zambezia in Portuguese East Africa, Tete used stamps of Mozambique until 1913.

From 1913 to 1920, it had its own stamps. These first comprised stamps of the Vasco da Gama issue of the Portuguese colonies overprinted "REPUBLICA TETE," followed in 1914 by the Ceres key type inscribed "TETE."

From 1920, Tete used stamps of Mozambique.

The capital of the district is the town of Tete,

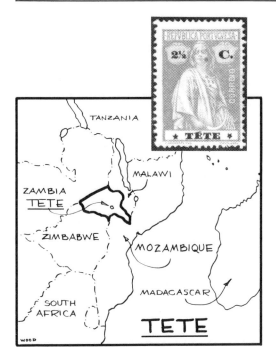

TETE

TETUAN (TETOUAN)

fer many examples.

In the early days of French stamp production, tete-beche varieties occurred when a cliche (q.v.) was placed in the printing plate upside down in relation to the others.

It is possible for dissimilar stamps to exist both tete-beche and se-tenant (q.v.) simultaneously.

Tetuan (Tetouan): The town of Tetuan is located some 10 miles from the Mediterranean on the peninsula of Africa that juts up towards Spain at the Strait of Gibraltar.

It is the capital of Tetuan Province and the Jabalah region of Morocco.

A corsair stronghold in the 14th century, it became populated by muslim refugees from Spain.

Spain occupied the town in 1860 and again in 1913, when it became the residence of the Spanish high commissioner.

In 1908 stamps of the Spanish offices in Morocco were overprinted diagonally with the name "TETUAN" for use at the Spanish post office in the town.

Tetuan later became the capital of the protectorate of Spanish Morocco. (See Morocco, Spanish.)

Texas Postal History Society: The Texas Postal History Society exists to encourage the collection and study of the postal history of Texas.

Its publication, the quarterly *Texas Postal History Society Journal*, contains articles and serves as a means of informing members of news and information pertaining to the subject.

Information may be obtained from Dr. William H.P. Emery, 1421 Schulle Dr., San Marcos, TX 78666.

located on the Zambezi River. It was established by the Portuguese in the mid-1500s.

The area of the Tete district was 36,041 square miles, and the population is estimated at about 500,000.

The area is now part of the People's Republic of Mozambique. (See Mozambique.)

Tete-beche: A French expression used in philately to refer to stamps joined together, one of which is inverted in relation to the other.

Naturally, such varieties must be left unsevered, since, once separated, the stamps are normal.

Most tete-beche varieties come about in the course of printing stamps in specially arranged sheets for stamp booklet production. Germany and Switzerland, to name just two countries, of-

A tete-beche pair from Germany.

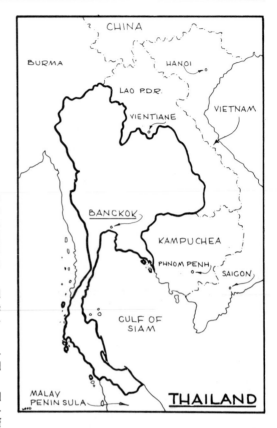

Thailand: Once known as Siam, the area that is now the Kingdom of Thailand can trace its history back to the middle of the sixth century. At that time, the Thai people moved into the area. By AD 1160 they had penetrated to the tip of the Malay Peninsula, and by 1284 east to Cambodia.

A Thai kingdom was established by 1350, and it flourished for the next 400 years, until the Burmese invaded the country. But Burma's incursion was brief.

In 1826 Britain and Thailand signed a commercial treaty, and British influence in Thailand was strong during the 19th century.

The Thai government and France disputed the border with Indo-China, and France prevailed upon Thailand to give up territory. Part of the Malay Peninsula was transferred to Britain in 1909.

In World War I, Thailand sided with the Allies, but in WWII it declared war on Britain and the US when Japan attacked Pearl Harbor.

In return, Thailand received some of the territory that Japan had conquered. However, with the defeat of Japan, Thailand was forced to return it. Since then, Thailand has followed a pro-Western policy.

The country's economy is based on rice, of which it is the world's largest single exporter. Milled rice is the keystone of Thailand's income. Tin is the most important mineral, and Thailand produces more than any other country.

The latest per capita income figure is $444 and the literacy rate 82%. The unit of currency is the baht, which in 1981 was 20.78 to the US dollar.

The population is estimated at 46,687,000.

The first stamps were issued in 1883 and feature King Chulalongkom. Most of the succeeding issues of the 19th century were surcharges, and during the first half of the 20th century, comparatively few stamps were issued. Recent issues depict a wide variety of Thailand's culture, flora, and fauna, plus its architectural beauty.

The address of the philatelic bureau is Philatelic Promotion Center, Posts and Telegraphs, Bangkok 5, Thailand.

Thai Philately, Society for: The

Society for Thai Philately exists to serve collectors of the stamps and postal history of Thailand (Siam).

Its quarterly journal, *Thai Philately,* offers articles and news. The group holds auctions, publishes monographs, and offers a translation service.

Information may be obtained from Gary A. Van Cott, Box 1118, Aiea, HI 96701.

Thaler: A currency unit widely used in

Europe and from which the word "dollar" is derived. It was "thaler" in German and "daler" in low German.

The word "thaler" is an abbreviation of "Joachimsthaler," a large silver coin picturing St. Joachim, first minted about 1518, from silver mined at Joachimsthal, Bohemia.

One famous thaler is the Maria Theresa thaler (dollar) used in international trade and still circulating in Middle East areas.

The thaler was a unit of currency in a number

of German areas, including the German states of Brunswick, Hanover, Mecklenburgh-Strelitz, Oldenburg, and Saxony, plus the northern district of the Thurn and Taxis postal service.

It was also used in the North German Confederation and the northern district of the German Empire.

The African country of Ethiopia used a currency unit known as the thaler from 1936.

The Gambia:
Once a British colony, the Republic of The Gambia claims to be the only functioning democracy in Africa.

It began in 1618, when James I of England granted a charter to a company to trade with The Gambia.

A settlement was established on the Gambia River, but wars with France resulted in considerable instability in the area.

A British protectorate was not established until 1894, following an 1889 agreement on boundaries. But the Gambia is recognized as the oldest British colony in Africa, on the basis of a 1588 sale of treaty rights to England by the Portuguese, although this did not result in European settlement of the area at that time.

During World War II, The Gambia was an aerial staging post on the route from the United States to the Middle and Far East.

The colony was granted independence in 1965, and in 1970 The Gambia became a republic within the British Commonwealth. There has been political unrest, and in 1981 a coup was attempted.

In December 1981, The Gambia agreed to a merger with the Republic of Senegal, effective Feb. 1, 1982. The new name of the combined countries is Senegambia (q.v.).

Peanuts are the country's main export, although some rice is grown.

The unit of currency is the dalasy (100 bututs), which in 1981 was 1.85 to the US dollar.

The latest per capita income figure is $275, and the literacy rate is 12%. Severe famine struck the country in 1977-78.

The land area of the country is 4,000 square miles, and the estimated population is 600,000.

The Gambia's first stamps were the famous "Cameos," or embossed heads of Queen Victoria. Following these, the British Empire key types were used until 1922, when the King George V issue featured the elephant badge of the colony.

In recent years, a moderate stamp-issuing policy has been maintained, and stamps have featured scenes and subjects relating to the country.

The address of the philatelic bureau is Postmaster, GPO, Banjul, The Gambia. (See Cameos.)

Thematic Collecting:
An alternative name for topical collecting (q.v.) used in many areas of the world, especially Great Britain.

In North America, attempts are often made to ascribe to it other meanings.

Thus, you will often hear collections of, for example, Red Cross stamps, certain omnibus issues (q.v.), issues honoring the Universal Postal Union (q.v.), etc., described as "thematic collections."

It is also not uncommon to hear of a form of

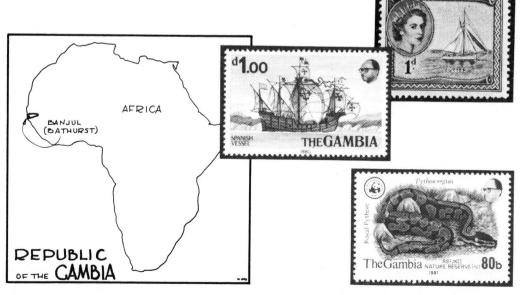

topical collecting in which a story is being told with the use of appropriate postal material, called a theme collection.

Such uses are not necessarily inaccurate, but because of the confusion surrounding the term "thematic," they are not desirable.

Theresienstadt:
The horror of the German concentration camps during the 1930s and 1940s lives on in a seemingly innocent, non-denominated postal label issued by the Germans on July 10, 1943.

The purpose of this item was to frank parcels sent to victims in the camp at Theresienstadt. Its use was obligatory.

The design features a peaceful rural landscape, which lends even greater horror to the

name it bears — "THERESIENSTADT."

We must assume that the motif was chosen deliberately to lull families into thinking that their loved ones were being well treated.

The stamp was intaglio printed in dark green in sheets of 25 stamps and perforated 10.

The use of this label required that the sender make application to the Gestapo for permission to send a parcel and to receive a certificate of permission, which then had to be presented in order to purchase the postal label.

It cost 1,000 crowns (about $20) and was affixed to the parcel, which was then delivered to the camp.

Upon arrival, the wrappings were removed by the guards, who censored the contents, accounting for the label's scarcity in used condition.

The use of this label thus in no way guaranteed that the prisoner would receive all or any of the parcel's contents, according to *Bohemia, Moravia, and Slovakia*, edited by Ray Van Handel Jr., published by the Czechoslovak Philatelic Society in 1958.

Thessaly:
A district in northern Greece on the Aegean Sea and south of Macedonia, Thessaly was ceded to Greece by Turkey in 1881.

The area was the scene of fighting during the war between Greece and Turkey in 1897. In 1898 the Turkish postal authorities issued a set of stamps for use by its occupation forces in Thessaly.

The stamps were issued on April 21 and are hexagonal in shape. Their designs feature a tughra (q.v.) and the bridge at Larissa.

Forgeries exist, which are perf 11.5 instead of perf 13.

Thick:
Foreign words for "thick" include dik (Dutch), epais (French), dick (German), spesso (Italian), and grueso (Spanish).

Thies, James H.:
James H. Thies was the brother of Thomas Thies, postmaster of St. Georges, Bermuda. He was filling in for his sick brother when he created the Thies type of postmaster provisional stamp, similar to the famous Perot stamps of Bermuda. (See Perot Stamps.)

Thin:
The term "thin" is used to describe a condition of the paper upon which a stamp is printed. It consists of an area where a portion of the stamp's paper has become removed, usually from the back.

It can result from the careless removal of a hinge, poor quality hinges that do not peel properly, a stamp becoming partially stuck to an album page by careless hinging, or exposure to humidity.

A thin can usually be detected by holding a stamp up to light. It should be remembered that a watermark will often give the appearance of a thin, for indeed it is one. But an awareness of the stamp's watermark will enable you to discount its presence.

Sometimes, a stamp with a portion of its gum removed may look like a thinned stamp, but the paper would not be damaged, and thus it will be a gum defect rather than damaged paper.

As an example, collectors should always be wary of the French 5fr stamp of 1869. It is particularly susceptible to thinning and has undoubtedly attracted the attention of "restorers."

Thins can be filled and thus not be detected by visual examination. Watermarking will often show up a thin whether or not it has been filled. The use of an ultraviolet lamp will also be of use.

Since an unused stamp (a mint stamp from which the gum has been removed) will often be regummed after the repair of a thin, you should not make any assumptions on the basis of gum condition. (See Condition.)

Thin:
Foreign words for "thin" include dun (Dutch), mince (French), dunn (German), sottile (Italian), and delgado (Spanish).

Thormond: (See Bogus.)

Thrace: The name of Thrace lives on only as the name of the easternmost province of Greece.

Once, it applied to an area encompassing most of what is now Bulgaria, northeastern Greece, and the area of Turkey in Europe. Turkey dominated the Balkans for 400 years but began to disintegrate in the late 1800s.

The area of Thrace was a battleground for a number of years, with Turkey fighting Bulgaria, and Greece and Serbia also becoming involved. The first result was the creation of an autonomous area under the title of Eastern Rumelia (q.v.).

The second Balkan War resulted in the Treaty of Bucharest in 1913. This restored Eastern Thrace to Turkey and gave Bulgaria Western Thrace with a stretch of coast on the Aegean Sea and the port of Dedeagach (q.v.).

The settlement following World War I, in which Bulgaria and Turkey had sided with the Central Powers of Germany and Austria-Hungary, resulted in just about today's boundaries.

During 1919-20, there was a period of Allied occupation north of the Aegean Sea, and stamps were issued.

These were Bulgarian stamps overprinted "THRACE INTERALLIEE" or "THRACE OCCIDENTALE." Greek stamps were also overprinted with the inscription "ADMINISTRA-

TION OF WESTERN THRACE" in Greek.

Shortly thereafter, Greece occupied a portion of Eastern Thrace, and Greek and Turkish stamps were overprinted — "ADMINISTRATION OF THRACE" on Greek stamps, and "HIGH COMMISSION OF THRACE" on the Turkish stamps. Both overprints are in Greek.

Previously, in 1913, Turkish stamps had been issued overprinted in Greek for use in the Giumulzina district.

THRACE INTERALLIEE: During the Allied occupation of Thrace (q.v.) in 1919-20, Bulgarian stamps were overprinted "THRACE INTERALLIEE" for use in the area while national boundaries were being determined in the area of what are now Bulgaria, Turkey, and the eastern Greek province of Thrace.

An overprint reading "THRACE OCCIDENTALE" was also used.

THRACE OCCIDENTALE: An overprint on Bulgarian stamps used by the occupying Allied forces in Thrace (q.v.) in 1919-20. (See THRACE INTERALLIEE.)

Three-skilling Banco Error: The three-skilling banco error of 1855 is a Swedish error of color that occurred on the first stamp of that country.

The one known copy is believed to be unique and is thus a fitting rival to the British Guiana 1c (q.v.) of 1856.

It is thought that the error occurred when a cliche (q.v.) of the three-skilling banco was accidently inserted in a plate of the eight-skilling banco stamp. It thus came to be printed in the orange color of the eight-skilling banco denomination instead of the green of the normal three-skilling banco.

The one known example is reported to have been found in 1885 by Georg Wilhelm Backman, a Stockholm schoolboy visiting his grandmother in the country, according to L.N. and M. Williams (Stamps of Fame, Blandford, London, 1949).

Backman sold it to a Stockholm dealer named Lichtenstein, who bought it at the price he had offered to pay for normal specimens of the three-skilling banco denominations.

Lichtenstein sold it some years later, and the stamp found its way into the Ferrary collection. It subsequently passed through the collections of several persons.

Though it is understandable that a cliche of the three-skilling banco denomination could have easily been inserted into a plate of eight-skilling banco stamps, it has been claimed that the color does not match that of the eight-

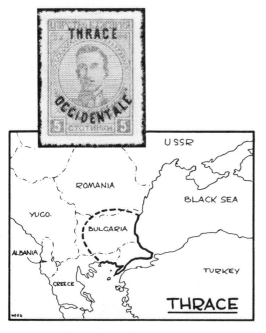

THRACE

skilling banco stamps and that it is, in fact, a fake.

Such a claim was made in 1975 by Gilbert Svensen, director of the Swedish Postal Museum, who also claimed that the paper of the upper portion of the stamp did not match that of the rest. Other experts have contradicted this claim and stated that the stamp is genuine.

In October 1978, the stamp was reported to have been sold by a Hamburg, Germany, auction firm for the sum of $550,000. If true, this would have made it the most costly single stamp at that time. The British Guiana 1c of 1856 has since sold for $850,000 to clinch top spot, at least for the time being.

Nevertheless, the Swedish stamp is still regarded as one of the world's major rarities, and though there are doubts as to its status, no proof appears to have been offered to support them.

Thuringia: Thuringia was an area of what is now the German Democratic Republic. Following World War II, it was occupied by Soviet forces.

Prior to the release of stamps for use throughout the areas of occupied Germany, the Soviets issued local stamps for the various provinces on the basis of the Higher Postal Directorates (Oberpostdirektionen, or OPDs) of the principal cities.

The Stanley Gibbons catalog lists 17 items released during 1945-46 and inscribed "THURINGEN."

Designs of the various stamps feature a posthorn and the poet and playwright Johann von Schiller, and a semi-postal set to raise funds to rebuild various bridges pictures some of the destroyed bridges.

Thurn and Taxis: Though usually grouped with stamps of the German states,

This stamp was issued by the Federal Republic of Germany in 1952 to mark the centenary of the first Thurn and Taxis stamps.

those of Thurn and Taxis were in fact stamps of a private postal operation, rather than of a geographic entity. The service operated under monopolies granted by the various rulers.

From the 1500s to 1867, the family of Thurn and Taxis ran a mail service that, at its height, served the greater part of Europe.

At first restricted to the carriage of official messages, the service was opened to the public in 1574. At its peak, it employed 20,000 people and had offices in most of the major towns of Europe. A yellow trumpet on the front and back of a messenger's jacket was a familiar sight. Messengers used posthorns and carried special passports.

Eventually, a growing desire in many of the states to establish their own national postal services led to a gradual erosion of the family's operations, and the Napoleonic Wars caused communications problems and further stimulated a growing nationalism. The House of Thurn and Taxis was never to fully recover its former glory.

For almost 400 years, the family had carried the mail of Europe, and in 1867 it sold its remaining rights to the government of Prussia.

Because of currency differences, the adhesive stamps issued by Thurn and Taxis in 1852 were divided into two issues, one for the north in silbergroschen (or groschen) and thalers, and the other for the south in kreuzer and gulden.

When the operation was sold to Prussia, part of the deal was that the family should have free use of the postal services, and it had labels printed to that effect. These were used on family letters up to the outbreak of World War I, according to Otto Hornung's *The Illustrated Encyclopedia of Stamp Collecting,* (Hamlyn Publishing Group Ltd., England, 1970).

An excellent short history of the operations of Thurn and Taxis appears in *Collecting Postal History* by Prince Dimitry Kandaouroff (Larousse and Co., New York, 1974.

Tibet: After a long period of Chinese rule, Tibet became independent in 1911 and remained so until 1951, when the People's Republic of China (q.v.) seized the country. It created the Tibet Autonomous Region in 1965.

Tibet is an area north of India (q.v.), Nepal (q.v.), and Bhutan (q.v.) and has what is believed to be the world's highest town — Jiachan, located at an altitude of 15,870 feet.

The average altitude of the whole country is about 15,000 feet, and it covers an area of 470,000 square miles. The capital is La-sa (Lhasa).

The Himalayas form the southern boundary,

This cover mailed from Tibet to the US bears three Indian stamps in addition to Tibetan postage. The Tibetan stamp carried the letter to a post office of British India, one of three in Tibet, where Indian stamps were affixed to frank the letter to its destination. The stamps of Tibet were only valid within the country.

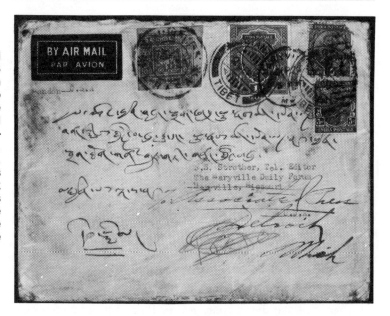

A full sheet of the four-trangka stamp in Tibet's 1933 issue. Each cliche was hand carved individually and thus each varies in detail. The lower-right cliche is a replacement. It is somewhat larger than its neighbors and is called the "13th Cliche," according to Tom Matthiesen of Duvall, Wash., who supplied the photograph.

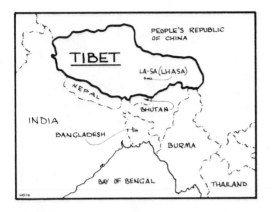

and high passes connect the country with India, Nepal, and the People's Republic of China. The population is estimated to be about two million.

There was an uprising in Tibet in 1959 and the Dalai Lama, ruler of the country, fled to India together with 100,000 followers.

It is reported that unrest continues. In 1961 the International Commission of Jurists charged the People's Republic of China with following a policy of genocide in Tibet.

In 1911 the Chinese issued a set of stamps for use at the post offices set up in Tibet by the Chinese army.

A year later, when the country became independent, it released its own stamps. These were valid only within the country, and mail to points outside Tibet had to bear stamps of a neighboring country (usually India) before being placed in the international mails.

Tical: A unit of currency once used in Siam (Thailand). (See Thailand.)

Tied: A stamp is said to be "tied" when the cancelation marking falls partially on the stamp and partially on the cover or wrapper of the mail item that the stamp franks.

It is especially necessary in the case of bisected stamps (q.v.) that the cancelation tie the bisect to the cover across the cut made to bisect the stamp.

An example of a cancelation tying stamps to a cover.

Tief: German word for "deep," as in deep color.

Tien: Numeral ten (10) in Dutch.

TIENTSIN: Beginning in 1908, stamps of Italy were handstamped and overprinted "TIENTSIN" for use at the Italian post office in that Chinese city.

The overprint is sometimes accompanied by a surcharge.

Tierra del Fuego: Philately rears its head in the strangest places, even at the very tip of a continent.

Down in desolate Tierra del Fuego (Spanish for "Land of Fire"), there once was a postage stamp issued. The single stamp was the result of a would be dictator's desire to exercise his authority over the island at the southern tip of South America.

In 1890 Julio Popper, a Romanian engineer, obtained a concession to mine gold in the part of the island under Argentina's administration, and

TIERRA DEL FUEGO

in order to help establish his authority over the local inhabitants, he issued a single postage stamp in January 1891.

The stamp was intended to frank internal mail or outgoing letters to the nearest post office on the mainland.

Its red design features a miner's pick and hammer. Its denomination of 10c is expressed in centigrammes of gold dust.

Little is known of the stamp's usage, and although covers are said to exist, they are reported to be extremely rare. The stamp was in use only a short time, as Popper died in Buenos Aires in 1893.

Separated from South America by the Strait of Magellan, Tierra del Fuego has an area of 28,434 square miles and is divided between Chile and Argentina.

Its climate is wet and cold the year round, although considering its southerly position, it has a relatively small amount of freezing weather. The small islands off the very tip of Tierra del Fuego constitute Cape Horn, named "Cape Hoorn" by two Dutch navigators in 1616.

Sheep farming is the chief activity, although the discovery of gold in 1890 brought settlers.

Air services operate from the Chilean mainland town of Punta Arenas and from Rio Gallegos in Argentina.

TIMBRE/COLIS POSTAUX:

Overprint on stamps of Indo-China to convert them to parcel post stamps.

TIMBRE COMPLEMENTARIO:

Inscription on postage due labels of Mexico.

Timbre Coupe: French expression for "bisected stamp."

Timbre Fiscal: French expression for "revenue stamp."

TIMBRE IMPERIAL/JOURNAUX:

This inscription is found on newspaper stamps of France.

Timbre Poste: French expression for "postage stamp."

TIMBRE TAXE: Inscription on postage due labels of France.

Timbrologie, Timbromanie, and similar: These were early French names for what was then the infant hobby of stamp collecting, which later became universally known by its present name of philately (q.v.).

They were derived from the French word "timbre," meaning stamp. Thus "timbre-poste" translates to postage stamp.

TIMBRU/DE AJUTOR: Found as both inscription and overprint on some postal tax stamps of Romania.

TIMBRU DE BINEFACERE:

Inscription on some early semi-postal stamp of Romania.

TIMBRUL AVIATIEI: Inscription on 1931-32 postal tax stamps of Romania to benefit the National Fund for Aviation.

Timor: (See Portuguese Timor.)

Tin Can Mail:

Many unusual mail services have operated in various parts of the world. Some were strictly gimmicks established to provide souvenirs for sale to collectors and tourists, but there have been those that did serve a useful and practical function.

The Tin Can Mail Service of Niuafo'ou was a little bit of both.

Niuafo'ou is an island on the outskirts of the Tongan group, to which it belongs, and lies some 400 miles north of the Tongan island of Tongatapu, roughly between Samoa and Fiji. It uses the stamps of Tonga.

Three and one-half miles long by three miles in width, it is volcanic in origin. There are no good landing places, and because the sea bottom drops away sharply, it is dangerous to anchor offshore.

Such is its postal fame that the island is much better known to collectors by its popular name of Tin Can Island than by its proper title.

It is said that by the mid-1880s, whaling ships chained barrels to buoys and left letters in them to be picked up by passing ships and mailed at US or British ports.

Later, mail was placed in sealed tins and thrown overboard in the hope that it would drift ashore.

Sometime between 1902 and 1915, A.E.F. Tindall established a trading post on the island, and during this period rockets were used in attempts to get mail ashore. A considerable amount was lost in the sea or fell in the dense jungle ashore.

Another trader, Charles Stuart Ramsay, lived on the island and claimed to be the first to deliver mail to ships.

Ramsay is said to have used buoyant fau wood poles to support the swimmers who carried the mail on sticks held out of the water.

After a swimmer was killed by a shark, mail was sealed in 50-pound biscuit tins and taken out by canoe, which picked up the inbound mail and took it ashore.

Ramsay's first swim is reported to have been in August 1921, with the last taking place in 1932.

The first of the "modern" tin can covers originated in August 1930, when the US Navy sent an Eclipse Expedition to the island. Covers are known canceled "NIUAFOO" within seven lines.

But it was Walter George Quensell who made Niuafo'ou famous. He lived there from October 1919 to August 1946, when the island erupted and was evacuated.

Covers by Quensell appeared during the years 1931-34. It was during this period that the first South Seas Exploration Cruise occurred, and he made covers with a "Tin Can Mail" handstamp and a paquebot marking on the face.

Although these covers bore stamps of Tonga, they were machine-canceled at Honolulu on April 13, 1934. The reverse bears a round "Dispatched by Tin Can Mail" marking.

Covers exist from a second cruise, following which many types of covers with numerous cachets in many languages were made.

Quensell claimed that he was not a postal employee, but the "Tin Can Mail Man." He collected a fee from passengers on passing ships along with their covers, affixed stamps, applied cachets, etc., and took covers out to the next ship for transmission.

He estimated that he handled 300,000 letters in the 750-900 mail shipments to arrive and leave the island.

Hard-to-find censored covers of World War II vintage do exist, as do hand-painted cards and covers.

During the 1946 eruption on the island, Quensell lost all his covers.

In the 1960s, the Matson Line resumed a Tin Can Mail Service as a publicity scheme, with mail being carried by Pacific Far East Line ships. Imitations of the Quensell cachets were utilized. (See Tonga.)

A Tin Can Mail cover that has received the full treatment from Walter George Quensell, the man who made the Tin Can Mail Service famous. Quensell had cachets made up in a great variety of foreign languages and applied them to mail quite without regard for their actual necessity, as the back of this cover (see opposite page) illustrates very well. Postmarked at Niuafo'ou on Oct. 17, 1941, it arrived at Maplewood, N.J., on Jan. 22, 1942, and thus traversed the Pacific area during a rather hectic period of world history. It was subsequently redirected to Santa Monica, Calif. Quensell also signed this cover, in addition to applying six handstamp markings identifying the cover as a genuine Tin Can Mail cover!

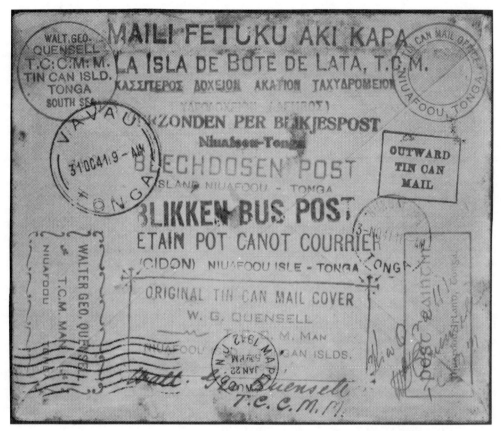

The reverse of the Tin Can Mail cover shown on the opposite page.

Tint: (See Color, Tint.)

Tinted Paper: (See Paper, Tinted.)

Tio: Numeral ten (10) in Swedish.

Tipo: Italian and Spanish word for "type."

Tipografia: Italian and Spanish word for "typography."

Tira: Spanish word for "strip."

Tirada: Spanish word for "printing."

Tirage: French word for "printing."

Tiratura: Italian word for "printing."

TJANSTE FRIMARKE: Inscription on some Official stamps of Sweden.

TJENESTE FRIMAERKE: Inscription found on some Official stamps of Denmark and Sweden.

Tlacotalpan: A Mexican village in the state of Veracruz that issued one stamp in 1856. (See Mexico.)

Tobacco Sale Tax Stamp: (See Stamp, Tobacco Sale Tax.)

Tobago: (See Trinidad and Tobago.)

Tocado: Spanish word for "touched."

Toccato: Italian word for "touched."

Toe: A unit of currency used since 1975 by Papua New Guinea. One hundred toea make up one kina.

Toeslag: Dutch word for "surcharge."

Toga: From the late 1800s up to 1950, the stamps of Tonga (q.v.) were inscribed "Toga."

Togo: The Republic of Togo is an independent state located in West Africa between Ghana (q.v.) and Dahomey (q.v.).

Prior to World War I, it was a German colony carved out of Africa by German military expeditions between 1888 and 1897.

The boundaries thus established were recognized by Great Britain in 1899. France had given similar recognition in 1897.

When WWI began, British and French troops occupied the colony, and following Germany's defeat, the League of Nations gave both Britain and France mandates over the territory in 1922.

The British portion was eventually incorporated into what was then the neighboring British colony of the Gold Coast, later Ghana. The French portion remained a separate entity until 1934, when an economic union was formed with Dahomey. In 1936 French Togo became associated with French West Africa (q.v.) until the end of WWII.

Britain and France placed their respective portions under United Nations trusteeship in 1946, and after a plebiscite, the British portion became a permanent part of the Gold Coast and is now a part of Ghana.

French Togo remained a colony until it achieved partial autonomy within the French Community, and on April 27, 1960, it became the independent Republic of Togo.

Stamps were first used by the German col-

onial administration in 1897 and consisted of German stamps overprinted "Togo."

In 1900 the well-known Kaiser's Yacht key type inscribed "Togo" was introduced. Following their defeat of the German garrison, the British and French overprinted this German issue — the British, "Anglo-French Occupation," and the French, "Occupation franco-anglaise." Later, they also used stamps of the Gold Coast and Dahomey with similar overprints.

Though the British area of Togo used Gold Coast stamps when it became a part of that colony, the French area continued to use its own stamps until 1957, when stamps bearing the inscription "Republique Autonome du Togo" were introduced. When complete independence came in 1960, this inscription was changed to "Republique du Togo,"

The capital city is Lome, located at the western end of the country's coastline.

The population of Togo is estimated at about 2½ million. The latest per capita income figure is $319, and the monetary unit is the CFA franc (q.v.).

For information on available philatelic services, collectors may direct inquiries to Direction Generale des PTT, Service Philatelique, Lome, Republique Togolaise.

Tokelau Islands: A territory of New Zealand, the Tokelau Islands are administered from Apia, Western Samoa.

The group of three atolls is located 300 miles

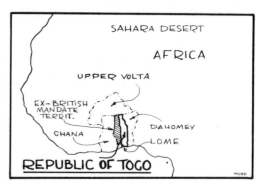

north of Samoa and has a total land area of four square miles.

They were formerly known as the Union Islands and were part of the Gilbert and Ellice group (q.v.) prior to the transfer to New Zealand on Nov. 4, 1925.

Their present name was adopted in 1946, and they became part of New Zealand on Jan. 1, 1949.

The first stamps were issued in 1948, and since then a relatively modest stamp-issuing policy has been followed.

The definitive issue of 1976 provides a colorful look at life on the remote islands.

Tolima:
Tolima is a department of the Republic of Colombia (q.v.).

It is located to the west of the national capital city of Bogota, between that city and the Pacific

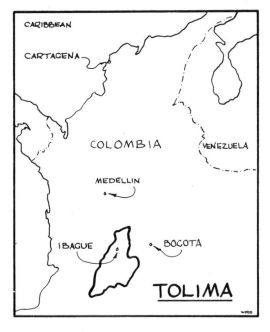

coast, although it does not border on the ocean. The capital city is Ibague.

The Magdalena River flows through the southern portion and forms the eastern border in the northern part of the department.

Like other departments that were originally states of the United States of Colombia prior to 1886, Tolima issued its own stamps.

The first issue came in 1870, and releases continued until the early 1900s.

These stamps were discontinued in 1904 and since then stamps of Colombia have been used.

Toman:
A unit of currency used in Persia (Iran) during the 19th century.

Tombstone Marking:
A tombstone postal marking is a postmark that has a vertical format with a rounded top and a square bottom.

An example of this type of marking was used at Liverpool, England, as a receiving mark on incoming mail from 1852 to 1870.

Tonga:
Once called the Friendly Islands, Tonga is an independent Polynesian kingdom located about 180 miles southeast of Fiji.

The country comprises about 150 islands in three main groups known as Tongatapu, Haapai, and Vavau. The capital is Nukualofa, situated on the north coast of Tongatapu, the largest island in the group.

The islands have a total land area of 269 square miles and a population estimated at 100,000.

The Vavau group is volcanic and mountainous, but the other two groups are of coral origin.

The Dutch first visited the islands in the early 17th century. In 1900 the islands came under British protection and were granted complete independence on June 4, 1970.

Coconuts, bananas, and tourism are the main source of income. The latest per capita income figure is $430.

Tonga's first stamps were issued in 1886 featuring the profile of King George I of Tonga.

A remarkably handsome set picturing island scenes was issued in 1897, and the regal Queen Salote is seen on an attractive 1938 issue. Until 1950, stamps were inscribed "TOGA," but since

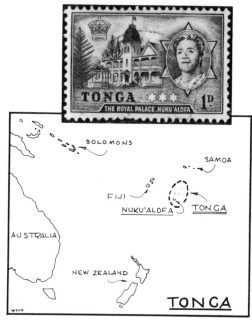

then they have borne the inscription "TONGA."

Unfortunately, since 1963, the country has released a stream of gaudy, free-form, self-stick items in every shape and conformation that merchandising imagination can devise, and as a consequence, the country is pretty well ignored by the philatelic community.

The unit of currency is the pa'anga (100 seniti), worth about .89 to the US dollar.

The philatelic bureau is located at Stamp Section, Treasury Building, Nukualofa, Tonga. A minimum order of $15 is required. (See Tin Can Mail.)

Tongareva: Native name for Penrhyn Island (q.v.).

Tongs: An implement used for handling stamps, tongs are often erroneously referred to as tweezers. Such incorrect terminology can lead new collectors to believe that cosmetic tweezers can be used to handle stamps. Because of their serrated tips, tweezers can easily cause damage to stamps.

Tongs are especially made for philatelic use. They come in a number of shapes and sizes. Some have pointed tips, and others are known as spade-ended tongs. All will do an effective job if you take the trouble to become used to them, and the type selected is not very important.

I prefer the sharp, pointed type, since it slides under a stamp easily and does not bend the perforations during this operation. Great care, however, must be taken, since sharp tongs can go through a stamp almost as easily as they go under it!

The new collector should buy the type that feels most comfortable and then stick with it. I have found that a pair of tongs will last a lifetime, unless left unguarded at a stamp show or other philatelic gathering!

Tonkin: (See Annam and Tonkin.)

Too Late: Stamps inscribed "TOO LATE" were used to indicate payment of a fee on a letter deposited after a specific mail had closed. (See Stamp, Late Fee.)

Top: Foreign words for "top" include bouvenkant (Dutch), haut (French), oben (German), alto (Italian), and arriba (Spanish).

To Pay: The inscription "To Pay" appears on some British postage due labels.

Topical Collecting: This is a form of collecting in which the subject of the design is

the focus. Examples would be ships on stamps, flowers on stamps, etc.

This form of collecting is also called "thematic collecting" (q.v.) in some countries other than the US, notably Great Britain.

In simple terms, topical collecting is the collection, arrangement, study, and display of stamps and other postal material with reference to the subjects of the designs, regardless of the country of origin.

Though topical collecting is one of the least stereotyped branches of philately, and forms of presentation can be varied to a high degree, there are two basic formats into which all topical collections can be segregated.

The first is a straightforward subject collection, such as trains, coats of arms, animals, fish, etc., on stamps.

The second, and probably the most challenging, is the "story" or "narrative" form of presentation. In this form, the collector will attempt to tell a continuing story, such as a segment of history, the life of a famous person, and so on.

A good comparison between the two would be the history of railroads as opposed to a collection of trains on stamps.

Topical collecting is the area of the hobby that is most likely to attract a new collector. This is not surprising, since you can combine it with your profession or any other non-philatelic interest. For instance, many doctors collect stamps with medical-related designs, a sports fan can easily relate to sports on stamps, a keen gardener will find it easy to become absorbed by the many stamps featuring the world's flora, and an outdoor lover can develop into an enthusiastic collector of stamps depicting wildlife.

It is this ability to relate topical collecting to just about any subject you could name that accounts for its enormous popularity, not only among new collectors, but also for a large percentage of those experienced in the hobby.

The newcomer to stamps can immediately see the attraction of a collection of animals or historic buildings, whereas a collection of stamps with an emphasis on perforation or watermark variations is an acquired taste that must be

Here are just a few of the more popular topical subjects shown on stamps. There are literally thousands of different topics you can collect, ranging from vases to volcanos, art to automobiles, chiefs to churches, and birds to begonias. No matter what your interest, there are related stamps to collect.

developed over a fairly long philatelic apprenticeship.

Many people believe that topical collecting is a recent phenomenon, but there is evidence that it began as early as the 19th century.

In *Stamp Collector* of Sept. 20, 1980, topical authority George Griffenhagen reports the discovery, by topical collectors George T. Guzzio and Mary Ann Owens, of philatelic literature in the literature collection of Guzzio referring to topical collecting as early as 1863.

The Reverend Henry H. Higgins, writing in the British *Stamp Collector's Magazine* of June 1, 1863, states: "The possessor of an album must be of a singularly apathetic disposition, if he is not incited to make some investigations into the history of the personages whose portraits are so often before him."

In the same article, Higgins writes: "The analogy between the groups into which it is found convenient to distribute a series of postage stamps, and the families, genera, species, and varieties recognized in zoology and botany, is so manifest, and the method of identification of species, etc., by description is so much the same in one as in the other, that a collector who had honestly made out his stamps for himself, and had arranged his book accordingly, would have no small advantage in commencing the study of classification in any branch of natural history."

Higgins goes on to indicate that this method of arranging stamps had been enthusiastically adopted by "...the junior members of the community with a zeal which has not a little astonished their elders." He continues, "this relationship between these trifling bits of stamped paper...has affected a very large number of the rising generation throughout Europe and even in America."

Griffenhagen also reports the finding by Owens and Guzzio of a July 1, 1870, article in the *Stamp Collector's Magazine* entitled "A Collection of Heads" that begins: "I think that some of your readers may be interested to learn of a little supplementary collection of stamps which I have formed, consisting solely of which are ornamented with portraits."

This early topical collector concluded with a comment that many more modern topicalists can appreciate: "...I have found that it is useless to expect mere philatelists to comprehend or take anything more than a coldly complimentary interest in my collection."

Despite this rather pessimistic attitude, in an article in the February 1887 issue of *The Philatelic Journal of America*, a writer indicates an increased interest in topical collecting when he states that "the subject of Philatelic Portraits has been dwelt upon by able writers" and goes on to give the opinion that his article will establish this form of collecting "as a legitimate branch of philatelic science."

Despite these early glimmerings of topical interest, it is believed that it was not until 1928 that a collector named Bernard Fetter of Luxembourg became the first to exhibit a topical collection, according to Hornung *(The Illustrated Encyclopedia of Stamp Collecting*, Hamlyn, London, 1970).

It is said to have caused much head-scratching among the judges, and Hornung does not indicate whether it won an award!

I recall British stamp firms in the early 1930s offering packets of stamps by topic, including the more popular subjects such as maps, trains, ships, etc.

However, it is since World War II that topical collecting has really snowballed in popularity, and nowadays it is very possibly the most popular method of collecting stamps, at least in North America.

At the national and international level of exhibiting, you now see topical displays exhibiting the same degree of research and technical skill as that applied to other areas of philately.

In this country, the American Topical Association (q.v.) is the nation's second largest in membership, and there are few philatelic exhibitions that do not include topical entries.

Toppan, Carpenter, Casilear & Co.: The printing firm of Toppan, Carpenter, Casilear & Co. printed the US issue of 1851-56.

The firm maintained offices in New York, Boston, and Cincinnati, although its printing plant and main office were located in Philadelphia.

The stamp printing contract that it gained in 1851 was for a period of six years, but it was extended for a further four years until June 10, 1861, according to Brookman *(The 19th Century Postage Stamps of the United States*, Lindquist, 1947).

Tornese: A currency unit in the Kingdom of the Two Sicilies (q.v.). Two hundred tornesi equaled one ducat.

Torn Stamps: As a general rule, a stamp with a tear is considered to be damaged and is usually not worthy of a place in a collection.

In some cases, a stamp with a small closed tear is acceptable as a space filler only providing that no part of the stamp is missing and that is an otherwise attractive specimen.

A closed tear is one that is not noticable except on close examination.

One exception to the rule that a torn stamp is a damaged specimen occurs in the early issues of Afghanistan (q.v.). These stamps were officially canceled by tearing off a portion of each.

TOSCANO: This inscription identifies stamps of the Italian state of Tuscany (q.v.).

Tou: The inscription "Tou" is found at the foot of Iranian revenue stamps overprinted for use as air mail stamps in 1928.

The overprint features an aircraft, probably a Junkers F-13, and the words "Poste aerien."

Touche: French word for "touched."

Touched: Foreign words for "touched" include touche (French), beruhrt (German), taccato (Italian), and tacado (Spanish).

TOUVA: Inscription found on the stamps of Tannu Tuva (q.v.).

Town Mark: A town mark usually takes the form of a circular marking known as a circular date stamp (CDS).

It identifies the town and date of mailing and can be used as a transit or receiving marking. The CDS of a machine canceler can also be called a town mark. (See Cancelation; Postmark; Circular Date Stamp.)

TPO: (See Traveling Post Office.)

T.R.: Prior to the introduction of stamps overprinted "O.S." in 1874 for general Official use, South Australia used a number of different overprints to indicate use by specific government departments.

The overprint "T.R." stood for Titles Registry.

Traditional Philately: (See Philately, Traditional.)

Traffic Lights: On the sheet margins of multicolor stamps from Great Britain, there is a series of round dots arranged vertically.

Because of their likeness to traffic signals, these have come to be called "traffic lights" and are collected quite widely by collectors who find marginal markings of interest.

For a period, traffic lights were also placed in the gutters of twin-pane sheets, but this practice has now been discontinued.

The color dots are an aid in checking stamps for color registration and presence. If the dots

The US version of the British "traffic lights" are seen in the selvage of this Christmas stamp.

A gutter pair of British stamps showing "traffic lights."

to rock in the design on the soft steel of the plate, thus creating a duplication of the original female die. The operation is repeated until the required number of subjects (q.v.) is entered on the plate.

Because the design stands out in relief on the transfer foller, it is sometimes referred to as the relief roller.

The illustrated Swiss stamp, issued on Sept. 5, 1980, to mark the 50th anniversary of the Swiss PTT's security printing plant at Bern,

A transfer roller at work, as seen on a Swiss stamp.

are all there and lined up, then they must be correct on the stamp.

Stamps of the US usually have a column or row of square boxes filled with the various colors. These are at the edge of the selvage and are often partially trimmed off.

Transcaucasian Federation: This was a federation of Azerbaijan, Armenia, and Georgia in the 1920s and early 1930s known as the Transcaucasian Soviet Federated Socialist Republic.

Two sets of stamps were released in 1923 picturing Mt. Ararat and oil wells. (See Azerbaijan; Armenia; Georgia.)

Transfer: Foreign words for "transfer" include report (French and German), riporto (Italian), and transferencia (Spanish).

Transfer, Double (or Triple): A double transfer occurs when for some reason the transfer roller (q.v.) is moved during the process of rocking in, or entering, a subject onto the printing plate.

It results in either complete or partial duplication of the design. This will vary depending upon the degree of movement that took place.

A triple transfer is similar and is the result of two shifts in registration between the transfer roller and the subject being entered. It will result in the main design plus two duplications. (See Reentry.)

Transferencia: Spanish word for "transfer."

Transfer Roller: The transfer roller is a male version of the engraved female die. It is made on a transfer press by exerting great pressure and forcing the soft steel of the transfer roller into the recesses of the hardened die in a rocking motion.

The transfer roller is then hardened and used

depicts a transfer roller transferring the stamp design to a cylindrical printing plate. Sometimes the plate is flat and curved afterwards to fit onto a rotary press. (See Printing, Intaglio; Reentry.)

Transfer, Short: A short transfer occurs when a transfer roller (q.v.) does not rock in a subject on the plate to its full length. Part of the design will be omitted either at the top or the bottom. (See Reentry.)

Transit Mark: A transit mark is a postmark applied to an item of mail during the course of its journey from point of mailing to destination.

It was often the marking of a post office where the item was transferred from one route to another.

Such markings are usually applied to the back of a letter, but this is not always the case.

Transjordan: (See Jordan, Hashemite Kingdom of.)

Transkei: (See South Africa, Homelands of.)

Transparent: Foreign words for "transparent" include transparent (French), durchsichtig (German), and trasparente (Italian and Spanish).

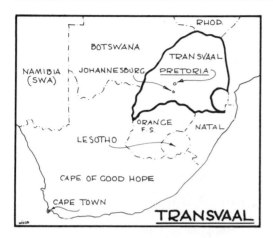

Transvaal: Located in South Africa between Southern Rhodesia and the Orange Free State, the 110,450-square-mile Transvaal is the source of much of the world's gold and diamonds.

The Transvaal's capital city of Pretoria is also the current capital of the Republic of South Africa (q.v.). The largest city of the Transvaal is Johannesburg.

When the Boers first migrated to the area north of the Vaal River, it became known as the Transvaal.

They founded the South African Republic in 1848, but hostile native inhabitants, who objected to their country being taken from them, and bickering within Boer ranks led Britain to annex the Transvaal in 1877.

The Boers rebelled in 1880 and persuaded Britain to grant them autonomy.

But the discovery of gold resulted in the Boers being swamped by a mass of outsiders, and in 1899 many British subjects in the Transvaal signed a petition for help addressed to Queen Victoria.

But it was to no avail, and as both Briton and Boer hardened their positions, the situation drifted into the South African War.

At the end of the war, with the Boers defeated, the Transvaal was a British colony from 1902 to 1906, when self government was again granted.

In 1910 it became one of the four colonies forming the Union of South Africa (q.v.).

The vast majority of the population is native African and includes people of the Bechuana, Basuto, Zulu, and Anaswazi tribes.

Stamps of the first Boer republic were released in 1869 and feature the country's coat of arms. There are numerous varieties because a number of different printers were used, and counterfeits exist.

During the first British occupation, stamps were overprinted "V.R./TRANSVAAL" until 1878, when stamps featuring Queen Victoria were used.

The second Boer republic was marked by a return to the coat-of-arms motif on stamps, but in a different format.

When the second British occupation began, stamps of the previous Boer regime were overprinted "V.R.I." prior to the release of stamps featuring King Edward VII.

A number of other stamps of a local nature were issued in the area, and except for the Pietersburg issue of 1901, they are overprints on stamps of the republic.

They were issued in the towns of Lydenburg, Rustenburg, Schweizer, Renecke, Volksrust, and Wolmaransstd.

Transylvania: Transylvania was the eastern part of Hungary until the end of World War I, when it was occupied by Romania.

In December 1918, Romania declared it a part of that country, and the Treaty of the Trianon on June 4, 1920, fixed its boundaries.

A variety of Hungarian stamps were overprinted with a circular device containing the inscription "REGATUZ ROMANIEI." with the word "BANI." below.

The catalogs list two issues, one for Cluj (Kolozsvar or Klausenburg), and the second for Oradea (Nagyvarad and Grosswardein).

The stamps are reported to have also been valid throughout Romania.

Trasparente: Italian and Spanish word for "transparent."

Travancore: An Indian Feudatory State, Travancore was located in the very southwest area of India. Its capital city was Trivandrum.

It issued its first stamps in 1888, and these continued in use until the formation of the Travancore-Cochin union on July 1, 1949, when stamps of both Cochin (q.v.) and Travancore were overprinted and surcharged. Two specially designed stamps inscribed "STATE OF

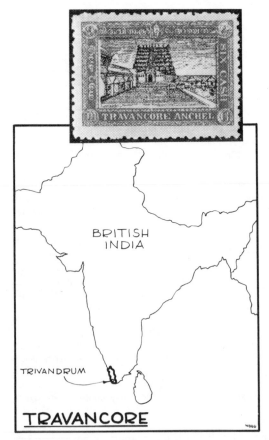

British Treasury decided upon a public competition to determine the best form of indicating the payment of postage.

The Treasury had announced that the new "stamp" would be in four forms. There would be a "stamp" struck upon paper supplied by the public; a "stamped" official cover comprising a sheet of paper that would show the "stamp" when folded, sealed, and addressed; a "stamp" struck upon a cutout sheet of paper that, when folded, would form an envelope; and finally, the format that was to outdo all the others — the adhesive postage stamp.

The competition was intended to obtain suggestions on the best form for these varied "stamps."

A first prize of £200 and a second prize of £100 were to be awarded for the two best ideas offering practical use, reasonable cost, and security against forgery.

Some 2,600 ideas were received. Some had considerable merit, but many were of little value.

Treasury officials decided not to use any, but they awarded four £100 prizes. These went to Bogardus and Coffin working as a team, Cleverton, Whiting, and Cole.

Henry Cole submitted the illustrated essay, which was printed by Charles Whiting, according to Robinson *(The British Post Office: A History,* Princeton University Press, 1947), although Philip Halward *(Stamp Collector,* April 28, 1979) credits the design to Whiting.

The essay is described as about an inch square, printed from a complicated machine engraving in blue and red, on watermarked paper.

It has a denomination of 1d and is inscribed "NOT TO EXCEED HALF OUNCE."

Another competitor, Benjamin Cheverton,

TRAVANCORE - COCHIN" were issued in 1950.

In July 1951, the Republic of India took over the postal services, and its stamps have been used since then.

Traveling Post Office: Generally, these were post offices on trains that applied special TPO markings to the mail they handled. Similar to RPO and PTS (railway post offices and postal transportation service). (See Ambulant, Railway Mail Service.)

TRD: A TRD is a temporary rubber date stamp that is issued for use while a regular marking is being replaced. Post offices in some countries keep these devices on hand for use during a period when a post office's regular date stamp is not available.

Tre: Numeral three (3) in Italian and Swedish.

Treasury Competition: In the course of implementing Rowland Hill's postal reforms in Britain during the late 1830s, the

One of the 2,600 ideas the British Treasury Department received in a competition for a postage stamp.

suggested that a female head be used in the design as "the eye being better educated to the perception of difference in the features of the face, the detection of any deviation in the forgery would be more easy." The authorities seemed to agree, and when Hill undertook to create the first stamp design himself, it bore a female head — that of Queen Victoria.

It is interesting that John Chalmers (q.v.) was an unsuccessful competitor and strange that his entry did not involve the use of the adhesive stamp that was later claimed to be his invention and which his son accused Hill of appropriating.

Whether or not Hill made use of any "outside" ideas in his adhesive postage stamp, the fact remains that history has given him the credit for putting it to work in a practical manner.

Treaty Ports:
The so-called treaty ports were cities in China and Japan at which European nations operated their own postal facilities.

At the end of the Opium Wars in 1842, the Treaty of Nanking permitted Great Britain to engage in trade at Canton, Shanghai, Ningpo, Amoy, and Foochow, according to Charles W. Dougan *The Shanghai Postal System*, American Philatelic Society, 1981).

Because of the lack of a national postal ser-

vice in China, consular postal agencies were opened at these cities and, later, at others including Swatow, Chefoo, Hankow, Kiungchow (Hoi Hao), and Tientsin. Consular postal agencies were also opened in Japan at Nagasaki (1859), Yokohama (1859), and Kobe (1868).

These offices were under the British Post Office in London until Jan. 1, 1868, when administration was transferred to Hong Kong. Eventually, the governments of Germany, France, Italy, Japan, Russia, and the United States operated consular post offices in various Chinese treaty ports.

A number of local posts were also established by foreign businessmen. In all, there were 11 Chinese cities in which local posts were operated using local post stamps.

The local posts and their stamps were discontinued when the Imperial Chinese Post opened in 1897.

The British Post Office at Wei-hai-wei is not considered to be a treaty port office, since it was leased to Great Britain from 1898 to 1930. It was administered from Hong Kong but had the same status as a treaty port.

In 1917 the British overprinted stamps of Hong Kong with the word "CHINA" for use at the treaty port post offices.

Britain closed its treaty port post offices in

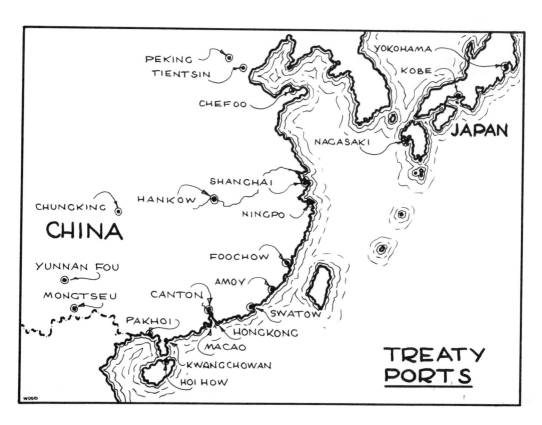

November 1922, according to Robson Lowe's *Encyclopedia of British Empire Postage Stamps, Volume III.*

Of the foreign countries operating post offices in treaty ports, Germany used German stamps overprinted "CHINA."

Italy used stamps overprinted "PECHINO" (Peking) and "TIENTSIN."

Japan used Japanese stamps overprinted with Japanese characters.

France, from 1894, used a large number of French and Indo-China stamps at post offices it operated at Canton, Hoi How, Kwangchowan (leased territory), Mongtseu, Pakhoi, Tchongking (Chungking), and Yunnan Fou (Kungming).

The United States operated a postal agency in China at Shanghai, and US stamps overprinted and surcharged "SHANGHAI/ (denomination)/ CHINA" were issued at Shanghai on July 1, 1919. They were used until December 1922.

Russia began to overprint Russian stamps in 1899 for use at Russian post offices in China. (See China, US Postal Agency in.)

Trebizonde: Stamps issued by Russia in 1909 for use in the Turkish Empire were overprinted with the names of various Turkish cities in which there were Russian post offices.

These overprinted issues commemorate the 50th anniversary of Russian post offices in the Turkish Empire. Trebizonde was one of the cities.

The others were Beyrouth, Constantinople, Dardanelles, Ierusalem (Jerusalem), Jaffa, Kerassunde, Metelin, Mont Athos, Salonique, Smyrne, and Rizeh.

Trengganu: Trengganu became a British protectorate in 1909 after being under Thai rule.

It joined the Federation of Malaya (q.v.) in 1948 and is now a state in the Federation of Malaysia (q.v.)

The state comprises a number of settlements along the coast of the South China Sea and is isolated from the rest of the Malay Peninsula by a high, forested range of mountains that in some cases exceed 7,000 feet in height.

The capital city is Kuala Trengganu, located about midway along the coast of the state.

Much of Trengganu is forest, and the people who inhabit the coastal area grow rice and fish and harvest small amounts of rubber.

The first stamps were issued in 1910 and feature Sultan Zenalabidin, the ruler. During World War II, the Japanese issued stamps for the area. (See Malaya, Japanese Occupation of).

Trengganu used stamps of the Federation of

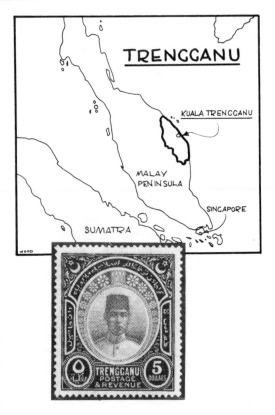

Malaya from 1957 until it joined the Federation of Malaysia in 1963.

Stamps inscribed "TRENGGANU" appeared as part of Malaysia's omnibus issues in 1965 (featuring orchids), 1970 (marking the Silver Jubilee of the sultan of Trenggau), and 1971 (showing butterflies).

Trentino: (See Italian Austria.)

Tres: Numeral three (3) in Portuguese and Spanish.

Trieste, Free Territory of: The ex-Italian province of Venez Giulia (q.v.) was occupied by an Allied military government of the US and Great Britain (Zone A) and Yugoslavia (Zone B) at the end of World War II.

Stamps issued for use in Zone A, which included the city of Trieste, were Italian stamps overprinted "A.M.G. F.T.T."

Stamps for Zone B were either specially printed or overprinted "VUJA-STT" (q.v.) on stamps of Yugoslavia.

The area was designated a Free Territory from 1947 to 1954, when it was divided between

Italy and Yugoslavia. Italy regained the northern part including the city of Trieste, and Yugoslavia received the southern Zone B including the towns of Fiume (q.v.) and Pola.

Trinidad and Tobago:

The twin-island Republic of Trinidad and Tobago is located at the South American end of the chain of Lesser Antilles, which descends east and south from Puerto Rico.

In 1493 Columbus named the island "La Trinidad" for a group of three hills he saw when approaching the island.

At one time connected to the South American mainland, Trinidad has flora and fauna quite different from that of the islands to the north.

Its chief mountain range runs along the northern coast of the island and is an extension of a range that runs along the coast of Venezuela. Its highest point is 3,000 feet.

There is a wide variety of scenery, ranging from open savannah to the desolation of the Pitch Lake and from rolling cane fields to dense tropical jungle. On the east coast, long rolling breakers wash up white sandy beaches to the fringe of coconut palms that march as far as you can see, like a line of soldiers guarding the land from the Atlantic Ocean's onslaught.

Trinidad's Carib Indian name is "Iere" — Land of the Humming Bird, — and these beautiful little creatures shimmer in a rainbow of irridescent colors as they flit from flower to flower. Other birds abound in as many colors as there are varieties.

The flora is equally exotic, and virtually every type of tropical tree, shrub, and flower can be found.

The island was not settled by Spain until 1577, and although its possession was fought for by Britain, France, Spain, and the Netherlands, it did not change hands as much as the other islands. However, its cultures are as varied, since it was a place to which refugees from the other islands came.

Britain gained possession of Trinidad in 1797 and retained it until granting its independence in 1962. Its diverse economy and oil reserves have made it the most prosperous country in the area.

Agricultural products include sugar, cocoa, coffee, citrus, and bananas. Rum is also an important product.

Asphalt from the Pitch Lake and its oil production seems to ensure a bright future for the country.

The latest per capita income figure is $2,090, and the literacy rate is 92%.

Trinidad has an area of 1,864 square miles and is about 65 miles from north to south and 48 miles from east to west. Its capital city is Port of Spain, overlooking the Gulf of Paria.

Tobago, Trinidad's partner is located about 21 miles northeast of Trinidad and has an area of 116 square miles.

It has a relaxed pace compared with the bustle of Port of Spain and is an ideal haven for those seeking peace and quiet. The population of both islands is estimated at 1,150,000.

Tobago changed hands many times between

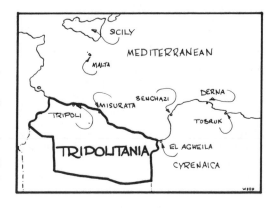

the British, French, Dutch, and Spanish, but it has remained British since 1803.

Trinidad's first stamp was the famous "Lady McLeod" issue (See Stamps, Local) of 1847, but the first government postage stamps came in 1851 in the attractive and simple "Britannia Seated" design.

Until 1913, the stamps were inscribed "TRINIDAD," but after that date issues bear the inscription "TRINIDAD AND TOBAGO."

The stamps of the country reflect much of its wide cultural variations, scenery, and its flora and fauna. Recent issues have not proliferated to the same extent as those of other newly independent nations.

Tobago's first stamps were released in 1879 and feature the usual profile of Queen Victoria. They were used until 1896, when stamps of Trinidad were used.

From 1913, Tobago has used the stamps of Trinidad and Tobago.

The unit of currency is the dollar (100 cents), which is 2.40 to the US dollar.

The address of the Trinidad philatelic bureau is Postmaster General, GPO, Port of Spain, Trinidad.

Tripoli di Barberia: Stamps of Italy overprinted "Tripoli di Barberia" were issued in 1909 for use in Tripoli. (See Tripoli.)

TRIPOLI, FIERA CAMPIONARIA:

This inscription is found on stamps of Libya used during the 1930s while under Italian control.

Tripolitania: Tripolitania was one of the provinces into which the Italian colony of Libya was divided. It is now part of the Socialist People's Libyan Arab Jamahiriya (q.v.)

Triptych: A triptych is a strip of three stamps that form a single design unit but which can be separated and used individually.

Tristan da Cunha: The island group known as Tristan da Cunha comprises three islands in the South Atlantic.

The islands are Tristan da Cunha, Inaccessible, and Nightingale, of which only Tristan da Cunha is inhabited.

Gough Island, about 250 miles to the south-southeast, is also associated with the group.

The islands became a dependency of St. Helena (q.v.) in 1938.

The inhabitants are mostly descendants of British soldiers stationed there in the early 1800s and of various shipwrecked sailors. The group was discovered by the Portuguese admiral Tristao da Cunha in 1506, and the Dutch attempted to settle them in 1656. By 1886, there were 97 people living in Tristan da Cunha.

During World War II, a naval weather and radio station was established on the island, and in Royal Navy tradition, the island was commissioned as HMS *Atlantic Isle.*

In 1961 a volcanic eruption occurred, and the population had to be evacuated to Britain. But the settlers found it impossible to adjust to life in the hectic outside world, and as soon as it became possible, they returned.

Fishing for crawfish is the main occupation, and potatoes are the mainstay of the islanders diet.

Tristan da Cunha has an area of 40 square miles, and the central peak rises to 6,760 feet. The average temperature ranges from a low of 52 degrees F. to a high of 65 degrees F.

The first stamps were issued in 1952 and consisted of the contemporary issue of St. Helena overprinted "TRISTAN/ DA CUNHA."

Since then, various island scenes and activities, together with events related to the island's history, have been its stamps subjects.

Stamps of Tristan da Cunha may be purchsed from the Postmaster, Jamestown, St. Helena, South Atlantic.

The official unit of currency is the pound sterling.

Trois: Numeral three (3) in French.

Tropical Staining: Tropical stains, rust, and mold, are names for a condition that occurs on paper in areas subject to conditions of temperature over 65 degrees F. and humidity over 65% where there is little or no free air circulation.

It is a fungus growth that takes the form of brownish spots usually on mint stamps or on an area around a stamp on cover, although I have seen it on used stamps and paper not adjacent to a stamp's gum in a climate such as that of the Caribbean area.

Tropical staining is a condition that can be treated by a household bleach solution. This treatment is tricky and dangerous, since even a very weak solution can cause damage not only to the printing and cancelation ink but to the structure of the paper itself.

Unless the gum is to be sacrificed, mint stamps are hard to handle, not because the weak bleach solution cannot be placed directly onto the stain on the surface of the stamp with a small camel-hair brush, but because the bleaching action must be "stopped" with a good wash in clear water.

Writing in the October 1977 issue of *The Mail Coach,* journal of the Postal History Society of New Zealand, Robin Gwynn tells us that sometimes a mold spot can be dislodged by the careful use of a needle point under a magnifying glass or may be removed by a soft art gum eraser. Both methods would be much preferred to the bleach treatment.

Nonetheless, if bleach must be used, take great care to apply it only to the stain and to neutralize it immediately with clear water. Be prepared for damage to printing ink and any cancelation.

Robson Lowe, in his book *The Diseases of Philately and their Treatments* (Robson Lowe, London), states: "...it is better and more natural to under-treat than to over-treat...immersing any used stamp in water or any other liquid will remove something of the pristine freshness of the color."

Cabeen (*Standard Handbook of Stamp Collecting,* Crowell, N.Y.) suggests the use of a solution of one or two drops of Clorox in a teaspoon of water, or, as an alternative, he notes that a hot bath in salted milk has been reported to be successful in treating early US stamps!

Thus, the collector must consider whether the patient is worth the risk of treatment. It is not hard to see that, in many cases, the cure might be just as bad as the disease, and that prevention by proper storage is by far the best solution.

Trub: German word for "dull," as in dull color.

Truboliv: German word for the color "olive drab."

Trucial States: Sometimes known as the Trucial Coast and sometimes as Trucial Oman, the area along the Arabian Coast of the Persian Gulf from the Oman Peninsula, at the mouth of the Gulf, to the peninsula of Qatar is now the United Arab Emirates (q.v.).

The Persian gulf area has always been a place where East meets West. From 700 BC, the Babylonians were trading with India. Islam came to all of the gulf countries in the seventh century, and the Chinese are known to have visited the Gulf in the ninth century.

Portuguese traders had by the early 1500s attempted to close the gulf to all other shipping, but they were eventually joined by the British and Dutch.

Trouble came in the early 19th century when the area became known as the Pirate Coast, with piracy being a way of life for the many small sheikdoms around Arabian coast of the Gulf.

Following negotiations between the British and the local sheiks, a treaty was signed, after which the area was named the Trucial Coast.

In 1853 the Perpetual Maritime Treaty was signed and the British assumed responsibility for policing the gulf. (See British Postal Agencies in Eastern Arabia.)

British influence remained strong throughout the area until after World War II, and on Jan. 7, 1961, seven of the sheikdoms — Abu Dhabi (q.v.), Ajman (q.v.), Dubai (q.v.), Fujeira (q.v.), Sharjah (q.v.), Ras al-Khaima (q.v.), and Umm al-Qiwain (q.v.) — joined to form a political entity known as the Trucial States.

It lasted only 2½ years, when the sheikdoms opted for more independence than that offered as part of a group.

Then, several of the sheikdoms began to issue what was to become a veritable flood of gaudy, inappropriate, agent-inspired stickers.

It was this mass of material aimed solely at collectors that sparked the derogatory name for the whole area: "Sand Dune States."

During its 2½-year life, the Trucial States issued just one set of stamps. These stamps plus one aerogramme, were only used in Dubai, since that town had the only post office in the seven sheikdoms.

The designs of the low-denomination stamps feature seven palms symbolizing the seven sheikdoms, and an Arab dhow is seen on the high values.

The stamps were withdrawn when the sheikdoms began to issue their own postage stamps.

Later, on Dec. 2, 1971, the seven sheikdoms united once again to form what is now the United Arab Emirates. (For a map of the Trucial States, see United Arab Emirates.)

Tsingtau: The port and pre-World War I German naval base of Tsingtau was part of the German colony on the Chinese mainland known as Kiauchau (q.v.)

T.Ta.C.: This inscription is found on Turkish postal tax air post stamps of 1931-33.

These stamps were required to be used during 21 days each year. The money so raised was used for the benefit of the Turkish Aviation Society, according to Scott.

The stamps were withdrawn on Aug. 21, 1934.

Tughra: A tughra was the royal cypher of the former sultans of Turkey. Examples can be seen on the first stamps of Turkey and Saudi

Arabia and some issues of Hejaz-Nejd.

The tughra is believed to date from the mid-1300s, when the sultan of those days, unable to write, dipped his fingers in ink and "made his mark."

Since that time, it has been the monogram of Turkish sultans.

Tugrik (Tuhrik, Tugrog): A unit of currency used in the Mongolian People's Republic. It comprises 100 mung.

Tunisia: An independent republic in North Africa between Algeria and Libya, Tunisia is the dividing point between the Eastern Mediterranean and the western part.

Its coastline is to the north and to the east, and the southern part of the country blends into the northern Sahara region.

Tunisian history is of great significance as the area is the site of Carthage, that ancient civilization that tried to fight both the Greeks and the Romans.

The Romans won the last of the Punic Wars in 146 BC, but Carthage has left its mark on the world.

The Romans continued the development of Tunisia, and its surviving remnants indicate a state of prosperity never equaled since those days. Islam came to Tunisia in AD 670, but it took a number of years before the country was completely converted.

The Turks were in control of the area by the 16th century, and it became part of the Ottoman Empire.

Piracy and the holding of European slaves had ceased by 1819, and in 1830 France's conquest of Algeria was looked upon with favor by the Turkish-dominated and poverty-ridden country.

Eventually, Tunisia came under French domination, and by the 1880s France was master. It declared Tunisia a French protectorate in 1883.

French control resulted in a rapid recovery from the former inept rule, and a large measure of prosperity followed.

The period between the two world wars was one in which the voice of nationalism began to be heard, but France was not listening.

After World War II, France tried to eliminate the independence movement by declaring that Tunisia had cooperated with the Germans during their occupation of the country.

But the voice of freedom was not to be denied. The French bowed to changing times and granted the country the right to run its own affairs. Independence was finally achieved in 1956. The country became a republic in 1957.

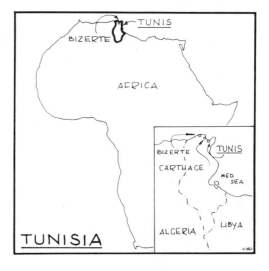

Tunisia has an area of 63,378 square miles and a population estimated at 6,360,000.

The latest per capita income figure is $934, and the literacy rate is 40%. The unit of currency is the dinar (1,000 millimes), which in 1981 was 4.91 to the US dollar.

The first stamps of Tunisia were issued in 1888 under the French protectorate. They feature the country's coat of arms. Succeeding stamps picture Tunisian scenes and its Carthaginian heritage.

With independence, Tunisian stamps became more symbolic and less scenic, but the country has followed a fairly modest stamp-issuing policy.

The address of the philatelic bureau is Service Philatelique des PTT, Bureau Directeur de Tunis Recette Principale, Tunis, Tunisia.

Tunisie: Inscription identifies stamps of Tunisia under French administration.

Turbio: Spanish word for "dull," as in dull color.

Turkestan, Russian: Russian stamps of 1917-18 were surcharged supposedly for use in Russian Turkestan. Scott state that these are bogus.

Turkey: The site of early civilization, the Asian part of what is now the Republic of Turkey (Asia Minor) was a refuge for Mohammedan Turks fleeing from Iran in advance of the Mongols under Genghis Kahn early in the 13th century.

This was the seed that germinated and sprouted into the Ottoman Empire. As Ottoman power grew, territory in Europe on the other side of the narrow waterway between Europe and Asia was annexed, and the Turks began to nibble away at the rotting Byzantine Empire. By 1453, Constantinople (Istanbul) fell, and the Byzantine Empire was no more.

The Turks surged into the Balkans and around the Black Sea, even obtaining a toehold at Otranto, on the Italian "boot." Then Persia, Syria, Egypt, and Arabia, including the holy city of Mecca, came under Ottoman rule.

In Europe, even Vienna was besieged, and Hungary was converted into a Turkish province.

The Eastern Mediterranean became a Turkish lake, except for Malta, which held off the Turkish invaders in 1565.

Nonetheless, the tide began to turn in 1571, when the Turkish fleet was defeated by Spain and the Papal States at the naval battle of Lepanto. The Turkish occupation of Tunis was little more than a dying gasp, and from then on,

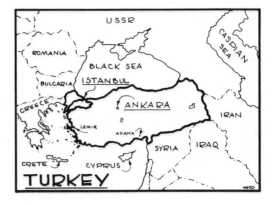

the Ottoman Empire began to decline, although it remained in existence through World War I.

By the time Napoleon appeared on history's stage, Turkey was unable to offer much resistance, and it remained to the British to drive the French out of Egypt at the beginning of the 19th century.

Even Egypt itself attacked Turkey in 1839, and the nations of Europe rallied to prevent the complete disruption of the Ottoman Empire for fear that Russia might move into the vacuum if this would leave.

When Russia did attack Turkey in 1853, Britain and France joined against the Russian threat and in the Crimean War were able to stem the Russian tide.

This alliance brought Turkey into the European community and prompted some liberalization within the Ottoman Empire.

The Balkan pot continued to bubble toward the end of the 19th century as the various peoples began to rebel against what was perceived as a weakening occupation.

One of Turkey's last terrible acts before the complete disaster of the WWI alliance with the Central Powers of Germany and the Austro-Hungarian Empire was the massacre of many thousands of Christians in Armenia and later in Bulgaria. This shocked the world and generated much anti-Moslem hostility in several parts of the crumbling empire.

But, before WWI broke out, the "Sick Man of Europe," as Turkey was regarded, received a shot in the arm from a young and agggressive group known as the Young Turks, which claimed to want to modernize Turkey. Once in power, however, the group reversed all of its hitherto liberal policies, and an even more repressive regime was born.

In 1911-12, Italy occupied Ottoman territory in Africa and even took over islands in the Aegean. (See Dodecanese Islands.)

WWI spelled final doom of the Ottoman Empire, and at war's end a new leader appeared. He was Kemal Ataturk, who finally led his people out of the Middle Ages and created a modern republic.

Turkey remained neutral through WWII, only declaring war on an already beaten Germany in February 1945.

Long at odds, Greeco-Turkish relations continued strained, and post-war hostilities in the area became focused on the island of Cyprus. Turkey finally invaded the island in 1974 and still occupies a portion of northern Cyprus.

Although more progressive than in the days of the Ottemen Empire, Turkey is still a poor country, plagued with internal unrest and with an economy in bad shape.

With an area of 301,380 square miles and a population estimated at 45,360,000, it has a per capita income of $1,140 and a literacy rate of 60%.

The unit of currency is the lira (100 kurush), which in 1981 was 99.18 to the US dollar.

The capital city is Ankara, but the main population center and chief port is Istanbul on the European side of the Bosporus, the waterway leading into the Black Sea.

The philately of Turkey and the Ottoman Empire is broad and interesting. In addition tc Turkish stamps, there are those of the many foreign countries that maintained post offices in the empire. (See Levant.)

The first Turkish stamps were issued in 1863 and feature the tughra, or monogram, of the sultan.

Just before WWI, an attractive pictorial set was issued. During the war, Turkey prepared a set of stamps for use in reconquered Egypt, but the event did not come to pass, and the stamps were overprinted and issued later.

As the Turkish nation changed into a more modern republic after the war, so did its stamps. They lost their hitherto Asian flavor and took on a decidedly European appearance.

Turkey has the dubious honor of having released what must be the world's longest set of stamps. Between 1958 and 1960, the country issued a set of 134 stamps picturing various Turkish scenes.

The address of the Turkish philatelic bureau is Direction Generale des PTT, Department of Posts, Stamp Section, Ankara, Turkey.

Turkey in Asia: (See Anatolia.)

Turkis: German word for the color "turquoise."

TURKIYE CUMHURIYETA: Inscription identifying the stamps of Turkey.

Turks and Caicos Islands: The British crown colony of the Turks and Caicos Islands comprises about 30 islands extending east-southeast of the Bahamas. They are located north of the island containing Haiti and the Dominican Republic.

The Turks group is to the east of the Caicos and comprises the main islands of Grand Turk and Salt Cay. The capital is the town of Grand Turk on the island of the same name.

There are seven main islands in the Caicos group, the largest of which is Grand Caicos. The combined area of the two groups is 166 square miles, and the population is about 6,000.

Salt is the basis of the islands' economy, and

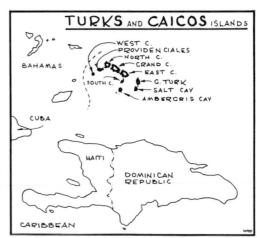

Britain has to provide considerable financial aid.

The climate is generally good, but the islands are frequently struck by Caribbean hurricanes.

Ponce de Leon, the first European visitor, came across the islands in 1512.

In 1678 settlers from Bermuda established the salt trade with the American colonies, and it was maintained despite much harassment by the French and Spanish.

At first administered by the Bahamas, the Turks and Caicos groups were transferred to Jaimaica in 1848.

Now they are a Crown Colony administered by Great Britain.

The Turks Islands issued stamps from 1867 until 1900 when the inscription was changed to "TURKS AND CAICOS ISLANDS." The Turks stamps feature the profile of Queen Victoria, but in 1900, under the new title, the badge of the islands was featured.

The Turk's Head cactus, for which the islands were named, is seen on a design first issued in 1910.

With the accession of King George VI, stamps were released showing the salt pans, and these have been followed by a number of stamps showing various aspects of the islands' scenery and history.

The unit of currency is the dollar (100 cents), which is at par with the US dollar.

Stamps of the Turks and Caicos may be purchased from Postmaster, Grand Turk, Turks and Caicos Islands. (See South Caicos.)

Turks Islands: (See Turks and Caicos Islands.)

Turned Covers: In periods of severe paper shortage, as in Great Britain during WWII and during the American Civil War, it was common to get as much use out of an envelope as possible. Indeed, in World War II the British government encouraged this and required its own departments to use envelopes over and over again.

In many cases, this was done by the use of labels pasted over old addresses, but some persons went a step further and got maximum usage out of both sides of the paper by taking the envelope apart and refolding it so that the inside became a brand new outside.

These are called turned covers.

Today's awareness of the need to conserve all natural resources and get the most possible mileage out of everything is causing people to once more resort to turning and reusing envelopes.

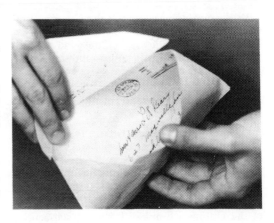

The interior of a modern turned cover.

Turquoise: Foreign words for the color "turquoise" include turquoise (French), turkis (German), azzurro turchese (Italian), and azul turquesa (Spanish).

Tuscany: Now a department of Italy, Tuscany is located in the north central portion of the country. The capital city is Florence.

The area is largely agricultural and is noted for

its fine wines, particularly those of the Chianti district, which are widely exported.

In addition to Florence, other noted cities are Pisa and Siena.

On March 22, 1860, the constituent assembly of Tuscany voted for annexation to the kingdom of Sardinia, and on Feb. 18, 1861, the kingdom of Italy, including Tuscany, was formed from that of Sardinia.

Stamps for the Grandy Duchy of Tuscany had been issued in 1851. They feature the arms of the grand duchy.

In 1860 a provisional government issued a second set, which features the arms of Savoy.

In 1861 the stamps of Sardinia began to be used in Tuscany, and these were followed in due course by those of the kingdom of Italy.

Reprints and forgeries of the stamps of Tuscany are plentiful.

Tussenstrook: Dutch word for "gutter."

Tuva: (See Tannu Tuva.)

Tuvalu: Tuvalu is a group of islands in the Pacific Ocean comprising the group formerly called the Ellice Islands. It was part of the British Crown Colony of the Gilbert and Ellice Islands (q.v.)

The division of the two groups took place on Jan. 1, 1976.

Included in Tuvalu are the islands of Fanning, Washington, Christmas, and Ocean. They total some 10 square miles.

The islands have a population of about 7,400, and the capital is Funafuti. The United States had claimed the islands of Funafuti, Nukufetau, Nukulailai, and Nurakita but has since withdrawn that claim.

The unit of currency is the Australian dollar, and the address of the philatelic bureau is Tuvalu Philatelic Bureau, GPO, Funafuti, Tuvalu, Pacific Ocean.

Tuvalu Philatelic Society: The Tuvalu Philatelic Society is a group of collectors interested in the stamps and postal history of the South Pacific country of Tuvalu. (q.v.)

Information on the society's activities is available from the secretary, Gregory Osowski, Box 38, Riverside, IL 60546.

Tva: Numeral two (2) in Swedish.

Twee: Numeral two (2) in Dutch.

Two Kingdoms of Sicily: (See Sicily, Two Kingdoms of.)

Twopenny Blue: (See Penny Black.)

Tyosen: Name once used for the area of what is now Korea. (See Korea, Republic of.)

Type: The word "type" is used to refer to shaped pieces of metal, plastic, or wood with raised letters or a design that, when inked and applied to paper, will leave an inked impression.

The typewriter "writes" by applying its type to paper through an inked ribbon.

In philately, overprints and surcharges are

often applied to stamps by means of type set into forms on a printing press that is inked before application of the paper.

Various styles of letters are known as "typefaces."

Type: The word "type" is used in reference to a stamp design, as in the variations of the US Washington Head design. There are numerous variations of this design, and they are referred to as Type I, Type II, etc.

Another common usage is that of the Briish Commonwealth "key type," a standard design that was used, varied only by the country name and denomination.

Many omnibus issues in a common design are referred to as types, for example, "the 1935 Silver Jubilee type," "the 1937 Coronation type," etc.

Typeset: (See Printing, Typeset.)

Typographie: French word for "typography."

Typography: Foreign words for "typography" include boekruk (Dutch), typographie (French), buchdruck (German), and tipografia (Italian and Spanish).

Typography: (See Printing, Relief.)

Typewritten Stamps: (See Printing, Typewriter.)

A selection of "T" country stamps.

UAE: The first issue of the United Arab Emirates comprised stamps of Abu Dhabi bearing the overprint "UAE" plus an Arabic inscription.

The stamps were issued in August 1972 and followed the union of the sheikdoms of Abu Dhabi, Ajman, Dubai, Fujeira, Sharjah, Umm al Qiwain, and Ras al Khaima. (See under individual names, also United Arab Emirates.)

Ubangi-Shari: Ubangi-Shari was a French colony in Central Africa. It was part of the French Congo and later became the Central African Republic (q.v.). For a short period, it was known as the Central African Empire before reverting to the name of Central African Republic.

Uberdruck, Aufdruck: German words for "overprint."

UEPT: The letters "UEPT" refer to the European Union of Posts and Telecommunications.

This was a short-lived union established by Germany in the European countries it occupied during World War II.

It came into being at the European Postal Congress in Vienna on Oct. 19, 1942.

The occupied countries included in the organization were Albania, Bulgaria, Croatia, Denmark, France, Hungary, Italy, the Netherlands, Norway, Romania, San Marino, and Czechoslovakia, plus Germany.

Ufficio Postale: Italian expression for "post office."

UG: The letters "UG" are the only identification on the first typewritten stamps of Uganda (q.v.).

The stamps were produced in 1895-96 by a missionary, Rev. Ernest Miller, on a Barlock typewriter.

Uganda: The Republic of Uganda's written history does not begin until the middle of the 19th century, when European influence made itself felt.

The name of Uganda is derived from the Swahili name for the Kingdom of Buganda, the base upon which the present state is built.

Captain John Hanning Speke was the first European to visit what is now Uganda when he arrived in 1862. Henry Morton Stanley, of "Dr. Livingston, I presume" fame, also traveled to the area, in 1875.

In May 1890, the Imperial British East Africa Company assumed administration of the area (see British East Africa), but on July 1, 1895, control of the territory was transferred to the British government, and it became a protectorate.

In 1902 the postal services of British East Africa and Uganda were amalgamated, and stamps issued in 1903 are inscribed "East Africa and Uganda Protectorate."

World War I and the Depression of the early 1930s caused a slowdown in Uganda's

economic development, but it was able to recover faster than many of the other African countries.

The move toward independence gained momentum during the 1950s, and internal self-government was achieved on March 1, 1962, with complete independence coming on Oct. 9 of the same year.

In recent years, the lot of the estimated 13,225,000 Ugandans has not been a happy one. The Amin regime was marked by barbarity, and the economy was virtually wrecked. The corruption and crimes against humanity charged at the 1977 Commonwealth Conference caused the Western nations to end their economic aid programs.

Amin made himself president for life and brought the nation to the brink of economic disaster before he was ousted.

The unit of currency is the shilling, which is about 7.72 to the US dollar. The latest per capita income figure is $240.

In the world of philately, Uganda is probably best known for its early typewritten postage stamps. In 1895 George Wilson, later deputy commissioner of the Uganda Protectorate, enlisted the aid of a missionary named Rev. Ernest Miller, who had recently brought a Barlock typewriter to Uganda. Rev. Miller created the famous stamps using a unit of currency called the "cowrie."

For about two years, he typed Uganda's postage stamps.

Dr. Ansorge of the Congo Free State Company persuaded Rev. Miller to create some stamps in denominations of 35 and 45 cowries, but these were not made for postal use, and no postal rate existed for them.

Additionally, varieties were created because of a switch to a different typewriter, plus ribbon changes.

These primitive stamps are now among the world's philatelic rarities. From 1898 to 1903, stamps picturing Queen Victoria and inscribed "Uganda Protectorate" were used.

In 1902 the postal services of British East Africa and Uganda were merged. Beginning in 1903, stamps of "East Africa and Uganda Protectorate" were used, being replaced in 1922 by issues inscribed "Kenya and Uganda."

By the terms of the East African Customs and Postal Union of 1935, the postal services of Kenya (q.v.), Uganda, and Tanganyika (q.v.) were combined, and subsequent stamps bear all three names.

There was a period of overlap beginning in 1962 with the release of a set of stamps marking the centenary of Speke's discovery of the River Nile's source. These stamps were inscribed "Uganda."

This was followed the same year by a definitive set for the newly independent state.

Uganda also shared in the communal issues of the East African Postal and Telecommunication Administration from 1964 to 1977. (See East Africa.)

The address of the Ugandan philatelic bureau is East African Posts and Telecommunications, Dept. of Posts, Box 7171, Kampala, Uganda.

U.H.: The letters "U.H." are overprinted, together with a "10 ctvs." surcharge, on a stamp of Ecuador for use as a Late Fee stamp.

Uitgave: Dutch word for "issue."

UK: The letters "UK" stand for United Kingdom, a contraction of United Kingdom of Great Britain and Northern Ireland (q.v.). It includes England, Wales, Scotland, and Northern Ireland.

UKRAINE: Overprint on stamps of Germany for use in occupied territory of the Soviet Union during World War II.

Ukraine, Western: Following World War I, a portion of what had been the Austro-Hungarian Empire, known as Eastern Galicia, was briefly independent before being made part of Poland.

In 1918 a set of Austrian stamps of 1916-18 was overprinted "Ykp. H.P." and surcharged.

In May 1919, further Austrian stamps were overprinted with symbols similar to "3. Y. H. P.," with each item being in one of the four corners of each stamp and with a trident emblem in the center.

These symbols are in the cyrillic alphabet and are the initials of "Western Ukrainian National Republic."

The issues for Western Ukraine are divided into what are described as the Kolomyya issue and the Stanislav issue.

Forgeries of all overprints abound, and collectors should exercise care when purchasing.

Ukrainian Philatelic and Numismatic Society: The Ukrainian Philatelic and Numismatic Society is an organization devoted to the collection and study

of material relating to the Ukraine and Ukrainian culture.

It publishes the *Ukrainian Philatelist*, a bilingual journal, and operates an expertizing service for members.

Information concerning membership is available from the society at Box C, Southfields, NY 10975.

Ukrainian Soviet Socialist Republic: Known as the "Mother of Russia" and the "granary of Russia," the Ukraine was the center of a Rus principality during the 11th and 12th centuries.

Although at times a part of both Poland and Lithuania as well as the USSR, the Ukraine has managed to remain independent-minded and to retain its identity.

The goal of Ukrainians has always been independence, and after the Russian collapse during World War I, Ukrainians proclaimed themselves a republic in 1918, with their capital at Kiev.

Stamps were issued, that at first were overprints of the trident emblem on stamps of Russia, but these were soon followed by specially designed stamps, all of which incorporated the trident.

A number of stamps were either prepared for

use but not issued or are completely private productions.

German stamps were overprinted "UKRAINE" in 1941 and used during the WWII occupation.

In 1919 the republic declared war on the new state of Poland in an attempt to obtain Galicia, but it was soon allied with Poland against the greater threat of the oncoming Russian Bolsheviks. It was to no avail, however, and the Ukraine was soon overrun.

It joined the other Soviet republics in 1922 to form the present USSR, and the Communists made great efforts to supress the Ukrainian spirit of nationalism.

The Ukraine's dislike for the Communists was demonstrated when Germany invaded the Soviet Union in 1941 and the people hailed them as liberators, little knowing that German brutality was to be even worse than that of the Communists.

Since WWII and its return to the Soviet fold, the Ukrainian SSR has acquired territory in the form of Bessarabla and North Bucovina from Romania and the Carpatho Ukraine region from Czechoslovakia.

The Ukraine SSR is a charter member of the United Nations despite its status as part of the USSR, stamps of which have been used in the Ukraine since 1923.

Currently, the Ukraine produces about 90% of Soviet grain and is also an important manufacturing center.

Ulster: (See Northern Ireland.)

Ultramar: Spanish word for the color "ultramarine."

Ultramar: The inscription "Ultramar" on certain Spanish stamps indicates that they were intended for use in Spanish colonies overseas.

Ultramarin: German word for the color "ultramarine."

Ultramarine: Foreign words for the color "ultramarine" include outremer (French), ultramarin (German), oltremare (Italian), and ultramar (Spanish).

Ultraviolet: (See Luminescent; Paper, Fluorescent; Phosphorescent.)

Um: Number one (1) in Portuguese.

Um: (See Ouguiya.)

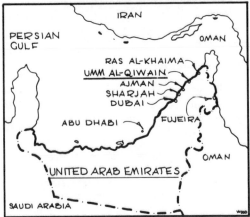

Umm al-Qiwain: One of the seven sheikdoms forming the United Arab Emirates (q.v.), Umm al-Qiwain is located on the Persian Gulf side of the Oman Peninsula.

With an area of some 300 square miles, its population is reported to be about 6,000.

In the period between the break-up of the Trucial State (q.v.) and the formation of the UAE, about 1,500 stamps were issued bearing the name of Umm al-Qiwain, according to R. Howard Courtney writing in The Arab World Philatelist.

Umm Said: Umm Said is a town in Qatar (q.v.).

The British established a postal service at Umm Said that operated from February 1956 to March 31, 1957.

It used the stamps of the British Postal Agencies of Eastern Arabia (q.v.).

Un: Numeral one (1) in French.

Underprint: Usually, an underprint takes the form of a design or tint applied to the face of a stamp to render counterfeiting more difficult.

Winchester paper (q.v.) is an example.

Underprinting does not refer to printing on

the back of a stamp. This is correctly termed "back printing."

The illustrated example is from the 1937-39 issue of Lithuania, which is printed on paper having an underprint in the form of a grey network pattern. (See Burelage; Paper, Winchester.)

UNEF: The letters "UNEF" were overprinted on stamps of India in 1965 for use by Indian forces serving as part of the United Nations Emergency Force in Gaza.

UNESCO (United Nations Educational, Scientific, and Cultural Organization): Beginning in 1961, special stamps inscribed "UNESCO" were issued by France for use on mail posted at the UNESCO headquarters building in Paris.

Several issues have followed.

Unexploded: The term "unexploded" refers to a stamp booklet that is retained by a collector in the state in which it was sold by a post office.

Its antonym is "exploded," which refers to a booklet taken apart for mounting in a collection. When this is done, all parts are usually mounted, including covers, interleaving, and even the thread or staples with which the booklet might have been bound. (See Booklet, Stamp.)

U.N. FORCE/ INDIA/ CONGO: This overprint appears on Indian stamps of 1962 for use by the Indian contingent of the United Nations forces in the Congo. (See Indian United Nations Forces in the Congo.)

U.N. FORCE W. IRIAN: This overprint appeared on a definitive stamp of Pakistan on Feb. 15, 1963, to mark the departure of Pakistani troops that were to serve with the United Nations force in western New Guinea.

Ungebraucht: German word for "unused."

Ungefalzt: German word for "unhinged."

Ungestempelt: German word for "uncanceled."

Ungezahnt: German word for "imperforate."

Ungummed: The term "ungummed" refers to a stamp that is issued without gum.

It would not be correct to describe as "ungummed" a stamp that has lost its previously applied gum, and such a stamp should be referred to as being "without gum."

It was not unusual for stamps to be used in hot and humid climates to be issued ungummed and for paste pots to be supplied at post offices for patrons to use in affixing stamps.

Many older issues of China were released in an ungummed state, as have more recent stamps of Brazil.

Nowadays, since the development of adhesives more resistant to heat and humidity, the release of ungummed stamps is less common.

Ungummiert: German word for "ungummed."

UNIAO DOS ATIRADORES CIVIS PORTO FRANCO: Inscription on Portuguese franchise stamps issued to benefit civilian rifle clubs.

Union Islands: (See Tokelau Islands.)

Union of Soviet Socialist Republics: Often incorrectly referred to as "Russia," the Soviet Union is a federation of 15 so-called Soviet Socialist Republics, of which the Russian Soviet Federated Socialist Republic is the largest.

Two republics, Ukraine and Byelorussia,

have the status of independent countries in the United Nations.

The USSR's population is 266,670,000, and its area is 8,649,490 square miles.

The present federation of "republics" was formed as a result of the Russian Revolution of 1917, which toppled the creaking and corrupt Russian Empire.

Just prior to World War I, it comprised 8,764,586 square miles and included a sixth of the world's land area.

Peter the Great became czar of Russia in 1682 and was largely responsible for orienting his country towards the West. He did much to transform Russia into a European power.

One of his more significant acts was the foundation of Saint Petersburg — later Petrograd, and now Leningrad — as his "window on Europe." He made it his capital in 1714.

In time, Russia edged its way into Europe and came to control the Baltic Sea. In 1721 Peter proclaimed the Russian Empire.

Weak rulers followed him, until Catherine the Great became empress in the latter part of the 18th century. She carried on where Peter had left off and adopted French culture.

After the French Revolution, however, she changed her attitude and became not just less liberal, but something of a despot.

Russian power in Europe grew after the defeat of Napoleon and his retreat from Moscow in 1812. The 19th century saw the expansion of the empire in Asia, although the Crimean War in the 1850s was a disaster for Russia. It continued to exert pressure at points of least resistance in an attempt to reach the Persian Gulf and the Pacific. The latter ambition was achieved, but the former continues to elude the leaders of the Soviet Union, although the incursion into Afghanistan indicates that the ambition might still exist.

In 1861, in a move towards liberalization, the serfs of Russia were emancipated. In a local government reform, Zemstovs, or district governments, were set up to handle local problems, among which was mail service, and local postage stamps were issued in many areas. These are known as "Zemstovs" (q.v.)

These reforms, though, were only a drop in the bucket of oppression, and there was continued unrest, flaring at times into open revolt and terrorism.

This came to a head with the assassination of Czar Alexander II in 1881. At this point, the coming explosion was set in train as the weak Czar Nicholas II came to the throne. Unable to direct affairs and easily led, he tried to rule by oppression.

In 1905 another revolution came, and although it was put down with considerable brutality, the oppression was only the lid on the boiling pot of Russia. That pot finally exploded in the revolution of 1917.

Russian forces experienced loss after loss in their hopelessly inept fight against the organized and ruthless Germans, and as Russia was beaten to its knees, the revolution could be no longer contained.

Soviet history began on Nov. 8, 1917, when Vladimir Ilich Lenin came to power. His first task was to end WWI, and this was done by the Treaty of Brest Litovsk.

Then came a period of civil war and the intervention of foreign military forces, which lasted until 1922.

The following years were ones of struggle, and the new regime worked to build a modern nation. Instead of doing this by means of private enterprise as in the West, the Soviet government did it by force, repression, and bloody purges.

WWII caused intense suffering and destruction in the USSR, as Germany attempted the conquest that had spelled doom for Napoleon 129 years earlier. It resulted in doom on an even greater scale for the Germans, as the Soviet Union exacted a terrible retribution.

Since recovering from the war, the Soviet Union has made massive efforts to achieve worldwide power and, together with the US, has become one of the two dominant forces of the modern world.

Sadly, the Soviet Union has used this power to impose its will, regardless of the desires of other smaller countries unfortunate enough to have such a ruthless neighbor.

At the end of WWII, the USSR had established puppet regimes in many neighboring states and, in the case of the Baltic states of Estonia, Latvia, and Lithuania, enacted outright annexation — annexation that the US still refuses to recognize.

During the years since WWII, the cold war between the Soviet Union and the West has alternated between periods of mutual suspicion and of outright confrontation.

There has been a series of crises, such as the Berlin Blockade, the invasion of Czechoslovakia, the Hungarian bid for freedom, the Cuban missile affair, the invasion of Afghanistan, and the encouragement of recent repression by the military regime in Poland.

Rich in natural resources, the Soviet Union is handicapped by a climate that often makes adequate food production a real problem, and large grain purchases have been made from the US and other Western grain producers.

The latest per capita income figure is $2,600 and the literacy rate is 99%. The unit of currency is the ruble (100 kopeck), which is .64 to the US dollar.

The most prolific of all stamp-issuing nations, the Soviet Union is not generally popular with collectors in other countries, although there is some interest in the Czarist period and in specific older philatelic areas, such as the Zemstovs.

The first stamps were issued in 1857 and, like most Czarist issues, feature the royal coat of arms.

With the revolution came a new look for the country's stamps,   and workers replaced coats of arms and bewhiskered royal features.

It is interesting to trace on stamps the cataclysmic history of the USSR since the days of the czars. Because of the enormous number of stamps, they reflect many aspects of the social change, and since the change is still going on, it is likely that they will continue to do so.

At times the emphasis has been on industrial

production, with workers, factories, and tractors sharing the philatelic limelight, and other periods show the arts. WWII was a time of heroes and military might, but more recently, space and sports have been prominent.

The 1980 Olympic Games sparked an enormous number of gaudy, sports-related stickers, which, like all Soviet commemorative stamps, are aimed primarily at obtaining foreign currency.

Within the country, most domestic mail is in postal stationery form, and very seldom do you see the large and colorful commemoratives actually serving a postal purpose. Most of the "used" material is canceled to order.

Union of South Africa: (See South Africa.)

Union Postale Universelle: (See Universal Postal Union.)

Unique: The word "unique" means "one and only" and is only used correctly to describe a stamp or other item that is the only one of its kind in existence.

It is much misused in philately and is often used when the words "scarce" or "rare" would be more accurate. It is also often incorrectly qualified as in "almost unique" or "virtually unique."

There is an old philatelic story concerning an auctioneer who included in the description of a lot the word "unique." The following lot was described "as above"!

Unissued: A stamp that has been prepared for use but not issued is said to be an unissued stamp.

Unissued: Foreign expressions for "unissued" include non emis (French), nicht ausgegeben (German), non emesso (Italian), and no emitido (Spanish).

United Arab Emirates: The United Arab Emirates is a union of sheikdoms bordering on the southern coast of the Persian (Arabian) Gulf and the Gulf of Oman.

On Dec. 2, 1971, the sheikdoms of Abu Dhabi (q.v.), Ajman (q.v.), Dubai (q.v.), Fujeira (q.v.), Sharjah (q.v.), and Umm al-Qiwain (q.v.) joined to form the UAE.

The sheikdom of Ras al Khaima (q.v.) joined the union in February 1972.

The UAE possesses a great reserve of oil, and the nationalized oil deposits give the country a very high per capita income. It was most recent-

ly reported at $16,000, compared with $8,612 for the US.

The capital city of the UAE is Abu Dhabi, which has a population of some 60,000. The second city is Dubai.

The area is bordered on the north by Qatar, with Saudi Arabia to the west and south, and Oman on the east. The barran, flat coastal strip gives way to an area of uninhabited sand dunes in the interior.

The first stamps of the UAE comprise stamps

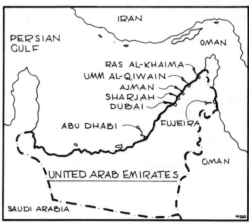

of Abu Dhabi overprinted "UAE" and with an Arabic inscription.

The effect on philately of the creation of the UAE was to bring to a halt the enormous flood of agent-inspired stamps of the individual sheikdoms, most of which remains unlisted, and to introduce a policy of philatelic responsibility and moderation.

In the years since 1971, a modest number of stamps have been released with subjects related to the area.

The total population is estimated at about 900,000 slightly more than over 70% of whom are Arabs, with the remainder being Iranians, Pakistanis, and Indians.

The currency unit is the dirham, which in 1981 was about 3.67 to the US dollar.

The address of the philatelic office is Philatelic Bureau, GPO, Dubai, United Arab Emirates, Arabian Gulf.

United Arab Republic:

The United Arab Republic was formed in 1958 by the merger of Syria and Egypt. The capital was Cairo, and similar stamps were issued by each country.

The union lasted only until 1961, when Syria withdrew.

United Kingdom:

The United Kingdom of Great Britain and Northern Ireland, or UK, as it is commonly known, includes England, Wales (q.v.), Scotland (q.v.) and the six counties of Ulster, or Northern Ireland (q.v.), plus numerous small islands around the coast of the British Isles.

People have been arriving in the UK for many years. First came the Celts in about 1,000 BC, and their language still can be heard in parts of Wales, Scotland, and Cornwall.

The Romans came in AD 43 and stayed to build roads, castles, and cities until AD 410. Then came the Jutes, Angles, and Saxons, all of whom battled the raiding Danes, who also stayed for a while.

The last time an invasion of the UK was successful was in 1066 when the Normans crossed the English Channel and landed near Hastings.

They fought their decisive battle a few miles inland, near a town that now bears the name "Battle," and beat the resisting inhabitants under King Harold, who had rushed south from defending his kingdom in the north.

The Norman Conquest united England with much of France, but over the years the situation changed to the point at which England was the leader with possessions in France, instead of the other way around.

In 1215 King John was forced to sign the Magna Carta, that forerunner of a later American document known as the Bill of Rights, and the years that followed saw the development of the parliamentary system of government.

For several hundred years, the British Isles enjoyed peace and a time of development unknown on the other side of the British moat that was the English Channel.

There was a period of civil war from 1642 to 1649 that resulted in a republican form of government under that humorless man Oliver Cromwell, but the British liked to enjoy themselves, and the monarchy was restored in 1660.

At the end of the 18th century, there began the Industrial Revolution that was to do more to change the face of Britain than could any military or political revolution. It led to a period of decline in agriculture as the population move to industrial centers developed and the country came to depend on the colonies for much of its food. This was a dependence that was to almost cause disaster in two world wars.

Nevertheless, for a number of years, Britain led the world in industrial technology and during the Victorian age became the world's leading power.

This was an age of glory and strength; the empire was secure, and many of the colonies were already being groomed for eventual independence. But war clouds were looming as Europe became tied up in the bonds of treaty obligations, and in 1914 came catastrophe for Britain.

World War I cost Britain a generation of its best men and left the country weakened and apathetic.

During the early 1920s, Ireland gained its independence except for the six counties in the north that chose to remain part of the United Kingdom.

The years between the wars were ones of drift, as Britain just coasted along. While Hitler gained power, Britain stood by, along with the rest of a tired and depressed world, and let Germany gain such power that it is entirely possible that if Germany had invaded Britain immediately after the fall of France, Hitler might just have become another William the Conqueror.

The country, however, could not accept the thoughts of an "Adolf the Conqueror," and perked up. With Churchill for inspiration, Britain fought on alone for a year while others used the time as a breathing space in which to gird their loins.

For that breathing space, the world will ever be in Britain's debt.

At the end of WWII, Britain, again the winner, was drained and almost bankrupt. Its effort had reduced it to a second-class power, and as

the colonies were given their independence, it withdrew from the seat of world power.

In recent years there has been a resurgence, and with the discovery of oil in the North Sea, Britian has become one of the few major nations to be self-sufficient in terms of oil.

This will undoubtedly place it in a very good position in the future as other nations, including the US, become ever more dependent on uncertain imports of energy.

The UK has an area of 94,214 square miles and a population estimated at 55,901,000.

Great Britain will always live in philatelic history as the first to use government-issued, nationwide, adhesive postage stamps.

The famous Penny Black and Twopenny Blue (q.v.) of 1840 was the start of a hobby that has become one of the world's most popular.

Sir Rowland Hill (q.v.) was remembered for his development of the idea of adhesive postage stamps with issues from all over the world in 1979, the centennial year of his death.

Though the British stamps that followed the early intaglio-printed issues (q.v.) are not con-

Much of Britain's heritage is pictured on her stamps.

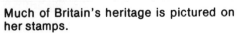

Seascapes and land-
scapes featuring
water abound in the
British Isles.

sidered as beautiful, recent issues show a dramatic change from the extreme conservatism of former years.

There have been regional issues for Wales (q.v.), Scotland (q.v.), North Ireland (q.v.), the Isle of Man (q.v.), and the Channel Islands of Jersey (q.v.) and Guernsey (q.v.).

There is a mass of stamp-like labels bearing the names of many of the small islands around the coast of Britian, but these are not official postage stamps. They are considered at best to be British private local issues and at worst to be items simulating postage stamps produced solely for collectors.

Britain's unit of currency is the pound (100 pence), which in 1981 was .47 to the US dollar. The latest per capita income figure is $4,955 and the literacy rate 99%.

The address of the philatelic office is British Post Office Philatelic Bureau, 20 Brandon St., Edinburgh, Scotland, EH3 5TT, United Kingdom.

United Kingdom, Regional Issues:
(See Northern Ireland; Scotland; Wales; Isle of Man; Jersey; and Guernsey.)

United Nations, Geneva: Since 1969, the United Nations has issued stamps with French inscriptions and bearing denominations in Swiss currency.

These stamps are only valid to frank mail posted at the UN's Geneva, Switzerland, office.

United Nations Member Countries: At the beginning of 1981, member countries of the United Nations were:

Afghanistan, Albania, Algeria, Angola, Argentina, Australia, and Austria.

Bahamas, Bahrain, Bangladesh, Barbados, Belgium, Benin, Bhutan, Bolivia, Botswana, Brazil, Bulgaria, Burma, Burundi, and Byelorussia.

Cambodia (Kampuchea), Cameroon, Canada, Cape Verde, Central African Republic, Chad, Chile, China (People's Republic), Colombia, Comoros, Congo, Costa Rica, Cuba, Cyprus, and Czechoslovakia.

Denmark, Djibouti, Dominica, and Dominican Republic.

Ecuador, Egypt, El Salvador, Equatorial Guinea, Ethiopia, Fiji, Finland, and France.

Gabon, Gambia, Germany (East), Germany (West), Ghana, Greece, Grenada, Guatemala, Guinea, Guinea-Bissau, and Guyana.

Haiti, Honduras, Hungary, Iceland, India, Indonesia, Iran, Iraq, Ireland, Israel, Italy, Ivory Coast, Jamaica, Japan, Jordon, Kenya, and Kuwait.

Laos, Lebanon, Lesotho, Liberia, Libya, Luxembourg, Madagascar (Malagasy), Malawi, Malaysia, Maldives, Mali, Malta, Mauritania, Mauritius, Mexico, Mongolia, Morocco, Mozambique, Nepal, Netherlands, New Zealand, Nicaragua, Niger, Nigeria, Norway, and Oman.

Pakistan, Panama, Papua New Guinea, Paraguay, Peru, Philippines, Poland, Portugal, Qatar, Romania, and Rwanda.

St. Lucia, St. Vincent and Grenadines, St. Thomas and Prince, Samoa (Western), Saudi Arabia, Senegal, Seychelles, Sierra Leone, Singapore, Solomon Islands, Somalia, South

Africa (currently under suspension), Spain, Sri Lanka, Sudan, Surinam, Swaziland, Sweden, and Syria.

Tanzania, Thailand, Togo, Trinidad and Tobago, Tunisia, Turkey, Uganda, Ukraine, USSR, United Arab Emirates, United Kingdom, United States, Upper Volta, Uruguay, Venezuela, Vietnam, Yemen (Arab Republic), Yemen (People's Democratic Republic), Yugoslavia, Zaire, Zambia, and Zimbabwe.

United Nations, New York: Since 1951, the United Nations has issued its own stamps in US denominations for use on mail posted at the UN headquarters building in New York.

The United Nations Postal Administration has an agreement with the United States Postal Service by which the USPS carries mail so franked and introduces it into the international mail if it is addressed outside the US.

There is one exception to this. When the UN participated at EXPO '67 in Montreal, Canada, a set of stamps was issued for use from the UN pavilion and was valid only on mail posted there that was carried by Canada Post under a special arrangement with UN postal authorities. (See United Nations, Geneva; United Nations, Vienna.)

United Nations Philatelists: The United Nations Philatelists is a group organized to meet the needs of collectors of United Nations stamps and postal history.

Its bimonthly journal, *The Journal of United Nations Philatelists*, provides articles and information on this area of the hobby.

Services to members include free ads in the journal, an award program to encourage exhibition of UN material at stamp shows, auctions, and slide programs.

Information is available from Secretary Ronald Hollinger, 712 N. Broadway, Lombard, IL 60148.

United Nations, Swiss Offices: (For issues supplied by the Swiss Post Office to the League of Nations, the United Nations Geneva offices prior to October 1969, and the International Bureaus, see Switzerland, International Bureaus.)

In October 1969, the United Nations Geneva office (q.v.) began to issue its own stamps.

United Nations, Vienna: Since 1979, the United Nations has issued stamps with German inscriptions and bearing denominations in Austrian currency.

These stamps are only valid to frank mail posted at the UN's Vienna, Austria, office.

United Postal Stationery Society: The United Postal Stationery Society is a group devoted to the collection and study of postal stationery, both US and foreign.

It publishes two bimonthly journals, *Postal Stationery,* which features in-depth articles on worldwide stationery, and *The Pantograph of Postal Stationery,* which is intended to keep members up to date on society activities, new issues, and society services.

These latter include a sales circuit department, bimonthly auctions, slide programs, a library, and a number of society handbooks and catalogs.

There are several local chapters across the country.

The society has published several editions of its two catalogs, *The United States Postal Card Catalog* and *Postal Stationery of the US Possessions and Administrative Areas.* Work is currently in progress on a revision of the Thorp *US 19th-Century Stamped Envelope Catalog.*

Information is available from Executive Secretary Joann Thomas, UPSS Central Office, Box 48, Redlands, CA 92373.

United State of Saurashtra: (See Soruth.)

United States of America: As has been the case with a number of relatively new nations, the United States was born of revolution.

A federal republic, the country comprises 50 states and a federal district, plus the possessions of Puerto Rico (q.v.), Guam (q.v.), American Samoa, the American Virgin Island, and the Pacific Trust Territory.

The modern history of the new country began with the voyages of Christopher Columbus for Spain and John Cabot for England in the late 1400s.

After the voyage of Cabot, England claimed the entire continent, but the first mainland settlement was made in 1565 by Spain at St. Augustine, Florida. The first English settlement was at Jamestown in 1607. The French and Dutch also moved in to claim colonies in North America.

The Plymouth Colony inaugurated a significant period of English activity, and settlements along the East Coast soon became permanent colonies.

The English attempted to control colonial trade and levy taxes, which the colonies objected to paying, claiming that they did not have the representation to which taxpayers were entitled.

The resulting American Revolution gained freedom for the 13 American colonies. But freedom did not end the problems, and the new country found that without a strong central government, it would have a hard time surviving.

The US Constitution was adopted in 1788, and the country was on a course headed for nationhood. Alexander Hamilton established the first bank in the US and placed it on a firm financial footing, although fiscal problems were massive.

As the nation grew, it expanded westward and, with the addition of Spanish California and the Pacific Northwest, soon stretched from ocean to ocean.

During the 19th century, friction arose between the slave-owning states in the south and the free states in the north, and emotions ran so high on both sides that a number of southern states declared themselves out of the union and founded the Confederate States of America.

This resulted in a bitter and bloody civil war, but though it ended in defeat for the industry-lacking and cotton-dependent southern states, the nation had survived the test, and it would not be so severely tried in the future.

The Civil War not only tested the bonds of nationhood but brought an end to slavery, and no longer could one man own another once the 13th Amendment to the Constitution was enacted.

Economic progress followed in bursts, with a period of prosperity followed by a depression,

but each time the nation seemed to emerge a bit better than before.

The next major event was the Spanish-American War, and since Spain was not much of a foe, it was easily and quickly won. The result was new territory for the US in the Caribbean and the Western Pacific.

Although US participation in World War I was not extensive, owing to its late entry into the conflict, the moral effect on the Allies was great.

The period between the two world wars was one of prosperity followed by devastating depression, the effects of which were not removed until WWII pulled the economy together.

The US emerged from WWII richer and

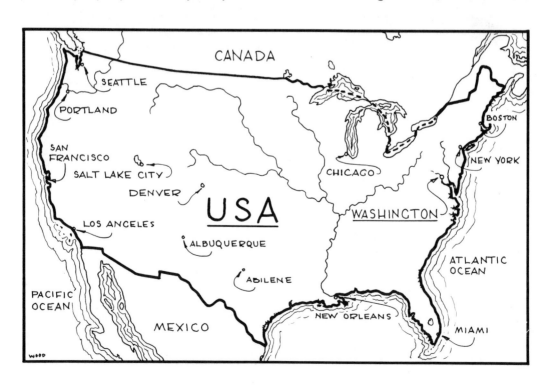

Stamps of the United States of America portray history, politics, and achievements. They run the gamut of artistic and technical quality from mediocre to superb.

stronger than ever before while other major nations involved were bankrupted and bled dry from their efforts.

For a few years, the US was the world's one major power, but the Soviet Union soon recovered from its massive wartime suffering, and the years since have been ones of constant competition and periodic confrontation between the two.

The US has an area of 3,628,150 square miles and a population estimated at 226,504,825. The per capita income figure is $8,612, and the literacy rate of 99%.

The first national government postage stamps were 5c and 10c stamps issued in 1847, but these had been preceded by a number of local issues from several cities, beginning in 1845, which are known as postmasters' provisionals.

During the Civil War, the Confederacy issues, at first various postmasters' provisionals, were followed by a number of national stamps. These are extremely popular with US collectors, as is the postal history of the period.

The first US adhesive commemorative stamps are the 1893 Columbian issue, a long set from 1c to $5. It was not at all popular for some years after its release, and it is only in comparatively recent years that it has shot up in value.

During the first part of the 20th century, not too many commemorative stamps were released. Since WWII, however, the rate has increased until the present, when a steady stream of new stamps, for all kinds of occasions, has descended upon collectors.

While the philatelic interest embodied in modern commemorative stamps of the US — as of other countries also — is minimal, there has been much to fascinate the collector and postal historian in the definitive stamps and in the workings of the postal system.

The tiny Indian Head Penny stamp of 1978, the non-denominated "A" stamp of the same year, and lately the "B" and "C" stamps, offer much to the collector who would specialize in material issued primarily for postal purposes rather than for sale to collectors.

The 1970s were marked by an enormous increase in the popularity of collecting and studying the material illustrating postal usage and the functioning of the postal service, popularly known as "postal history."

This trend has been accelerated by the investor invasion of philately, causing much of the more expensive material to become very much more expensive, with unreasonably high prices being paid.

Thus, collectors have been busy seeking other fields to collect, and postal history has benefited, enriching the hobby considerably in the process.

Another side effect of the investment boom in US philately has been the encouragement of collectors to investigate other, hitherto quite unpopular areas collectively known as "back-of-the-book" material. This includes postage dues, revenues, special delivery stamps, US possessions, postal stationery, etc.

Currently, the US Postal Service does not offer the deposit account service that many other countries have, and collectors must order each issue as it is released. The Philatelic Sales Branch has a $5 minimum order requirement and levies a 50c per order service charge.

A list of currently available stamps and stationery can be obtained from the Philatelic Sales Branch, US Postal Service, Washington, DC 20265.

United States Plate Blocks, Collectors of: (See Collectors of United States Plate Blocks.)

United States Possessions Philatelic Society: The United States Possessions Philatelic Society is a group devoted to the collection and study of stamps and postal history of the possessions of the US.

Information on the society's activities and services available to members can be obtained from the secretary, Kenneth M. Koller, 217 Tyler Ave., Cuyahoga Falls, OH 44221.

United States Postal Service:

Some form of postal service had been needed in North America almost from the time the British colonies were established.

What early services existed were primitive, unofficial, and uncertain. Letters were usually carried by special messenger or by travelers and merchants.

The captains of merchant vessels carried mail between England the colonies, and coffee houses often doubled as post offices for the collection of letters for the colonies.

In 1639 the Massachusetts General Court appointed Richard Fairbanks to be responsible for letters entering and leaving the colony by sea, "provided that no man shall bee compelled to bring his letters thither except hee please."

Benjamin Franklin — he laid the foundation.

(Rich, Wesley Everett, *The History of the United States Post Office to the Year 1829,* Harvard University Press, 1924. Reprinted in facsimile reproduction by Quarterman Publications, Inc., Lawrence, Mass.)

Fairbanks was not responsible for domestic mail, however.

In these early days, Indians were often employed as messengers and were highly regarded for their reliability and knowledge of the country.

The Dutch in New Amsterdam (now New York City) set up a mail box for outgoing mail in 1660 and introduced regulations forbidding anyone to visit newly docked ships until an official had taken charge of incoming mail.

In 1661 Virginia developed a system whereby mail was carried from plantation to plantation under penalty of supplying one hogshead of tobacco each time this was not done. This, however, only applied to official mail, and it was four more years before the requirement was extended to the letters of private individuals.

A mail service was set up from New York to Boston on Jan. 1, 1673, by Governor Lovelace of New York. In a letter to Governor Winthrop of Connecticut, Lovelace noted that mail was carried in sealed bags, while By Letters (See By Posts) were carried in an open bag, to be left at appropriate places along the route.

The service did not last long because of wars with the Indians and the Dutch.

Gradually, a system of post riders came into being in the colonies, but these were for official mail, and mail for the public continued on a very uncertain basis.

In 1683 William Penn established a post office and introduced a weekly service between Philadelphia, New Castle, the Falls, and Maryland, with rates from 3d to 9d per single letter. This is claimed to be the first successful postal service in the North American colonies.

On May 1, 1693, Andrew Hamilton became deputy postmaster general of the colonies under Thomas Neale, Master of the Royal Mint in

**In 1971 — symbol of a
new beginning.**

England, who had been granted a royal patent to operate a postal system in North America.

Hamilton was based in New York and controlled a service that reached from Maine to Georgia.

It was financially unsuccessful, however, and not until 1753 was a deputy postmaster general able to show a profit. This remarkable man was Benjamin Franklin, who had been postmaster of Philadelphia for 16 years.

Franklin held his new office for 21 years and made a spectacular contribution to North American postal services. He revamped the routes, instituted mail wagon service, began a penny post in the larger cities, and maintained an inexpensive rate for delivery of all newspapers.

As revolutionary fever swept the colonies to the south of Canada, the British dismissed Franklin in 1774, because of his political activities, but he was made postmaster general of the postal system established by the Continental Congress on July 26, 1775.

In 1789 the United States Congress was given control of the Post Office, and Samuel Osgood was appointed the first postmaster general of the new United States.

Gradually, but with considerable backsliding, the postal service grew and improved, and as the new nation expanded to the West so the Post Office moved with it.

By the 1840s, however, increasing postal rates were causing much protest, and although the postal authorities studied the newly reformed British system, not much was done to improve matters.

About this time, various postmasters began to issue their own postage stamps (See Stamps, Postmasters' Provisionals), and in 1847 authorization was given to issue the first United States government postage stamps, thus giving birth to the 1847 5c and 10c stamps.

The American Civil War and the rapid Westward expansion provided many problems

and headaches for the US Post Office, but the most positive development also came during this period with the introduction of mail service utilizing the growing network of railroads. Soon the bulk of US mail was being carried by rail.

In their turn came other significant developments in the form of special delivery service and rural free delivery. Then, as the country entered the 20th century, along came the first sputtering of a machine that was to make possible the US Post Office Department's most dramatic mail-carrying step forward. This was the airplane, and by the 1920s, mail by air was firmly established.

But air mail was not without its drawbacks. Though it made possible the rapid transportation of mail between airports, it caused enormous problems by dumping this vast quantity at the airports on the outskirts of cities instead of delivering it to the postal facilities right downtown, as did the trains. And that was to cause increasing problems as the volume of air mail grew when the jet age arrived following World War II.

From 1900 to 1970, the annual volume of mail grew from seven billion items to more than 80 billion. By the 1960s, the system was fast coming unglued, and the dramatic clogging of the Chicago Post Office in October 1966 indicated that drastic changes were necessary if the postal system was to survive.

It became obvious that the Post Office Department had to be removed from congressional control and that business methods rather than political patronage should be the guiding force.

A Commission for Postal Reorganization was formed and went to work. After a year, it recommended that Congress charter a government-owned corporation to operate the nation's postal service.

Congressional approval was eventually forthcoming, and President Nixon signed HR 17070 on Aug. 12, 1970, making it the Postal Reorganization Act of 1970, which created the United States Postal Service out of the faltering United States Post Office Department.

A board of governors was set up, which selected a postmaster general.

A Postal Rate Commission came into being, and all political recommendations for appointments were banned.

The new organization officially began work on July 1, 1971, and a special stamp bearing the logo of the USPS was issued to mark the event.

Since then, great efforts have been made to improve mail service, and in general it may currently be regarded as adequate. The Postal Service, however, has been a victim of massive inflation, and postal rates have continued to soar in a thus-far vain attempt to push postal income into the black.

The reorganization worked no miracles, nor, indeed, were any really expected, but the nation's postal system has survived and in some ways is giving better service than it was prior to 1971.

United States Post Office Department: (See United States Postal Service.)

Universal Postal Union: Claimed
to be the only international organization that really works, the Universal Postal Union (UPU) is one of the oldest international bodies.

It has survived global wars, depressions, and deep political divisions between nations.

It is a result of the efforts of the UPU that you can mail a letter and expect it to be delivered to virtually any part of the world.

Following a suggestion by US Postmaster General Montgomery Blair (q.v.) that the US call an international conference to discuss common postal problems, representatives of Austria, Belgium, Costa Rica, Denmark, France, Great Britain, the Hanseatic cities, Italy, the Netherlands, Portugal, Prussia, the Sandwich Islands, Spain, Switzerland, and the United States met at Paris, France, on May 11, 1863.

Though the Paris conference had not been intended to result in a permanent body for the regulation of the international mails, it could be said that it gave birth to what would become the UPU.

It was at the Postal Congress of 1874, in Bern, Switzerland, that a treaty was drafted and signed to form what was first called the General Postal Union. (This name was changed to the Universal Postal Union at the Paris Congress of 1878.)

The main purpose of the organization was to standardize and simplify postal rates and to devise methods of accounting so that participating countries would be reimbursed for transporting international mail through their postal systems.

Though it was Blair who was responsible for the 1863 Paris Conference, the man credited for setting in motion the events leading to the Postal Congress of 1874 was Heinrich von Stephan (q.v.), director of posts for the North German Federation.

Von Stephan had urged such a congress in 1868, but the Franco-Prussian War postponed it, and later hesitation by France and Russia delayed it further.

During the period that ended with the outbreak of World War I in 1914, the UPU caused

A stamp from the British Commonwealth omnibus issue marking the 75th anniversary of the UPU in 1949 and depicting the UPU monument at Bern, Switzerland, headquarters of the UPU.

to be instituted a number of services for those using the international mails.

These included arrangements for the exchange of mail, special delivery, parcel post, postal money orders, international reply coupons, and reply-paid postcards, plus an agreement that mail to and from prisoners of war should pass through the international mails free of charge.

WWI caused an extensive breakdown in "freedom of transit" for the mails, which had been a major achievement of the UPU, but with the war's end in 1918 things soon returned to normal, and members, including those from former enemy states, met at the seventh congress, held in Madrid, Spain, in 1920.

The period between the two world wars saw an increase in membership and was marked by the development of a new method of mail transportation in the form of air mail.

As international air services expanded, so international air mail service grew, limited only by the capabilities of aircraft of the day.

The matter of air mail postage rates engaged much of the attention of the UPU and led to the Hague Air Mail Conference in September 1927.

At that meeting, uniform rates were established for mail carried by air.

By the time of the European Air Mail Conference in Brussels in 1938, it had become obvious that air transport had developed to the point at which air mail was the normal means of carrying first-class mail in Europe.

WWII greatly disrupted the work of the UPU, although the organization remained in being and even functioned in a limited sense. It did much useful work by cooperating with the International Red Cross in helping to keep communications open for the exchange of mail between POWs and interned civilians, and their families.

In November 1947, the UPU became a specialized agency of the United Nations Organization.

Since WWII, strained relations between major powers have tended to reduce the universality of the UPU, although it still remains one of the most effective of all international organizations.

Of particular interest to philatelists was the UPU's attempts to standardize colors of stamps for the most-used denominations in the international mails.

At the 1898 Congress in Washington, D.C., it was recommended that the following stamp colors be adopted:

International single printed-matter rate — green.
International postcard rate — red.
International single letter-rate — blue.

The introduction of this standardization resulted in a number of member nations changing the color of their stamps to conform. Later on, however, as multicolor printing became more popular for stamps and as inflation began to cause increases in rates, the idea became more honored in the breach than in the observance, and the plan was finally abandoned at the 1952 Congress in Brussels.

The UPU and its various congresses and anniversaries have been the subjects of a great many commemorative stamp issues, and the organization is a popular topical subject for collectors.

There have been 18 congresses of the UPU, including the 1874 congress that resulted in its formation. The years and sites of the congresses are:

1874, Berne, Switzerland; 1878, Paris, France; 1885, Lisbon, Portugal; 1891, Vienna, Austria; 1897, Washington, D.C.; 1906, Rome, Italy; 1920, Madrid, Spain; 1924, Stockholm, Sweden; 1929, London, England; 1934, Cairo, Egypt; 1939, Buenos Aires, Argentina; 1947, Paris, France; 1952, Brussels, Belgium; 1957, Ottawa, Canada; 1964, Vienna, Austria; 1969, Tokyo, Japan; 1974, Lausanne, Switzerland; and 1979, Rio de Janiero, Brazil. (See International Bureau of the Universal Postal Union.)

Universal Postal Union Collectors:

The Universal Postal Union Collectors is an organization of collectors of the stamps and postal history of the Universal Postal Union.

The group offers a journal, *The Publication of the Universal Postal Union Collectors*, which is distributed to members quarterly.

Information is available from Raymond Reaber, 107 Rollingwood Dr., San Rafael, CA 94901.

Universal Postal Union Members:

As of the beginning of 1981, the following countries and groups of territories were members of the Universal Postal Union:

Afghanistan, Albania, Algeria, Angola, Argentina, Australia, and Austria.

Bahamas, Bahrain, Bangladesh, Barbados, Belgium, Benin, Bhutan, Bolivia, Botswana, Brazil, Bulgaria, Burma, Burundi, and Byelorussian SSR.

Cambodia, Cameroon, Canada, Cape Verde, Rep. of, Central African Republic, Chad, Chile, China, People's Rep. of, Colombia, Comoros, Congo, Costa Rica, Cuba, Cyprus, and Czechoslovakia.

Denmark, Denmark (Faroes and Greenland), Djibouti, Dominica, Dominican Republic, Ecuador, Egypt, El Salvador, Equatorial Guinea, and Ethiopia.

Fiji, Finland, France, French Overseas Departments, French Overseas Territories, Gabon, Gambia, Ghana, Greece, Grenada, Guatemala, Guinea, Guinea-Bissau, and Guyana.

Haiti, Honduras, Hungary, Iceland, India, Indonesia, Iran, Iraq, Ireland, Israel, Italy, and Ivory Coast.

Jamaica, Japan, Jordan, Kenya, Kiribati (applied), Korea (South), Korea (North), Kuwait, Laos, Lebanon, Lesotho, Liberia, Libya, Liechtenstein, and Luxembourg.

Madagascar, Malawi, Malaysia, Maldives, Mali, Malta, Mauritania, Mauritius, Mexico, Monaco, Mongolia, Morocco, and Mozambique.

Namibia (through UN), Nauru, Nepal, Netherlands, Netherlands Antilles, New Zealand, New Zealand (Tokelaus, Ross Island, Cook Islands, Western Samoa), Nicaragua, Niger, Nigeria, and Norway.

Oman, Pakistan, Panama, Papua New Guinea, Paraguay, Peru, Philippines, Poland, Portugal, Portugal (Macao), Qatar, Romania, and Rwanda.

St. Lucia, St. Thomas and Prince, St. Vincent and Grenadines (applied), San Marino, Saudi Arabia, Senegal, Seychelles, Sierra Leone, Singapore, Solomon Islands, Somalia, Spain, Sri Lanka, Sudan, Surinam, Swaziland, Sweden, Switzerland, and Syria.

Tanzania, Thailand, Timor (status uncertain), Togo, Tonga, Trinidad and Tobago, Tunisia, Turkey, and Tuvalu (applied).

Uganda, Ukrainian SSR, United Arab Emirates, United Kingdom, United Kingdom (Guernsey), United Kingdom (Isle of Man), United Kingdom (Jersey), United Kingdom (Overseas Territories), United States, United States Territories, Upper Volta, and USSR.

Vanuatu (New Hebrides), Vatican City,

Venezuela, Vietnam, Yemen Arab Republic, Yemen, Peoples Democratic Republic of, Yugoslavia, Zaire, Zambia, and Zimbabwe (Rhodesia).

The following is a breakdown of the territories and departments of the various national groupings:

France, Overseas Departments: Guadeloupe, Guiana, Martinique, Reunion, and St. Pierre and Miquelon.

France, Overseas Territories: New Caledonia, Polynesia, Southern and Antarctic Territories, and Wallis and Futuna.

Great Britain, Overseas Territories: Anguilla, Antigua, Ascension, Belize, Bermuda, Brunei, Cayman Islands, Falkland Islands, Gibraltar, Hong Kong, Montserrat, Pitcairn, St. Kitts-Nevis, St. Helena, Tristan da Cunha, Turks and Caicos, and Virgin Islands.

United States Territories: Guam, Puerto Rico, Samoa, and American Virgin Islands.

United States Pacific Trust Territories: Caroline, Marshall, and Mariana Islands.

Universal Ship Cancellation Society:

The Universal Ship Cancellation Society is an organization of collectors interested in the cancelations and history of US Naval ships and Coast Guard vessels.

The society's publication is *The USCS Log.*

The society holds mail auctions of material in its area of coverage, and sales circuits are also available.

There are a number of regional chapters, and information concerning membership is available from Frank M. Hoak III, 488 West Rd., New Canaan, CT 06840.

Un Milliardo: One million (1,000,000) in Italian.

Un Million: One million (1,000,000) in French.

Un Millon: One million (1,000,000) in Spanish.

UNO: United Nations Organization. (See United Nations.)

Uno: Numeral One (1) in Italian and Spanish.

Unordered Merchandise: (See Approvals.)

Unperforated: If a stamp that is normally perforated is found to exist without perforations, because of some accidental happening during its production, it is said to be "unperforated."

The term distinguishes an accidental condition from a deliberate action, as in the case of a stamp that is officially issued without means of separation, which would be termed "imperforate." (See Perforation.)

Un Quart: French expression for "one quarter."

Unsevered: The term "unsevered" applies to a pair, row (q.v.), or column (q.v.) of stamps that is still intact. It is often used to describe stamps in such a state used on cover.

UNTEA: The overprint "UNTEA" (United Nations Temporary Executive Authority) was applied to stamps of Netherlands New Guinea in 1962 for use during the period before it became West Irian (q.v.) the following year.

Unten: German word for "bottom."

Unterbrochen: German word for "broken."

Unused: This term is correctly reserved for a stamp that has not been canceled but that has had its gum removed.

Unfortunately, this is currently considered an undesirable state, although removal of a stamp's gum may have saved the stamp from eventual destruction because of the gum's action on the paper.

Many older stamps can be saved by the removal of deteriorating gum.

Unused: Foreign words for "unused" include ongebruikt (Dutch), neuf (French), ungebraucht (German), nuovo (Italian), and neuvo (Spanish).

Upper Senegal and Niger: (See Senegambia and Niger).

Upper Silesia: (See Silesia, Upper.)

Upper Volta: A landlocked state to the north of the West African country of Ghana, the Republic of Upper Volta was proclaimed in 1958 as a semi-autonomous state within the French Community and became fully independent on Aug. 5, 1960.

The land is mostly plain, with rainfall low in the north and increasing in the south. The chief crops are cotton, rice, peanuts, and grain. A severe drought in 1973-74 and again in 1977-78 brought famine to the area.

The area is desperately poor, and the latest per capita income figure is only $75, the world's lowest. The population is estimated at 6,910,000.

The French colony of Upper Volta was carv-

UPPER VOLTA

ed from Upper Senegal and Niger in 1919 and continued as a colony until 1932, when it was divided among French Sudan, Ivory Coast, and Niger Territory.

It was reconstituted in 1947 as an overseas territory of France until independence was granted. The capital is Ouagadougou.

The first stamps were those of Upper Senegal and Niger overprinted "HAUT-VOLTA" and released beginning in 1920. A number of surcharged issues followed, until specially designed stamps were issued in 1928.

Stamps inscribed "REPUBLIQUE DE HAUTE VOLTA" came in 1959.

Since then, stamps have been issued on a number of themes, some not directly relating to the republic. In a spirit of fine impartiality, the country's postal service has issued stamps honoring General De Gaulle, Queen Elizabeth II's Silver Jubilee, and Lenin!

The unit of currency is the CFA franc (q.v.).

The address of the philatelic bureau is Service Philatelique, Office des Postes et Telecommunications, Ouagadougou, Upper Volta.

UPU: (See Universal Postal Union.)

URGENTE: Inscription or overprint on special delivery stamps of Spain.

URI: A partial overprint on the first semipostal stamp of Yugoslavia.

The overprinted stamps had no franking power, according to Scott, and were given to an organization called the Uprava Ratnih Invalida (Society for Wounded Invalids), which sold them.

Urstempel: German word for "die."

Uruguay: The early European exploration of what is now the Oriental Republic of Uruguay occurred in the early 1500s.

Lack of mineral wealth and a native population very much inclined to hang on to its territory, tended to discourage early attempts at colonization. When the original inhabitants were eventually "pacified" by missionaries, the country became mostly cattle range. Border clashes with Brazil were frequent.

Strangely, it was the British in 1807 — during the Napoleonic Wars, when Spain was allied with Napoleon — who occupied the city of Montevideo and brought a taste of independence.

Their regime was less repressive than that of the Spanish, and the local population was im-

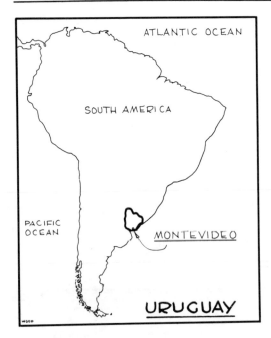

pressed. The first newspaper in Uruguay was founded by the British during their stay, and it was the British who suggested the formation of an independent Uruguay to serve as a buffer between Spanish Argentina and Portuguese Brazil.

Sadly, after independence did come in 1830, there were more than 40 years of internal strife before the people could set about building a nation.

But after its tumultuous beginning, Uruguay settled down, and by the early 1900s social measures had been enacted that made the country one of the most advanced in the world. Its standard of living was the highest in South America, and its government the most liberal.

Later, economic and political ups and downs rendered the economy unstable. By the 1960s, the economy was declining, and terrorist activity added to the problems facing a series of governments unable to cope. Recently the country has been under military government.

In the period between 1968 and 1976, inflation was 1,200%.

The area of Uruguay is 68,548 square miles, and the population is estimated at 2,910,000. The latest per capita income figure is $1,710, and the literacy rate is 94%.

Meat, wool, textiles, and wine are the chief industries, with wheat, citrus, rice, and oats being important crops.

The unit of currency is the new peso, which in 1981 was 10.44 to the US dollar.

The first stamps were issued in 1856 and are the so-called carrier issues of Adminstrator-General of Posts Atanasio Lapido. They are inscribed "DILIGENCIA."

The first general government issues were released in 1859 but bear the inscription "MONTEVIDEO." The country name did not appear on stamps until the 1866 issue. Subsequent stamps have followed the usual South American pattern, including a large proportion of air mail issues.

The address of the philatelic bureau is Direccion Nacional de Correos, Oficina Filatelica, Casilla de Correos 1296, Montevideo, Uruguay.

Urundi: (See Ruanda-Urundi.)

Usado: Spanish word for "used."

Usato: Italian word for "used."

US Automatic Vending Company:
(See Perforation, US Automatic Vending Company.)

US Cancellation Club:
The US Cancellation Club is a club for collectors of postal markings and cancelations.

It offers members a sales circuit; a research department; a bimonthly publication, *U.S. Cancellation Club News;* and a library.

Information is available from Alyce Evans, Box 286, Bonsall, CA 92003.

Use: French word for "worn."

Used: The term "used" refers to an adhesive postage or revenue stamp or item of postal stationery that has performed the service for which it was created and bears positive evidence that it has done so.

This evidence takes form of a postal cancelation or an appropriate revenue cancelation.

In the case of postage stamps and postal stationery, the term will often be qualified as "postally used" to distinguish it from a canceled-to-order specimen (q.v.) or a stamp that is valid for both postal and revenue use but that has been used to frank mail. (See Stamp, Postal Fiscal.)

Used: Foreign words for "used" include gebruikt (Dutch), utilise (French), gebraucht (German), usato (Italian), and usado (Spanish).

Used Abroad:
The term "used abroad" refers to stamps bearing evidence of usage outside the country of issuance.

Both Great Britain and France had post offices in foreign countries and colonial areas before local stamps were placed in use, and a great many of their stamp can be found bearing markings of those areas.

Stamps of Spain, Italy, and Russia are also known used outside those countries.

British stamps in particular can often be identified by the letters and/or numerals incorporated in the canceling device.

For example, "AO1" was used at Kingston, Jamaica; "G" was used at Gibraltar; "942" identifies Larnaca, Cyprus; and "C56" was used at Cartagena, Colombia.

US stamps have also been used in foreign countries, notably in China and Japan, with US consuls acting as postal agents.

US stamps were also used at military post offices in Puerto Rico in 1898-99 and at Vera Cruz, Mexico, in 1914.

Another source of stamps canceled out of their own country is the reply-paid postcard. When the card is sent out of the country, the stamp is still valid to prepay the reply portion of the card from UPU-member countries.

Though in the US this is usually a postal stationery item with imprinted indicia, cards bearing adhesive postage stamps have been used, and thus an adhesive can receive a "foreign" cancelation.

US 1869 Pictorial Research Associates:
The US 1869 Pictorial Research Associates is a specialist organization of collectors of the US 1869 issue.

It publishes a quarterly journal, *The 1869 Times,* and a book-length publication of articles called *The Register.*

A current project is to list and publish a book containing data on all existing 1869 covers.

Information is available from the association's secretary-treasurer, Rex H. Stever, Bank and Trust Tower, BT167, Corpus Christi, TX 78477.

USIR: The letters "USIR" are found watermarked on paper used to produce many US revenue stamps.

During the 1950s, the $1 stamp in the US 1938 Presidential definitive postage series was discovered printed on USIR-watermarked paper.

Two values in the 1895 definitive series, the 6c and 8c denominations, were also printed on USIR-watermarked paper.

Uskub: In 1911, Turkey issued a set of 18 stamps overprinted to mark the Sultan's visit to Macedonia.

Four different sets were issued, each bearing the name of a different city, one of which was Uskub.

The others were Monastir, Pristina, and Salonika.

US Philatelic Classics Society:
The US Philatelic Classics Society is an organization devoted to the study of 19th-century US material and its related postal history.

It publishes the *Chronicle,* a quarterly containing articles about the group's area of interest.

Information is available from Robert R. Hegland, Box 1011, Falls Church, VA 22041.

USPOD: The letters "USPOD" stand for United States Post Office Department. (See United States Postal Service.)

USPS: (See United States Postal Service.)

USPS: The letters "USPS" form the watermark for the paper on which US stamps were printed between 1895 and 1916. In some cases, the letters are single-lined; in others they are formed of two lines.

USSR: (See Union of Soviet Socialist Republics.)

USSR, German Occupation of:
In 1941 Germany overprinted "OSTLAND" on a set of 20 German stamps for use in the German-occupied areas of the USSR.

During the same year, a second set of 20 stamps was overprinted "UKRAINE" for use in that area.

U.S.T.C.: Overprint on stamps of Cochin for use in the United State of Travancore-Cochin in India.

Utilise: French word for "used."

UV (Ultra violet): (See Luminescent; Paper, Fluorescent; Phosphorescent.)

A selection of stamps from ''U'' countries.

V

V: Prior to the introduction of stamps overprinted "O.S." in 1874 for general Official use, South Australia used a number of different overprints to indicate use by specific government departments.

The overprint "V" stood for Volunteers.

V: The overprint "V" on air mail stamps of Colombia indicates that the stamp was sold in Venezuela to frank mail from that country to an interior point in Colombia and carried by the airline SCADTA (q.v.).

It was also necessary that such mail be franked with appropriate Venezuelan stamps.

The mail would be handed either to a Colombian consulate or to an agent of the airline.

V: The letter "V" overprinted on 1935-41 stamps of Belgium mark victory at the end of World War II.

The overprint on stamps of Norway issued in 1941 by the Quisling regime commemorated the successful invasion of the country by the Germans.

V.A.: Prior to the introduction of stamps overprinted "O.S." in 1874 for general Official use, South Australia used a number of different overprints to indicate use by specific government departments.

The overprint "V.A." stood for Valuator.

Vale: Overprint found on stamps of Nicaragua together with surcharge to indicate new denomination.

Valencia Stamps: Stamps with the appearance of Spanish postage stamps but inscribed "PLAN SUR DE VALENCIA" and bearing denominations of 25c or 50c are obligatory tax stamps.

In 1962 the Spanish government approved a redevelopment plan for the city of Valencia. It included the rebuilding of areas, land reclamation, and construction of a university.

This plan, which was called the Valencia Southern Plan, or the "Plan Sur De Valencia," was to be financed by local rather than state or national funds.

One of the schemes to raise money took the

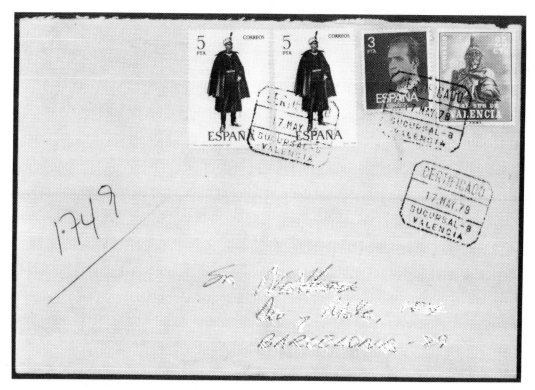

A Valencia stamp used from that city in 1978.

Two of the nine different designs issued between 1963 and 1978.

form of an obligatory tax stamps to be used on every letter mailed in Valencia.

The tax amounted to 25c, and special stamps were used beginning in 1963.

The stamps that have been issued in varying designs are 25c and 50c (1963), 25c (Oct. 14, 1964), 25c (May 20, 1966), 25c (1968), 25c (Jan. 3, 1971), 25c (May 11, 1973), 25c (Aug. 1, 1975), and 25c (1978).

Valeur: French word for "denomination."

Valevole/ per le stampe: Overprint on Italian parcel post stamps. Issued in 1890 for ordinary postage.

Valladolid Province: In 1868-69, provisional stamps were released for use in the Spanish province of Valladolid. They consisted of Spanish stamps overprinted "HABILITADO/ POR LA/ NACION."

VALLEES d'ANDORRE: Identifies some stamps of the co-principality of Andorra (q.v.).

VALONA: Overprint on stamps of Italy for use in the Italian post office at Valona in the Turkish Empire. (See Levant, Italian.)

VALPARAISO MULTADA: Inscription identifies early postage due labels in Chile.

Value: The term "value" is sometimes applied to describe the denomination (q.v.) of a stamp, as in "a 10c value." The word also expresses the monetary collectible worth of a philatelic item.

Sometimes, collectors will speak of a stamp's "catalog value," although this represents little more than an approximation of the item's market value.

The value of any philatelic item is what anyone is willing to pay for it at the time the owner wishes to sell.

Vancouver Island: Until Nov. 19, 1866, when it united with the colony of British Columbia (q.v.), Vancouver Island was a separate British colony.

Located off the west coast of Canada, it was discovered by Juan de Fuca in 1592. Spain claimed it in 1774, and Captain Cook visited in 1778. After a dispute with Spain over possession, Great Britain gained control.

The diplomatic Captain George Vancouver charted the island and named it "Quadra and Vancouver's Island" in tribute to the commander of the Spanish settlement at Nootka, on the island's west coast.

Although the Spanish left in 1794, it was not until 1843 that James Douglas established Fort Victoria, now known as Victoria, and provincial capital city of British Columbia.

In 1860 a 2½d stamp was released. It was inscribed "British Columbia and Vancouvers Island" and was used by both colonies.

Soon after the stamp appeared, the island's name was shortened to "Vancouver Island."

When Vancouver Island switched to decimal currency and British Columbia retained sterling, separate stamps were necessary, and two were issued in 1865 in denominations of 5c and 10c.

These were in use until union with British Columbia in 1866.

The largest island on the west coast of North America, it is 282 miles long with an area of 12,408 square miles.

At its southern tip it is separated from the state of Washington by the Strait of Juan de Fuca. Logging and the timber industry is most important to Vancouver Island's economy, although fishing and tourism are also significant.

The island is served by a number of ferry routes to Victoria and to the mid-island city of Nanaimo, from Washington State and the British Columbia mainland. (For map, see British Columbia.)

Van Diemen's Land: (See Tasmania.)

Vanuatu: Independence came to Vanuatu, formerly the New Hebrides, on July 30, 1980. It had been administered by both France and Great Britain for many years.

The strange arrangement had given rise to considerable confusion, and if the camel is an animal that was designed by a committee, then that same committee must have designed the

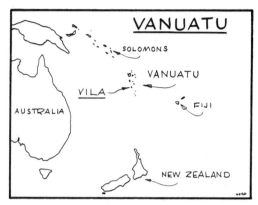

form of government known as a "condominium," which ruled the South Pacific island colony from 1906 until independence was achieved.

The administration by Great Britain and France was not merely joint, it was duplicated! The two governments exercised separate control over their own nationals and jointly over the native inhabitants, who, with some justification, felt a bit left out of the picture in their own land.

Vanuatu comprises a group of 11 main islands and some 70 islets located about 500 miles west of Fiji. The land area is about 5,800 square miles and the population numbers some 112,600.

The economy is based on copra but is not prosperous because of primitive methods that produce a low-grade product.

As might be expected in a land where there were two separate but equal administrations and everything had to be done in duplicate (with some things affecting the native population being done in triplicate), there were two separate but equal stamp issues!

Since the area's independence, the stamps have continued thus, and the first stamps bearing the name of Vanuatu differ only in the expression of denomination and in some of the island names on the maps depicted. The country name remains the same on both.

The islands' first stamps were issued in 1908. The French stamps were overprints on stamps of New Caledonia; the British ones were created by overprinting stamps of Fiji.

Prior to 1908, stamps of New Caledonia and New South Wales had been used.

In 1911 stamps featuring the arms of Great Britain and France were issued. On the British stamps, the coat of arms of France was on the left and that of Britain on the right. The denomination was in British currency.

On the French stamps, the coats of arms were reversed, and the denomination was in French currency.

After that, stamps were issued in similar designs but in duplicate, one in English and one in French.

The currency name has been changed from the New Hebrides franc to the vatu. In 1981, it was 64 to the US dollar.

The address of the philatelic bureau is Philatelic Section, Main Post Office, Vilna, Vanuatu, South Pacific.

Variedad: Spanish word for "variety."

Varieta: Italian word for "variety."

Variete: French word for "variety."

Variety: A variety is a stamp that differs in some way from a normal copy. But first, you must define what is normal, and that is sometimes not as easy as it sounds.

In most cases, it will be the stamps that exists in the greatest quantity and in the condition that the printer intended.

A variety can come about in any number of ways. It can be a die variety, occurring when a number of different dies and plates made from them are use in the course of a stamp's production, in which case the stamps will be identified as coming from die one, two, etc. Here the problem of which is normal comes up, since really both are normal, even though one may have two stamps that differ to some degree but that are both supposed to be the same!

Nonetheless, since all stamps printed from their respective dies are the same, they are both normal for their dies.

Apart from die variations, every stage of a stamp's production can result in the creation of varieties. The two perforation varieties of some US commemorative stamps (see Perforation) are excellent examples of the type of variety that is of philatelic interest, since it indicates that the stamps were perforated on two different pieces of equipment.

If a printing plate became damaged during printing and production continued, that would be classed as a constant variety, since all subsequent stamps from that particular plate position would bear the evidence of that damage. The same would apply if the damage was repaired and the repair was detectable.

If a variety is caused by, for instance, a piece of foreign matter on the plate, it might show up only once, or it might move around on the plate. This would be a non-constant variety and consequently of minimal philatelic interest.

This, together with other one-time varieties, including paper folds, missing or misplaced perforations, color shifts, and missing colors, are correctly known as EFO (errors, freaks, and oddities) material. In most cases, it is nothing more than printer's waste that came about during press start-up or at other times during the press run, perhaps while making press adjustments. It ought never to have left the printing plant and should have been caught and destroyed.

It is intersting to note how so much of this type of material becomes available to the philatelic public almost as soon as a new stamp appears. Its philatelic value is mostly minimal, except to show what can go wrong in both the printing process and the security that should protect it.

More significant are the varieties that come from work on the printing base, expecially in recess/ intaglio production.

These include such things as reentries, which can occur when a weak subject is strengthened, evidenced in the doubling of the design. A second application of a transfer roll during the making of the plate can also double some or all parts of a design to a greater or lesser degree.

Over- or under-inking can cause a stamp's appearance to be dramatically changed, but this is a non-constant variety that would properly be classed as a freak.

Even the startling, and often expensive, inverts are a type of freak occurrence, as would be a missing center (vignette).

In the Giori multicolor recess/ intaglio and other similar printing methods, in which the plate is inked with several colors at the same time, a number of variations can happen.

These include wiping smears or streaks, accidental blending of color on the plate, and color where it should not appear. Again, these are not constant and would fall in the EFO classification.

In photogravure printing, there are streaks and smears known as doctor blade flaws (q.v.), which are also not constant.

In other methods of printing, you can find set-offs — where sheet printed stamps can pick up a mirror image impression on their backs from being placed on top of another still damp sheet — plus color shifts and missing colors.

Of most philatelic interest are varieties caused by work on the printing base that can be noted on the stamp and which appears during the production run from the printing base while in that state.

Other significant varieties are those caused by wrongly watermarked paper, watermark in the wrong position (inverted, sideways, etc.), perforation variations (as in the 1977 US $1 vending machine booklet), and paper variations. (See Errors, Design; Errors, Production; Freaks; Printer's Waste.)

Variety: Foreign words for "variety" include soort (Dutch), variete (French), abart (German), varieta (Italian), and variedad (Spanish).

Varnish Bars: Diagonal bars of uncolored varnish have been applied across the face of a stamp to prevent the removal of a cancelation and subsequent reuse of the stamp.

The 1901-02 issue of Austria is an example of this security measure.

west bank of the Tiber. A special rail line runs into the Vatican City station.

Agreements with the Italian government provide for Vatican City postal, telegraph, and radio services. Though its currency is the Italian lira, it has its own coinage.

The area of the Vatican City is 109 acres, and the population is about 1,000.

The first Vatican City postage stamps were issued on Aug. 1, 1929, and feature the Papal Arms and Pope Pius XI.

Since then more than 700 stamps have been issued. Their designs feature religious themes, art, architecture, etc.

The address of the philatelic bureau is Ufficio Filatelico Governatorato, Vatican City.

VATICANE: Inscription identifies stamps of the Vatican City (q.v.).

Veglia: Veglia is an island in the Adriatic Sea off the northern coast of Yugoslavia. It is now named Krk.

In 1920, during the period when d'Annunzio occupied Fiume (q.v.), his army also occupied the islands of Veglia (Krk) and Arbe (q.v.).

Six regular stamps of Fiume and two express letter stamps were released overprinted "Veglia."

The island is the largest and most northerly of

Vathy (Vathi):
Vathy is a town on the island of Samos. In 1893 stamps of France were overprinted "VATHY" for use at the French post office there, which operated from 1893 to 1914.

Samos is a fertile island, much of it covered with vineyards, located in the Aegean Sea off the coast of Asia Minor. About 27 miles long by 14 miles at its widest point, it is separated from Turkey by a mile-wide strait. Cigarette making and boat building are industries of importance.

After years under Turkish control, the island was annexed to Greece in 1912.

In 1832 the town of Vathy (Vathi) became the capital of Samos, but it is now a part of the larger capital city bearing the same name as the island and formerly known as Limin Vatheos. It is located at the head of a bay on the north coast of the island. Samos is still part of Greece and uses Greek stamps.

Vatican City:
Formed in 1929 by the signing of the Lateran Treaty, the State of the Vatican City has independence and sovereignty in its international relations.

It is located within the city of Rome on the

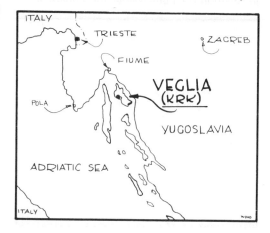

the Yugoslav offshore islands. It has a population in excess of 15,000 and an area of 157 square miles.

Austrian territory until 1918, it came under Italian occupation for two years and then became part of Yugoslavia, acquiring its new name at that time.

It is the most fertile of the Adriatic islands and grows grapes, olives, and figs. It is known for the quality of its red wine.

Vel: Dutch word for "sheet."

Velijnpapier: Dutch word for "wove paper."

Velletje: Dutch word for "souvenir sheet."

Venda. (See South Africa, Homelands of.)

Vending and Affixing Machine Perforations:
In the early 1900s in the US, a number of firms made vending machines that dispensed postage stamps.

These firms purchased stamps from the US Post Office in imperf sheets, cut them into strips, glued the strips together, applied their own types of perforation, and made them up into coils for use in their machines.

The names of the various companies were the Brinkerhoff Co., the Farwell Co., the International Vending Machine Co., the Schermack Co. (which included the Mailometer Co., the Mail-om-eter Co., and the Mail-O-Meter Co.), and the US Automatic Vending Co. (See under the various company names.)

Vending Machine Franking Label:
At the end of the 1970s and during the early 1980s, a new postal development began to appear as several countries introduced vending machines that dispenses gummed labels imprinted with an indicium indicating the amount of postage paid.

These are, in fact, postage stamps, and the only difference is that with some exceptions, the denomination is imprinted to correspond with the amount of money deposited by the mailer. Nonetheless, the labels bear a closer resemblance to a postage meter tape.

The following is a brief outline of this mailing system as operated in the various countries currently using the franking label dispensers.

Belgium: On Nov. 16, 1981, the Belgian Post Office introduced franking label vending machines at six locations in the country. The impressions are rectangular, with the figure of denomination impression in the center.

According to a Belgian Post Office announcement, the impressions were available in denominations of six, nine, 14, and 59 Belgian francs.

Finland: On April 1, 1982, Finnish postal authorities introduced franking label vending machines at the Helsinki railroad station, the Helsinki-Vantaa Airport, and outside the Turku 10 Post Office.

By inserting the correct amount, mailers can obtain labels in fixed denominations of 90 pennia, 1.10 markka, and 1.20 markka.

France: The Meter Stamp Society *Bulletin* #156 (Winter 1976) reported a self-service meter installed at the 75 PARIS 102 Post Office on Boulevard de Vaugirard in France.

This device uses preprinted labels onto which the machine imprints only the date, hour, and postage value. The identification number shown on the label is "G1 75702," "G" being the abbreviation for "Guichet d'Affranchissement Postal Automatique," meaning "automatic postage stamp window." The number "75702" is connected with the postal code number system used in France.

Germany: For some years, large-volume mailers in West Germany were able to use their computers to print the date of mailing and the postage amount on envelopes or address labels within a preprinted indicium prescribed by postal authorities.

According to a report in the MSS *Bulletin* #164 (Winter 1978), proof of such mailers' postal license is shown by a small posthorn printed in front of the denomination. This arrangement was simplified, according to the *Bulletin* report, whereby the indicium on the envelope could be completely preprinted with the inscription "Freimachung im Fenster" (meaning "postage in window").

As the computer prints up the invoice it also includes the date and postage denomination on the invoice. The invoice is then inserted in the envelope so that the name and address of the customer, as well as the computer-printed postage amount, shows through a window on the front.

This poses problems for collectors since the indicium on the envelope itself is more of the "permit" type, while the actual postage appears on the content of the mailing, such as an invoice, which does not lend itself to preservation by collectors.

A report in MSS *Bulletin* #171 (1981) noted that on Jan. 2, 1981, the West German postal administration began experimentally to install up to 15 self-service, coin-operated automats that supply metered postage stamps of 14 different denominations from 10 to 280 pfennigs. Coins up to five marks can be inserted, and the machine will return the balance automatically after the selection of the desired denominations.

The imprints appear on coils that show a posthorn and the inscription "DEUTSCHE/BUNDESPOST" in green. The upper half of the label has a yellow-orange-green background on which the automat prints the selected denomination together with the letters "DBP" in black. The German philatelic agency is reported to sell these automat stamps in all 14 denominations.

An additional report, in MSS *Bulletin* #172-73 (combined issue, 1981), notes that "roving stamp dealers had a field day on Jan. 2, 1981, as they offered first-day covers to the crowd waiting for their (sic) turn at the automats at $22 for the complete set, which cost $7. In several instances, the automats broke down and supplied lables without any value imprint or with double prints of the denomination."

It is further reported that the automatic machines cost about $13,000 each, and that so far 29 have been installed, one in the postal department's laboratory, 15 in front of various post offices, 11 at the postal philatelic sales office, and two at the Hanover Fair for promotional purposes.

Great Britain: Six coin-operated postage vending machines were scheduled to be installed by the British Post Office during June or July 1982, five in London and one in Edinburgh. They dispense stamps in 31 fixed denominations printed on a security-design background. The

A cover bearing a Japanese franking label.

Switzerland's vending machine franking label.

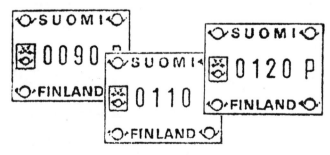

The three denominations of the Finnish vending machine franking labels.

One of the metered postage stamps used by the West German Postal Administration.

denominations range from ½p to 15½p in ½p steps.

Japan: A coin-operated postage vending machine was first installed at the Shibuya 1 Post Office, Japan, on June 23, 1975, according to MSS *Bulletin* #155 (Fall 1976). Subsequently, additional machines began operating at Tokyo and Nakano post offices. A Japanese legend at the bottom of the impression translates as "Valid for the day of issue only."

Switzerland: Coin-operated devices manufactured by the firm of FRAMA were put into operation in Switzerland beginning on Aug. 8, 1976. These devices, called "Self-Service Value Ticket Automatons," or SSVTA for short, contain a printing mechanism described as "a line-printer (Zeilendrucker) with cliche-print" developed especially for this apparatus.

The SSVTA labels or indicia measure 4x3.2cm and have a bluish safety underprint. They resemble closely the regular meter indicia from meters manufactured by the firm. The SSVTAs are capable of printing denominations from 0005 to 9995 Rappen.

The first SSVTA device was used at Zurich on Aug. 8, 1976, the labels showing the identification "A1" below the denomination. Imprints were canceled with a postmark reading "8023 Zurich 23 Hauptbahnhof" at the central railroad station post office.

Other such devices were subsequently used at Bern (A2); Grindelwald (A3); and Geneva (A4).

A report in MSS *Bulletin* #156 (Winter 1976) states that between 3,000 and 4,000 of the SSVTA labels were sold on the first day, presumably mostly to collectors. An account of these devices is contained in an article by E.J. Roscoe in *Stamp Collector*, March 26, 1977.

A related development from FRAMA is the "Desk Top Ticket Producer," which prints labels (Roscoe, *Stamp Collector*, June 25, 1977). These desk-top devices are not coin-operated but are used at parcel counters in post offices. Desired denominations are punched up on a 10-key keyboard and printed by the same mechanism as contained in the SSVTAs.

The only differences between the desk-top indicia and those from the SSVTAs are in the designation in the bottom-center rectangle and the wording and numerals printed to the left of the indicia from the desk-top devices (Roscoe, *Stamp Collector*, June 25 and March 26, 1977).

I am grateful to Ernest Roscoe for his cooperation in supplying much of this information.

Vending Machine Gripper Marks:

Frequently, collectors will come across what seems at first glance to be a variety of a US coil stamp.

This takes the form of varied and assorted markings on the face of the stamp, usually somewhere near the center and having mostly a vertical character.

In the case of those illustrated, it is fainter than most and gives the impression of being a crack or mark on the printing plate.

Unfortunately, the truth for those collectors who "discover" such items is a bit disappointing. They are not varieties at all, but merely damage caused by a vending machine mechanism.

Depending on the money inserted, the machine will feed out so many stamps, and then a gripper will hold the next stamp so that more stamps cannot be pulled out of the machine.

This gripper mechanism will gradually pick up a coating of ink from the faces of the stamps it holds and tend to smear the ink back on as it operates on successive stamps.

The Eisenhower coil stamp often shows these gripper marks and has been seen advertised as a variety dubbed the "Weeping Ike" variety. Needless to say, there are collectors who have

Vending machine gripper marks on the Eisenhower 6c coil stamp and the 10c Jefferson Memorial coil stamp.

acquired such items thinking they have desirable plate varieties.

In fact, these items are nothing more than damaged stamps and are only noted here in an attempt to ensure that collectors do not buy them thinking that they are adding desirable stamps to their collections. As in all things philatelic, knowledge will protect you.

Venetian Red: Foreign terms for Venetian red include rouge brun terne (French), Venezianischrot (German), rosso Veneziano (Italian), and rojo Veneciano (Spanish).

Venezia Giulia: Venezia Giulia was an Italian province on the Yugoslav-Italian border and included the city of Trieste (q.v.).

At the end of World War II, it was occupied by the Allies, and in 1947 the Free Territory of Trieste was created with the balance of the area going to Yugoslavia.

Italian stamps were overprinted "A.M.G. V.G." by the combined US-British Military Government from 1945 to 1947.

In the Yugoslav area prior to 1947, stamps inscribed "Istria Slovensko" were used by the Yugoslav military government. (For post-WWI issues, after Italy took the area from Austria, see Italian Austria.)

Venezianischrot: German word for the color "Venetian red."

Venezia Tridentina: (See Italian Austria.)

Venezolano: A unit of currency used in Venezuela during 1879. It was composed of 100 centesimos.

Venezuela: To the Peninsula of Paria, opposite the island of Trinidad, goes the honor of being the first spot on the South American continent upon which Columbus set foot. This event occurred in August 1498.

The name of Venezuela, meaning "Little Venice," was acquired when Spanish explorers saw native houses on stilts over the shallow Lake Maracaibo.

It was not until the 1520s that a settlement on the mainland was established. In 1528 ownership of western Venezuela was transferred to a German banking house as payment of a loan by King Charles V of Spain.

The 18-year occupation by the Germans was a period of unsuccessful searches for gold and other sources of wealth. Little did they realize the treasure of oil that lay beneath their feet!

Caracas, the capital city of Venezuela, was founded in 1567, and soon other settlements along the coast sprang up.

The economic potential of the area was recognized more by foreigners than by the Spanish, and the Dutch, British, and French were active along the Venezuelan coast during the 16th and 17th centuries.

The winds of change began to rustle through the Venezuelan countryside in the early 1800s. While Spain was occupied by Napoleon, independence was declared in 1811.

But it was not until 1821 that Simon Bolivar was able to bring freedom to a population decimated by the struggle.

The new country first united with Colombia and Ecuador as the Republic of Gran Colombia but became an independent nation in 1830.

For much of its life, Venezuela has been ruled by military governments, but in recent years, democratic governments have been freely elected.

Oil is the mainstay of the country's economy, and Venezuela is believed to have one of the world's largest oil reserves. Oil profits are currently providing the country with enormous revenue, but inflation is high. The latest per capita income figure is $2,772, and the literacy rate is 82%.

Venezuela has an area of 352,143 square miles and a population estimated at 14,529,000.

The unit of currency is the bolivar (100 cen-

timos), which in 1981 was 4.29 to the US dollar.

The first stamps of Venezuela were issued in 1859 and feature the country's coat of arms. Most of the other 19th-century issues picture the national hero, Simon Bolivar.

During the 1950s, a continuing series of stamps was issued depicting the coats of arms of the various districts of the country. In common with other South American countries, Venezuela has issued a large proportion of air mail stamps.

The address of the philatelic bureau is Direccion de Correos, Oficina Filatelica Nacional, Caracas, Venezuela. (See Guayana; Carupano.)

Verde: Spanish, Italian, and Portuguese word for the color "green."

Verde Manzana: Spanish expression for the color "apple green."

Verde Mar: Spanish expression for the color "sea green."

Verde Mare: Italian expression for the color "sea green."

Verde Mirto: Italian and Spanish expression for the color "myrtle green."

Verde Muscosa: Italian expression for the color "moss green."

Verde Musgo: Spanish expression for the color "moss green."

Verde Salvia: Italian and Spanish expression for the color "sage green."

Verfahren: German word for "method."

Verfalscht: German word for "falsified."

Vergato: Italian word for "laid," as in laid paper.

Verge: French word for "laid," as in laid paper.

Vergroessern: German word for "magnify."

Verkaufpreis: German word for "selling price."

Verkehrt: German word for "inverted."

Vermelho: Portuguese word for the color "red."

Vermiglio: Italian word for the color "vermilion."

Vermilion: Foreign words for the color "vermilion" include vermillion (French), zinnober (German), vermiglio (Italian), and cinabrio (Spanish).

Vermillion: French word for the color "vermilion."

Verschlussmarke: German word for "label" or "seal."

Versleten: Dutch word for "worn."

Verso: French word for "back."

Versteigerung: German word for "auction."

Vert: French word for the color "green."

Vert de Mer: French expression for the color "sea green."

Vert Emeraude: French expression for the color "emerald."

Vert Mousse: French expression for the color "moss green."

Vert Myrte: French expression for the color "myrtle green."

Vert Pomme: French expression for the color "apple green."

Vert Sauge: French expression for the color "sage green."

Vervalsing: Dutch word for "forgery."

Very Fine: Generally, the highest standard of condition, although some use is made of more impressive sounding grades above this called "superb," "extra fine," "very fine plus," etc. (See Condition.)

Very Good: A standard of condition, rating between good and fine. (See Condition.)

VF: The letters "VF" are frequently noted in price lists, advertisements, auction catalogs, etc.

They are an abbreviation of "very fine," a standard of condition generally held to be the top grade, although such expressions as "superb," "extra fine," and "very fine plus" are sometimes noted. (See Very Fine; Condition.)

VG: The letters "VG" represent a standard of condition and are an abbreviation of "very good."

This is not a particularly high grade and rates between "good" and "fine." (See Condition.)

Vichy Administration: During the World War II Vichy administration in France, which was a puppet government under its German overlords, a number of stamp issues for the colonial possessions of France were prepared bearing the names of a number of the French colonies.

Many of these issues also bear the portrait of Petain, the head of the French puppet regime.

These stamps, however, were generally not placed on sale in the colonies, and though some catalogs list them, they are correctly described as "prepared for use but not issued."

Victoria: The second smallest, after Tasmania, of the states making up the Commonwealth of Australia, Victoria has the second largest population.

Strangely, it was first settled during the 1830s in violation of a government order barring settlement in the area, then a part of the colony of New South Wales (q.v.).

In the beginning it was an agricultural community, and the first settlers were farmers who crossed from Van Diemen's Land (q.v.) in search of grazing land.

In 1836 the government backed down and authorized settlement. By 1850, there was a population of 76,000 people and six million sheep!

Becoming dissatisfied with their representation in the government of New South Wales, the settlers soon demanded more of a say in their affairs, and in 1851 Victoria became a separate colony.

With the discovery of gold near Melbourne, a rush ensued, and by 1860 there were a half-million people living in the colony.

During the 1890s, Victoria suffered a massive depression triggered by the speculative boom of the 1880s, and this was felt for the next 20 years.

With federation in 1901 came a growing industralization and a trend for population to become more concentrated in urban centers. By 1961, more than 65% of Victoria's residents lived in metropolitan Melbourne, the state's capital.

The first stamps were issued in 1850 and differed from most in that they featured a full-face portrait of Queen Victoria on her throne. An interesting range of various designs followed, including several high values depicting King Edward VII.

In 1897 and 1900, semi-postal issues appeared. The latter comprised a pair showing the Victoria Cross, Britain's top award for bravery and scouts during the South African War. Modern collectors would likely object strongly to the surtaxes — the stamps were 1d + 1/- and 2d + 2/-. The fact that their mint and used catalog values are equal is a clue as to their popularity during their period of use.

A number of postal-fiscal stamps are included in the catalog listings. These stamps, inscribed "STAMP DUTY" (q.v.), were valid for postal use from Jan. 1, 1884, according to the Gibbons catalog, but collectors should be sure that they bear postal cancels.

VICTORIA: The word "VICTORIA" inscribed on stamps of Cuba identifies World War II-era postal tax stamps.

Victoria Land: A number of the ½d and 1d 1909 stamps of New Zealand were overprinted "VICTORIA LAND" and supplied to Capt. Scott for use by members of his expedition on their mail from Antarctica during his 1910-1912 effort to be the first to reach the South Pole.

The tragic story of that journey to the pole

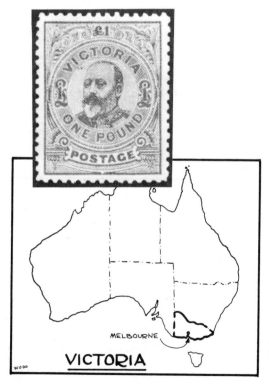

and the return, during which Scott and his party died, is one of exploration's epics.

Robson Lowe, in his *Encyclopedia of British Empire Postage Stamps, Volume IV,* reports that 2,400 of the ½d stamp and 24,000 of the 1d denomination were overprinted.

Lowe also notes that there were four mails sent back from a post office established at Cape Evans on Jan. 3, 1911, and that the ½d stamps was only used on the last one.

Forgeries exist.

Virgin Islands: (See British Virgin Islands.)

Virgin Islands (American): (See Danish West Indies.)

Vienna: In 1945 German stamps were overprinted diagonally "Osterreich" for use in Vienna, Lower Austria, and Burgenland.

Vier: Numeral four (4) in Dutch and German.

Viererblock: German word for "block of four."

Viertel: German word for "one quarter."

Vietnam: The area that is now the Socialist Republic of Vietnam was under the control of China from 111 BC to AD 939.

Modern history in Vietnam dates from 1858,

when the French began their penetration of Indo-China.

Vietnam continued as part of French Indo-China (q.v.) until World War II, when Japan occupied most of Southeast Asia.

After the war, the French tried to reestablish their regime by force of arms. Following their defeat at Dienbienphu, the country became split between the southern part, under Bao Dai, and the Communists in the north, under Ho Chi Minh.

Thus the scene was set for the long and unsuccessful struggle to avert a Communist takeover of the entire country. Gradually the US became involved in the South Vietnamese fight against the north.

After a long and bitter war, the north was victorious, US forces were withdrawn, and the country declared unified by the Communists on July 2, 1976.

In recent years, the USSR has supported Vietnam. Relations with the People's Republic of China grew worse to the extent that China invaded Vietnam for a short while, reportedly as a punitive measure.

The US Treasury Department forbids the importation of all stamps issued by the Democratic Republic of Vietnam (North Vietnam), and on April 30, 1975, it extended the prohibition to include the issues of the Socialist Republic of Vietnam.

Stamps were issued by South Vietnam, North Vietnam, and the National Front for the Liberation of South Vietnam.

The latter organization issued its own stamps for use in the areas of South Vietnam it controlled.

During the 1950s, Indian stamps were overprinted for use by Indian forces serving with an international commission in Vietnam.

The population is estimated at 52,300,000, and the latest per capita income figure is $150.

The unit of currency is the dong (100 xu), which in 1981 was 2.18 to the US dollar.

VIETNAM CONG HOA: Inscription identifies stamps of South Vietnam.

VIETNAM DAN CHU CONG HOA: Inscription identifies stamps of North Vietnam.

Vif: French word for bright, as in "bright color."

Vignetta: Italian word for "vignette."

Vignette: Foreign words for "vignette' include vignette (French and German), vignetta (Italian), and vineta (Spanish).

Vignette: A vignette is the central portion of a stamp that is in a different color from that of the frame and that requires a separate pass through the press.

This central portion can be a portrait, a landscape, or other subject. It is usual for the vignette to have edges that tend to fade out, so that any misregistration within the frame will be less obvious.

Where the same vignette is used in stamps with varied frame colors, country names, or

Misregistration of the vignette can change the appearance of a stamp.

denominations, its plate is termed a key plate.

The various colonial key types (q.v.) of Great Britain, France, Spain, Portugal, and Germany are examples.

Upside-down centers and inverted frames can result from production of stamps with vignettes. A classic example is the US 24c air mail invert.

This patriotic label is called a vignette in France.

Vignette: This term used in France to describe a non-postal label in the format of a postage stamp.

Vijf: Numeral five (5) in Dutch).

Vilnius: The first stamp issues of Lithuania are called the Vilnius issues.

Vilnius was the capital city of the once-free and independent country of Lithuania. It was invaded and occupied by the Soviet Union and has since been made a part of that country.

The vignette and the frame.

Vinaccia: Italian word for the color "claret."

Vineta: Spanish word for "vignette."

'Vineta' Bisect:
When the German cruiser *Vineta* visited New Orleans in 1901, during a goodwill cruise, a ball was held by the German community to celebrate the kaiser's birthday.

The local press reported the grand affair in detail, and since most of the crew attended, they wanted to send the newspapers home to family and friends.

The ship's stock of 3pf stamps needed to frank the newspapers proved inadequate to handle the volume of mail. And so came into being one of philately's gems, as the ship's officer in charge of postal affairs cut in half vertically a number of 5pf stamps and handstamped each half "3PF."

The use of the bisects caused a great fuss in Berlin, and word was sent to the ship to cease and desist at once.

However, the word from on high took five months to reach *Vineta,* and by then a supply of 3pf stamps had been received. So the question of bisecting stamps was quite academic.

The quantity of bisects made is reported not to exceed 600, since only three sheets of 100 5pf stamps were bisected and handstamped. Not all are believed to have been used, however.

Vin Fiz Label:
Only eight years after that first flutter along the ground at Kitty Hawk by the Wright brothers, a man flew from the Atlantic to the Pacific across the width of the United States.

His name was Calbraith Perry Rodgers, and he took 84 days, had 12 major crashes, and had replaced virtually every part of his Wright Flyer aircraft by the time he sighted the Pacific Ocean.

But, most important to philately, he took along some mail franked with a special label plus regular postage.

The label was the famous Vin Fiz label, a black stamp with a face value of 25c and reproducing the Wright Flyer.

Rodgers left Sheepshead Bay, Long Island, on Sept. 17, 1911, on a flight sponsored by a soft drink firm that made the grape drink known as "Vin Fiz."

He finally landed at Long Beach, Calif., taxied his aircraft to the water's edge, and wet the wheels in the Pacific Ocean.

Despite the crashes and the injuries — he was on crutches by the end of the flight — his was the greatest adventure so far in a heavier-than-air craft, and he captured the attention of a continent.

More important to our hobby, he had also made philatelic history with the Vin Fiz label.

Violet: Foreign words for the color "violet" include violett (German and Swedish), violet (French), violetto (Italian), and violeta (Spanish).

Violeta: Spanish word for the color "violet."

Violett: German and Swedish word for the color "violet."

Violetto: Italian word for the color "violet."

Virginia Postal History Society:
Concentrating on the postal history of Virginia, including West Virginia, the Virginia Postal History Society works to further research about the state's postal history.

A quarterly journal, *Way Markings,* publishes original articles, reprints of US and Confederate postal records, and other material of interest to members.

A continuing *Catalog of Virginia Postal Markings, Colonial-1865,* is a major project.

Annual meetings are held in conjunction with the exhibition VAPEX. Information is available from the society at Box 29771, Richmond, VA 23229.

Virgule: A virgule is a short, oblique stroke or slash, thus /. It is used to indicate line endings in quotations and to express British shilling and fractions; for example, 2/6 for two shillings and sixpence or 2½ shillings. (See Shilling Mark.)

A virgule is also used to indicate that a choice may be made between two stated words, as in "and/ or."

Vit: Swedish word for "white."

Vivo: Italian and Spanish word for "bright," as in bright color.

Vladivostok Issue:
Two issues of stamps, one in 1922 and the other in 1923, for use in the Far Eastern Republic (q.v.) are known as the Vladivostok issues.

The first consisted of the overprint "1917/ 7-XI/ 1922" on earlier stamps. The second was a Cyrillic overprint and surcharged on Russian stamps.

V-Mail: (See Airgraph.)

V.N.: Prior to the introduction of stamps overprinted "O.S." in 1874 for general Official use, the colony of South Australia used a number of different overprints to indicate use by specific government departments.

The overprint "V.N." stood for Vaccination.

VOJENSKA POSTA: Inscription on stamps of the Czechoslovak Legion Post in Siberia.

VOJNA UPRAVA JUGOSLA-VENSKE ARMIJE: This overprint is found on stamps of Yugoslavia for use in Zone B, Istria, and Slovene coastal area.

Volksrust: The town of Volksrust is located in what was once Transvaal, near the border with Natal.

In 1902 stamps of an earlier regime were issued for local purposes overprinted "V.R.I." and used from the town. (See Transvaal.)

VOLKSSTAAT WURTEMBERG: Inscription or overprint identifies some Official stamps of Wurttemberg.

VOM EMPFANGER EIN-ZUZIEHEN: Inscription identifies postage due labels of Danzig.

VOM EMPFANGER ZAHLBAR: Inscription on postage due labels of Bavaria.

Von Stephan, Dr. Heinrich: (See Stephan, Dr. Heinrich von.)

Voor Het Kind: The inscription "Voor Het Kind" on stamps of the Netherlands denotes semi-postal issues for child welfare.

The inscription translates as "For the Children."

VR Essay: When the Penny Black of Great Britain was conceived, it was also intended that a version bearing the letters "VR" in the upper left and upper right corners, respectively, would be issued for Official use.

Such a stamp was prepared but never officially placed in use. It is known in used condition, however, and thus must have somehow "escaped" and been used on mail.

Since it was printed in a quantity of 3,500 sheets, it should properly be regarded as "prepared for use but not issued" rather than being considered an essay. (See Penny Black.)

V.R.I.: Overprint on various stamps of the areas occupied by the British in South Africa. Stands for "Victoria Regina Imperatrix."

V.R. SPECIAL POST: An overprint on stamps of the Transvaal for the British occupation of Vryburg, Cape of Good Hope.

V.R. TRANSVAAL: Overprint on stamps of South African Republic for use in the Transvaal during the British occupation.

Vryburg: During the South African War, the town of Vryburg, located some 120 miles north of Kimberley, was occupied by the Boers in 1899.

In the course of their occupation, the Boers produced several stamps comprising issues of the Cape of Good Hope overprinted and surcharged.

In addition to the new figure of denomination, the overprint consists of the letters "Z.A.R.," which stand for "Zuid Afrikaansche Republiek" (South African Republic).

When British forces reoccupied the town in 1900, they issued stamps of the Transvaal overprinted sideways "V.R./ SPECIAL/ POST."

VUJA-STT: Stamps overprinted or inscribed "VUJA-STT" were created by Yugoslavia for use in Zone B of the ex-Italian province of Venez Giulia (q.v.). (See Trieste, Free Territory of.)

The initials "VUJA-STT" refer to "VOJNA UPRAVA JUGOSLOVENSKA ARMIJE, SLOBODNA TERITORIJA TRSTA" (Military Adminstration Yugoslav Army, Free Territory of Trieste), according to the Scott catalog.

The overprints vary and include "STT VUJA," "VUJA-STT," or "STT VUJNA."

This area included the cities of Fiume (q.v.) and Pola.

A selection of stamps from ''V'' countries.

W: Prior to the introduction of stamps overprinted "O.S." in 1874 for general Official use, South Australia used a number of different overprints to indicate use by specific government departments.

The overprint "W" stood for Waterworks.

Waagerecht:
German word for "horizontal." Thus, when combined with German word "paar (pair), "waagerechtes paar" means "horizontal pair."

Waddington of Kirkstall Ltd.:
John Waddington of Kirkstall Ltd. is a firm of British security printers currently producing postage stamps for a number of postal administrations.

The firm accepted its first postage stamp commission in 1968 from Guyana.

Since then, Waddington has produced stamps for 79 British Commonwealth countries and offers both design and production facilities, using the four-color lithographic process.

Wadhwan:
An Indian Feudatory State located in Western India, Wadhwan issued a total of three stamps in 1888-89.

These stamps feature the state's coat of arms and were valid only within the state.

Wadhwan is now part of the Republic of India and uses its stamps.

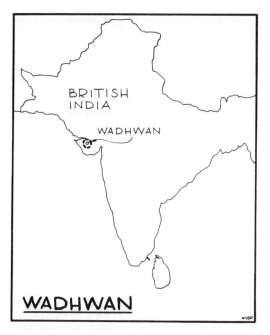

WADHWAN

Waghorn, Thomas:
Thomas Waghorn was a British sailor who established a letter-forwarding agency in Egypt in 1845.

The inscription "Care of Mr. Waghorn" identified letters that were carried between Great Britain and India much more quickly than if they had gone all the way around Africa by ship.

Waghorn set up overland transportation between Alexandria and Suez.

He had served in the Royal Navy, and as captain of the East India ship *Matchless* he saw the need for a fast mail service between India and Great Britain.

As part of his organization, he built hotels between Cairo and Suez and operated steamers on the Red Sea.

He also found that overland European travel to Trieste and down the Adriatic to Alexandria was 13 days faster than the route across France and through the length of the Mediterranean Sea.

Despite his efforts and the pioneering work he performed, he died in 1850 tired and worn out by his efforts and deeply disappointed at what he perceived as a lack of success. (See Forwarding Agents.)

Walachia:
(See Moldavia-Walachia; Romania.)

Wales:
The Principality of Wales is located in the western part of Great Britain.

The Romans subdued the tribes of Wales between AD 69 and 79, and following their withdrawal from Britain, the Celtic inhabitants of England fled to the west before the Anglo-Saxon invaders and eventually merged with the tribes in the Welsh mountains.

Although in 1062-64 an English army subdued Wales and William the Conqueror persuaded the Welsh to recognize him as king, it was not until 1284 that King Edward I annexed Wales to England as a principality.

Then, in a master-stroke of public relations that would be remarkable even today, he had his son made Prince of Wales. Since then, each eldest son of the British monarch has been made Prince of Wales.

There was to be only one final Welsh uprising against "foreign" domination. It occurred in the early 1400s. Since then, Wales has been relatively peaceful, except for when Wales and England play rugby!

Wales has an area of 8,017 square miles, and its population was estimated in 1976 at 2,766,800. The capital is Cardiff.

The principality's main economic asset is coal

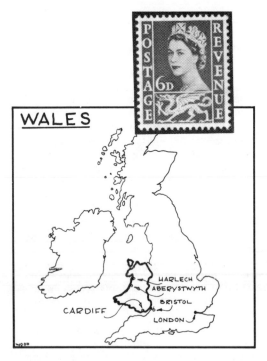

WALES

HARLECH
ABERYSTWYTH
CARDIFF
BRISTOL
LONDON

and the largest single employer is the coal-mining industry.

Prior to World War II, the coal-producing area of South Wales was in a state of deep depression, and I remember the coal town of Merthyr Tydfil as being a bleak, barren wasteland of crumbling houses with ancient streetcars rattling along the deserted streets.

The activity of WWII gave the Welsh coal industry a shot in the arm, but I will never forget the atmosphere of depression that hung over South Wales in the late 1930s.

Stamps for Wales were first issued in 1958 and were part of the regional issues of Great Britain.

First bearing the Wilding portrait of Queen Elizabeth II, and from 1971 the Machin Head design, the stamps all feature the Welsh dragon emblem.

The stamps are available only from post offices in Wales and the British philatelic service (British Post Office Philatelic Bureau, 20 Brandon St., Edinburgh, Scotland, EH3 5TT, United Kingdom).

Wallis and Futuna Islands: This
French island group comprises the Wallis group (Uvea and eight islets) and Futuna, which consists of Futuna (or Hoorne) and Alofi.

The two groups lie west of Samoa and northeast of Fiji. They are about 120 miles apart.

Discovered in the late 1700s, the Wallis group

was occupied by the French in 1842. At first attached to Tahiti, it became a dependency of New Caledonia in 1887.

The Wallis group is about 40 square miles in area, and the nine islands within the reef vary in circumference from one to 10 miles.

The Futuna, or Hoorne, group was annexed by France and placed under the administration of New Caledonia along with the Wallis group.

Fortuna is about eight miles long by five wide and rises to an altitude of 2,500 feet.

Uninhabited Alofi is six miles long and three wide.

They all became the French colony of Wallis and Futuna Islands in 1917, being raised to the status of a French Overseas Territory on July 29, 1961.

The population was estimated in 1971 at 10,000, and the capital is Mata Utu on Wallis Island.

The colony's first stamps were released in 1920 and are overprints on the stamps of New Caledonia. During World War II, a number of stamps were overprinted "FRANCE LIBRE" to show support for the Free French.

Many of the recent issues are very attractive and feature the scenery, history, and culture of the group.

The address of the philatelic bureau is Service Philatelique, Direction General des PTT, Matu Utu, Wallis and Futuna Islands, South Pacific.

The unit of currency is the CFA franc (q.v.).

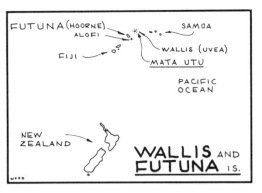

FUTUNA (HOORNE)
ALOFI
FIJI
SAMOA
WALLIS (UVEA)
MATA UTU
PACIFIC
OCEAN
NEW
ZEALAND
WALLIS AND FUTUNA IS.

Wallpaper Covers: A severe shortage of paper in the Confederacy during the American Civil War resulted in the use of all kinds of unusual paper to make envelopes.

Wallpaper was one such paper, and covers made of it are highly prized by collectors of Confederate material.

Walsall Security Printers Ltd.: The firm of Walsall Security Printers entered the stamp-printing business in 1963 and currently produces stamps for some 50 countries.

The firm, located in Walsall, England, is reported to offer its clients a package stamp deal, whereby its research and art departments create the stamp design which is then printed on the firm's varied printing equipment.

The free-form, self-stick stamps of Tonga and Sierra Leone are produced by Walsall.

Walzendruck: German word for "rotary printing."

Want List: A want list is a listing, usually by catalog number, of stamps that a collector requires for his collection.

It is usual for a collector to send such a list to a stamp dealer, who will supply those items on the list that he has in his stock.

In the case of a large list, a dealer may fill items up to an amount specified by the collector. He may also be requested to retain the list and supply shipments at specified intervals.

Many dealers' advertisements note that want lists are welcomed.

War Board of Trade: In 1918 stamps of the Swiss 1908-18 issue were overprinted "Industrielle/ Kriegs-/ wirtschaft" for use by the War Board of Trade.

War Cover Club: The War Cover Club is a group devoted to the collection and study of military covers, censored mail, POW covers, patriotics, and all aspect of military postal history.

Members' interests range from stampless covers of the Revolutionary War to Korea and Vietnam.

The club was formed in 1937 and is unit #19 of the American Philatelic Society. A bulletin is published, and regular auctions of appropriate material are held.

Information is available from Secretary-Treasurer Lincoln E. Kieffer, Box 173, Jamesburg, NJ 08831.

War Tax Stamp: (See Stamp, War Tax.)

Wasserzeichen: German word for "watermark."

Waterlow & Sons Ltd.: Waterlow & Sons Ltd. was a British security printing firm known for many years as a producer of stamps for many countries.

On Jan. 9, 1961, its stamp-printing operation was taken over by De La Rue & Co. Ltd., another of Britain's famous security printing firms.

Waterlow had printed the first British Commonwealth Giori-printed stamps when it pro-

The first British Commonwealth stamp printed by Waterlow & Sons using the firm's Giori press.

duced Jamaica's Postal Centenary issue of Jan. 4, 1960.

In 1940-41, when the facilities of De La Rue had been destroyed by German terror bombing, Waterlow had taken over the perforation of certain stamps for New Zealand, gauging 12, 14, and 14x15, creating the so-called "Blitz Perforations."

Watermark: A watermark is a pattern impressed into paper during its manufacture.

While it is in a semi-soft pulp state, the paper is passed under a roller in the form of a wire gauze cylinder called a "dandy roller."

If the paper is to be watermarked, shapes known as "bits" are affixed to the roller at regular intervals, and as the paper passes this roller, the "bits" cause a slight thinning where they are impressed into the pulp.

Thus, when the paper is held up to a light source, the watermark shows, since the paper is thinner at that point and thus more transparent.

An exception to this is a type of watermark in which the design shows up darker instead of lighter, because the watermark area of the paper has been made thicker instead of thinner.

L.N. and M. Williams, in *Fundamentals of Philately,* note that the 1858 issue of Russia, the 10k, 20k, and 30k values, utilize this form of watermark, as do some of the Hitler-era German stamps.

This type of watermark is created by passing the drying pulp over a smooth roller into which the watermark design has been engraved. The

A variety of watermarks.

pulp is pressed into the design and thus is thicker in the area of the watermark design.

Watermarked paper has been used from the very earliest days of adhesive postage stamps in an attempt to discourage counterfeiting.

The first adhesive postage stamp, the British Penny Black, was printed on paper watermarked with a small, simple crown. Areas such as British Commonwealth countries still use watermarked paper, and there are many different designs.

Reflecting a modern trend, Great Britain issued its first stamp produced on unwatermarked paper in 1967.

France has never used watermarked paper for stamp production, if you except the 1892 15-centime stamp printed on paper with a quadrille pattern impressed into it during manufacture. But this is not a watermark so much as a paper type, although it came about in a similar way.

The United States printed stamps on watermarked paper for a period from 1894 to 1915.

The watermark consisted of the letters "USPS" (standing for United States Postal Service) repeated across the sheet.

There were two types used, the first employing letters best described as "double lined," and the second, beginning in 1910, with the same letters, but in single-line form.

An interesting exception was the unintentional use of paper watermarked "USIR" intended for revenue stamps.

This occurred in 1895 and again in 1951, when the then-current $1 stamp was produced on paper intended for revenue stamp production.

Getting back to the normal USPS double- and single-lined watermarks, often only one letter and sometimes only a portion of a letter appears on a single stamp, and it is frequently very difficult to identify the letter especially the single-line version.

The designs of watermarks are many and varied. They can take the form of letters, symbols, or combinations of both. Probably the most widely used watermark is the so-called "Crown CA" type used for Crown Colonies within the British Commonwealth.

For philatelic purposes, watermarks can be divided into four main types. These are:

Sheet Watermark: In this type, one large design is used to cover an entire sheet of paper. There may be some stamps in sheets printed from such paper that receive no portion of the watermark.

An example of sheet watermark can be seen on the stamps issued by Brazil on Oct. 7, 1933, to mark the visit of the president of Argentina to Brazil.

Continuous Watermark: This type consists of a repetition of various combinations of letters or words over and over across an entire sheet. The United States' "USPS" watermark is an example of continuous watermark.

Unit Watermark: A unit watermark is one where a symbol or a symbol-letter combination forming a single unit appears on each stamp in a sheet. The pineapple watermark of Jamaica's first issue illustrates this type.

Multiple Watermark: Multiple watermarks are similar to unit watermarks, except that they are usually smaller and more closely spaced. One complete design and portions of several more will appear on a single stamp.

The "Multiple Crown CA" watermarks of the British Crown Colonies are of this type.

Other types of watermarks should be mentioned. There are the various papermaker's watermarks, which represent the trademarks of the paper manufacturers, but which do not usually appear on that part of the sheet of paper upon which the stamps are printed, although this has been known to happen.

When the average collector runs across such a variety, he is usually confused and tends to believe that he has discovered a variety of great value.

There is also what is known as a "stitch watermark," which is not an intentional watermark but, nevertheless, is a watermark.

It consists of a series of short, parallel lines across a stamp and is formed by the stitches joining the ends of the belt that carries the pulp over the drying rolls. These stitches become impressed into the pulp in exactly the same way as do the "bits" on the dandy roll. Such stitch watermarks are not usually very prominent.

A country that, until recent years, was considered to be a bit on the conservation side has used a very wide variety of watermarks from the very earliest years of adhesive postage stamps.

This country is Great Britain, and an examination of the catalog will show watermarks in the form of the simple small crown used on the Penny Black, the initials "VR," a more elaborate crown in two types, plus small, medium, and larger garters, heraldic emblems, a spray of roses, a Maltese cross, a script "Half Penny," an anchor, and an orb. All of these were used during the first 40 years of British adhesive postage stamps!

Going beyond the realm of adhesive postage stamps for a moment, I should mention that paper watermarked "USPOD" was used on US postal cards from 1873 to 1875, and a great variety of attractive and complex watermarks have been used on the paper from which US stamped envelopes have been produced.

During 1893, there was even a com-memorative watermark, which shows the busts of Columbus and Liberty within a belt formed by the words "Liberty-US-Columbus" and the dates "1492" and "1892." As far as can be determined, this is the sole example of a commemorative watermark and was used on US stamped envelopes in 1893, according to Scott.

Stamp catalogs illustrate the various watermarks used in the past and those in use today. Though the significance of watermarks in philately is less than it once was, collectors would do well to retain their sense of curiosity, since there surely are varieties still to be discovered.

Probably the most common watermark varieties are those known as "watermark inverted" or "watermark sideways," where the stamp design is printed upside down or sideways in relation to the watermark.

Strictly speaking, it is not the watermark that is inverted or sideways, but the printed design of the stamp.

In some cases, these are intentional variations caused by the printing of stamps to be made into booklets, for which some stamps are printed inverted in relation to others in the same sheet. In other cases, they are accidental and merely the result of paper being fed into the press incorretly.

With US stamps printed on watermarked paper, the position of the watermark was not considered, and thus stamps may be found with the watermark normal, reversed, inverted, inverted reversed, and sideways as seen from the back of the stamp. None of these should be considered in any way unusual or a variety.

Stamps of Great Britain with watermarks sideways are usually from coils used in vending machines. British coil stamps are perforated on all sides, and this is one way in which coils can be identified.

There are some true error varieties in watermarks, and one of the most spectacular is the St. Edward's Crown error. This consists of early 1950s stamps printed on paper watermarked "Multiple Script CA," which shows the imperial crown and the letters "CA" in script. It seems that in a couple of instances a crown became detached from dandy rolls. In one case the crown was replaced but with the St. Edward's crown instead of the imperial crown. This resulted in stamps showing a missing crown and, in other cases, the two types of crowns.

Other watermark errors are the result of wrong paper being used for a stamp. In the case in which a stamp printer produces the stamps of a number of different countries, it is possible for the stamps of one country to bear the watermark of another. Stamps of the Transvaal are known on paper having the watermark of the Cape of Good Hope.

Watermark Detection: The detection and identification of watermarks range from very easy to virtually impossible.

Some can be seen by holding a stamp up to a light source or placing it face down on a dark surface. Others, such as those printed on colored paper, are extremely difficult to identify.

You can usually determine if a stamp is watermarked or not; the difficulty arises when varieties of watermark have to be distinguished. The normal way of establishing a stamp's watermark is to place it face down in a watermark tray and drop a small quantity of benzine on it.

As the liquid penetrates the paper, there will be an instant in which the watermark shows up because of the faster penetration of the thinner paper constituting the watermark design.

If the moment is missed, the stamp can be allowed to dry and the operation repeated.

Benzine is highly flammable, and great care should be observed in its use. There are also many stamps with printing ink that is affected by the liquid, especially those printed by the photogravure process as the ink is often fugitive. Gum is unaffected by benzine.

At one time, carbon tetrachloride was popular, but this is now considered so hazardous to health that it should never be used.

There are a number of patent watermarking fluids on the market, as well as electrical or photograhic devices, and you should make a point of trying them out before purchase, since some are only effective in the easier cases in which their use is often unnecessary.

There is no single solution to the problem of watermark detection, and collectors must do the best they can in each individual instance. One old trick, often used by longtime dealers, is to look at a stamp against a light source while wearing an old-fashioned green eyeshade. This probably has the effect of filtering some of the color out of the stamp, enabling the watermark to become more easily seen.

Topical Watermarks: Topical collectors will want to consider watermarks, since they can picture symbols related to their topics.

The island of Cyprus has used a watermark, part of which reproduces a map of the island, and this would be of interest to the cartographic collector.

Crowns of all types abound, and a number of watermarks feature eagles and other birds. South African watermarks feature a springbok head, Jamaica shows a pineapple, and Cochin used an umbrella!

Chess stamp collectors may want to include Spain's castle watermark, which looks very much like the chess piece known as a rook.

An interesting story in philatelic lore is that the Sudan nearly had a revolt on its hands over a stamp watermark. This is said to have occurred when stamps went into use printed on paper watermarked with what is known as a rosette or Maltese Cross. It seems that towards the end of the 19th century, the Moslem population took violent exception to kissing a Christian symbol whenever they licked a stamp!

Whether the story is true or not, the fact remains that the watermark was soon changed to the Crescent and Star.

Watermark: Foreign words for "watermark" include watermerk (Dutch), filigrane (French), wasserzeichen (German), and filigrana (Italian and Spanish).

Watermark, Bothwell: Stamps of Canada's 1868 Large Queen issue are known printed on paper watermarked "E.&G. Bothwell/ Clutha Mills."

Robson Lowe (*Encyclopedia of British Empire Postage Stamps, Volume V*, Robson Lowe, London, 1973) reports that the portions of the letters are found on either 13 or 20 stamps, depending on the position.

It is also noted that forged watermarks are known. These have been made by impregnating the paper with wax.

Watermark, Pirie: The papermaker's watermark of the Scottish firm of Pirie & Sons reads "Alexr Pirie & Sons."

Such paper was used by the British American Bank Note Company to print a small quantity of the 15c value in the Large Queens issue of Canada.

The watermark takes the form of a single line of script about seven inches in length diagonally across the sheet. Thus portions only appear on a few stamps in each sheet.

Watermark, Pseudo: A pseudo watermark is actually not a watermark at all, but a device applied in such a manner as to simulate a true watermark.

Sometimes this consists of a device applied by a die under pressure after the paper has been made. The 1862 issue of Switzerland has a device consisting of a cross in a circle that was applied in this manner.

Another type of pseudo watermark is made by printing a design on the paper in a light color. New Zealand's 1925 issue of types of its 1909 and 1915 definitives has "NZ" and a star printed on the back in blue.

A gum watermark is another type of pseudo watermark. In this case, the watermark-like device is imprinted into the gum.

Since 1968, the Cook Islands have intermittently used what it terms a "fluorescent security underprinting" in a multiple coat-of-arms pattern. Some issues come both with and without this pseudo watermark.

Watermerk: Dutch word for "watermark."

Waxed Paper: It is dangerous to use waxed paper for any philatelic purpose.

It can cause permanent damage through the absorbtion of the wax into any philatelic material that is placed in contact with it.

Waxed paper should never be used for interleaving or to prevent sheets of stamps from sticking to each other. (See Glassine.)

Way Letter: A way letter is one that was handed to a post rider or mail carrier for deposit at the next post office.

As far as the United States is concerned, Konwiser (*The American Stamp Collector's Dictionary,* Minkus, New York, 1949) quotes Joseph Habersham, who was US postmaster general from 1795 to 1801, as defining Way Letters as "...such letters as are received by a mailcarrier on his way between two post offices and which he is to deliver at the first post office he comes to, and the postmaster is to enquire of him at what places he received them, and in his post-bills charge the postage from those places respectively to the offices at which they are to be finally delivered; writing the word 'way' against such charges in his bills. The word 'way' is also to be written upon each Way Letter."

Calvet Hahn, in an article awaiting publication in *Stamp Collector* at the time of this writing, notes that the use of way letters in the US dates from the original inland post of 1672-73, but he states that the first legislative reference he can find on the subject in American postal laws is that of the Act of May 8, 1794, which contains an extensive section devoted to the way letter.

He quotes it as follows:

"Sec. 15. AND BE IT FURTHER ENACTED, That the deputy-postmasters and other agents of the Postmaster-General, shall duly account, and answer to him, for all way-letters, which shall come to their hands. And for this purpose, the post-riders and other carriers of the mail, receiving any way-letters or letters (and it shall be their duty to receive them, if presented more than two miles from a post-office) shall deliver the same, together with the postage, if paid, at the first post-office, to which they shall afterwards arrive, where the postmaster shall duly enter the same, and specify the numbers and rate or rates in the post-bill, adding to the rate of each way-letter, one cent, which shall be paid by the deputy-postmaster, to the mail carrier from whom such way-letters shall be received. And that letters directed to persons living between post-offices, may be delivered, and the postage thereof duly collected, it shall be the duty of the carriers of the mail, to take charge of, and deliver all such letters as shall for that purpose, be committed to them, by any deputy-postmaster, and collect the postage thereof,

This letter is dated New York May 5, 1794, and addressed to Brunswick (New Brunswick), N.J. according to Hahn. The "Way 6" in manuscript represents the under-30-mile rate of the Act of Feb. 20, 1792, with the way fee paid in cash. As New Brunswick was 35 miles from New York, this had to be handed to the post rider somewhere in northern New Jersey (photo courtesy of Calvet M. Hahn).

which shall be paid over to such deputy-postmaster, on demand. And for every letter, so delivered, the mail-carrier delivering the same shall be allowed to demand and receive two cents, to his own use, besides the ordinary postage. And if any deputy-postmaster, or other agent of the Postmaster-General, shall neglect so to account, he or they so offending, shall on conviction thereof, forfeit for every such offense a sum not exceeding fifty dollars. PROVIDED, That no mail-carriers shall make such deliveries at any place not on the post-road. PROVIDED ALSO, That the receipt and delivery of letters on the way, between post-offices, shall not be required of the mail-carriers, in cases, where, in the opinion of the Postmaster-General, the time or manner of carrying the mail, or the speed of conveyance is incompatible with such receipts and deliveries."

Hahn further notes that with the exception that the word "postmaster" was substituted for "deputy-postmaster," this section was repeated verbatim as section 13 of the "Act to Establish the Post-Office of the United States," approved March 2, 1799.

In Canada, prior to 1867, a way letter was also to be accepted by a mail carrier on a coach road only if it was more than one mile to the nearest post office.

In Great Britain , during the time Ralph Allen (q.v.) contracted to provide mail service, way letters (also known as by letters) constituted one of the four classes of mail.

It was defined by Allen as a letter from one town to another on a post road, but which did not go into London. (See By Post, Cross Post.)

Wayzata Air Mail Stamp: This

label, now either only a footnote in the Newfoundland section of a stamp catalog or ignored completely, almost became an official postage stamp of the Newfoundland government. Under an illustration of the label, which has puzzled new collectors for years, the Scott catalog notes that the stamp was produced in the US by a private company under an agreement with the government of Newfoundland. The government, however, canceled the contract, and the stamps were never valid to prepay postage.

During 1932, the Newfoundland government faced a financial crisis. The situation that was to result in the 1934 appointment of a Commission of Government, in lieu of one elected by the people, was bleak, and the government was inclined to look with favor on any scheme likely to increase its revenue, according to Lorne Bentham, writing in *Western Stamp Collector* of Oct. 29, 1968, who also cites *Newfoundland Air Mails* by R.E.R. Dalwick and C.H.C. Harmer.

The stamp that never was, for the flight that never took place.

Thus it agreed to a plan proposed in June 1932 by Aerial World Tours, Inc., of Wayzata, Minnesota. The plan involved a passenger and mail flight across the Atlantic to be financed by an issue of 400,000 air mail postage stamps.

The company arranged for the stamps to be printed in Minneapolis.

The $1 stamp was designed by L.S. Clark and P.T. McCarty, with Northcraft Engraving Co. of Minneapolis doing the engraving and printing under a subcontract from the Minneapolis Bureau of Engraving, according to a report in the first issue of *Stamps* on Sept. 17, 1932.

The design features the Sikorsky aircraft that was to be used for the flight.

The stamps were printed in sheets of 20 from one plate made up of 20 separate engravings, thus resulting in variations on each subject, most noticeably in the clouds.

After trimming and perforation, the stamps were delivered to the Northwestern National Bank at Minneapolis.

The company took 300,000, which it was to draw from the bank in lots of 25,000 against a payment of $5,000, while the Newfoundland Government was to sell the other 100,000 through its post offices, giving the stamps official status, but only after the company's 300,000 were sold. The company was to retain 80c for each stamp it sold.

The flight was planned to depart no later than Aug. 31, 1932, and Aerial World Tours planned to purchase a Sikorsky S-40 four-engine amphibian capable of carrying 44 passengers.

The route was to be from Wayzata to Toronto, Montreal, St. Pierre and Miquelon, St. John's, Greenland, Iceland, Norway, Sweden, Finland, Leningrad, Latvia, Germany, Denmark, and finally to London, where the flight would end.

If the company had sold all 300,000 stamps, it would have received $240,000 to cover the expenses of the flight, including the cost of the aircraft, and the Newfoundland government would have made $100,000, if it sold all its stamps, plus $60,000 representing 20c on each of the 300,000 stamps sold by the company.

Following publication of the plan, there was much opposition in Newfoundland, and the Aug. 25, 1932, issue of the St. John's *Evening Telegram* went so far as to say: "The scheme would be tantamount to a prostitution of the postal service. The special issue of air mail stamps now contemplated is an effort to impose upon collectors and cannot be successful. But what is more serious is that it involves the transference by the Government of a very definite privilege to a private group of speculators."

Would that the lay press be similarly concerned with the welfare of stamp collectors today!

There was opposition also from the philatelic press, and a contemporary story in *Stamps* stated: "The circumstances surrounding the issue of this transatlantic stamp cause the whole affair to give off a somewhat offensive odor."

It went on to note that since the stamps were being produced by a private company, the stamp would fall into the same category as the semi-official stamps of Canada and thus not achieve Scott catalog status.

As a result, financing of the project became difficult, and the promotors reportedly were forced to purchase a much smaller, twin-engined flying boat for the flight.

But the great flight was not to take place, for, on Sept. 13, 1932, the following notice appeared in the St. John's newspapers: "The Newfoundland Government has canceled its special issue of 400,000 stamps which were to have been sold during a world flight sponsored by Aerial Tours, Inc. of Minneapolis.

"This action was taken because the flight has not started.

"About 25,000 stamps have been issued and the government has demanded their return."

This compounded the problems of Aerial World Tours, which had received thousands of covers from collectors specially prepared for the flight. The company had also paid $5,000 for the first 25,000 stamps and spent a considerable sum of money on an aircraft, not to mention the cost of publicizing the flight.

Despite company appeals, the Newfoundland government was adamant, and the transatlantic passenger and mail flight was canceled.

Soon after, the 25,000 stamps were placed on the philatelic market at face value, and the Newfoundland government destroyed the remaining 375,000.

Web: The term "Web" refers to paper in a roll. When a press is described as "web-fed," it means that it is fed from a continuous web of paper as opposed to a press into which individual sheets are inserted.

Web-fed presses became possible when a rotary mechanism was developed. Prior to this, most stamp presses printed from flat plates using individual sheets of paper.

Nowadays, extremely fast presses through which paper from large rolls speeds are virtually universal.

Weeping Eisenhower Variety: (See Vending Machine Gripper Marks.)

Weeping Princess: The variety known as the Weeping Princess is one of the best-known Canadian varieties.

It occurs on the 1c denomination in the 1935 King George V Silver Jubilee issue and consists of a small ink spot below Princess Elizabeth's right eye.

It is found on stamp #21 on the upper right pane of plate one. The variety is thought to

The stamp and the teardrop.

have come about from damage to the subject during the rock-in process when the plate was being made up.

It is also known in a repaired state, according to Hansen's *Guidebook and Catalogue of Canadian Stamps, 1970-71*, (Regency Publishing, Winnipeg, 1970).

Weinrot: German word for the color "claret."

Weiss: German word for "white."

Wells, Fargo & Co.: No one can

think of the winning of the Old West without the name Wells, Fargo & Co. coming to mind.

The firm was the leader in the carriage and distribution of mail in the days following the discovery of gold in California.

In 1852 Henry Wells, already experienced in the express business, joined with William G. Fargo to form the Wells, Fargo Express Company.

The company was a joint stock association with a capitalization of $300,000.

An announcement of the business that appeared in the May 20, 1852, *New York Times* is published in a booklet prepared by the History Department of the Wells Fargo Bank in San Francisco:

"This company having completed its organization... is now ready to undertake the general forwarding agency and commission business; the purchase and sale of gold dust, bullion and specie, also packages, parcels and freight of all descriptions in and between the City of New York and the City of San Francisco and the principal cities and towns in California connecting at New York with the lines of the American Express Company, the Harnden Express, Pullen, Virgil & Co., European Express.

"They have established offices and faithful agents in all the principal cities and towns throughout the eastern, middle and western states; energetic and faithful messengers furnished with iron chests for the security of treasure and other valuable packages accompany each express upon all their lines as well as in California and in the Atlantic States.

"Samuel P. Carter, for many years connected with the American Express, and R.W. Washburn, late of the Bank of Syracuse, have been appointed principal agents in California."

Thus was born a firm that was to become a part of Western lore.

The company soon established agencies in the gold country and offered a number of banking and express services.

Wells, Fargo was the only major banking and express house in California to survive the panic of 1855, and it immediately assumed the leading position.

Soon its activities extended from Oregon to San Diego and from Honolulu and Panama to New York, Boston, and Philadelphia.

The era that followed brought the company further development, including its association with the Overland Mail Co. and participation in the Pony Express (q.v.).

This culminated in the consolidation of 1866 when the Wells, Fargo empire included overland mail routes from Missouri to the Pacific and well as hundreds of miles of stagecoach

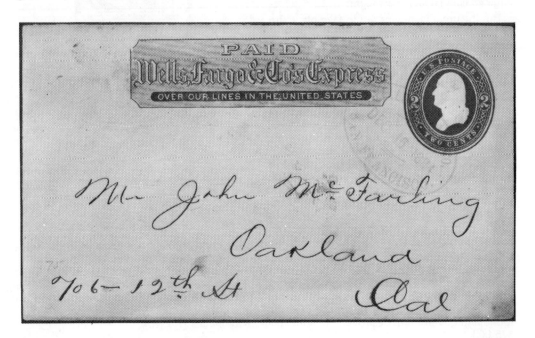

A cover carried by Wells, Fargo and bearing its corner card, with the word "PAID" indicating that the mailer had paid the Wells, Fargo charge for carrying the letter, in addition to the US Post Office Department's 2c rate. The cancelation reads "WELLS, FARGO & CO./ DEC 16 1884/ SAN FRANCISCO."

lines in California, Nevada, Utah, Idaho, Montana, Wyoming, Colorado, and Kansas.

It was supreme in stagecoaching after it took over the Overland Mail Co., leading to ownership of the Pony Express for the last six months of its existence.

During the heyday of Wells, Fargo stagecoaching, the Concord Coach (q.v.) gained its fame.

It was under Wells, Fargo that the Pony Express stamps were issued. Prior to the release of stamped envelopes by the US Post Office Department, the express companies, including Wells, Fargo, sold envelopes franked with adhesive stamps for the transmission of letters. Later, US stamped envelopes were printed with the firm's corner card and sold for a fee over the US postage rate to cover the cost of transmission by the express company.

Between 1861 and 1870, newspaper stamps were issued, of which there are six types listed in the Scott *Specialized Catalogue of United States Stamps.*

With the completion of the transcontinental railroad in 1869, the Concord Coach became "the terrible rattling stage," according to a contemporary description, and the puffing smoke of the steam locomotive wrote the obituary of the stagecoach in the Western sky.

Now the express business was virtually in the hands of the railroads, and they were disinclined to allow an outside firm to operate such services using railroad facilities.

Nonetheless, an agreement between Central Pacific and Wells, Fargo gave the latter express rights, and a new order began.

In 1872 the firm moved its headquarters from New York to San Francisco, and it had by then managed to survive the transition from stagecoach to railroad.

It also survived the earthquake and fire of 1906, although its building was destroyed.

During World War I, the domestic express business of Wells, Fargo was consolidated into the government-formed American Railroad Express, later the Railway Agency, Inc., which as the REA Express, Inc., went into bankruptcy in 1975.

Now, the name of Wells, Fargo lives on in the Wells Fargo Bank, still with its headquarters in San Francisco, where in its History Room visitors may journey into the past and relive the era of the stagecoach.

Wenden (Livonia):

The town and district of Wenden was part of Russia from 1721 to the end of World War I, when it became included in the state of Latvia, with some of the district going to Estonia.

The town was German-speaking and is on the

main railway from Riga to Pskov.

Now named Cesis, Wenden was one of the 13th-century Hansa towns and is a popular summer resort in the area known as the "Livonian Switzerland."

It was swallowed up by the USSR in 1940, when that country took the Baltic states of Estonia, Latvia, and Lithuania.

Beginning in 1863, stamps inscribed in German were issued, and they continued until 1901, when a set inscribed in Russian was released.

A circular stamp was prepared in 1862, but it was not issued and is claimed to be an essay.

Most of the German-language stamps have been reprinted.

Western Australia:

There are few collectors who are not familiar with that symbol of Western Australia, the black swan, which featured so extensively on the early stamps of that one-time colony.

One of the world's great rarities is Western Australia's famous invert. It occurs on the 4d stamp, and though many collectors think of it as the "inverted swan," it is really the frame that is inverted.

Western Australia is the largest of the states making up the Commonwealth of Australia (q.v.). It has an area of 975,920 square miles and a coastline of 4,350 miles.

Though it is possible that the early Portuguese explorers sighted the Western Australian coast, the first recorded landing occurred in 1616,

WESTERN AUSTRALIA

when the Dutch captain Dirck Hartog landed on the island that now bears his name.

Because of fears that the French might try to establish a settlement in Western Australia, the British government sent a party of soldiers and convicts under Major Edmund Lockyer from Sydney in 1826. This settlement was governed from Sydney until 1831.

In 1828 Captain C.H. Fremantle arrived to take possession of Western Australia. Development continued, spurred by a large supply of cheap labor in the form of convicts sent from Britain prior to 1868, when the transportation of convicts ceased.

In due course, the colony prospered, and when the time came for federation with the other colonies of the continent, Western Australia became one of the states of the new Commonwealth. During the depression of the late 1920s, however, a move for secession grew, and in 1933 a referendum actually favored secession by 138,653 to 70,706.

The arrival of World War II and the great economic surge it triggered caused secession to be forgotten, and the movement disappeared.

Although Western Australian has a third of the continent's area, it has less that 7½% of the population, much of which is concentrated in the urban areas of the southwest. Perth, the capital, has a population of more than 500,000.

Much of the state's interior is desert and is unsuitable for habitation.

Stamps for the colony were first issued in 1854 and feature the black swan emblem already mentioned.

It was not until the issue of 1902 that Queen

Victoria made a philatelic appearance, and then only on the high values.

Whether this represents an overly independent attitude on the part of the colonists is not clear. It was, however, an unusual, although not unique, policy for a colony to follow during the heyday of the British Empire. (See Swan's Inverted Frame.)

Western Cover Society: The Western Cover Society is an organization of collectors interested in covers and postal history of the far West.

A quarterly journal, the *Western Express*, is published, and an annual meeting is held in San Francisco in conjunction with WESTPEX.

Information is available from Everett Erle, 9877 Elmar Ave., Oakland, CA 94603.

Western Samoa: (See Samoa.)

Western Thrace: In 1920 stamps of Greece were overprinted "Administration Western Thrace" in the Greek alphabet. (See Thrace.)

Western Ukraine: (See Ukraine, Western.)

West Irian: The western half of the island of New Guinea comprised Netherlands New Guinea until 1963.

In May 1963, it was transferred to the Republic of Indonesia (q.v.) after negotiations with the United Nations.

The agreement was that Indonesia would hold a plebiscite in 1969 to ascertain the wishes of the inhabitants, but after gaining possession, the Indonesian president, Sukarno, reneged. As soon as Indonesia took over, all Dutch place names were changed, but following Sukarno's ouster, some were changed a second time!

The city of Hollandia, capital of Netherlands New Guinea, is now Djajapura (Jayapura).

Once part of the Dutch East Indies (q.v.), Western New Guinea used its stamps until 1950,

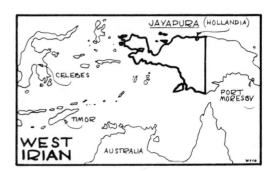

WEST IRIAN

when the Netherlands issued stamps inscribed "NIEW GUINEA."

While the transfer to Indonesia was being worked out, the territory was administered by the UN, and stamps of Netherlands New Guinea were overprinted "UNTEA" (United Nations Temporary Executive Authority) and issued in 1962.

These were followed in 1963 by Indonesian stamps overprinted "IRIAN BARAT."

The stamps of Indonesia are now used.

West New Guinea: (See West Irian.)

Wet Printing: The term "wet printing" refers to the condition of paper during the moment of printing.

It was once common for paper to be dampened before printing in order to improve the quality of the impression, but this is no longer necessary, and paper is mostly used in its normal dry state.

A characteristic of stamps printed on dampened paper is one of size. As the paper dries, it shrinks across the grain, and the resulting stamp will measure less in one direction than the plate from which it was printed.

The degree of shrinkage depends on the moisture content of the paper.

In cases in which the same plate has been used for both wet and dry printing, the resultant stamps are of different sizes. This led some early philatelic students to believe that more plates were used to print a given issue than was the case. (See Dry Printing.)

Weun: A unit of currency used in Korea. In 1953, 100 weun formed one hwan.

White: Foreign words for "white" include hvid (Danish), wit (Dutch), blanc (French), weiss (German), bianco (Italian), blanco (Spanish), and vit (Swedish).

White Back: The term "white back" is sometimes applied to stamps printed on paper that had a background color applied to the face.

This gave the impression that the stamps were printed on colored paper, but examination of the back reveals the normal paper color — hence the name.

White Russia: Once a part of Imperial Russia, the area known as White Russia (Belorussia) proclaimed its independence in 1918, following the Russian Revolution.

It called itself the Byelorussian Democratic Republic but was crushed by the Bolsheviks in 1919 and made a Soviet republic.

Poland also claimed the area and in the same year invaded it in an attempt to re-establish historic boundaries.

The treaty of Riga in 1921 gave West Belorussia to Poland, with the eastern portion remaining in Soviet hands. Together with other territory, it now forms the Belorussian (Byelorussian) Soviet Socialist Republic within the Soviet Union.

During the fighting in 1920, a set of labels was prepared for postal use in the area by General Bulak-Balakhovitch.

At one time, these were believed to have been issued, but Gibbons reports that used copies have not been seen and that it has no evidence of issue.

The unissued stamps exist in five denominations and are reported by Minkus to have been printed by the Latvian State Printing Office, perforated 11.5 and imperforate.

W.H.W.: Overprint together with surcharge on regular issue of Danzig indicated in 1934 semi-postal issue.

Wilson, Sir John: Sir John Mitchell Harvey Wilson (1875-1975) Bt. KCVO, was one of the world's better known philatelist.

He joined the Royal Philatelic Society, London, in 1921 and became president in 1934, continuing in that office until 1940.

He was appointed chairman of the expert committee in 1926 and held that office until his death, according to the London Philatelist, journal of the Royal Philatelic Society, London.

He was the moving spirit behind the exhibition held at the home of the Royal Philatelic Society, London, to mark the Silver Jubilee of King George V in 1935. He was made chairman of the exhibition to celebrate the centenary of the postage stamp in 1940, an exhibition that was preempted by World War II.

In 1938 he was appointed Keeper of the Royal Collection, a position he held until his retirement in 1969.

During that period, he wrote his most important philatelic work, a massive book entitled The Royal Philatelic Collection, which is a catalog of the royal collection from 1840 to 1935.

Winchester Paper: (See Paper, Winchester.)

Windmill Study Unit: (See American Topical Association Study Units.)

Wing Margins: Wing margin stamps are those from a position adjacent to a centrally perforated, vertical gutter separating a sheet of stamps into panes.

Such stamps will have three sides of normal

This variety, known as a wing margin stamp was once called a "flapper."

margins, and the fourth, adjacent to the gutter, will have an extended perforated margin, or "wing."

This extended margin represents half the width of the gutter.

This variety exists on many stamps of Great Britain and some of the colonial countries, including Jamaica and British Honduras, dating from the 1860s.

This form of perforating down the center of the gutter was used on stamps perforated at Somerset House, London, the headquarters of the British Inland Revenue Service (similar to the Internal Revenue Service of the US).

Wing margin stamps have also been referred to as "extended margins" or "flappers."

Winston Spencer Churchill Study Unit: (See American Topical Association Study Units.)

WINTERHILFE: This overprint together with a surcharge on a stamp of Austria indicates a semi-postal issue of 1933.

WIPA Sheet: The Austrian WIPA souvenir sheet was issued in 1933 to mark the Vienna International Philatelic Exhibition.

It is inscribed "Wien Internationale Postwertzeichen-Ausstellung/Wein 1933."

The sheet contains four stamps reproducing a painting of a mail coach by Moritz von Schwind.

The stamps sold for 50g + 50g for charity. There was also a surcharge of 1.60s representing a single fee for admission to the exhibition.

The sheet is a major rarity and commands a high price.

Wisconsin Federation of Stamp Clubs: Founded at a meeting in Fond du Lac, Wis., on March 19, 1932, as the Wisconsin

Association of Philatelic Societies, the federation assumed its present name in 1935.

From the nine founding societies of Appleton, Fond du Lac, Green Bay, Milwaukee, Oshkosh, Ripon, Sheboygan, Madison, and Waupun, the federation has grown to a membership of 50 philatelic organizations located in the state.

It publishes a monthly newsletter, *Across the Fence,* edited by federation President Howard Sherpe, 1017 Chieftain Lookout, Madison, WI 53711.

Wisconsin Postal History Society:
The Wisconsin Postal History Society has as its aim the collection and dissemination of information on the postal history of the state.

It publishes a journal, *Badger Postal History,* and has prepared a number of handbooks.

Information is available from Executive Secretary Frank Moertl, N. 95 W. 32259 County Line Rd., Hartland, WI 53029.

Wit: Dutch world for "white."

Wmk: This is the usual abbreviation of "watermark" (q.v.).

Wolmaransstd: (See Transvaal.)

Women on Stamps Study Unit: (See American Topical Association Study Units.)

Won: A unit of currency used in Korea from 1962. It is made up of 100 chun.

Woodblocks: The name "Woodblock" is given to a provisional issue of two Cape of Good Hope triangular stamps printed in Cape Town in 1861.

The stamps came into existence because of an unexpected shortage of the two denominations normally produced in Great Britain by Perkins, Bacon & Co.

The Woodblocks comprise the 1d red and 4d blue denominations, plus errors of color in which the 1d was printed in blue and the 4d in red.

The stamps follow the same design as the Perkins, Bacon products except that they are primitive in nature.

Some sources claim that they gained their name because their appearance suggested that they were printed from woodcuts.

It seems more likely, however, that they were so named because they were produced from stereos mounted on blocks of wood, and this is the explanation given by Stevenson *(The Triangular Stamps of Cape of Good Hope,* Harmer, London, 1950).

The Woodblocks were printed by Saul

A Cape of Good Hope "woodblock."

Solomon of Cape Town from steel engravings by C.J. Roberts, a local engraver.

The errors of color came about when a cliche of each value was accidently included in a plate of the other value.

Woodcut:
One definition of the term "woodcut" is printing from a plate carved from wood.

This technique has rarely been used in the production of postage stamps, but several examples may be found among the early stamps of Victoria. The 1854 6d stamp, for instance, was printed from a plate of 50 woodblocks, each engraved individually.

L.N. and M. Williams (*Fundamentals of Philately*, American Philatelic Society, 1971) note that a woodcut differs from a wood engraving. The former is a knife carving on a piece of wood; the latter is made on the endgrain of a piece of hardwood with a graver.

The art of printing from wooden plates is known as xylography. (See Printing, Xylography.)

The resulting print from a wooden printing base is also termed a "woodcut."

Working Die:
The term "working die" describes an intermediate die that is created through a transfer process (see Printing, Intaglio) from the original engraved die and that is multiplied to create a printing base (plate).

L.N. and M. Williams (*Fundamentals of Philately*, American Philatelic Society, 1971) note that the term "subsidiary die" is sometimes used.

"Working die" also describes the female die, sometimes called the embossing die, used for embossing stamps or stamped paper. Examples are US stamped envelopes, stamps known as the "Cameos" (q.v.) of The Gambia, stamps of Heligoland, etc.

The Williams brothers note that the term "printing die" is properly used in embossing when the female "working die" is inked to apply color and emboss in one operation.

The male portion that forces the paper into the female, or "working," die is called the "force" or "counterpart."

World's Fair Collectors Society, Inc.:
(See American Topical Association Study Units.)

Worn:
Foreign words for "worn" include versleten (Dutch), abgenutzt (German), logoro (Italian), and gastado (Spanish).

Wove Paper:
(See Paper.)

Wrangel Government:
(See Russia, South.)

Wrapper:
A wrapper is an item of postal stationery used in the mailing of newspapers. It comprises a strip of paper gummed along one end and bearing an indicium.

It was wrapped around a rolled newspaper and sealed at the gummed end.

The first use of wrappers was in the US. They were authorized by an Act of Congress dated Feb. 27, 1861, and first issued in October of that year. They were discontinued in 1934.

A number of other countries have used wrappers. (See Postal Stationery.)

Wrapper, Newspaper:
(See Wrapper.)

Wreck Cover:
A wreck cover is one that has been salvaged from the wreck of a ship or from a railroad accident.

The term "crash cover" (q.v.) is usually used to describe mail recovered from the crash of an aircraft in which the mail was being transported.

In his book *A History of Wreck Covers* (Robson Lowe, London), A.E. Hopkins uses the term to include mail salvaged from ships, aircraft, and accidents on land, and mail damaged during the London Blitz of 1940-44.

Write-up:
The writing-up of a collection, whether it is simply for your own personal pleasure or for a competitive exhibition, is one of the areas into which you can inject something of your own personality.

For a personal collection, you can include as much or as little as you choose, and it can range from pencil notes to an elaborately hand-lettered manuscript. The only limits are your own desires and the space available.

Writing-up a display to be entered in competition is another matter altogether.

It then becomes necessary to conform to what seems to be generally preferred by the judges. Unfortunately, the judges themselves do not alway agree, and there are few guidelines except those dictated by your own common sense.

Obviously, too much is just as bad as too little, so you should strive for some middle course consistent with the display format you have chosen.

Although a light, open format is always attractive, you should beware of creating a scattered effect, so write-up is often a useful layout tool to hold a page together. It then becomes more than just the required chunk of information necessary to explain the material, and it can be used as an element of the overall design.

One tip: though an open layout containing plenty of white space can be effective as an individual page, it can be a disaster when a number of similar pages are viewed together, as in an exhibit frame. You might, therefore, want to draw the material more to the center of the page and provide a bit more white space around the outside to act as a cutoff between pages.

Lay out a number of pages in the quantity and arrangement that they will have in the frames. Design faults that are not apparent on individual pages will immediately be obvious.

As to quantity of write-up, keep it as brief as possible without sacrificing clarity. Never use a long word if a short one will do, or two words if you can tell it with one.

But this is the challenge and the pleasure of creating an exhibit. You are the boss. You are the writer, editor, and printer, and since you do the coordinating, you are also your own publisher.

How to do the writing-up is something that bothers many collectors. Some prefer to type, some like to hand letter, and others prefer the "rub-on" letters available at drafting and art supply stores.

The method used is not as important as how well it is done, so do it in the way that feels most comfortable and as effectively as you can.

Fortunately, the simplest way is usually the most effective and seems to show off the philatelic material to the best advantage. (See Albums; Albums, Do It Yourself; Collateral Material; Hinges; Judging; Mounts; Philatelic Exhibiting; Presentation.)

Wurttemberg:

Now part of the "land" of Baden-Wurttemberg in the Federal Republic of Germany (q.v.), the Republic of Wurttemberg had been a countship, a duchy, and a kingdom before becoming a republic just after World War I.

It is located in southern Germany between Bavaria (q.v.) and Baden (q.v.). The capital is Stuttgart.

The recorded history of Wurttemberg dates back to 1081, when a Conrad of Wirtemberg was noted as being a member of the local nobility of Stuttgart.

In 1495 Wurttemberg became a duchy, and in

1525 the great peasant rebellion began there.

During the 16th to 18th centuries, wars ravaged the area. Support of Napoleon led to formation of the kingdom in 1806, after the battle of Austerlitz in which Napoleon defeated Austria.

When Napoleon's power began to wane, Wurttemberg quickly changed sides and fought with the nations allied against France.

During the Seven Weeks War, Wurttemberg chose the side of Austria, and when that war was lost, it had to pay an indemnity to Prussia.

The side of Prussia was chosen in the Franco-Prussian War of 1870-71, and when that was won, Wurttemberg became a member of the German Empire with special privileges in 1871.

Wurttemberg's first stamps were issued in 1851 and continued, as one of the special privileges, until 1902.

A large number of Official stamps were released and used until 1923. Some of these were used for official purposes throughout Germany.

During the French occupation of part of Wurttemberg after WWII, stamps were again issued inscribed "Wurttemberg" for a short period in 1947-49.

Stamps of the Federal Republic of Germany are now used.

X: Sometimes you come across a large "X" on a blank, stamp-sized tab adjacent to a stamp. Such a marking is called a St. Andrew's Cross (q.v.) and is used to avoid making blank, gummed, and perforated paper available that could be used for purposes of counterfeiting.

Some early Austrian stamp sheets included four such items, and British stamp booklet panes have featured them.

XEIMAPPA: Partial inscription and overprint on stamps of Epirus (q.v.).

Xmas: A large cross and "MAS" appears on cancels used in Great Britain in the early 1900s to identify mail deposited and held for delivery on Christmas Day. (See Christmas Day Mail Delivery.)

XMAS 1898: The inscription "XMAS 1898" appears on the 1898 Map stamp of Canada. (See Canadian Map Stamp.)

Although, because of the inscription, it is considered by many collectors to be a Christmas stamp, it was not intended to celebrate Christmas, but to mark the inauguration of Imperial Penny Postage.

Xylography: (See Printing, Xylography.)

Yang Yin: An oriental symbol of the two principles of life, indicating opposites such as active and passive, male and female, night and day, etc.

The symbol identifies the stamps of South Korea and is seen on that country's flag.

It was used as a watermark device for the stamps of China in 1885-98.

Yca: Now the Peruvian town of Ica, the town, when named Yca, issued its own provisional stamps during the 1879-84 war with Chile.

These took the form of "YCA" and "YCA VAPOR" overprinted on various stamps of Peru in both black and violet.

The town is located near the coast, south of Lima.

Yellow: Foreign words for the color "yellow" include gul (Danish and Swedish), geel (Dutch), juane (French), gelb (German), giallo (Italian), amarelo (Portuguese), and amarillo (Spanish).

Yemen Arab Republic:

The Yemen Arab Republic was once part of the kingdom of Sheba. The Bible refers to gold, spices, and precious stones as gifts from the Queen of Sheba to King Solomon.

This provides a very different picture from the poverty-stricken country that is the Yemen Arab Republic today.

After many years as part of the Ottoman Empire, the country gained its freedom in 1918 after Britain's defeat of Turkey in World War I.

The country remained backward and poor and in the early 1960s was wracked by civil war between royalist and republican forces.

In the beginning, Egypt supported the republicans, and Saudi Arabia aided the royalists.

Fighting came to an end in 1970 with the establishment of a republican regime, although unrest and border clashes with the People's Democratic Republic of Yemen (Aden) con-

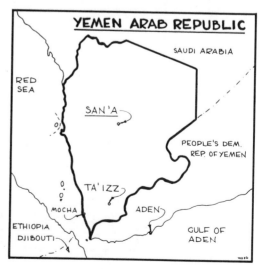

tinued and a number of recent leaders have been assassinated.

The country is still poor, the latest per capita income figure is $475 and the literacy rate a low 12%.

With an area of 75,290 square miles, the country has a population estimate at 5,930,000. It is split almost equally between Sunni and Shiite Moslems.

During the civil war, the country had two capitals — the royalist of San'a, and the republican one at Ta'izz. San'a is now the national capital.

Except for a local stamp issue in 1926, the country did not issue its own stamps until 1930.

During the civil war period, both sides continued to issue their own stamps, many of which are unrecognized by the major catalogs.

The philatelic office's address is Director of Stamps Bureau, Ministry of Communications, GPO, San'a, Yemen Arab Republic.

The unit of currency is the riyal (100 fils), which is about 4.56 to the US dollar.

Yemen, South: South Yemen, or the People's Democratic Republic of Yemen, contains the former British Crown Colony of Aden (q.v.), its capital, plus the surrounding area once known as the Aden Protectorate (q.v.).

Aden is located about 100 miles east of the Strait of Bab-el-Mandeb, at the southern end of the Red Sea, and is on the southern coast of Arabia.

The island of Perim, located in the Strait of Bab-el-Mandeb, and the five Kuria Muria Islands off the coast of Oman were administered from Aden. The latter group is now part of the Sultanate of Oman (q.v.).

During its colonial period, Aden had a population estimated in 1952 at about 130,000.

The first stamps of Aden appeared in 1937, when Crown Colony status was achieved. They depict a type of vessel widely used in the area, known as dhow. Previously, the stamps of India had been used.

At the time of the first stamps for Aden, there were four post offices in the colony: Aden GPO, Aden Camp (Crater), Sheikh Othman, and Maala.

These stamps were valid for use in the protectorate area, which also had offices and agencies.

Aden has been a trading port for Arabia for hundreds of years. British interest in the area dates from Napoleon's conquest of Egypt, at which time British communications with India were seen to be endangered.

With steamships came the need for coaling stations, particularly on the Red Sea route to India, and Aden was selected for this purpose.

Later, the surrounding territory was acquired, and this became the Aden Protectorate.

The Crown Colony of Aden and the protectorate area achieved a degree of self rule in 1963 as the Federation of South Arabia (q.v.), but

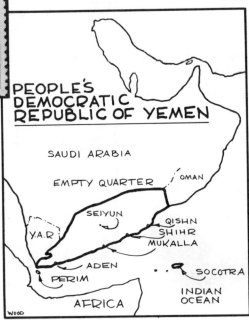

when independent status was promised for 1968, a struggle for power began between two nationalist organizations. These were The Front for the Liberation of Occupied South Yemen (FLOSY) and The National Liberation Front (NLF).

On Nov. 30, 1967, the People's Republic of South Yemen came into being, comprising the colony and protectorate area, with Aden as the capital city.

Despite its late entry into the adhesive stamp-issuing area, Aden has a postal history that is extensive and interesting. Its position as a major area seaport, a coaling station, and a crossroads point resulted in much mail being routed through the former colony.

The country is reported to have a current population of about 1,863,000, and its area is estimated by the US Department of State at 111,000 square miles. The latest per capita income figure is $310.

The country's unit of currency is the dinar, which in 1981 was .35 to the US dollar.

A philatelic agency is said to operate, and its address is Director General of Posts and Telegraphs, Postal Division, Aden, People's Democratic Republic of Yemen.

Yen: The yen is the unit of currency used by Japan.

Ykp. H.P.: This inscription is found on Austrian stamps for use in Western Ukraine during World War I.

Yuan: The yuan is the unit of currency used in the People's Republic of China. It comprises 100 fen.

The yuan was also used in Manchukuo.

Yucatan: Six stamps, of which only four were issued, were prepared by the Mexican state of Yucatan in 1924. Examples of Mayan architecture are featured on the stamps. (See Mexico.)

Yugoslavia: When the Austro-Hungarian Empire collapsed at the end of World War I, the Kingdom of Serbs, Croats, and Slovenes was created from Croatia (q.v.), Dalmatia (q.v.), Bosnia and Herzegovina (q.v.), Slovenia (q.v.), Voyvodina, and Montenegro (q.v.).

Shortly thereafter, its name was changed to Yugoslavia, and it became a constitutional monarchy under King Alexander I, son of King Peter of Serbia.

The new country faced an almost impossible task just to hang together. The Balkan states had never been noted for their spirit of brotherly love, and the chances for the new country seemed dim indeed.

Alexander soon found that the only way to achieve agreement among his diverse subjects was by a royal dictatorship, but even that was not the answer, and bickering continued.

On a visit to France, Alexander was assassinated at Marseilles by a Macedonian terrorist.

Despite its problems, the country continued

to struggle along under regents for Alexander's son, the young King Peter.

Although Yugoslavia tried to keep out of World War II, Germany invaded it anyway and occupied it from 1941 until its liberation at the end of the war.

During the German occupation, King Peter had been in exile, but the partisans under Josip Broz, later Marshal Tito, carried on the fight against the German and Italian occupation. At the end of the war, Tito was in effective control of the country, having eliminated the other partisan leader, Draja Mikhailovich.

After the war, King Peter transferred his power to the Communist government under Tito, who continued to rule the country until his death in 1980.

His was one of the few Communist satellite countries to stand up to the Soviet Union, and he attempted to steer a middle course between East and West.

The area of Yugoslavia is 98,766 square miles, and the population was estimated in 1978 at 22,340,000. The unit of currency is the dinar (100 paras), which in 1981 was 32.92 to the US dollar. The per capita income figure is $3,109.

A general issue of stamps for Yugoslavia was first released in 1921 and features King Alexander on some denominations and his father, King Peter of Serbia, on others.

After WWI and prior to the 1921 general issue, there had been a number of issues for various regions of the country, including Bosnia and Herzegovina, Croatia-Slavonia, and Slovenia.

Like its Communist neighbors, Yugoslavia has released a large number of stamps since WWII, but its policies have been a little more restrained, and it is a great deal more popular among Western collectors than other Eastern European countries.

The address of the Yugoslav philatelic bureau is Biro Za Postanske Marke, Palmoticeva 2, Belgrade, Yugoslavia.

Yugoslavian Military Government of Venezia Giulia: (See Venezia Guilia.)

Yugoslavian Occupation of Fiumi: (See Fiume.)

Yugoslavian Occupation of Istria: (See Istria and Trieste.)

Yugoslavian Occupation of Trieste: (See Trieste, Free Territory of.)

Yunnan Fou (Kunming): In 1900 an Indo-Chinese post office was opened in Yunnan Fou, the capital city of Yunnan province.

From 1903, stamps of Indo-China were overprinted "Yunnanfou," "Yunnan-Fou," or "Yunnansen." They were also surcharged with the denomination in Chinese characters.

The post office closed in 1922.

The name was subsequently changed to Kunming.

YUNNANSEN: Overprint on stamps of Indo-China for use at French post office in Yunnan Fou, China.

Yvert et Tellier: Publisher of the widely used French stamp catalog.

Z: On May 6, 1930, Bolivia issued its 1928 air mail stamps overprinted "Z" to designate mail carried on the airship *Graf Zeppelin*.

The stamps were also overprinted "1930" and surcharged.

Z. AFR REPUBLIEK: The inscription "Z. AFR REPUBLIEK" identifies stamps of the first South African Republic, later known as the Transvaal.

Zaire: The Republic of Zaire was previously known as the Congo Democratic Republic (Kinshasa), which in turn had been the old Belgian Congo.

The beginnings of the Belgian Congo must surely be some of the most unusual of any colonial possession.

It was formed as the personal and private possession of one man, King Leopold II of Belgium, who had a hankering for a colonial empire but could not persuade his government to go along with him.

He therefore appropriated a large part of central Africa and on July 1, 1885, made it an independent state with himself as king! He was assisted in this venture by Henry Morton Stanley of "Dr. Livingstone, I presume" fame, who explored, negotiated treaties with local chiefs, and generally got the kingdom organized.

During the 1890s, an outcry was raised at the methods Leopold was using to ensure that the natives put his kingdom on a profit-making basis.

This resulted in an independent investigation, which confirmed many of the stories of abuses against the native population.

After long debate and much disagreement, the Belgian parliament finally agreed to annex the Congo Free State, as it was called, as a colonial possession under the control of the

Belgian government, to better protect the welfare of the native population. This finally came about in 1908, and it became the Belgian Congo.

By the 1920s, the riches of the area were being realized, and it was second only to South Africa as a source of diamonds.

During World War II, the Belgian Congo played a vital role as a supplier of raw material, especially after Southeast Asia was invaded by the Japanese.

Belgium tried to avoid the problems of other colonial areas by eliminating the right to vote entirely in the colony, until elections could be organized with the assurance of an African majority. Thus was minority control by whites prevented.

This resulted in a speedy road to independence, which came on June 30, 1960, when the Belgian Congo became the Congo Democratic Republic (Kinshasa).

The road was far from smooth, however, and widespread violence followed. This caused Europeans to leave and the southern province of Katanga (q.v.) to secede for several years.

A UN peace-keeping force was in the troubled country until 1964.

Late in 1964, rebel forces murdered many white hostages and thousands of Congolese. Belgium sent in paratroopers dropped from US aircraft to rescue hundreds, and by mid-1965 the rebels were controlled.

In 1971 the country changed its name to the Republic of Zaire and at the same time ordered all citizens with Christian names to change to African names.

In 1974 foreign owned business were forced to sell to citizens of Zaire, but when the economic situation grew very bad, the original owners were asked to return.

There are estimated to be 28,090,000 people in Zaire, which has an area of 905,063 square miles.

Kinshasa (Leopoldville) is the capital city, and the unit of currency is the zaire, which in 1981 was 3.11 to the US dollar.

The latest per capita income figure is $127.

Stamps were first issued in 1886 and depict Leopold II, the king and sole proprietor!

Subsequent issues reflect the many changes in name and status of this beautiful but violent land.

The early pictorial colonial issues show some very beautiful scenes, and current stamp-issuing policy seems quite restrained when compared with other newly independent areas.

The address of the philatelic bureau is Agenses Philateliques Gouvernementales, Chaussee de Waterloo 868-70, 1180 Brussels, Belgium.

It is not known what, if any, services are available to individual collectors.

Zaire: The zaire is the unit of currency used in the African country of Zaire (q.v.). It is composed of 100 ma-kuta.

Zambezia: (See Quelimane.)

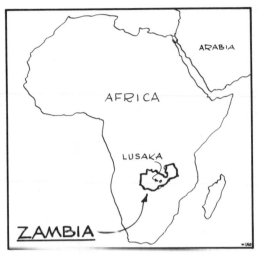

Zambia:

Once known as Northern Rhodesia, the area that is now the Republic of Zambia was administered by the British South Africa Company from 1889 to 1924.

In that year, the area was divided into Northern and Southern Rhodesia. Called Northern Rhodesia until 1954, it became part of the Federation of Rhodesia and Nyasaland (q.v.) until 1963.

On Oct. 24, 1964, the country became an independent republic within the British Commonwealth under the name of Zambia.

To the north are Zaire and Tanzania, to the east Malawi and Mozambique, to the south Rhodesia, and to the west Angola.

Remains found in Zambia indicate that man has lived in the area for at least 25,000 years.

The Portuguese were the first in modern times to have explored Zambia, doing so early in the 19th century. Later, slavers from Zanzibar (q.v.) decimated the area's population.

The British South Africa Company made treaties with the native tribes in the 1890s, and the company administered the area until 1924, when a British Protectorate was declared.

With an area of 290,724 square miles, Zambia is larger than the state of Texas. It has a population estimated at 5,649,000.

Copper is the main export, but other minerals including cobalt, lead, zinc, gold, and coal are exported.

The first stamps were issued in 1890 and feature the coat of arms of the British South Africa Company.

In 1905 a very handsome set depicted Victoria Falls, and a 1910 issue featured portraits of King George V and Queen Mary.

Stamps inscribed "Northern Rhodesia" were issued from 1925 until stamps of the Federation of Rhodesia and Nyasaland appeared.

The first issue inscribed "Zambia" was released in 1964, and the inscription has been retained unchanged.

The unit of currency is the kwacha (100 ngwee), which in 1981 was .82 to the US dollar. The latest per capita income figure is $414.

The address of the philatelic office is Philatelic Bureau, Box 1857, Ndola, Zambia.

Zante: (See Ionian Islands.)

Zanzibar:

The name of Zanzibar, known also as the Isle of Cloves (the main islands are Zanzibar and Pemba), conjures visions of a tropic isle, with Sidney Greenstreet and Peter Lorre doing their sinister deeds in seedy hotels where lazy ceiling fans circulate the scents of exotic flowers and spices.

Long a center of the slave trade, Zanzibar could doubtless live up to the reputation bestowed on such places by movies and mystery novels.

Able to boast its own turbulent history, the island of Zanzibar has played host to Arabian invaders, Portuguese colonists, dealers in human beings, and traders of many countries.

Its islands are located in the Indian Ocean

ZANZIBAR

some 22 miles off the east coast of Africa.

Between the eighth and 11th centuries, Persian and Arab moslems fled to East Africa to escape religious persecution. They founded city states in Zanzibar and along the adjacent mainland coast.

Early in the 16th century, the Portuguese arrived and attempted to colonize Zanzibar, but in 1698 more Arabs arrived and occupied the islands.

In 1741 Ahmed bin Said became Imam of Muscat and founded the Al-Busaid dynasty, which ruled Zanzibar from 1744 to 1964.

About the middle of the 19th century, British influence began to make itself felt, and by 1885, the Germans had established themselves in German East Africa, across the narrow channel from Zanzibar.

In return for German recognition of British interests in Zanzibar, the North Sea island of Heligoland (q.v.) was ceded to Germany by Great Britain in 1890.

French interests in Zanzibar were terminated in exchange for recognition by Great Britain of French interests in Madagascar. A French post office operated in Zanzibar from 1894 to 1904, while a German post office opened Aug. 27, 1890, and closed on July 31, 1891.

British rule continued until 1963, when independence was granted. Despite this long period as part of the British Empire, only one stamp issue, the 1948 Silver Wedding omnibus issue, depicted a British monarch.

In 1964 the sultan was overthrown and the People's Republic of Zanzibar established. This government later merged with the mainland republic of Tanganyika (q.v.), with Dar es Salaam as the capital city. It is now part of the United Republic of Tanzania (q.v.).

Zanzibar's beginning as a stamp-issuing area came in 1895 when the Indian stamps previous-ly used were officially overprinted "Zanzibar" at the office of the Zanzibar Gazette.

The first Zanzibar designs appeared on Sept. 20, 1896, when a set reproduced the portrait of Sultan Seyyid Hamed-bin-Thwain. This was one year after his death, the stamps having been delayed because De La Rue's cost estimate for the production had been higher than that of Bradbury Wilkinson. Nevertheless, De La Rue produced this issue and succeeding issues up to 1944.

Over the years, various stamps have depicted sultans, scenes, and ships, the latter being that graceful vessel the Arab dhow.

Some 50 miles from north to south and about 24 miles from east to west, Zanzibar is the largest island of coral origin off the African east coast; neighboring Pembina is the second largest.

The climate is hot and dominated by monsoons, with an average annual rainfall of 58 inches.

The chief export is cloves, and about 80% of the world's supply is grown on the island. Second only to cloves is the production of copra, the dried meat of the coconut, and increasing amounts of oranges, pineapples, and other tropical fruit are being grown in an effort to create a more diverse economy.

Nowadays, the ghosts of Greenstreet and Lorre must look down with mixed emotions as they see a country engaged in the modern struggle to achieve an independent prosperity.

Z.A.R: Overprint on stamps of the Cape of Good Hope, accompanied by a surcharge, identifies stamps issued in the town of Vryburg (q.v.) in 1899 while occupied by the Boers.

The letters "Z.A.R." stand for Zuid Afrikaansche Republiek.

Zehn: Numeral ten (10) in German.

Zeichnung: German word for "design."

ZEITUNGSMARKE: Inscription on some Austrian newspaper stamps.

ZEITUNGS STAEMPLE: Inscription on first newspaper stamps of Austria.

Zelaya: A province of Nicaragua (q.v.), on the country's east coast, Zelaya had a currency based on silver at a time when the rest of the Central American country used paper currency.

Because of the different value of the currency used in the province, it was necessary that the area have its own postage stamps. Beginning in 1904, Zelaya, also known as Bluefields, used the stamps of Nicaragua overprinted "B" and "Dpto Zelaya."

There were also other overprints ("COSTA ATLANTICA," "B VALE 5 cts," "Oficial B," etc.), but Scott notes that overprints reading "B Dto. Zelaya" were made only for the philatelic trade and never placed on sale for postal use.

The last such issue appeared in 1912. (See Cabo Gracias a Dios.)

Zemstvos: The word "zemstvo" means "district" in Russian and is the name given to a large number of Russian local postage stamps (q.v.).

Zemstvos were units of local government established in Russia in the 1860s to bring order and extend services of government to the more remote areas of the country.

One of their functions was to organize and operate local postal services in the absence of a national postal service.

These were official services, unlike many local posts in other countries, which were mostly private mail services.

The government provided a charter, and the local mailbags were adorned with the national coat of arms.

In *Collecting Postal History* (Larousse & Co., New York, 1974), Prince Dimitry Kandaouroff reports that the state eventually took over 82 of the local posts between 1870 and 1900, but that 170 others issued a total of 2,427 local postage stamps.

Some services were still in operation at the time of the 1917 revolution.

Colonel Hans Lagerloef *(The Stamp Specialist,* Lindquist, 1945) states that Alexander II signed an authorization in 1864 enabling the zemstvos to begin their own local postal services between their towns and a point at which they could link up with the imperial post roads.

As the zemstvo services grew and prospered, additional powers were granted by the imperial government.

In 1870 a decree stated that the rural zemstvo services must not infringe upon the imperial postal service, zemstvo mail pouches must not bear the crossed posthorns emblem of the imperial post, and zemstvo postage stamps must differ in design from those of the imperial post.

A letter franked with a zemstvo stamp, according to Lagerloef, could be carried within that zemstvo, but one addressed to another zemstvo required three stamps — one of the originating zemstvo, an imperial post stamp, and a stamp of the destination zemstvo.

Many of these local issues were quite primitive, and Lagerloef notes one amusing example in which the design was made in the form of a handstamp and carved as it should have appeared when impressed, so that the impression is in reverse and must be held to a mirror to be read!

ZENTRALER KURIERDIENST: Inscription identifies some Official stamps of the German Democratic Republic (East Germany).

Zentrierung: German word for "centering."

Zeppelin Philately: During the years between the two world wars, the German Zeppelin dirigibles captured the public's imagination, both as carriers of mail and as passenger vehicles.

To an even greater extent, they captured the fancy of philatelists, and this interest lingers, as witness the enormous prices being paid for Zeppelin stamps and covers.

The single event that generated the most interest was the round-the-world flight of *Graf Zeppelin* in 1929.

In many ways, the story of the Zeppelin dirigibles is a follow-up to that of balloon mail (q.v.), since a dirigible is nothing more than a balloon with a propulsion and steering system, so that it can travel from point to point without being carried at the whim of the winds.

Dirigibles are of two main types: the rigid dirigible, in which the gas bags are contained within a fabric-covered frame, and the non-rigid type, such as today's Goodyear "blimps," which are merely balloons with motors.

The heyday of the dirigible came in the period of the airplane's infancy. As the airplane developed, it caught and passed the "gasbags" as a practical means of transporting people, goods, and mail.

Not all dirigibles were Zeppelins, and that name should only be applied to the dirigibles

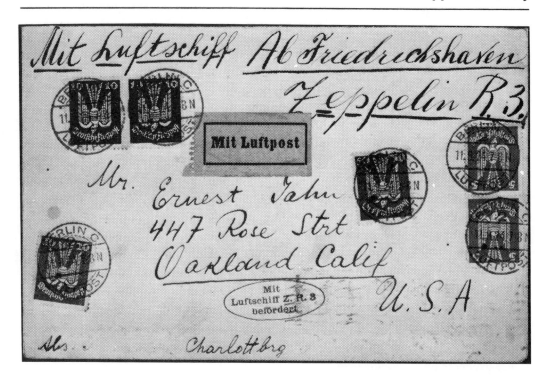

A cover carried on the delivery flight of the ZR-3 *Los Angeles* from Germany to the US.

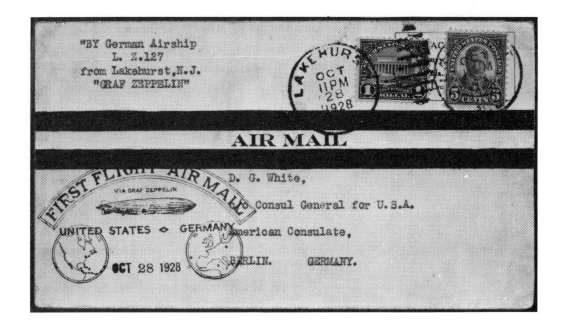

A cover carried on the first west-east transatlantic flight of the LZ-127 *Graf Zeppelin*.

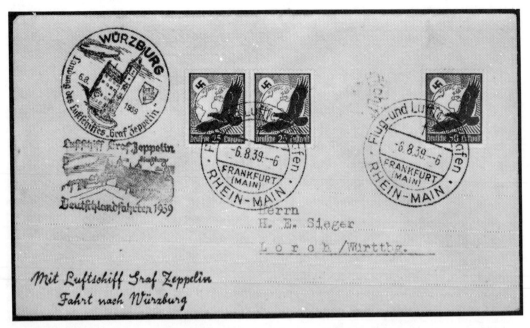

A cover carried on one of the few flights made by the LZ-130 *Graf Zeppelin II*. The dirigible was dismantled two months later.

This stamp pictures *Los Angeles* making the first air mail flight from Lakehurst to Bermuda.

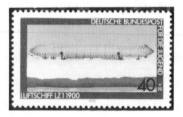

The first Zeppelin, LZ-1.

The impressive LZ-127 *Graf Zeppelin*.

The three US Zeppelin stamps of 1930.

built by the German Zeppelin company, which had been formed by Count Ferdinand von Zeppelin.

Britain built several dirigibles, but these were only marginally successful and played no real role in mail carrying.

The US began its dirigible career by building the ZR-1 *Shenandoah*, which went into military service in 1923.

The most successful of the US dirigibles was a Zeppelin-built dirigible, *Los Angeles*. It was built in Germany in payment of war reparations and was delivered by being flown across the Atlantic to the US in 1924.

It was one of the few dirigibles that lived to be decommissioned, and it went out of service in 1932.

Although some mail was carried on the Zeppelins that operated a passenger service in Germany prior to World War I, it was not until *Graf Zeppelin* began to fly that philately and the Zeppelin really came together.

After WWI, although the US, Britain, and France adopted programs of dirigible development, disaster after disaster eventually led to the abandonment of the rigid dirigible, and the field was left to a reborn Germany. By the end of the 1920s, Germany once more led the world in dirigible design.

The LZ-127 *Graf Zeppelin* first flew on Sept. 18, 1928, and it was this enormously successful craft alone that created the Zeppelin philatelic cult.

Many countries issued Zeppelin stamps on the occasion of the 1929 globe-circling flight, and these issues include the four US Zeppelin stamps so popular today.

Other spectacular flights followed until it was decommissioned in the late 1930s.

In all, *Graf Zeppelin* flew more than a million miles, carried 13,110 passengers without scratching or denting a single one, and transported 235,300 pounds of mail.

It was succeeded by the more modern LZ-129 *Hindenburg*, which came to such a spectacular end at Lakehurst on May 6, 1937.

An even larger Zeppelin had been built and named *Graf Zeppelin II* (LZ-130), but because Hitler was fanning the flames of war, the dirigible never went into commercial service, and the Zeppelin era went up in flames with *Hindenburg*.

Now, only a few small non-rigid blimps are left. Those in the US are used mostly as television camera platforms for sporting and other outdoor events and to give a few passengers a taste of what lighter-than-air flight was like.

Stamps and covers in great variety exist, and their collection seems to be ever growing in popularity as what was once the latest thing in transportation becomes an object of nostalgia for a bygone age.

Zes: Numeral six (6) in Dutch.

Zeven: Numeral seven (7) in Dutch.

Z Grill: (See Grill, Z.)

Ziegelrot: German word for the color "brick red."

Ziffer: German word for "numeral."

Zijkant: Dutch word for "side."

Zil Eloigne Sesel: In 1980 the postal administration of the Seychelles (q.v.) announced that separate stamps would be issued for the

portion of the country comprising all the islands located to the south of the main Seychelles group.

Prior to independence, most of the islands were included in the British Indian Ocean Territory (q.v.), but since the Seychelles was granted independence, these islands have been part of the Republic of the Seychelles.

Although the official announcement stated that for some years, the outer islands had been without postal service, there seems no reason why this could not have been provided by the Seychelles Post Office using the country's stamps. The prospect of multiple stamp sales to collectors, as in the case of several Caribbean countries, must be considered to be the prime reason for the separate stamp issues.

The 25 islands served by this postal "entity" include three island groups, Amirante, Farquhar, and Aldabra, plus Coetivy Island.

The total population is estimated at 3,000.

Stamps of Zil Eloigne Sesal are available from the Seychelles Philatelic Bureau, Victoria, Mahe, Seychelles.

Zimbabwe:

The country now known as Zimbabwe began its modern history as a colony administered by the British South African Company formed by Cecil Rhodes.

The company issued stamps bearing its name from 1890 to 1924, when the area was divided into Northern Rhodesia, later to become the Republic of Zambia, and Southern Rhodesia.

In 1924 stamps inscribed "Southern Rhodesia" were issued, and this continued until 1965, when the inscription was changed to "Rhodesia."

In that year, Prime Minister Ian D. Smith declared the colony independent, but this was never recognized by Great Britain, which was concerned about African rights in the white-dominated colony.

In 1966 the United Nations imposed economic sanctions, and the United States continued to regard Rhodesia as a British colony.

The US Treasury Department's Foreign Assets Control Section prohibited the purchase abroad and importation of Rhodesian stamps issued after July 29, 1968, until these restrictions were lifted on Dec. 17, 1979.

The objectives of the British South Africa Company, back in the 19th century, had been to encourage immigration and colonization, to promote trade, and to secure mineral rights.

The original African inhabitants were not too happy about this, and it was not until 1897 that the area was "pacified."

The white population grew and by 1977 numbered some 237,000. But there were 6,500,000 Africans, and their voice was getting louder and louder.

After a period of unrest and virtual civil war, Great Britain, by a miracle of diplomacy, was able to bring the rebel colony to a point at which free elections could be held. At midnight on April 17, 1980, the colony of Southern Rhodesia officially became the independent nation of Zimbabwe.

Thus, while another colony disappeared from the African scene, a nation emerged, and a new page of the stamp album will reflect this change.

Salisbury is the capital city, with a population of 568,000, and the second city is Bulawayo, with some 340,000 inhabitants.

The unit of currency is the dollar (100 cents), worth $1.54 US in 1981.

The per capita income figure is $501.

A philatelic office is reported to operate, and its address is Philatelic Bureau, Post and Telecommunications Corporation, P.O. Box 4220, Salisbury, Zimbabwe.

ZIMSKA POMOC: During the German occupation of Yugoslavia in World War II, stamps of Italy were overprinted "WINTERHILFE ZIMSKA POMOC" together with a heraldic eagle and surcharge.

Zincography: Zincography is a term used to describe printing from zinc plates.

Zinnober: German word for the color "vermilion."

ZIP Code: The Zoning Improvement Plan, or ZIP Code was introduced by the US Post Office Department in 1963. Previously, there had been zone numbers in the major cities.

The ZIP Code is a five-digit national coding system identifying each postal delivery area.

The first digit identifies one of 10 (0 through 9) geographical areas. The second digit indicates a state, a portion of a heavily populated state, or two or more less populated states.

The third digit indicates either a major metropolitan post office or a sectional center, and the fourth and fifth digits identify either a delivery station of a metropolitan post office or a smaller office served through a sectional center.

Most large post offices have several ZIP Codes, identifying various branches or postal stations.

The objective of the US ZIP Code system is the same as the postcode systems (q.v.) of other countries — to speed up the handling of today's heavy mail volume by the use of automated equipment, optical scanners, etc.

The five-digit US system currently in use guides the sorting of mail to 40,000 post offices, stations, and branches serving more than 70 million homes, farms, and businesses.

In 1978 about 92% of all US mail carried the ZIP Code, and an extension of the code to nine digits is planned for the future.

These extra four digits would narrow the sorting down to individual blocks on a street, which codes used in some other countries, with their combination of letters and numerals, are better adapted to do than is the five-digit system used in the US.

The added numbers will provide up to 9,999 possible delivery points, such as street blocks, office buildings, and other large users, in a given area.

When the ZIP Code was introduced, the US Post Office Department created a cartoon figure known as Mr. ZIP to publicize the new system.

Mr. ZIP began to appear in publicity and on the selvage of postage stamps, beginning with the Sam Houston issue of 1964. Often the slogan "Use ZIP Code" was also included.

This initiated a new area of philatelic study, and the collection of the single stamps and blocks with the adjacent Mr. ZIP figure and the inscriptions became popular. (See Zippy Collectors Club.)

Zippy Collectors Club: The Zippy Collectors Club is a group for collectors interested in all aspects of the Mr. ZIP and other marginal

This 1974 US stamp was issued to publicize ZIP Code.

The various figures of Mr. ZIP in the selvage of US stamps.

markings on US stamp selvage and all related material.

Information on the group's activities is available from the secretary, Thomas Hensler, 2021 West Ninth, Emporia, KS 66801.

Zitronengelb: German word for the color "lemon."

Zloty: The zloty is a unit of currency used by Poland since 1924. It is made up of 100 groszy.

ZOMERZEGEL: Inscription on some semi-postal stamps of the Netherlands.

ZONA DE PROTECTORADO ESPANOL EN MARRUECOS:

Overprint on stamps of Spain for use at Spanish post office in Morocco.

ZONA FRANCAIS BRIEFPOST:

Inscription on early issues of the French Zone of occupation of Germany following World War II.

Zone A, Trieste: (See Trieste, Free Territory of.)

Zone B, Trieste: (See Trieste, Free Territory of.)

Zululand: Now a territory of Natal Province in the Republic of South Africa, Zululand was once the scene of battles "for Queen and Country" and even had its own stamps.

A major portion of the area today is a reserva-tion for use by the native inhabitants, mainly Zulus.

The area of Zululand is 10,427 square miles, and its administrative center is Eshowe.

Trouble began back in the 1870s, when border scuffles between Boers and Zulus continued after British annexation of the Transvaal.

When the Zulus ignored a British cease-and-desist order, war ensued. At Isandhlwana in 1879, Britain lost more than 1,000 men but restored its pride at Ulundi later the same year, and the Zulus admitted defeat.

By 1887, Zululand was British, and it was incorporated into Natal in 1897.

Stamps of Zululand were first issued in 1888 and consisted of issues of Great Britain overprinted "ZULULAND," followed by stamps of Natal bearing the same overprint.

In 1894 the British Colonial key type design was issued inscribed "ZULULAND."

Natal revenue stamps were also used for postage in Zululand.

Stamps for the area were discontinued on June 30, 1898, following the area's incorporation into Natal.

Zumstein & Co.: Swiss publishers of a well-known stamp catalog that is widely used in Europe.

Zurich: (See Cantonal Issues.)

Zusammendruck: German word for "se-tenant."

Zuschlag: German word for "surcharge."

Zwart: Dutch word for "black."

Zwei: Numeral two (2) in German.

Zwischensteg: German word for "gutter."

CATALOGS

A.C. Roessler: Photo Cachet Catalogue, Barry Newton, FDC Publishing Co., Stewartsville, N.J., 1976.

American Air Mail Catalogue, American Air Mail Society, Washington, D.C.

Australian Commonwealth Specialists Catalogue, 1980, Hawthorn Press, Melbourne, Australia.

Campbell Paterson Loose Leaf Catalogue of New Zealand Stamps, Campbell Paterson Ltd., Auckland, New Zealand.

Catalog of British Local Stamps, Rosen, editor, B.L.S.C. Publishing Co., London.

Catalog of Local Post Issues, Rowcroft, editor, S. Ozone Park, N.Y., 1961.

Collect British Stamps, Stanley Gibbons Ltd., London, England.

Discovering the Fun in First Day Covers, Michael Mellone, editor, FDC Publishing Co., Box 206, Stewartsville, N.J.

Durland Standard Plate Number Catalog, Sterling Stamp Co., Boston.

Elizabethan Specialized Catalogue of Modern British Commonwealth Stamps, 1980 Edition, Stanley Gibbons Ltd., London, England.

Facit Specialkatalog, Frimarkshuset, Stockholm, Sweden.

Gibbons Part I, British Commonwealth Stamp Catalogue, Stanley Gibbons Ltd., London, England.

Handbook of the Private Local Posts, Hurt, E.F. and L.N. and M. Williams, published as Volume 6 of Billig's Specialized Catalogues, Fritz Billig, Jamaica, N.Y.

Minkus New American Stamp Catalog, Minkus Publications Inc., New York.

Minkus New Worldwide Stamp Catalog, Minkus Publications Inc., New York.

Postal Stationery of the United States Possessions and Administrative Areas, United Postal Stationery Society.

Regent Stamp Catalog, Robson Lowe, Herbert Joseph Ltd., London, 1937.

Sanabria World Airmail Catalogue, 1966, Nicholas Sanabria, Ridgefield, Conn.

Scott Specialized Catalogue of United States Stamps, Scott Publishing Co., New York.

Scott Standard Postage Stamp Catalogue, Scott Publishing Co., New York.

Specialized Catalog of United States First Day Covers, The Washington Press, Maplewood, N.J.

Stamps of Finland, 1856-1976, Suomen Postimerkkeily oy, Helsinki.

Stamps of Ireland, 1980 Edition, Feldman, Dublin, Ireland.

Stamps of the World, Simplified, Stanley Gibbons Ltd., London, 1982.

Standard First Day Cover Catalog, James Helzer, editor, Fleetwood Publications, Cheyenne, Wyo.

Switzerland Catalogue, The Amateur Collector, London, England.

United States Postal Card Catalog, United Postal Stationery Society.

United States Postal Slogan Cancel Catalog, Moe Luff, editor, Spring Valley, N.Y., 1975.

GENERAL

Allen, Jon L., and Paul H. Silverstone, Stamp Collector's Guide to Europe, American Topical Association, Milwaukee, Wis.

Argenti, Nicholas, The Postage Stamps of New Brunswick and Nova Scotia, Quarterman Publications Inc., Lawrence, Mass., 1976.

Attwood, J.H., Ascension: The Stamps and Postal History, Robson Lowe, London, 1981.

Barnes, Robert, The Postal Service of the Falkland Islands, Robson Lowe, London, 1972.

Baxter, James H., Printing Postage Stamps by Line Engraving, American Philatelic Society, 1939.

Bierman, Stanley M., The World's Greatest Stamp Collectors, Frederick Fell, New York, 1981.

Billig Handbook Series, HJMR Co., North Miami, Fla.

Boggs, Winthrop S., Foundations of Philately, Philatelic Foundation, New York, 1955.

Bohemia, Moravia, Slovakia: A Philatelic Handbook, Czechoslovak Philatelic Society of North America, 1958.

Branston, A.J., Thematic and Topical Stamp Collecting, Batsford, London, 1980.

Branston, A.J., Introducing Postal History, Stanley Gibbons Ltd., London, 1978.

Burgess, Gerald H., Minimum Essentials in Stamp Collecting, Lindquist, New York, 1939.

Cabeen, Richard McP., Standard Handbook of Stamp Collecting, Crowell, New York, 1957.

Canadian Philately: Bibliography and Index, 1864-1973, National Library of Canada, Ottawa, 1979.

Castle, Wilfrid T.S., Cyprus: Postal History and Postage Stamps, Robson Lowe, London, 1971.

Chaintrier, Louis A., Balloon Post of the Siege of Paris, 1870-71, American Air Mail Society, 1976.

Codding, George Arthur, The Universal Postal Union, New York University Press, 1964.

Dalwick, R.E.R., and C.H.C. Harmer, Newfoundland Air Mails, Harmer, 1953.

Davis, Gerald, and Denys Martin, Burma Postal History, Robson Lowe, London, 1971.

Dehn, Roy A., Italian Stamps, Heinemann, London, 1973.

Dehn, Roy A., Philatelic Exhibiting, Stanley Gibbons Ltd., London, 1978.

Dougan, Charles W., The Shanghai Postal System: The Stamps and Postal History, American Philatelic Society, 1981.

Eisendrath, Joseph L., Crash Covers: An Aerophilatelic Challenge, American Air Mail Society, 1979.

Felix, Ervin J., Watermarks and Perforations, Whitman, 1966.

Foster, C.E. How to Prepare Stamp Exhibits, New Mexico Philatelic Association, 1970.

Foster, C.E., Showcasing Your Stamp Collection, Hobby Publishing Services, Albuquerque, N.M., 1978.

Foster, Thomas, The Postal History of Jamaica, 1662-1860, Robson Lowe, London, 1968.

Fletcher, Leslie H.G., Postal Forgeries of the World, Hayes, Batley, England, 1977.

Frajola, Richard, *The Postage Stamps of Siam to 1940: A Descriptive Catalog,* Postilion Publications, Southfield, Mich., 1980.

Goodman, Roland A., *Guatemala 1 and 2,* The International Society of Guatemala Collectors, Robson Lowe, London, 1969 and 1974.

Green, Irving I., *The Black Honduras,* The Collectors Club of New York, 1962.

Griffenhagen, George, and Jerome Husak, *Adventures in Topical Stamp Collecting,* American Topical Association, 1981.

Hallgren, Mauritz, *All About Stamps,* Knopf, N.Y., 1940.

Hals, Nathan, and Phil Collas, *The New Hebrides,* The Collectors Club, New York, 1967.

Hargest, George E., *History of Letter Post Communication Between the United States and Europe,* Smithsonian Institution Press, Washington, 1971.

Haverbeck, Harrison D.S., *Commemorative Stamps of the British Commonwealth,* D. Van Nostrand, New York, 1955.

Herst, Herman Jr., *Fun and Profit in Stamp Collecting,* Meredith Press, New York, 1962.

Holmes, Dr. L. Seale, *Specialized Philatelic Catalogue of Canada and British North America,* Ryerson Press, Toronto, 1959.

Hornadge, Bill, *Stamp Investment Guidelines,* Review Publications Pty. Ltd., Dubbo, Australia, 1979.

Howes, Clifton A., *Canadian Postage Stamps and Stationery,* Quarterman Publications Inc., Lawrence, Mass. 1974.

Hurt, E.F., and Denwood N. Kelly, *The Danube Steam Navigation Company,* American Philatelic Society, 1950.

Jacques, W.A., *Andorra/Andorre,* Robson Lowe, London, 1974.

Julsen, Frank W. and A.M. Benders, *A Postal History of Curacao,* Vandieten, the Netherlands, 1976.

Kandaouroff, Prince Dimitry, *Collecting Postal History,* Larousse, New York, 1974.

Kehr, Ernest A., *The Romance of Stamp Collecting,* Crowell, New York, 1947.

Kronstein, Dr. Max, *Pioneer Airpost Flights of the World, 1830-1935,* American Air Mail Society, 1978.

Langford, Frederick, *Flag Cancel Encyclopedia,* published by the author, 1976.

Linn's World Stamp Almanac, Amos Press Inc., Box 29, Sidney, OH 45367.

Lowe, Robson, *The Encyclopedia of British Empire Postage Stamps, Volume 3, The Empire in Asia,* Robson Lowe Ltd., 1951.

Lowe, Robson, *The Encyclopedia of British Empire Postage Stamps, Volume 4, Australasia,* Robson Lowe Ltd., 1962.

Lowe, Robson, *The Encyclopedia of British Empire Postage Stamps, Volume 5, North America, The Empire from Panama to the North Pole,* Robson Lowe Ltd., 1973.

Ludington, M.H., *The Postal History and Stamps of Bermuda,* Quarterman Publications Inc., Lawrence, Mass., 1978.

Meyer, K.F., *Disinfected Mail,* Gossip Printery, Holton, Kan., 1962.

Morris, Margaret, *Thematic Stamp Collecting,* Stanley Gibbons Ltd., London, 1977.

Mott, Dr. Rodney L., *Postal Stationery: A Collector's Guide,* United Postal Stationery Society, 1968.

Mueller, Barbara R., *Common Sense Philately,* D. Van Nostrand, New York, 1956.

Nathan, S., *The Railway Theme in Spanish Philately,* Spanish Philatelic Society Bookclub, 1978.

Nicklin, John W., *Fabulous Stamps,* Metro Publications, New York, 1943.

Patterson, Frank E., *Afghanistan: Its 20th Century Postal Issues,* Collectors Club, New York, 1964.

Patrick, Douglas and Mary, *The International Guide to Stamps and Stamp Collecting,* Dodd, Mead & Co., New York, 1962.

Poole, B.W.H., *Pioneer Stamps of the British Empire,* D. Van Nostrand Co., Princeton, N.J.

Putzel, Ralph F., *Handbook of Postmarks of South West Africa under South African Administration,* Collectors Mail Auctions, Bergvliet, South Africa, 1977.

Rhein, Francis, *The Postal History of the Grand Duchy of Luxembourg,* Chambers, Kalamazoo, Mich., 1941.

Richter, John Henry, *Judaica on Postage Stamps,* Judaica Historical Philatelic Society, 1974.

Robinson, Howard, *Carrying British Mails Overseas,* New York University Press, 1964.

Rogers, Col. Henry H., *A Century of Liberian Philately,* Bileski, Winnipeg, Canada, undated.

Rosenblum, Alec A., *The Stamps of the Commonwealth of Australia,* Acacia Press, Melbourne, Australia, 1966.

Rowe, Kenneth, *The Forwarding Agents,* The Philatelic Specialists Society, Toronto, 1966.

Schmid, Paul W., *How to Detect Damaged, Altered, and Repaired Stamps,* Palm Press, Huntington, N.Y., 1979.

Staff, Frank, *The Transatlantic Mail,* John de Graff, Inc., New York, 1956.

Stiles, Kent B., *Postal Saints and Sinners,* Theo. Gaus' Sons Inc., Brooklyn, N.Y., 1964.

Stone, Robert G., *French Colonies, the General Issues,* The Collectors Club, New York, 1961.

Sutton, R.J., *Stamp Curiosities,* New York Philosophical Library, 1957.

Thorp, Prescott H., *The Complete Guide to Stamp Collecting,* Minkus Publications Inc., New York, 1964.

Tranmer, Keith, *Austrian Post Offices Abroad,* published in the UK by the author, 1976.

Tranmer, Keith, *The Postal History of Austria,* Austrian Stamp Club of Great Britain, Hornchurch, England, 1974.

Tyler, Varro E., *Philatelic Forgers: Their Lives and Works,* Robson Lowe, London, 1976.

Tyrrell, M. William, *The Universal Postal Union: Members and Stamps,* Van Dahl Publications, Albany, Ore., 1974.

Wagenheim, Kal, *Paper Gold,* Peter H. Wyden, New York, 1976.

Ward, W., *The Postage Stamps of France,* Harris, London, 1926.

Watson, James, *Stamp Collecting,* Stanley Gibbons Ltd., London, 1975.

Watson, James, *Stamps and Aircraft*, Faber and Faber, London, 1961.

Watson, James, *Stamp Varieties Explained*, Stanley Gibbons Ltd., London, 1978.

Williams, L.N. and M., *Fundamentals of Philately*, American Philatelic Society.

Williams, L.N. and M., *Stamps of Fame*, Blandford Press, London, 1949.

Williams, L.N. and M., *The Postage Stamp*, Penguin Books, London, 1956.

Williamson, Omega, *American History Through United States Stamps*, Western Postal History Museum, 1975.

Wolf, Fred S., *Germany's Post-War Local Post Issues: 1945-48*, American Philatelic Society, 1964.

Wood, Kenneth A., *Basic Philately*, Van Dahl Publications, Albany, Ore., 1979.

Van Dam, Theo., *A Postal History of Spain*, Collectors Club, New York, 1972.

Zilliacus, Laurin, *Mail for the World*, John Day Co., New York, 1953.

Zirkle, Helen K., *The Postage Stamps and Commemorative Cancellations of Manchukuo*, Collectors Club, New York, 1964.

GREAT BRITAIN

Channel Islands Stamps and Postal Stationery, Stanley Gibbons Ltd., London, 1979.

Great Britain Specialised Stamp Catalogue, Vols. 1-4, Stanley Gibbons Ltd., London.

Houseman, Lorna, *The House That Thomas Built, the story of De La Rue to 1940*, Chatto & Windus, London, 1968.

Massy, A.J.P., *Isle of Man Postmarks, Surface and Air*, Harry Hayes, Batley, West Yorkshire, 1977.

Potter, David, *British Elizabethan Stamps*, Batsford, London, 1971.

Robinson, Howard, *The British Post Office: A History*, Princeton University Press, Princeton, N.J., 1948.

Rose, Stuart, *Royal Mail Stamps: A Survey of British Stamp Design*, Phaidon, Oxford, England, 1980.

Willcocks, R.M., *The Postal History of Great Britain and Ireland to 1840*, Heinemann, London, 1972.

Wilson, H.S., *TOP: A History of the Travelling Post Offices of Great Britain*, The British Railway Philatelic Group, 1971.

METER STAMPS

Barefoot, S.D. and Werner Simon, *The Meter Postage Stamp Catalogue*, Universal Postal Frankers Ltd., London, 1953.

Cahn, William, *The Story of Pitney-Bowes*, Harper, New York, 1960.

Pyle, Robert, editor, *The Classification of United States Postage Meter Prints*, Meter Stamp Society, Publication Number 3.

Rugg, Harold H., *A Guide to Meter Stamp Collecting*, MSS Bulletin #s132-33.

Steiger, William C., *Handbook of United States Postage Meters*, Stephen G. Rich, Verona, N.J., 1940.

Swan, Walter M., *The Basic Type Meter Catalog*, published privately, 1959.

Walsh, David P. and Simon Werner, *The United States Postage Meter Stamp Catalog*, Indicia Associates, San Francisco, 1976.

Werner, Simon, *Foreign Meter Stamp Catalogs*, MSS *Bulletin*, 1977.

PERIODICALS, PHILATELIC
AUSTRALIA

Australian Stamp Monthly (monthly), Box 178, PO Carlton South, Victoria, Australia, 3053.

Stamp News (monthly), Review Publications Pty. Ltd., Sterling St., Dubbo, New South Wales, Australia, 2830.

CANADA

Canadian Stamp News (every other week), Box 11,000, Bracebridge, ON, Canada, POB 1C0.

GREAT BRITAIN

Gibbons Stamp Monthly (monthly), Stanley Gibbons Magazines Ltd., Drury House, Russell St., London, England, WC2B 5HD.

Philatelic Magazine (monthly), Stamp Collecting Ltd., 21 Maiden Lane, London, England, WC2E 7LL.

Stamp Collecting (weekly), Stamp Collecting Ltd., 42 Maiden Lane, London, England, WC2E 7LL.

Stamp Magazine (monthly), Robert Rogers House, New Orchard, Poole, Dorset, England, BH15 1LU.

US

Linn's Stamp News (weekly), Box 29, Sidney, OH 45367.

Mekeel's Weekly Stamp News (weekly), Severn-Wylie-Jewett Co., Box 1660, Portland, ME 04104.

Minkus Stamp & Coin Journal (quarterly), 116 West 32nd St., New York, NY 10001.

Scott's Monthly Stamp Journal (monthly), Scott Publishing Co., 3 East 57th St., New York, NY 10022.

Stamp Collector (weekly), Van Dahl Publication Box 10, Albany, OR 97321.

Stamp Show News and Philatelic Review (thly), West Rock Show Associates, Inc. Palmer Ave., Larchmont, NY 10538.

Stamps Magazine (weekly), 153 Waverly New York, NY 10014.

PERIODICALS PHILATELIC (Trade)

Philatelic Exporter (monthly), Philate Ltd., Box 4, Edgware, Middlesex, 7HY.

Stamp Dealer (monthly), Hentzel Box 33467, San Diego, CA 92103.

Stamp Trade International (wee Ave., Larchmont, NY 10538.

The Stamp Wholesaler (twice Albany, OR 97321.

PHILATELIC DICTIONARIES

Bennett, Russell, and Jam Terms Illustrated, Stanle don, 1972.

German-English Philatel Philatelic Society, 1979

Graham, Harold T., Terms, The Philateli London, 1951.

Konwiser, Harry M., *American Philatelic Dictionary and Colonial and Revolutionary Posts*, Minkus Publications Inc., New York, 1947.

Konwiser, Harry M., *American Stamp Collector's Dictionary*, Minkus Publications Inc., New York, 1949.

Patrick, Douglas and Mary, *The Musson Stamp Dictionary*, Musson, Toronto, 1972.

Philatelic Vocabulary in Five Languages, Philatelic Foundation, New York, 1978.

Sutton, R.J., *The Stamp Collector's Encyclopedia*, Bonanza, 1966.

UNITED STATES

Boerger, Alfred G., *Handbook on US Luminescent Stamps*, Alfred G. Boerger, Fort Lauderdale, Fla.

Boggs, Winthrop S., *Ten Decades Ago, 1840-1850: A Study of the Work of Rawdon, Wright, Hatch, and Edson of New York City*, American Philatelic Society, 1949.

Bowyer, Mathew J., *They Carried the Mail*, Robert B. Luce, Inc., Washington, 1972.

Brett, George W., *The Giori Press*, Bureau Issues Association, 1961.

Brookman, Lester G., *The 19th Century Postage Stamps of the United States*, Lindquist, New York, 1947.

Crown, Francis J. Jr., *Confederate Postal History*, Quarterman Publications Inc., Lawrence, Mass. 1976.

Jerry B., and Richard B. Graham, *lishment of the First US Government Post in the Northwest Territory*, American ociety, 1975.

C., *Encyclopedia of Plate Varieties eau-Printed Postage Stamps*, ociation, 1979.

Overland Mail, Quarterman ence, Mass., 1976.

ates Postage Stamps, York, 1935 (republish- s Inc., Lawrence,

dt, *20th Cen- celations*,

Rotary d by

Schoen, Robert H., and James T. DeVoss, *Counterfeit Kansas-Nebraska Overprints on 1922-34 Issue, including the California Varieties*, American Philatelic Society, 1973.

Schriber, Les, *Encyclopedia of Designs, Designers, Engravers, Artists of United States Postage Stamps, 1847-1900*, American Philatelic Society, undated.

Segal, Dr. Stanley B., *Errors, Freaks, and Oddities on U.S. Stamps*, Bureau Issues Association, 1979.

Sloat, Ralph L., *Farley's Follies*, Bureau Issues Association, 1979.

Stern, Edward, *History of the 'Free Franking' of Mail in the United States*, Lindquist, N.Y., 1936.

Summerfield, Arthur E., *U.S. Mail: The Story of the United States Postal Service*, Holt, Rinehart, and Winston, New York, 1960.

Townsend, Capt. A.C., *United States Commemorative Stamp Facts*, Linprint, Columbus, Ohio, 1935.

Vecchiarelli, Carlo E., *U.S. Duck Stamps*, PATO Publications, 1979.

Vlissingen, Arthur Van, and Morrison Wald, *New York Foreign Mail Cancellations*, Collectors Club of Chicago, 1968.

Wells Fargo and Company, *Wells Fargo: A Brief History*, San Francisco, undated.

Wiltsee, Ernest A., *Gold Rush Steamers of the Pacific*, Quarterman Publications Inc., Lawrence, Mass., 1976.

Wiltsee, Ernest A., *Pioneer Miner and The Pack Mule Express*, California Historical Society, 1931, reprinted by Quarterman Publications Inc., Lawrence, Mass., 1976.

NON-PHILATELIC ATLASES

Atlas of European History, Oxford University Press, 1957.

Atlas of World History, Rand McNally, 1947.

Collier's Encyclopedic Atlas and Gazetteer of the World, 1912 Edition.

Hammond Medallion World Atlas, Hammond, Maplewood, N.J., 1971.

Rand McNally Standard Atlas of the World, 1890 Edition.

Schonberg's Standard Atlas of the World, 1867 Edition.

Times Atlas of the World, Comprehensive Edition, 1975.

NON-PHILATELIC GENERAL REFERENCE

Encyclopedia Britannica, 200th Anniversary Edition, 1970.

ndom House Unabridged Dictionary of the lish Language, Random House, New York,

Reference Encyclopedia, Funk & 1970.

of the World's Nations, Bureau of In- gence and Research, United States Depart- ent of State, Superintendent of Documents, GPO, Washington, DC 20402.

Webster's New World Dictionary, Second College Edition, World Publishing Co., New York, 1970.

World Almanac and Book of Facts, 1982 Edition, Newspaper Enterprise Inc., New York.